Saints' Lives and the Rhetoric of Gender

Saints' Lives
and the Rhetoric
of Gender

∾

Male and Female in
Merovingian Hagiography

JOHN KITCHEN

New York   Oxford

Oxford University Press

1998

Oxford University Press

Oxford   New York
Athens   Auckland   Bangkok   Bogota   Bombay
Buenos Aires   Calcutta   Cape Town   Dar es Salaam
Delhi   Florence   Hong Kong   Istanbul   Karachi
Kuala Lumpur   Madras   Madrid   Melbourne
Mexico City   Nairobi   Paris   Singapore
Taipei   Tokyo   Toronto   Warsaw

and associated companies in
Berlin   Ibadan

Copyright © 1998 by John Kitchen

Published by Oxford University Press, Inc.,
198 Madison Avenue, New York, New York 10016

Oxford is a registered trademark of Oxford University Press

Library of Congress Cataloging-in-Publication Data
Kitchen, John, 1963–
Saints' lives and the rhetoric of gender : male and female in
Merovingian hagiography / John Kitchen.
p.   cm.
Includes bibliographical references and index.
ISBN 0-19-511722-0
1. Christian saints—France—History—Study and teaching.
2. Christian hagiography—History.   3. Sex role—History of
doctrines—Middle Ages, 600–1500.   4. France—Church history—
to 987.   5. France—History—to 987.   I. Title.
BX4682.K58   1998
270'.092'244—dc21   97-30893

1 3 5 7 9 8 6 4 2
Printed in the United States of America
on acid-free paper

For my mother and father

Fontem igitur demonstro, purae quidem aquae et
salubris, sed in obscura latentem silva, densis sep-
tum frutetis, musco obsitum, avio loco, difficili
aditu, nullis labris aut marginibus aliisve operibus
conclusum, ita tamen ut haurire ex eo facile
queas, aquamque deducere, quibus voles canali-
bus, lapideis, ligneis, plumbeis, argenteis, inde aut
virtutum praestantissimarum petendo exempla,
aut materiam sumendo quam stylo exornes ad
aliorum utilitatem, Divorum honorem; ea lege tamen, ne ipsum unquam obstruas fontem. . . .

—Jean Bolland, preface to
volume 1 of the *Acta Sanctorum*

PREFACE

This book is the fruit of an abandoned project. Originally, I had planned an extensive study devoted entirely to the literature on female saints and writers of the Merovingian Age (ca. 500–ca. 750). At the time, the need for such a study was apparent, even pressing, as I believe it still is. Generally speaking, previous scholars had ignored or, as some claimed, even depreciated the rich contributions women made to early medieval culture. As a valuable corrective to the earlier research, a new trend in scholarship, discernible by the early 1980s, had begun to focus exclusively on the sources pertaining to Merovingian women, especially the hagiography. Building on this recent work seemed to me a legitimate and promising enterprise.

In addition to filling a need, there was, to my mind, a more enticing reason for wanting to investigate these hagiographic texts. The more recent researchers had claimed to find distinctive features in the accounts associated with women, who left their mark on the literature mainly in two ways: either as innovative narrators reporting the religious experiences of other women or as saints whose "women-centered" spirituality is reflected not only in those few works composed by female authors but also in some of the male writers' hagiography on holy women. In either case, the newly discovered distinctiveness was thought to be indicative of a female alternative to the religious ideals expressed in the *Vitae* written wholly by and about men. An investigation of the literature on women thus offered the chance to study the artifacts of a literary and religious subculture that once flourished in late antique Gaul.

However, I came to see the argument for distinctiveness as relying more on assumption than on a thorough and systematic investigation of the hagiographic literature. And as an assumption, it became an untenable starting point for treating the narratives on women. Frankly, it simply could not be maintained as I read more widely in hagiography, especially in light of the texts written by the prolific male authors whose works represented the standard—as opposed to what is now regarded as the distinctive—literature of the period. In short, a major premise for investigating the Merovingian hagiography on women collapsed, and with it went the validity of the conclusions that the leading scholars in the field had reached.

Thus I came to believe that the narratives written by and about women cannot be packaged so neatly into a gender study isolating the female hagiography from the main trends that characterize the evolution of the literature. Rather than a discussion exclusively devoted to female saints and writers, I saw a greater need for something broader and more fundamental (though I realize that what I have offered, basically a traditional *Topoiforschung* and *Quellenforschung*, may well be singled out as an example of theoretical impoverishment). In attempting to fill that need, I have sought to lay the cornerstone of a foundation for the systematic study of the hagiographic literature pertaining to the female saints and writers of the Merovingian period.

The present book, then, is an attempt to reformulate, through a source-derived methodology, the approach to the question of female sanctity and writing, a question that has come to the forefront of the modern debates on the role of women in the literature, spirituality, intellectual life, and history of the Middle Ages. The work is therefore intended to be a preliminary treatment that is needed just to begin to address the problems concerning the study of Merovingian holy women and their biographies. As will become apparent in the following pages, a paradox is inherent in the approach insofar as the reformulation tries to develop a method to treat the sources on female saints and writers by examining extensively the material pertaining to their male counterparts.

The book is a revised version of my 1995 doctoral dissertation done at the Centre for Medieval Studies in the University of Toronto. I wish to thank formally the advisors, readers, and members of the examination committee who gave their careful consideration to the work and made valuable criticisms: Professors Patricia Eberle, Alexander Murray, and Robert Sinkewicz. As the external appraisers of the dissertation, Professors Dorothy Bray (McGill University) and Giulio Silano (Saint Michael's College, University of Toronto) painstakingly examined the study and offered precise suggestions for improvement through their written evaluations. Thanks are also due to the anonymous readers who provided such perceptive comments in their assessment of the manuscript for Oxford University Press.

The particular instances in which I am obliged to these people, especially for their bibliographical suggestions, seem too numerous for me to note in the study itself. Let me, instead, express my gratitude here with a general acknowledgment of their contribution to increasing my awareness of the various issues and vast research related to the discussion. Their advice, which was not always followed, has also kept me mindful of the study's limitations and flaws, for which I am fully responsible.

In addition to the advisors and readers, I am indebted enormously to my former supervisor, Professor John Corbett. His fundamental, interdisciplinary course on early Latin hagiography will remain one of the most gratifying experiences of my life. As the dissertation director, he offered sound advice and unfailing support. Whatever merit the book has is due to the diligent guidance he so kindly bestowed.

I am also grateful to Professor Virginia Brown of the Pontifical Institute of Mediaeval Studies. Thanks to her, I did not have to write the drafts of this work in longhand. At a time when my impecunious circumstances made even the essentials seem extravagant, she generously gave me her personal computer.

There are also many individuals, especially in Canada, who assisted me, so many that I am bound to forget some if I try to name them all. Begging their forgiveness for leaving them anonymous now, I shall look forward to thanking them personally again and again in the years to come. In addition to giving me much practical help with preparing the manuscript, they offered generous hospitality and warm, lasting friendships, which still sustain me in a place often too cold for a born and raised Californian.

Finally, the book is dedicated to my mother and father, Eleanor and William Kitchen, whose many sacrifices on my behalf give me life and hope in abundance.

Toronto, Ontario   J. K. K.
December 1997

CONTENTS

ABBREVIATIONS

AASS	*Acta Sanctorum* (Paris, 1863–)
AB	*Analecta Bollandiana*
ACM	Acts of the Christian Martyrs, ed. and trans. Herbert Musurillo (Oxford, 1972)
BT	Bible de tous les temps
carm.	*carmen/carmina*
CCSL	Corpus Christianorum Series Latina (Turnhout, 1953–)
CSEL	Corpus Scriptorum Ecclesiasticorum Latinorum (Vienna, 1866–)
DACL	Dictionnaire d'archéologie chrétienne et de liturgie, ed. F. Cabrol and H. Leclercq (Paris, 1924)
Dial.	*Dialogus/i*
DVSM	*De virtutibus sancti Martini*
EM	*Études mérovingiennes: actes des journées de Poitiers, 1952* (Paris, 1953)
Ep.	*Epistula/ae*
GAG	Göppinger Arbeiten zur Germanistic, ed. Ulrich Müller et al.
GC	*Liber in gloria confessorum*
GM	*Liber in gloria martyrum*
HS	Harvard Studies in Classical Philology
JEH	*Journal of Ecclesiastical History*
JRS	*Journal of Roman Studies*
LH/Histories	*Gregorii episcopi Tvronensis libri historiarum X*
LVP	*Liber vitae patrum*
MA	*Liber de miraculis beati Andreae*
MGH	*Monumenta Germaniae Historica*
AA	*Auctores Antiquissimi* (Berlin, 1877–)

Ep. Mer.	*Epistolae Merowingici et Karolini Aevi*, ed. E. Dümmler and W. Gundlach (Berlin, 1887–)
SS	*Scriptores* (Hannover, 1826–1934)
SRM	*Scriptores Rerum Merovingicarum*, ed. Bruno Krusch and Wilhelm Levison (Hannover, 1885–)
MRW	*Medieval Religious Women*, 2 vols., ed. John A. Nichols and Lillian Shank (Kalamazoo, 1984 and 1987)
DE	*Distant Echoes*
PW	*Peace Weavers*
NF	Neue Folge
NTA	E. Hennecke, *New Testament Apocrypha*, 2 vols., ed. W. Schneemelcher (Eng. trans., London, 1963–1965)
PG	*Patrologiae cursus completus: series graeca*, ed. J. P. Migne (Paris, 1857–1866)
PL	*Patrologiae cursus completus: series latina*, ed. J. P. Migne (Paris, 1844–1864)
pref.	*praefatio*/preface
prol.	*prologus*/prologue
RH	*Revue historique*
RHE	*Revue d'histoire ecclésiastique*
RHEF	*Revue d'histoire de l'église de France*
SC	Sources Chrétiennes (Paris, 1940–)
SH	Subsidia Hagiographica
SP	*Studia Patristica*
TU	Texte und Untersuchungen zur Geschichte der alterchristlichen Literatur, begründet von O. von Gebhardt und A. Harnack (Leipzig, 1882–)
VA	*Vita sancti Albini*
VBA	*Vita beati Antonii abbatis*
VG	*Vita sancti Germani*
VH	*Vita sancti Hilarii*
VJ	*De virtutibus Sancti Juliani*
VM	*Vita sancti Martini*
VMarc	*Vita sancti Marcelli*
VP	*Vita sancti Paterni*
VR	*Vita sanctae Radegundis* (*VR* 1 refers to Fortunatus's text, *VR* 2 to Baudonivia's)

AUTHOR'S NOTE

To avoid confusion, the written narrative portraying a saint is referred to as a "Life." When this word denotes a holy person's existence, the lowercase "life" is used. Thus the distinction between the two meanings can be maintained. Similarly, to designate in general such narratives, the plural is "Lives," and the Latin *Vita* or *Vitae*.

As a matter of personal preference and convenience, the version of the Latin Bible used throughout is that edited by, among others, Robert Weber: *Biblia Sacra iuxta vulgatam versionem (editio minor)* (Stuttgart, 1984). Two versions of the Latin Psalter are printed side by side in this Bible—the "Gallican" and "Hebrew" Psalters. Unless stated otherwise, the Psalter cited here is the Gallican. Note that the numbering of the Psalms in the Latin Bible is different from that in the English Bible; it is one Psalm behind.

Finally, where no one is named for an English translation of a Latin or a modern foreign language text, that translation is my own.

Saints' Lives and the Rhetoric of Gender

I

INTRODUCTION

Methods and Metaphors

The enigma of sanctity is the temptation and often
the ruin of historians.
— Thomas Merton, *The Last of the Fathers*
(1954, p. 23)

Although Merton's comment appeared in 1954, its note of admonishing caution
recalls the earliest known reservation expressed by a modern thinker contemplating
the legitimacy of hagiographic studies. The renowned Counter-Reformation theologian Robert Bellarmine (1542–1621) discouraged such research in a letter to his
Jesuit colleague Heribert Rosweyde (1569–1629), the Belgian professor of philosophy who first proposed a hagiographic project that was to proceed according to
techniques characteristic of modern scholarship.[1] Despite Bellarmine's reservation
that publishing the colorful, "original histories" of the saints would too easily evoke
the ridicule of contemporary readers, Rosweyde proceeded with his plan. As is well
known, the vast enterprise that Rosweyde conceived and began was continued after
his death by that small but industrious group of hagiographic researchers in the
Society of Jesus who came to be known as "the Bollandists."[2]

Countless others have been as conscious as Bellarmine, Rosweyde, and Merton
were of the difficulties modern researchers faced when considering the recorded
history of holy men and women.[3] Indeed, for more than three centuries the vast
documentation of sanctity has received extensive, scientific treatment from historians
and other scholars representing a wide range of approaches.[4] But if, as Merton implies, these efforts to penetrate the meaning of sanctity have often failed, that failure
must lie in an understanding of the sources, for the saints of the past exist essentially
as texts; what is left of their sanctity survives through the written word, the "im-
probable" narratives that Bellarmine feared would be scorned in a milieu of enlightened rationalism. To find the reliable elements in these largely unreliable sources,
to legitimize the study of saints' Lives in the modern era, scholars devised elaborate
methodologies to investigate these texts, and the question of methodology remains

still the most difficult and contentious one to address for hagiographic researchers of today.

Certainly, the religious nature of the sources, which reflect a *mentalité* out of intellectual fashion even by Bellarmine's day, may be regarded as the chief difficulty researchers have in approaching hagiography. But the nature of the sources does not account for the ways in which they are problematized, for the problematization is the result of the questions scholars ask and the inadequacies of the approaches they develop. Hence the reasons for the persistent methodological admonishments and debates must be sought in the history of hagiographic research itself.

On turning to this history, we may find the past achievements of hagiographic studies as invaluable, significant to all those currently working in the areas of history, literature, religion, and philosophy. The methodological quest in the study of hagiography led to what are, arguably, some of the most significant accomplishments in the humanistic scholarship of the modern era. From the seventeenth century to the present, hagiographic sources have attracted the attention of the most advanced scholars, whose methods (as in the case of the Bollandists and certain Monumentists) became the hallmark of whole schools of research intimately connected with the major intellectual movements of the time. Indeed, within the history of hagiographic studies appear the figures who epitomize the essential characteristics of modern scholarship.

Yet behind every approach to hagiographic research is an assumption about what the goal of such scholarship should be. The confidence researchers once showed in their methods is now overshadowed by the aims of their studies, aims that now seem to have been determined largely by the philosophical, religious, or political allegiances of the scholars involved. Even though this history often shows the presence of a bewildering urgency for devising adequate methodologies, the legacy of the advances arising out of the earlier developments cannot be so easily detected in the current scholarly trends. In fact, to the contemporary researcher, the intellectual foundation of the earlier approaches to hagiography and to the historiographical genres as a whole may appear too tainted by biased, post-Enlightenment presuppositions regarding the criteria for determining truth to be actually adopted as a methodological principle.[5]

The approach outlined for this study arises largely out of a reflection on some of these more contentious views regarding the various developments in hagiographic research. Such developments deserve consideration in their own right because they readily illustrate some of the major advances and shortcomings that are worth recalling before embarking on an extensive study of saints' Lives. More important, when considered broadly and critically, some of these more salient features in the development of hagiographic research point to an ideal of method worth pursuing in light of the goals for the present inquiry.

Let us begin by considering the two researchers whose works represent the most remarkable yet divergent achievements ever made by scholars treating hagiographic material. They are the Bollandist Hippolyte Delehaye (1859–1941) and the social historian Peter Brown. An understanding of the reception of their scholarship by modern researchers will highlight perhaps the most significant shift in the study of hagiography during this century. As will become apparent, the comparison of the two also contributes to establishing a methodological scheme for the study of Merovingian saints' Lives.

To sense some of the most striking divergencies in the development of modern hagiographic research, consider Brown's groundbreaking *Cult of the Saints* in light of Delehaye's earlier and more methodologically comprehensive treatments, of which his *Legends* is a classic example. Brown's impressive, eloquent, perhaps even poetic observations on the function of saints and their shrines in a social context accord to hagiographic literature a distinction rarely granted by previous historians and suggest possibilities for studying such material as a source for late antique *mentalités* that have yet to be exhausted.[6] If Brown's work seems suggestive and open-ended with respect to what hagiography can offer historians of society, politics, literature, religion, or ideas, Delehaye's approach circumscribes the subject, defines and categorizes the sources so that their limitations in the search for objective data can be more easily detected. Unlike Brown, Delehaye offers a rigorous, systematic method, a technique that can be applied to a mass of literature that has persistently exasperated modern readers ever since hagiographic studies emerged as a legitimate field of research.

However, far more interesting than the obvious differences between the two is the impression that, in some fundamental way, each seems to succeed at what the other has set out to do. Delehaye, even as he tries to raise the study of hagiography to a science, relies, as Brown often does, on analogy or even metaphor at crucial points in the elaboration of his methodology or argument. To be sure, sometimes this strategy can lend a scientific air to his writing, as when he speaks of the "hagiographic coordinates,"[7] terminology derived from Cartesian geometry and not ill-chosen for a Bollandist, given what Descartes had learned from French Jesuits in the area of mathematics.[8] At other times, however, his explanations sound like sheer poetry, as when he attempts to answer the charge that hagiography draws heavily on pagan literature by coolly claiming that this aspect of the Christian narratives is merely "borrowed clothing."[9] Or, when struggling to square the sameness of hagiographic literature with the theological notion of sanctity as a distinctive and highly individualistic imitation of Christ, he offers the suggestive phrase "harmonious ensemble," words evoking the image of an orchestra and hence implying the possibility of genuine distinctiveness contributing to the overall impression of sanctity's sameness.[10] Similar to the descriptive power Brown would later display, Delehaye's use of metaphor (his "pithy expressions"[11]) sometimes leaves a penetrating image that offers an innovative, suggestive way to think about the literature rather than a methodology that treats it as a problem to be solved.

The introduction of such poetic imagery by so rigorous a researcher, who, after all, regards the literature itself—not his own writing—as poetry,[12] suggests that, when dealing with some fundamental issues concerning the sources, Delehaye's "science of hagiography" can break down, giving way to metaphor and an ingenious imagination. As Brown would do later in this century, Delehaye seems to reveal the nature of the literature most penetratingly when he offers vivid images rather than a systematic approach. If there is any validity to such an impression, then Delehaye, too, although not noted for doing so, advances some crucial arguments by relying, at least in part, on rhetorical techniques that would later make Brown so successful and popular an exponent of hagiographic literature.

Significantly, both Delehaye and Brown, when investigating hagiography, also turn to a scientific apparatus. Brown's hagiographic research, which does not adhere to a rigorously defined and applied methodology as Delehaye's does, derives cogency from the application of the social sciences to the literature pertaining to saints and their cults.[13] The important difference between them with respect to how the scientific structure functions in their work is that Delehaye's hagiographic coordinates attempt to be, like their Cartesian forerunner, an all-encompassing method of investigation seeking objective certainties, whereas Brown does not attempt to construct an entire system of hagiographic research based on the social sciences but merely utilizes the findings of anthropologists and sociologists to illuminate the social context and religious attitudes revealed by the literature.[14] Brown applies interpretive tools from other disciplines; Delehaye creates the interpretive tool, which, although based on a Cartesian analogue, is intended as a self-contained system of investigation suited specifically to the study of saints, their cults, and the related literature. In short, the work of the one uses social science, while that of the other aims at being a science, one as exacting as geometry.[15]

Obviously, this difference between the two arises out of the different aims of their scholarship (Brown is a social historian of late antiquity and Delehaye was purely a hagiographic researcher concerned with all manner of material spanning several periods). For this reason, comparing the two is more than a little unfair, even if Brown does consider his own approach in light of Delehaye's and the Bollandists'.[16] Nonetheless, the comparison is illuminating, if only for the way that the difference between the two regarding the role of a scientific structure in their work brings to light a great paradox in the hagiographic research of this century. Whether intended or not, Brown's approach, if we can call it that, although never formally outlined as a system of investigation, is now being followed, so that today a Brownian, rather than a Delehayean, methodology is in vogue.[17] Although lacking any elaboration and even consistent application of an advanced method for the systematic study of hagiographic literature, Brown's work has emerged as one of the most followed and engaging models of modern research, whereas the rigorous and clearly defined principles of hagiographic investigation carefully laid out by Delehaye and his successors attract little attention as a viable methodology and are sometimes even frowned on, with only the most superficial arguments usually passing for an adequate refutation.[18] Modern scholars normally turn to Delehaye and the work of the Bollandists when they want reliable information about saints and their cults or a modern edition of a hagiographic work, but for the facet of hagiographic research that Delehaye would consider his and the Bollandists' farthest reaching contribution—that is, developing a methodology by which all the sources can be soundly investigated—scholars look elsewhere, if they look at all.[19] In the case of the Brownians, researchers derive, paradoxically, an approach from a thinker who, notwithstanding the enormous contribution of his fascinating insights, offers no thoroughgoing methodological scheme for conducting hagiographic scholarship.

Of course, it is precisely because of the methodological loose ends in Brown's rich evocations of the religious past that others can take up the thread of his argument and weave it into new material, as if to conduct the experiments that verify an interesting hypothesis.[20] And as the body of Brown's hagiographically related research continues to be approached like a recently opened door leading to unexplored areas of study, Delehaye's tightly constructed system seems to be rapidly closing in on itself. Today, the culmination of his achievement amounts to an elaborate model so well ordered and thought out but also so alien to modern scholarship that it stands in the world of hagiographic studies like a magnificent, historic mansion, now too imposing and obsolete to make a home. Although the edifice is remarkably well designed and structurally sound, its legacy seems to be little more than a conspicuous landmark occasionally arousing nostalgic admiration or pointed criticism.[21] Given how modern scholars are using and evaluating the work of these two prominent students of hagiography, the impression is not unfounded that Brown has, in some fundamental way, succeeded at what Delehaye tried so rigorously to do.

By no means are these reflections intended to suggest that, in spite of the obvious paradox, hagiographic researchers have at last found an acceptable approach by building on Brown's work rather than on the writings of Delehaye and his Bollandist successors. On the contrary, Brown's approach continues to find formidable critics from those who more or less follow in his footsteps as well as from those who dispute his findings.[22] And even if the most attention that contemporary scholars seem to give to Bollandists such as Delehaye or Aigrain consists in superficial comments and a listing of some of their books in bibliographies, plenty of modern, secular researchers, especially historians, are more Bollandist in their critical outlook than they realize or care to acknowledge.

The original impression about the gulf between Brown and Delehaye, even after it is modified by seeing the unexpected points at which they converge, reflects the state of hagiographic research in general. In short, one cannot easily discern how or even if earlier scholarship bears any relation to the latest studies on hagiographic literature.[23] Apparently, hagiography as a field of inquiry does not develop as the sciences do, with previous researchers building on what came before, so that the conclusions of earlier findings can be tested against later ones. The area of hagiographic research has, evidently, no proven giants on whose strong shoulders we may stand. Considered in light of how hagiographic research progresses, the obvious questions that come to mind after an initial experience of reading Brown and Delehaye are never satisfactorily answered. How, for instance, should The Legends of the Saints be regarded today? Is its methodology really obsolete? If so, who made that decision and what has replaced this fundamental book and the others like it? These are questions that only a few scholars even care to raise, let alone answer, and the result is the current state of hagiographic research.

And what is the current state of hagiographic research? At the end of the twentieth century, hagiographic scholarship verges on becoming an amorphous field of study indiscriminately incorporating a variety of scholarly trends and disciplines, none of which, as an independent approach, is specifically suited to treat the sources in any satisfactory manner.[24] Yet precisely the opposite would seem to be the case, given how well scholars claim to know exactly what problems need to be addressed. Again and again, hagiographic researchers take up the same methodological questions in the introductions to their studies, and repeatedly they mention the old, tiresome problems so that, with their repetition and reliance on predictable scholarly conventions, their opening remarks exhibit the very qualities they find so perplexing in hagiographic literature itself. They go to great lengths to elaborate their methodologies and to offer an approach protecting themselves against the pitfalls encountered by modern readers.[25] Always the same issues arise: what to do with the swarming topoi, how miracles are to be understood, where the "historical kernels" are, and how they can be verified. These issues, to a varying extent, seem to concern all researchers, historian and literary critic alike. Yet for all the attention paid to methodology and the application of scientific, historical, or critical tools, no one has yet found any one modern approach that can adequately handle the totality that is hagiographic literature.

The last observation, however, may be qualified with a statement that is unlikely to win the approval of the various researchers dealing with hagiographic sources. The Bollandists come closer than any other scholarly movement to embracing all that hagiography is. There are instances, especially passages taken from Delehaye's *Legends* and *Cinq leçons*, in which the author accords to hagiographic texts, particularly *Vitae*, the lowest possible value of all the sources relating to the history of saints. Indeed, as one researcher has observed, the Bollandists in general and Delehaye in particular "sacrifice" (*geopfert*) the narratives to get at the historical saint.[26] Yet this universally accepted view, while highlighting as it does an obvious weakness in the way the Bollandists treat the narratives, is also an oversimplification that cannot adequately address what are either inconsistencies in or a genuine development of Delehaye's and the Bollandists' attitude toward the value of the sources as literature.

On this point, a challenging insight may be gained by considering the apparent incongruity in the way Delehaye's own research relates to his critique of the Bollandists themselves. In a work that the latest scholars consistently neglect,[27] Delehaye looks back over the history of his organization and frankly notes that one of its lowest points was the Bollandists' decision to provide only the most historically reliable *Vitae* as suitable material for the *Acta Sanctorum*. Here he not only comments on the fallacy inherent in this approach but also makes an extraordinary claim that does not conform with what later researchers attribute to him or to the so-called scientific hagiography of the Bollandists. The reason that all the versions of a Life ought to appear in the *Acta Sanctorum*, he argues, is to provide scholars with the necessary sources to conduct purely literary research. He hails the return to the earlier practice of providing numerous accounts of a saint's life as one of the great contributions the *Acta Sanctorum* made to literary scholarship. An overly fastidious concern with historical criticism is frowned on. In short, the historical veracity of hagiographic texts assumes a position subordinate to what the sources can offer as literature. Some of his remarks on this matter are worth quoting at length:

> Judged from the historical standpoint alone, many suppressions could in their case easily be justified. Literary interests, on the contrary, demanded the multiplication of texts and it cannot be denied that the volumes of the *Acta Sanctorum*, in which this principle has been acted upon most fully, are those which today render the greatest service. This had always been the practice of Bollandus and Henschenius, and Papebroch followed still more resolutely in the same path. After their day, a more exclusively historical tendency began to appear, to the detriment of a class of readers which increases constantly in proportion to the advance made by the study of literary history.

. . . After Papebroch, the editors failed only too often to preserve the breadth of mind he showed in this matter as in so many others. Nevertheless, it was no longer an anxiety for edification which prompted this increased severity, but a too exclusive desire to give first place to historical matter.[28]

Now a perplexing contradiction appears, one with which those who persist in generalizing about Delehaye and the Bollandists will have to contend: How is it that the very practice characteristic of a particular phase in the history of the Bollandists that most closely coincides with Delehaye's own treatment of the literature outlined in his *Legends* is precisely the approach that this same scholar regards as one of the most flawed methods ever employed by past editors of the *Acta Sanctorum*? How, in other words, can we make sense of the fact that some of the strongest criticism against the "historical tendency" of the Bollandists comes from the "scientific hagiographer" par excellence, that very Bollandist who himself always seems to display "a too exclusive desire to give first place to historical matter"? These are questions for which this discussion can provide no answer. Yet, one point seems certain: The study of hagiography as literature, along with the value accorded to the Lives on the basis of what they offer students of hagiographic narrative, cannot have been so consistently and uniformly held in such low esteem by Delehaye and the Bollandists as modern scholars continue to claim. The example given regarding the quality and number of versions worth publishing should caution us against speaking of the work and aims of the Bollandists as a generic whole, given that, as in this instance, significant divergencies can be detected throughout their history arising from methodological procedures sometimes deliberately introduced to eradicate a previous trend. Such divergencies reflect differences among the Bollandists themselves regarding what the literature was thought to offer and also show a conflicting vision of the purpose of the *Acta Sanctorum* itself, a purpose that was obviously redefined at various stages of the group's history, as much to solve practical and imposed problems as to compensate for previous methodological flaws.[29]

We must also acknowledge that at times this awareness of the potential for literary analysis went beyond a mere concession to philologists or folklorists. The section on Herbert, for instance, gives no fewer than seven versions of that saint's life.[30] More important, in the *Acta Sanctorum* the literary aspects of the literature can be seen as part of the total picture of all that hagiography embraces so that, as in the case of the offices of Saint Monegund, which consist largely of passages drawn from Gregory's *Life* of her found in the *Liber vitae patrum*, literature and liturgy merge in such a way that the relationship between the various elements of a saint's dossier offers a rich, irreducible amalgamation of integrated texts.[31] For this reason, as well as for the fact that the literary potential of the sources is not as categorically neglected by these researchers as it is generally assumed to be, the argument is compelling that none of the current scholarship comes closer to dealing with the totality of hagiography than the work of the Bollandists.

Another curious feature keeps surfacing in Delehaye's rarely cited narrative on his predecessors, a feature not only supporting the argument just made but also suggesting a major shift in the way hagiographic researchers see themselves in relation to their work. Again, it is a feature that seems at odds with what Delehaye says and implies elsewhere, particularly in his *Cinq leçons*, where he describes hagiography as a field belonging properly to historical research.[32] Significantly, through-out his history, he refers frequently to previous Bollandists as "hagiographers," and he obviously envisages both their work and the material they study as having un-paralleled literary significance.[33] In fact, there is good reason to think that the whole enterprise of the *Acta Sanctorum* is as much literary as it is a historical undertaking.[34]

This repeated designation of earlier researchers as hagiographers, an almost pe-jorative word in the *Legends*,[35] indicates that Delehaye is describing a scholarly move-ment that genuinely attempts to deal with every facet of the sources that it possibly can. Such a designation shows that the Bollandists view themselves and their work quite differently from the way in which today's most advanced researchers do. In-stead of calling themselves hagiographers, scholars currently studying the written sources are the representatives of one of several possible disciplines, each student applying a different technique to the study of the texts. The Bollandists, by contrasts, at least remain conscious of the great interdisciplinary breadth that is needed for the investigation of hagiographic literature. In doing so, they make a greater attempt at dealing with the many layers of the texts than do the latest researchers, who really represent the splintering of hagiographic studies into categories grossly inadequate for texts that have no such neat divisions to correspond with the various departments of a modern university.

These considerations highlight a salient feature of contemporary hagiographic research. When all the various movements are considered, no coherent methodo-logical evolution running from the earliest stages of scholarship to the present can be discerned. Instead, there is an impression of discontinuity, dissonance, or at least ambiguity; it is difficult—and becoming increasingly so—to determine how some forms of hagiographic research advance the field as a whole. This result is the in-evitable outcome of overspecialized scholars who are not hagiographers but histo-rians, literary critics, social scientists, or even, most recently, a "postmodern" phi-losopher.[36] In short, because hagiography is not really regarded as an area of study, a *Wissenschaft*, in its own right, there is no standard of research directly derived from the nature of the sources themselves to which a practitioner in one of the several fields of investigation would owe accountability beyond the demands set by his or her own discipline.[37] Thus the same mistakes made more than a century ago persist today precisely because the impoverishment of a particular methodology is rarely acknowledged.

On this point, historians seem to have enjoyed the greatest liberties, painstakingly extracting the "kernels" from the texts and being responsible for significant advances in treating the sources—as well as for the greatest failures ever known to the history of hagiographic research.[38] Earlier, a reference was made to the Bollandists' "sacri-ficing" texts in order to get at the historical saint. But we can say, at least, that one prominent representative of that organization expressed the view that the preferred approach is to provide as many literary sources as possible, so that the sacrificing will have to be done as part of an interpretive process rather than as an editorial practice. The "historical-critical" method of the *Monumenta* editors, however, with what amounts to a rational positivism as their guiding principle, is responsible for literally sacrificing the narratives, without any of Delehaye's awareness of how this jeopardizes the literary investigation of hagiography.[39] And besides bemoaning that hagiographic material fails to offer the kind of evidence that a charter would provide,[40] historians, especially those dealing with the Merovingian sources, showed themselves, and continue to show themselves, to be on the whole the most inept group of scholars ever to deal with the religious significance of the literature,[41] something that the Bollandists are consistently better at doing, notwithstanding the Catholic apologetical context of their enterprise and the scorn sometimes shown toward "popular piety."[42]

The attraction historians have for hagiography leads to one of the most mismatched unions perhaps ever encountered in humanistic scholarship. Historians continue to ask the questions that the hagiographic texts are the least likely to answer. They turn to hagiographic literature not only because they have to, there being, as is sometimes the case for the study of the early Middle Ages, a relative scarcity of sources outside hagiography,[43] but also, so it seems from their obvious disappointment, with the greatest expectations of acquiring sound information about a particular era.[44] These sources, so puzzling and challenging for the historian to deal with, seem, by that very fact, the most alluring, tempting the historian to try to understand the significance of evidence that pertains primarily to phenomena of which he or she is proudly ignorant in a modern, rational, and secularized society.[45]

If historians in general do not deal adequately with the religiosity of the texts, those who treat hagiography as literature generally show little concern with how the religious dimension may relate to the way in which the stories are told.[46] Here again, the sources offer a challenging temptation, an opportunity to explain their narratological nature in a few pages.[47] The sameness of hagiographic literature makes structural analysis especially enticing, and no doubt important insights have been gained precisely because this approach seems to be genuinely derived from the nature of the sources themselves.[48] But grappling with the homogeneity of the texts has also led to absurdities, such as one modern researcher's attempt to establish the three criteria of "a successful hagiographic work."[49] Within the literary approach, we may also include psychological interpretations and the application of theory, formerly employed in the study of more modern texts, to hagiographic sources, such as a Freudian, Rankian, or Jungian approach.[50] Again, absurdities appear,[51] and the decision over what critical tools can best penetrate a particular source will always remain a chief difficulty.[52]

On this point, the literary critic and the historian face a similar problem: how to avoid applying an interpretive tool that will lead to assessing the literature on the basis of what it is least likely to provide. The contemporary conditions under which the modern researcher lives and from which a critical perspective will obviously arise can facilitate new insights into the literature or lead to unfounded and misconstrued conclusions that show how utterly impoverished a modern vision may be when dealing with the sources. The example that comes immediately to mind is Ulrike Garbe's study of notable Frankish women, published in 1936. Although the subject of her discussion currently interests many modern researchers, the book itself apparently has only ever been cited in one recent work, which gives a description of its content that should suffice to show how dangerous the surrendering to contemporary trends can be: "A completely useless, bungled work of national-socialist racial ideology that has for its theme the 'moral degeneration' of the Franks in contact with the Gallo-Romans; the demoralization is demonstrated in the Queens, especially in Fredegund. As positive counterparts Clotild, Radegund and especially Brunhild appear."[53]

Lest there be any misunderstanding, the point here is not to equate modern theoretical approaches with Garbe's racism and the Nazi movement. What the existence of a work such as this shows—and, as we all know, there are others like it[54]—is that modern criticism, so much a part and creation of our own singular obsessions, is susceptible to a limitation that is usually regarded as the hallmark of what makes it so advanced—namely, a modern outlook facilitating new techniques that will allegedly help us uncover aspects of the literature that we ourselves are supposedly in a better position to see from our perspective than those who originally produced and used these texts. More and more, a modern perspective is thought to be capable of salvaging a source too unsophisticated on its own, reeking as it does of naive faith and bad literary taste.[55] But if Garbe's work teaches us anything, it is that the peculiar concerns of a scholar's contemporary society may color the texts beyond acceptable bounds of interpretation, assuming that there still are acceptable bounds of interpretation.

Today, we also hear much talk about how hagiography can be studied as a source for religious attitudes or ideas (l'histoire des mentalités, Ideengeschichte).[56] Indeed, Brown's work, and that of those indebted to it, has done much to uncover this aspect of the literature. Yet, the most striking feature of modern research in general is how little it actually engages the religious thought and theological outlook presupposed and expressed by the hagiographic texts.[57] Theologians themselves are the least likely of all researchers to show interest in hagiography.[58] Even a study purporting to deal with the ethical implications that hagiography has for developing a postmodern morality cannot face the most unsettling dissonances arising out of the religious beliefs and practices to which hagiography attests.[59] Moreover, for all the influence that the Bible exercises over hagiography, both historians and students of literature devote astoundingly little attention to the presence of a biblical worldview shaping the ideal of sanctity by the existence of countless explicit and implicit borrowings that can be detected in the narratives. Those works that do treat this issue elicit surprisingly little attention, as is especially evident from the general indifference shown toward them by North American scholars.[60]

Based on a critical understanding of hagiographic research in its historical development, two observations may be made. First, no one discipline appears to offer the preeminent methodology for investigating hagiography. Second, any approach is flawed that sets up a system of investigation that is alien to the spirit of the hagiographic texts and also allied entirely with what the modern researcher narrowly defines as valuable. The implication of the first observation is that the validity of the present study need not be contingent on the extent to which it conforms to the methodologies advocated by representatives of a particular field, whether historians of society and politics, literary critics, social scientists, or any of the other researchers who sometimes deal with these texts. The significance of the second observation concerns the area of research with which this study has a special interest.

If the history of past hagiographic scholarship teaches us that a narrowly defined focus on only those aspects of the sources held dearest to the modern researcher has led to significant failures because the literature is being expected to give answers that it often cannot provide, then the latest approach to the hagiography pertaining to Merovingian female saints and writers may also be flawed precisely because it is a specialty within a specialty, a trend that, by definition, attempts to study and to generalize about an aspect of the sources that at best plays a marginal role in the hagiographic texts themselves. If we briefly consider the nature of this approach, then we can gain a better sense of how its limited scope can lead to unreliable conclusions.

In 1965, Frantisek Graus noticed that at least one researcher had exaggerated the differences between the two Lives of Saint Radegund (ca. 518–587), the first of which was written by the poet Venantius Fortunatus (ca. 530–ca. 610) and the second by the nun Baudonivia (fl. ca. 600).[61] Since then, although not as extensively established as the growing proliferation of studies on women, sanctity, and writing in the later Middle Ages,[62] an entire scholarly trend has steadily developed, based largely on the assumption that the Merovingian hagiography produced by female authors, a corpus hitherto neglected or even depreciated by scholars, marks a decisive break with the way male writers portray sanctity and is, in fact, indicative of an altogether different religious and spiritual milieu, one that is consciously woman-centered.

While the seeds of the movement may be found, as Graus's comment suggests, in European scholarship,[63] the treatment of this literature as a major source for the understanding of early medieval women is, for the most part, the development of current North American researchers, in particular, Susan Wemple and Jo Ann Mc-Namara. To them a great debt is owed, for they have virtually rediscovered the literature and attempted to consider its relevance in light of a modern consciousness heightened by an awareness of gender issues. Through studies and translations, they have brought these relatively little-known texts into the mainstream of historical and literary research on the early Middle Ages. Their work is widely known and influential, attracting the attention not only of North American and European specialists working in Merovingian studies but also of medievalists in general and even a broader, popular audience that represents the growing interest in the lives of women throughout history.[64] On the whole, their conclusions have been accepted and, so far, rarely been challenged.[65]

Although they are social historians, they have attempted to treat the purely literary aspects of the works written by and about women in order to demonstrate the flourishing of a distinctive female sanctity. Hagiography produced by women played a decisive role in portraying this holiness by penetrating the spiritual experiences of female saints in a way that male writers allegedly failed to do. According to this view, the conventional depiction of the female saint as a "virago" imitating "male virtues" and transcending femininity is supplanted by female writers, who, unlike their male counterparts, show the nurturing, maternal, charitable side of holy women.[66] Indeed, the emphasis on charity is thought to be one of the chief contributions and innovations of this female hagiography. According to Wemple:

> Although Baudonivia's *Life of St Radegund*, the anonymous *vita* of St Balthild and the visions
> of St Aldegund synthesized rather than delineated stages of perfection in the exercise

of charity, they conveyed to posterity an awareness of the need and value of love in spiritual life. By recording the impulse of love in the religious development of Radegund, Balthild, and Aldegund, their biographies made an important contribution to monastic spirituality. They introduced a new motif into hagiography, providing an alternative to the male ideal of humility, penance, and renunciation of the self.[67]

Along similar lines, McNamara also views the hagiography pertaining to holy women of this era, including, apparently, the Lives of female saints written by men, as offering a sharp contrast to a previous ideal of sanctity: "Thus Merovingian Gaul produced a new model of sanctity: the great monastic lady, withdrawn from worldly power and worldly comfort but not from the world's misery and strife. Hagiographers praised her as a model of hospitality, a virtue antithetical to the original desert ideal."[68]

Obviously, we can immediately tell that what Graus had once regarded as an exaggeration in the way one scholar viewed the two Lives of Radegund has developed into a commonly accepted view about female saints and writers of the Merovingian age. On the issue of charity, moreover, even a superficial acquaintance with the pre-Merovingian literature is enough to demonstrate that Wemple's and McNamara's arguments cannot be substantiated. Here, there is no need to cite the various texts from the earlier sources to show the inaccuracy of their claims. That has already been done by two prominent exponents of the desert literature who, writing before the more recent scholarship on Merovingian holy women, found the emphasis on charity to be one of the chief characteristics of the "desert ideal" expressed in early hagiographic texts.[69] The position of Wemple and McNamara on this point is further weakened by consideration that Sulpicius Severus's paradigmatic Vita sancti Martini arguably records the most famous act of charity known to medieval Europe—Martin cutting his cloak at Amiens to clothe the cold beggar.[70]

On the question of a more maternal ideal of sanctity and the rejection of the virago, perhaps the view of McNamara and Wemple can find support.[71] It certainly cannot in their own treatment of this issue, however, for they have not attempted to substantiate their findings on the basis of a broad range of hagiographic texts. If we exclude the translations, most of their hagiographic research focuses on three or four compositions: Baudonivia's Life of Saint Radegund, the anonymous nun of Chelles's Life of Saint Balthild, and the visions that Aldegund is thought to have dictated to a scribe, which were eventually included in the text of her Vita.[72] Invariably, the only comparison done with other hagiographic literature occurs when Fortunatus's first account of Radegund is contrasted with the later one written by Baudonivia.[73] What we have, then, in the case of the current state of research on Merovingian female saints and writers, is a scholarly consensus that has yet to be adequately substantiated.

From the perspective of past hagiographic research, the recent interest in female saints and authors is thus characterized by a similar use of hagiographic texts that marks much of historical scholarship in general, only this time, rather than attempting to sift fact from fiction, the researchers try to distinguish the female elements of the literature from the male. But the focus is almost exclusively on texts written by or about women, while the question of how these sources relate to the larger corpus of Merovingian literature never receives adequate attention. The result is an assessment that cannot be upheld when the full range of hagiographic material is considered. The limited choice of sources, determined purely on the basis of what appear to the researchers to be texts that will address peculiarly modern concerns, has led to an inaccurate generalization about the special significance of charity.

My argument is not that the kind of evidence needed to show the traces of a distinctive history, literature, and spirituality of women is precluded by the nature of the hagiographic sources,[74] so that the current view of a special female sanctity flourishing at this time must therefore be regarded as an unfounded abstraction, something analogous to the concepts of "Germanism" (Germanentum) or "Volk" that were once so dear to the racially motivated historians of the late nineteenth and early twentieth century.[75] Rather, my point is that a basic methodology for even considering the question of female saints and writers has yet to be developed. A new approach is obviously needed, one that can substantiate its particular conclusions regarding female hagiography on the basis of a wider representation of the literature.

In light of this need for a new approach, the contributions of two major works in the history of hagiographic research deserve attention because of the critical and innovative methodological insights that they respectively offer. Significantly, the authors of these valuable studies were also concerned with sources dating from the Merovingian era.

The early sections of Graus's study on Merovingian hagiography are disturbingly illuminating. On these opening pages, the major movements of nineteenth- and twentieth-century historiography and hagiographic research receive their hardest blows. Giants like the Monumenta editors of the Merovingian Vitae and the great Bollandists seem on the verge of toppling, their successes much less compellingly portrayed than their failures. The reader is left actually doubting whether the earliest studies on Merovingian hagiography done by Bernoulli and Marignan have any merit at all after they have been subjected to Graus's scrutiny. Then, in a sudden contrast with what preceded, words of praise are showered on a book whose value seems to have eluded at least one contemporary researcher.[76] When Léon Van der Essen's work receives such acclaim in the context of Graus's highly critical opening statements, then the reader naturally wants to learn more about what makes this study so useful and distinctive from previous research, especially since the famous, towering achievements—what Knowles calls "the great historical enterprises"—have all but fallen. This work's innovation in approach is surprisingly simple: Unlike historians seeking information about the saint and his cult or using the Vitae only insofar as they pertain to social history, Van der Essen sets out to investigate the hagiographic literature as hagiographic literature—not to find historical kernels or establish the authenticity of a cult but to study the sources as they relate to each other. He thus establishes conclusions that have an intrinsic validity on the basis of the texts subjected to his examination. His starting point and focus, as Graus recognized, is the Lives. Everyone else up to that time—and, indeed, much like the current scholarship on holy women—started with the question of the historical saint. Although he initially engages the conclusions of earlier researchers,[77] his discussion generally avoids controversy, and his findings are almost banal, consisting of summaries describing the content of a Vita, information about the author if he or she is known, possible dates of composition, and the textual evidence showing the influences of other hagiographic sources on certain Lives, sometimes with useful line-by-line comparisons. By the end, however, a large, coherent picture emerges; the researcher has established the "hagiographic cycles" of the major Belgian dioceses and represented them in a flowchart showing at the top the paradigmatic Lives for each main diocesan cycle, with the lines of their influence carefully traced throughout the numerous *Vitae*.

Significantly, he begins by noting that hagiographic texts are not necessarily works of history but, as Delehaye suggests, literary productions meant to promote the cult of a saint. As such, rather than give what is generally regarded as historical information, they are more a reflection of the ideas and literary conventions of the age in which they flourished.[78] In his opening remarks, with their emphasis on how the historical deficiencies of the texts are compensated for by what they tell us about the literary life and religious attitudes of the past, the modern student of hagiography may finally begin to see a greater coherence emerging in the research and glimpse for a moment how the work of a Brown would be the natural development from Van der Essen, who, in turn, had built on one of Delehaye's postulates.[79]

Even though Van der Essen is not attempting to coordinate the *Vitae* with the more objectively usable data so valued by Delehaye, there still are "hagiographic coordinates"—that is, reference points that facilitate his approach and establish the foundation of his assessment. Here the Lives are coordinated with the dioceses. Starting with the ecclesiastical division where the oldest texts are found and gradually identifying "*un ensemble de Vitae*" for each region, he clearly reveals the individual literary cycles that distinguish one diocese from the next.[80]

What is needed for the study of the hagiography pertaining to Merovingian women is a method of coordinating the texts so that the differences and similarities between these *Vitae* and those produced by and about men may emerge as clearly and as naturally as those found in the Belgian cycles. The method I propose is not characteristic of the historian. I intend, as Van der Essen did, to begin with the Lives, not with the historical saint extracted from the text. Naturally, all discussion of historical issues will not be shunned. There are obvious occasions when material pertaining to ecclesiastical and social history blends completely into the literary conventions. But this study is not a history of Merovingian saints and society.[81]

This research is also not representative of what today is considered to be literary criticism. Although the discussion deals primarily with the literary characteristics of the *Vitae*, the latest critical techniques are not applied. At times, however, the findings of one critic have been introduced because of their obvious relevancy to the texts at hand. On this matter, I can hardly be said to be using the most advanced critical tools, however, because my reliance is on Northrop Frye, a critic who is increasingly out of fashion among students of theoretical approaches to literature.

Broadly speaking, what I try to do is situate the Merovingian sources within the phases of hagiography's early evolution and then see how the text of one writer of the period compares with his or her contemporaries, so that the *Vitae* eventually face each other both in their Merovingian context and in their relationship to past hagiographic trends. To the extent that this comparison is done, the study more or less conforms to what is usually regarded as a history-of-literature approach, which is rooted in a traditional examination of texts and hence philological in nature. The method is therefore derived from the sources and aimed at establishing the chief characteristics of a considerable body of hagiographic material.

Of course, only with qualifications can the method be labeled a history-of-literature approach. It is obviously more accurate to speak of a history-of-hagiographic-literature approach and to say that we shall focus on the writings of the most prominent authors of the Merovingian era more closely than is characteristic in sweeping surveys of literary overviews. Moreover, at the risk of sounding inconsistent, I stress that the investigation is not purely philological but also grapples with an issue perhaps more commonly associated with the study of spirituality. I try to get at and deal with, rather basically, the obvious religious dimension of the Vitae—namely, the particular ideal of sanctity that each author expresses through his or her writings. Those interested in reading about such technical issues as the proportion of accentual clausules, the presence of chiasmus, the corruption of the ablative absolute, the use of the passive paraphrastic, and other such matters raised by the Latinity of the Merovingian sources will have to look elsewhere.[82]

With respect to the comparative aspect of the study, much of the contrast between authors is brought out simply by the basic treatment of the often very different texts produced by each writer, especially for Venantius Fortunatus and Gregory of Tours (ca. 540–594). Given the aims of the study, it is not necessary to dwell on or even mention all the divergencies or similarities that can be detected throughout the various Vitae. For instance, the differences between the ways Gregory and Fortunatus preface their Lives will become obvious enough without my having to say so. To some extent, the texts "face each other" merely by the way the discussion proceeds, with elaboration on the rhetorical strategies of one author tacitly suggesting differences with those of another author whose work was previously treated.

This attempt to investigate in depth a relatively large body of texts marks a break with the current scholarship of the hagiography pertaining to Merovingian women. The discussion aims to go beyond the limited focus of contemporary research to gain a broader sense of the hagiographic literature written during the early Merovingian period. The main objectives of this study are therefore to establish the chief rhetorical strategies of the standard authors as they narrate the lives of male saints and then to situate what these same writers say about female saints within the context of their larger literary corpus. At this point, the comparison can occur at an internal level, so that the texts portraying sancti and sanctae can face each other within the context of each writer's separate corpus. By proceeding in this way, we shall be able to see if the usual approaches by male hagiographers to the genre—and hence the image of sanctity concomitant with them—change when the subject becomes a female saint. After this, we shall be in an excellent position to observe where a female writer's depiction of a holy woman falls within the previously established context of the hagiography produced by and usually about men. In other studies, the female writer to be discussed here is almost invariably compared only with one other author of the period. I am speaking, of course, of Baudonivia and her Life of Saint Radegund, a work that is being approached now more and more within the narrowly defined framework of a gendered reading of her text against the earlier Vita of that saint written by Fortunatus.[83]

In defining and elaborating the methodology, I have kept in mind three features related to some of the most fundamental work in the field of hagiographic studies: the rigor of Delehaye, the innovation of Van der Essen, and the critical insights into the failures of hagiographic research offered by Graus.

The study is thus posited on stylistic coordinates, derived from the sources and consisting in the constant elements that keep emerging in the literature and that reveal the dominant traits of a writer. By these reference points, the hagiographic texts can be compared and assessed in a way that preserves their integrity and also allows them to address an issue of special interest to scholars concerned with gender and writing (although, admittedly, these contemporary concerns must linger in the background for a considerable portion of the examination, and they are not treated with the intensity and sophistication that often characterize modern studies outside hagiography on medieval women, gender, and feminist criticism). The coordinates I propose can indicate a writer's reliance on convention as well as the favorite, peculiar strategies that distinctively characterize an author. These coordinates are the following: *prefaces* (perhaps the most important of all since prefacing matter often reveals an author reflecting on the aim of his or her work), the implicit and explicit use of *Scripture*, the various *saint types* represented, the presence of *previous hagiographic trends*, and the appearance of direct or indirect *borrowings* from other hagiographic works, especially paradigmatic texts. In focusing on these elements as the primary reference points, the methodology aims at uncovering the variations that appear within the regular features of hagiographic literature and thus protects the study against attributing originality to what is commonplace, as the current scholarship tends to do.

Let us consider the general nature of the discussion. Implicitly, the study develops a dialectic between what the sources contain and what the current scholars maintain, not by a simplistic, point-by-point argument against their conclusions but through a broad and careful examination of texts often having nothing to do with female saints and writers. Although not usually stated explicitly in the following discussion, the approach characterizing the recent scholarship, with its interest primarily in only a few texts concerned with or composed by women, becomes the trend against which this broader study develops. Thus, the discussion initially moves in exactly the opposite direction from that in which the current research starts. My premise is that, to study the works produced by or about women, it is first necessary to gain as broad a perspective of the literature as possible so that, when the Lives pertaining to women do become the focus of study, we have established a coordinated basis of comparison and assessment. The dialectic is thus gradually developed, first by an examination of male authors writing about male saints, then by observing how these same writers treat female saints, and, finally, by turning to the question of how a female writer portrays a female saint, so that I end where others invariably begin, and I reach the point where I can engage their conclusions in the full light of what a good sampling of the hagiographic literature has revealed.

To gain the broad sample of hagiography from this period, I have chosen texts written by the two most prolific writers of the era, Venantius Fortunatus and Gregory of Tours. Of the former, the six prose biographies are the focus; of the latter, the large collection of twenty Lives known as the *Liber vitae patrum* is the object of study.

In both cases, the body of material is handled thematically rather than given a consecutive *Vita*-by-*Vita* treatment that would begin with the first account of each corpus and end with the last. After studying the works of Fortunatus and Gregory, we shall turn to Baudonivia's *Life of Saint Radegund*. The advantages these choices offer are several.

First of all, as we shall see, although undoubtedly representative of the early phase of Merovingian hagiography, these two prolific writers strikingly contrast with each other, so the major sources of our sampling in no way constitute a generic collection of *Vitae*. If Fortunatus's hagiography, considered by itself, appears relatively uniform, the *Liber vitae patrum* is intrinsically a work of remarkable variety. The combination of the two makes for the richest, most complex, and diverse collection of texts that we can expect to find. And we are fortunate not only because these writings of Gregory and Fortunatus offer two very different representations of the literature but also for what each author includes in addition to the biographies of several holy men: a *Vita* devoted to a female saint. We can observe how the Lives of two holy women compare with the previously examined *Vitae* of holy men found in the broader hagiographic corpus of Fortunatus and Gregory. To the best of my knowledge, this issue has received no prior attention.

This selection and this way of proceeding are also advantageous because the text of Baudonivia, the last author to be considered in this study, who was familiar with the works of both writers and especially with Fortunatus's *Life of Saint Radegund*, can be treated in light of how it relates to hagiography never included in the limited studies comparing the two Lives of Radegund. We have not only the opportunity to examine how her version of Radegund's life compares with the first but also the chance to glimpse how Baudonivia's account of Radegund relates to and differs from the rest of Fortunatus's corpus. In the end, we may also gain a sense of the striking contrast offered by Gregory of Tours's *Liber vitae patrum* in light of the hagiography produced by Fortunatus and Baudonivia, a challenging consideration, given that current scholarship insists that female hagiography is the really distinctive corpus of the period.

A further reason for the appropriateness of this selection of texts is the lack of extensive studies on Fortunatus's prose biographies and Gregory of Tours's *Liber vitae patrum*. Most scholars have concentrated almost exclusively on Fortunatus's poetry, and research on his *Vitae* is still in its early stages.[84] It did not seem necessary to provide a preliminary overview of Fortunatus scholarship, since the conclusions of those few studies dealing specifically with his prose hagiography were more easily incorporated into the discussion at the moments when they bore the greatest relevance.[85] However, because so much scholarship touching on Fortunatus's writings also relates to studies on Gregory of Tours, a summary of how researchers generally tend to regard the two is given in chapter 3. There we shall find that, similar to the way Fortunatus's Lives have been inadequately treated in comparison with his poetry, Gregory's *Liber vitae patrum* has also received very little in-depth examination, with researchers preferring instead to study his *Histories*. Considerations related to the scholarly trends in the treatment of Gregory's writings were thus given to the extent that they bear some connection with the *Liber vitae patrum*.

The other obvious advantage of this approach is that no one disputes the authenticity of the sources serving as the main focus of this study, an important consideration given the ongoing debates regarding the uncertain authorship and dating of so many Merovingian or, as the case may be, Carolingian texts.[86] It is quite possible that more works will be shown to have been penned by Fortunatus,[87] but I have decided to include here only those that have been accepted by the overwhelming majority of scholars as the indisputable prose writings, or "*opera pedestria*," of the Merovingian poet who came from Ravenna, commonly known as Venantius Fortunatus. I have, however, excluded one piece attributed to Fortunatus because, even as it appears in the form of Levison's modern edition, this *Life* is virtually unreadable.[88] Regarding the authenticity of the *Liber vitae patrum* and the second *Vita sanctae Radegundis*, no one, to the best of my knowledge, has ever brought forth evidence suggesting that these are the products of writers other than Gregory of Tours and the otherwise unknown nun Baudonivia, respectively.

Furthermore, although the dates of composition for each *Vita* cannot be exactly determined, especially in the case of Gregory, who probably wrote his works gradually and simultaneously over a twenty-year period, the general consensus on the dating of these texts make it highly unlikely that any were produced long after the year 600, shortly after which Baudonivia is thought to have composed her *Life of Saint Radegund*.[89] And while I refer frequently in the main discussion to texts written prior to the Merovingian age, no works written after that period normally assume prominence in the investigation itself. On occasion, I refer, usually in the notes and rarely in the main body of the discussion, to hagiographic literature produced later but bearing some important connection to the issue at hand (for instance, when Fortunatus's influence on later hagiographers needed to be addressed or when the relevance of Radegund's dossier deserved attention).

What may be regarded as the study's chief limitations should also be acknowledged. In light of the inquiry's aims and the need it attempts to fill, the discussion strives at length to establish a literary context in which to place the sources dealing with women and to situate the Merovingian texts within hagiography's early evolution. While there is an adequate sample of how the two most prolific male writers of the Merovingian period depict female saints, no consideration is given to male authors who followed Fortunatus and Gregory and who also wrote Lives of holy women. More important, the texts of female authorship receive proportionally far less treatment in the discussion than do the works of the prolific male authors.

The disproportion, however, is not entirely due to the study's limited scope with respect to female hagiographers. Quite simply, there are few texts from the era that are unquestionably of female authorship.[90] Besides Baudonivia's *Life of Saint Radegund*, the *Vita* of Balthild (d. ca. 680) is the only other hagiographic document of the Merovingian period that is now indisputably attributed to a female writer.[91] While the latter biography is not extensively discussed here, its relevance to the hagiography on Saint Radegund does receive consideration. Other material possibly composed by women posed problems, the complexity of which would require another study altogether. For instance, while the visions narrated in the *Life* of Aldegund (d. ca. 684) may well be an accurate report that the saint herself gave to a scribe, at present there appears to be no one authoritative text of her *Vita* on which scholars consistently rely.[92] Whether Radegund is the author of the moving poem *De excidio Thuringiae* is also disputed and unlikely to be resolved.[93] Of course, there are the writings of

Hugeburc on Saints Willibald (d. 786) and Winnibald (d. 761), as well as some epistolatory sources that are unquestionably the products of female authors.[94] However valuable these pieces may be, they fall, respectively, outside the temporal scope and literary genre of this study, and so they have been excluded.[95] Hence, although the present treatment does not offer a complete survey of all the sources pertaining to women in the *regnum francorum* from the sixth to the mideighth century, it does come close to providing a comprehensive, comparative view of the main hagiographic trends that characterize the depiction of holy men and women during the early Merovingian period.

Acknowledging the study's limitations is reminiscent of an early chapter in Aristotle's *Metaphysics* on "*aporia*" and also the great medieval "*disputatio*" associated with scholastic theological debate.[96] Here we encounter authors who early on set out the obvious objections to the arguments they are about to make. These objections highlight some of the genuine difficulties that the writer must address to advance a convincing and valid argument on disputed issues. Well into this work, I came to realize that the most difficult problems related to the Merovingian *Vitae* have been barely acknowledged by scholars studying the early hagiographic sources on women.[97] Perplexing questions regarding the nature of the female voice and the legitimacy of associating certain characteristics of the depiction of holy women with only male writers, as current research tends to do, still need to be addressed. On such issues, the sources of the inquiry are pushed as far as they can go in grappling with these perplexities but only from within the context of the limited, methodological framework previously outlined. At times, the discussion reaches a point where others would want to introduce the observations of literary and historical theoreticians or to apply the findings of the social sciences in gender and religious studies. Indeed, in light of the advances made in those fields, the present work may seem rather "old-fashioned."[98] Yet, the approach that is used does offer a comprehensive method suited specifically to the sources and capable of pinpointing precisely where the interpretive difficulties lie. In the context of the present trend in the study of Merovingian hagiography and holy women, this discovering of the problems— which the recent scholarship, because of its limited approach, consistently overlooks and which became apparent to me only after a long and relatively thorough examination of the sources—is an advancement. By identifying the texts that pose the greatest difficulty to the current work in the field of Merovingian hagiography, the inquiry also serves, in part, as a kind of *aporia* engaging and challenging the now established research by raising objections that will have to be answered if the study of holy women and early medieval sanctity is to advance further.

Finally, in the selection of texts, I am reminded of Jean Bolland's elaborate remarks, which serve as the epigraph of the entire study. Here, once again, we notice a distinguished researcher—indeed, the one from whom the Bollandists take their name—relying extensively on metaphor to explain, or so it seems, the nature of his hagiographic enterprise.[99] Bolland claims to present the reader with a clear font that is fed by several channels. What this "salubrious" spring, with its various arteries, exactly is does not seem certain. However, given the marginal gloss, "*opus hoc fons est,*" I suspect that the different waterways feeding into the font could very well be the many genres and phases that hagiography has known throughout the ages, and that the gradual gathering together of the whole of this abundant textual material into the tomes that will become the *Acta Sanctorum* is the creation of a source into which all the channels can finally flow and from which the reader may now begin to drink. Bolland's metaphor offers an image that also encapsulates the present work's approach to the literature. The sampling of texts examined in this study may be considered one of those little *canales*, the early phase of Merovingian hagiography, with its own steady currents found in the writings of Fortunatus and Gregory. Whether Baudonivia in particular and female writers in general represent a strong countercurrent remains to be seen.

PART I

Sancti

2

THE PROSE HAGIOGRAPHY OF
VENANTIUS FORTUNATUS

> The experts in legitimation, the ones who labor
> to make what people in power do seem legiti-
> mate, are mainly the privileged educated elites.
> The journalists, the academics, the teachers, the
> public relations specialists, this whole category of
> people have a kind of an institutional task, and
> that is to create the system of belief which will
> ensure the effective engineering of consent.
> —Noam Chomsky, *Chronicles of Dissent*
> (1992, pp. 66–67)

The Image of Sanctity

To establish the main features that characterize the male saints portrayed by Fortunatus, we shall first concentrate on the depiction of the holy men in the earliest phase
of life. In the description of the young man, we find the profile of the whole saint.
If such an assertion seems to place undue importance on one aspect of what is
presumably a more comprehensive literary representation, that is because we generally expect biographical narrative to mirror the course of human life as it progresses
not only physically, which is obvious, but also psychologically through several distinct stages marking the passages from birth to death. The literature we are about
to examine, however, shows little correspondence to our modern scheme or even
our experience of human development. With respect to that gradual psychological
formation of a child into what we commonly call a "self-actualized" adult, the writing
of Fortunatus is a case in which art does not reflect life.[1] The gray-haired holy man described on his deathbed is fundamentally the same in character as the saintly youth depicted in the early portions of a *Vita*.[2] Even in death, the saint continues to perform
from the tomb virtually the same functions that he did while alive.[3]

From the perspective of a Merovingian hagiographer, the holy person is, as a
rule, not made but born—sometimes even with a tonsure.[4] Of course, not all early
Christian hagiography assumes that sanctity begins from birth and continues unin-
terrupted until death. Stories originating in the monastic circles of the East, but often
known to the early medieval West through Latin translations, told how profligates,
prostitutes, and even a brutal murderer abandoned the ways of sin to embrace in
the desert a life of humility and repentance.[5] Even Jerome, in his colorful account
of Malchus, allows his virginal but not quite unblemished saint to be temporarily

sidetracked from the religious quest—perhaps the hagiographic equivalent of Homer's diverted Ulysses.[6] But Merovingian authors in general—and Fortunatus in particular—show a remarkable resistance to literary trends that characteristically display the often tumultuous vicissitudes in a person struggling to attain holiness. The stories of "great sinners" becoming "great saints," of which Augustine's *Confessions* is an obvious example, never appear in the pages of Fortunatus's hagiography.[7] Even though the theme of repentance decisively marked Augustine's autobiography as well as the influential *Vita beati Antonii*, that dramatic moment in life known as "religious conversion" plays no role in the stories told by Fortunatus. As we shall discover later, the writings of Fortunatus reveal that the only major flaws requiring repentance and an actual change in the life of a Merovingian saint are the displays by independent holy men of excessive ascetic feats, which the more religiously moderate and control-oriented ecclesiastical authorities do not easily tolerate.

Because of this deliberate disregard for a detailed psychological profile of a saint's progression through life, we must forgo any attempt to discover in Fortunatus's literary portraits distinct phases representing actual changes in the personalities of the individuals described. Moreover, in the hagiography of Fortunatus, revealing distinctive traits in personality is subordinate to presenting a type of hero who embodies the ideal of Christian perfection. To divulge information such as whether a saint ever fell in love, harbored doubts about the religious calling, preferred summer to winter, or thought his nose too big has no functional value in a piece of writing that attempts to present a model of human achievement perfected by grace and self-sacrifice. Indeed, the peculiarities of an individual personality are, as Delehaye so aptly put it, "absorbed" by this "ideal figure" of hagiography's saint.[8] "Rebellious adolescence" and "mid-life crisis" do not entice Fortunatus and most Merovingian hagiographers the way they do modern biographers, who, instead of an idealized portrait, often want to give a "warts-and-all" display of their subjects.[9]

In the hagiography of Fortunatus, the features of this idealized portrait do not develop gradually but are explicitly present from a *Vita*'s inception. For this reason, attempts to categorize saints' Lives according to the periods in the course of a holy person's career overlook the fluid quality in the narrative of a writer like Fortunatus, who does not usually associate any particular moment in the hero's life with a corresponding sign of sanctity.[10] Such characteristics as fervent prayer or the ability to perform miracles appear throughout the whole *Vita* and are not correlated with the age of the saint.[11] Certainly, there is progression in Fortunatus's Lives; the holiness described is by no means static. But the progression really denotes the saint becoming more and more what he already is from the beginning of the *Vita*. Given, then, this religious precociousness of Fortunatus's holy men, a consideration of how he portrays a saint's early life will uncover some of the fundamental characteristics of the type of sanctity represented by his writing.

Fighting from the Womb

Fortunatus establishes sanctity at birth, even before birth if we consider the unusual description of a fetal Saint Germanus resisting the attempts of his mother to abort him. This episode in the *Vita sancti Germani* clearly illustrates how the hagiographer immediately frames the events of a saint's life by providing a religious context to an incident that, as other contemporary sources suggest, probably occurred on a regular basis.[12]

With an explicit reference to their high social status, the first sentence of the Life introduces the parents of Germanus. Other than social rank, we learn nothing about the father and only the most essential details about the mother, who poses the initial threat to the saint. Like most hagiographers before and during his era, Fortunatus dwells on the particular members of a saint's family only when they directly either promote or hinder religious development.[13] Occasionally, Fortunatus and other early medieval hagiographers mention an immediate member or relative of a saint's family who also lives a pious life,[14] and sometimes the attempt by a holy person to convert one of his kin receives attention.[15] Except for Fortunatus's insistence throughout most of his Vitae on the saints' noble origins, however, the attitude expressed toward the family is, in almost all cases, one of indifference. For example, in the beginning of Germanus's Life, we are told that the mother recently gave birth and refuses to bear another child—the future saint—so shortly after a previous pregnancy. About this earlier born child, we know virtually nothing. The most that can be determined is the gender since Fortunatus refers to this offspring as "*alterum*" rather than *alteram*. We never learn the infant's name, and his existence is never again mentioned. Thus, from the start, the narrative is conspicuously frugal in terms of the attention devoted to characters other than the saint.

In early medieval hagiography, the instances in which a familial relation actually appears prominently are often marked by opposition that is overcome when the saint rejects the ties of blood or some other bond commonly associated with family, such as marriage, children, filial obligations, or social status.[16] While the specific threat posed by Germanus's mother is certainly not common in early hagiographic literature,[17] the fact that Fortunatus presents a parent as the hero's first opponent is entirely in keeping with the earlier hagiographic tendency to accord the saint's kin a significant function in the narrative only when a member of the family initiates conflict. Again, to avoid drawing attention away from the main character, Fortunatus carefully focuses on the antagonism represented and generated in the form of a hostile relative. In Germanus's Vita, few particulars are given concerning the actual person who initially opposes the saint. Although much can be inferred from the passage about the anxieties of a wellborn Merovingian woman unable to bear alone an imposed burden of family planning, the attention given to the important role of the mother reveals only the bare facts of her situation. The author does not elaborate on the interior motive for the woman's desire to abort. Instead, by way of presenting the mother's highly personal motive, the writer offers only a suggestive phrase consisting of three words ("*pudore mota muliebri*") placed in a position subordinate to the rest of the sentence: "the mother, because she had conceived this child so shortly after another one, *moved by womanly shame* [emphasis added], wanted to kill the infant before birth."[18]

Noting the sense of shame certainly helps to explain the personal incentive of the mother, but the structure of the sentence itself draws attention primarily to a circumstance (unwanted pregnancy) and a proposed course of action (abortion) intended to remove that circumstance. Between the circumstance and the proposed action, lies, syntactically speaking, the emotional state of the woman. The position of the phrase *pudore mota muliebri* is significant because the reference to shame, although necessary as an explanation of behavior, cannot assume primary importance. To give greater prominence to the emotional factor by elaborating on it would risk casting the mother in a sympathetic light. If the mother is regarded sympathetically, then her role as an opponent would become ambiguous. Once ambiguity is introduced, the hagiographer loses the possibility of characterizing the circumstance as an occasion of highly polarized conflict between the hero and his mother. Rather than elaborating on the emotional and psychological implications, Fortunatus describes the course of action because the response to the unwanted pregnancy offers the hagiographer an immediate opportunity to introduce a facet of the holy individual's sanctity that will characterize the saint for the rest of the *Vita*: Germanus, even in his fetal state, is a Christian warrior.

The clash begins when the mother first ingests a drink capable of terminating the pregnancy. After Fortunatus matter-of-factly states that this procedure failed, his style begins to change; his language becomes more descriptive as the scene develops into a full-blown conflict between mother and son, the two fighting a contest that occurs entirely within the arena of the womb:

> The mother . . . wanted to kill the infant before birth, and a potion was taken in order to abort him. When she was not able to do any harm, she lay on her belly so that, with her weight she might suffocate him whom poison could not hurt. The mother fought with the little boy; the infant resisted from inside: it was a battle between the woman and her womb. The matron was being struck but the baby was not being injured. The bundle opposed the mother in order to prevent her from becoming a murderer. This happened so that he, kept safe and sound, might come out unharmed and render his mother innocent. To have performed a miracle before he happened to be born was, then, a foretelling of future events.[19]

The opening lines of the *Life* immediately define the saint as a holy warrior. In fact, Germanus comes close to being distinguished as a specific type of warrior since the characteristics of the *Vita*'s introduction—highly polarized opposition, an aggressor portrayed as immoral, the threat of death, and the victorious struggle of the hero in contest—recall several features of the drama that unfolds in the accounts of the martyrs. More important to our present discussion than noting similarities to a past hagiographic trend is the fact that the initial emphasis on the saint in conflict marks the entire *Vita*. Like the fetal saint fighting at the outset of the narrative, a holy "*belliger*" armed with prayers and the sign of the cross continues to appear prominently throughout the rest of the story.[20] Of course, new opponents take the place of the mother, and the hagiographer names many enemies specifically: Jews who refuse to convert, rebellious monks tired of fasting, disrespectful or cruel secular leaders, preoccupied workers neglecting their religious obligations, mean slave owners, and, occasionally, wily demons.

Besides the emphasis on conflict, we also notice that Fortunatus explicitly refers to the initial incident in the *Life* as a "miracle" (*virtutem*), a miracle anticipating similar *virtutes* that, like the instances of opposition, also occur throughout the story.[21] In fact, in the account immediately following his birth, Germanus again escapes a brush with death by his uncanny ability, demonstrated at the *Vita*'s outset, to avoid being poisoned.[22] Moreover, presenting Germanus as a fetus with the miraculous quality of indestructibility, as well as with an undaunted determination to live in spite of his mother's efforts, assumes that the saint's birth is predestined—no measure can be taken to prevent the holy man's coming into the world.[23]

In addition to establishing immediately the saint as a predestined warrior and thaumaturge, one other feature emerges from the opening scene in the *Life of Saint Germanus*. Even before birth, the saint possesses a moral consciousness. Fortunatus explains the struggle in terms of a heroic battle in which Germanus restores his mother's innocence by the very fact of his birth. The child in the womb already knows how he ought to act. His behavior assumes a religious and ethical sophistication characteristic of maturity. He is, in other words, a *puer-senex*—a child with the wisdom of an adult.[24]

Although they do not offer as vivid a scene of the saint's early development as the one found in the *Vita sancti Germani*, Fortunatus's other Lives show the same concern with immediately establishing the holiness of an individual. The attributes associated with sanctity are also combined in much the same way as in the case of Germanus. Hilary, for instance, receives not the milk of his mother but the nourishment of "wisdom." From the cradle, the infant saint realizes that he is a "soldier" of Christ, for whose causes he is destined to win victories. Like Germanus, the *puer-senex* Hilary senses his predestined role in life as one of God's warriors.[25] The same may be said of Albinus. Like a mature man, he leaves his family while still a child, even though, as Fortunatus carefully notes, infancy is the period during which a child usually clings to his parents. Albinus also wages war since he treats the "carnal desires" as if they were enemies.[26] Moreover, this freeborn infant, with the characteristic perception of a *puer-senex*, also "understands" that it is better to be a poor servant of Christ than a rich member of the upper class.[27] Likewise, after summarizing the qualities of the young Marcellus, Fortunatus claims that his complete devotion to religious training rendered the saint an adult even from childhood. With *infantia* placed directly beside *maturus*, the position of the words reflects precisely that juxtaposition inherent in the concept of the *puer-senex*: "*qui . . . se totum caelesti tradidit disciplinae, ut ab ipsa infantia maturus ascenderet.*"[28]

As in the Lives mentioned so far, the *Vita sancti Marcelli* is also marked by the combined depiction of the saint as a *puer-senex* and as a warrior.[29] But, in addition to these characteristics, Fortunatus uses a technique in his description of the young Marcellus that is not applied in the other *Vitae* at such an early stage in the narrative. Shortly after mentioning that "heavenly discipline" made Marcellus "an adult from infancy," Fortunatus relies heavily on military imagery to describe the saintly boy and then introduces biblical typology, which implicitly adds a richness to the notion of Christian warfare by associating the saint with a biblical figure who traditionally signifies a pivotal point in the history of salvation. The process culminating in the association is gradual and complex. To legitimize the analogy, a period in the saint's life must be molded or stylized to suit the anticipated comparison with the biblical model. Initially, the child-saint displays the typical *contemptus mundi* by rejecting worldly pomp. Fortunatus then proceeds to describe his ascetic training in terms of military service for Christ. This warfare qualifies him to serve as a lector. The hagiographer represents this liturgical appointment as an offering of the saint to the church. Once Marcellus's role as lector is related to a holy offering, a link with Scripture can be forged. Thus his formal acceptance into the clerical ranks is compared to Abel. The comparison has a twofold dimension based on the scriptural context. Like Abel offering his firstlings to the Lord, Marcellus offers himself as a new servant in Christ's church. In both instances, the offerings are accepted. This acceptance, however, entails not only the giving of gifts but also the sacrifice of the self. For Abel, the sacrifice leads to death at the hands of a jealous Cain; for Marcellus, the sacrifice calls for the death of bodily desires and the offering of a pure heart: "initiated in [the art of] divine weaponry, armed with the blessed hope, about to win back the palm from the public enemy and with training in the warfare of Christ, he was made a lector; offering himself as the firstfruits in the temple of Christ, like the sacrifice of Abel, he was received as a host of conquered flesh and pure heart."[30]

In the narrative leading to the comparison of Marcellus and Abel, Fortunatus introduces the features of a multifaceted sanctity. Like the ascetics of previous generations, Marcellus disciplines himself through almsgiving, chastity, and fasting.[31] A strong antagonism toward the body also marks Marcellus's sanctity; this Merovingian holy man shows no sign that he lives corporeally, the body being merely the physical form in which the saint is "placed."[32] In addition to the battle waged against the self and worldly enticements, the hero's life also entails conflict with the devil, here called the "public enemy." Although Fortunatus does not elaborate on the devil's role in Marcellus's life, the reference to winning back the palm branch of victory suggests, in keeping with previous traditions, that the saint's life of self-sacrificing warfare leads to the defeat of demonic forces.[33] But contrary to the early Christian ascetics described in the hagiography associated with the monks of the Egyptian desert, the sanctity of Marcellus functions from the start within the ranks of the church. However disciplined by fasts and sexual renunciation he may be, Marcellus still wages the "warfare of Christ" as an official member of the clergy. Despite the similarities with an ascetic style of Christianity, Fortunatus's description indicates from the outset that Marcellus is not preparing for the life of a wandering holy man but is, instead, being groomed for an ecclesiastical career that begins with the office of lector.[34]

Fortunatus thus combines various attributes of sanctity to portray the young Marcellus. The ascetic aspect is undeniably present, even if the religious practices are not described beyond the stock phrases characteristic of the genre. In addition, this ascetic element, formerly associated with independent—and especially Eastern—holy men, is amalgamated with a clerical sanctity. In other words, the asceticism typical of the hermit or self-mortifying monk and the active life characteristic of the cleric are fused. The young saint assumes the features of two types of sanctity so that, even at this early stage in the *Vita*, a syncretic saint emerges. We could even classify the type of holy person presented at this point as an ascetic-cleric or, more specifically, a monk-lector. Such a classification, however, would be misleading because the nature of the sanctity portrayed is expansive: First, Fortunatus can continue to add types as the *Vita* progresses (which he does) so that the *Life of Saint Marcellus*, or any Life, can end with a saint who is a monk-bishop-confessor-(bloodless) martyr.[35] Second, as the previous classification suggests, the fact that the hagiographer immediately describes Marcellus at a low rank in the clergy means that the expansion of sanctity can occur on the level of clerical progression, with the saint reaching higher and higher ecclesiastical grades until the episcopacy is finally attained. Third, Fortunatus introduces a biblical context that helps to explain or justify an aspect of or an event in the saint's life, as in the use of Genesis 4:4 to portray Marcellus as becoming a lector.[36]

Scriptural Resonances

The association of Marcellus with Abel may seem to present no interpretive difficulties because the comparison is presented in a straightforward manner and preceded by the appropriate stylization to lend plausibility to the simile. However, the application of biblical typology actually increases the complexity of Marcellus's sanctity, given that the comparison with Abel can legitimately assume multiple meanings in the context of Christian exegesis.[37]

As previously stated, for both Marcellus and Abel the sacrifice entails more than simply offering gifts; it also involves an experience of death. In the biblical account of Cain and Abel, this experience is explicitly related. With Marcellus, however, death occurs not from shedding blood but through conquering the flesh in ascetic warfare. Though the saint still lives in the body, he no longer requires, according to Fortunatus, a regular intake of food, and he shuns the pleasures of sex and worldly comforts. In a sense, then, the young Marcellus, as Fortunatus depicts him, acts as one who has already died, at least with respect to the flesh, which, for the most part, no longer needs to be maintained. Instead, the saint lives spiritually in a body, perhaps like one who has already died and then been resurrected.[38]

Of course, the image of the holy person offering his or her life as a religious sacrifice goes to the heart of what constitutes martyrdom. In fact, patristic biblical commentators commonly regarded Abel as the first martyr, an innocent victim whose death by the corrupt Cain foreshadows the coming of an equally corrupt and violent Roman state.[39] Although Fortunatus does not explicitly refer to Marcellus as a martyr, his description of the saint's self-sacrificing life as a religious offering made acceptable by the death of bodily desires at least suggests the experience of the so-called bloodless martyrdom attributed to rigorous ascetics in early hagiographic literature.[40]

The application of nominative typology, preceded by an emphasis on Marcellus's ascetic self-sacrifice, renders the saint a martyr by association, or rather, it can render him as such. The richness of the text lies in the fact that, even though Fortunatus does not explicitly refer to Marcellus as a martyr, that type of sanctity cannot be excluded from the saint's profile because the biblical context harmonizes with and points to the Christian experience of martyrdom and persecution. The application of the Bible facilitates the association of the saint with a prototype of Christian heroism, a prototype the hagiographer uses in precisely the same way as a patristic commentator would: In both biblical exegesis and in Marcellus's Vita, Abel signifies something beyond the scriptural text itself[41]; the murdered brother of Cain represents, or typifies, the holy person who dies as a sacrificial offering to God.[42] Given what Abel stands for, biblical exegetes could easily see in this figure of the Old Testament a foreshadowing of the Christian martyr, whose offering of life was unquestionably regarded as the supreme and literal fulfillment of Scripture. Fortunatus continues this line of reasoning in his use of the Bible by presenting the sacrificing Marcellus as a contemporary example of a saint reenacting an event in the history of salvation that early Christian literature commonly related to martyrdom.

But the expansion need not end with an implicit suggestion of bloodless martyrdom. The typology connects Marcellus's *Vita* to the important biblical theme of sacrifice. This theme is not only found in the accounts of Cain and Abel or Abraham and Isaac but also continued and "fulfilled" in the New Testament.[43] Exegetically speaking, Abel typifies, in addition to the martyr, the ultimate offering made by Christ, whose blameless life, accepted sacrifice, and cruel death were also thought by the fathers to be foreshadowed in the story of Abel.[44] When Fortunatus inserts into his text, by way of simile, a figure who typifies sacrificial offering, he is portraying the life of the saint as a fulfillment of Scripture.[45] In this respect, the writers of the Gospels and the author of Marcellus's *Vita* both present a holy man who conceived of his life and mission explicitly in terms of the themes found in the Old Testament, and the hagiographic account, insofar as it renews or fulfills the sacrifice of Abel, assumes the same relation to the Bible that the New Testament has to the Old.[46] In fact, the *Vita* becomes "a Bible actualized," a kind of contemporary Scripture narrating the deeds of a saint who really repeats—albeit under new circumstances and in a way quite different from the biblical version—the events described in Sacred Scripture.[47]

Although a detailed study on Fortunatus's use of the Bible lies outside the scope of the present discussion,[48] the comparison between Abel and Marcellus deserves further consideration because it illustrates how Scripture functions in the author's representation of sanctity.[49] As previously suggested, the typological significance of Abel facilitates an association of the saint with a specific kind of Christian heroism, one that derived from and continued the Judaic tradition of sacrificial offering. The comparison with Abel thus aligns the saint with other models of holiness so that the account in the Old Testament, its fulfillment in the New, and the hagiographic continuation of both biblical narratives all portray a sacrificial sanctity. Because Abel signifies in the text of Fortunatus a type of holiness that corresponds with that of the saint, the image of Marcellus's sanctity can be expanded to embrace Christ or the martyr, both of whom are also examples of the sanctity Abel typifies.[50]

Insofar as Abel, Christ, the martyr, and Marcellus represent the same sacrificial sanctity, a reference to the one can imply the others. This transparent quality of the typology allows Fortunatus to re-create the biblical episode by including the saint as one of the chief characters in the great events described in the scriptural accounts. To put it in another way, the Bible and the *Vita* are linked in what can rightly be called a "biblical-hagiographic chain."[51]

In contrast with the tension marking the literature's earliest development, when an antagonism can be detected between the "old examples of faith" found in the Bible and the "new proofs" of holiness described by hagiographers,[52] the *Vitae* of Fortunatus show no signs of apprehensiveness on the part of the writer in presenting the saint as a contemporary embodiment of a scriptural model. The link between the Bible and hagiography occurs when the author refers to the saint as continuing in the present the biblical deeds of the past. Miracle stories, in particular, dramatically link the deeds of a contemporary saint to this biblical past.

Because nearly all the miracles narrated in hagiographic literature derive directly from the Bible, the descriptions of *virtutes* are especially subject to stylization along biblical lines.[53] One type of miracle with obvious scriptural parallels is the ability of the saint to change water into wine or to maintain a sufficient amount of wine or beer without the supply ever diminishing.[54] A miracle attributed to Marcellus offers an instance in which both aspects—the transformation of water and a lasting supply of wine—are present. The hagiographer explicitly regards the saint's deed as a continuation of Christ's miracle performed during the wedding feast at Cana (John 2: 1–10).[55] But the scriptural reference appears in the context of a liturgical function so that the actualization of the Bible occurs within an ecclesiastical setting, where the saint's manifestation of *virtus* represents a contemporary reenactment of a biblical event.

The account of the miracle begins when Bishop Prudentius washes his hands with water drawn by the saint from the Seine. When the bishop notices that the water has turned into wine, he orders it to be poured into a chalice to be used "for communion." In elaborating on the miraculous properties of this wine, Fortunatus claims that the beverage never diminished, in spite of the "multitude of people" who drank it during mass. The wine also cures the sick. Fortunatus even calls the deeds associated with the drink "new miracles," a description anticipating the comparison with the older biblical account.[56] These *nova miracula* demonstrate, according to the hagiographer, that the miraculous event described in Scripture occurs again, with certain modifications, in the saint's own time and place:

> We see that the divine benefits are not limited to one place since what had preceded in Galilee succeeded in Gaul. There at the nuptial table Christ turned water into wine; here the altar received the new wine that sufficed for the table of Christ. The former [event] preceded in time, the latter in honor. For what the six jugs gave at that time, here a vessel and a half adequately supplied; whereas then it happened so that the Lord might proclaim himself, now [it was done] so that He might not hide His servant.[57]

In this passage relating the significance of Marcellus's thaumaturgic power, Fortunatus emphasizes the continuity between the saint's miracle and the scriptural account. The Bible also provides a foundation for—and lends authority to—the holy man's display of *virtus*.[58] In fact, the parallelism conveyed by the temporal and spatial references (*tunc . . . nunc; ibi . . . hic*) gives the impression that the hagiographic text functions as a contemporary sequel to the biblical story. Moreover, as the last sentence in the above passage suggests, Marcellus's miracle not only resembles Christ's but also is accomplished through "the Lord," who wishes to reveal the power of his saint. The mediating nature of the continuity implies that Marcellus's *Vita*, in addition to being a work about a contemporary holy man, is also an extension of Christ's biography, at least insofar as the Savior is represented by Fortunatus as continuing through the saint the same work described in the Gospels.[59]

All Christian hagiographers strive to associate the saint with the central figure of salvation's history so that the holy person described represents, either explicitly or implicitly, another Christ.[60] In addition to modeling the saint after Christ, often hagiographers regard their subjects as the successors of the patriarchs, prophets, and apostles.[61] For this reason, most *Vitae* undergo, as we have seen in Fortunatus's portrayal of Marcellus, a stylization that depicts the life of the saint in conformity with biblical models. However, the hagiographer's use of the Bible involves more than simply a contemporary adaptation of a scriptural figure or theme. As a "manifestation of the Gospel"[62] or a "Bible actualized," hagiography assumes a religious rationale for the nature and documentation of salvation, a rationale that justifies the function of biblical stylization and legitimizes the continuous relation between Scripture and hagiography, between the "preceding" biblical example, to paraphrase Fortunatus, and the "succeeding" embodiment of that example in a saint's *Vita*.

This rationale, of course, is not explicitly discussed by Fortunatus. Nonetheless, we can infer it, not only from texts associating Marcellus with Abel and Christ but also from a description such as this one of Paternus finding water for his thirsty companions: "When Paternus touched the ground with his staff, a spring burst from the abyss and, filling up, the water flowed out, as if another Moses with a piercing rod had drawn water from the rock."[63] Such an application of Scripture suggests that, as a book documenting the history of salvation, the Bible does not end but continues in the narratives on the lives of the saints.[64] In other words, to actualize the Bible—that is, to compare a holy man to Abel, to present a thaumaturgic display as a continuation of Christ's life or as a reenactment of a miracle performed by Moses, in short, to forge a link in the biblical-hagiographic chain—assumes that the events of sacred history are renewable, that a chosen people live on in the church and the holy elect known as saints.

Saints in Conflict

Even from these brief sketches of youth, we can detect a multifaceted type of sanctity marking the first stage of each *Vita*'s development. Generally speaking, the initial portrait presents a little saint who is predestined to holiness, as wise as an old man, ascetically disciplined, and ready to wage war against Christ's enemies. Furthermore, in two cases (those of Germanus and Marcellus), Fortunatus initially associates this warfare with the threat of death or an experience reminiscent of death. These themes, illustrated by numerous examples, continue to characterize the narrative as each saint's life rhetorically unfolds. The most dominant theme of all, which appears prominently in each *Vita* and is deftly adapted to the special historical circumstances of a particular holy person, is warlike conflict or struggle against a hostile force. This strategy of presenting the saint as a *belliger* has the advantage of giving coherence to the diverse expressions of sanctity because conflict surrounds all aspects of each saint's life. As the previous description of Germanus's *Vita* suggests, every holy man portrayed by Fortunatus fights a host of enemies, including himself. Furthermore, the confrontation is not limited to the obvious enemies who represent secular power or a heretical religious faction; the saint also battles the corrupt and compromising clergy within the church itself. Considering the military imagery Fortunatus sometimes uses to describe miracles, we should also include disease, poverty, and cruel enslavement among the saint's foes.[65] From the beginning of his life until his death, the holy man remains in constant combat. Given this persistent emphasis on combative struggle, an examination of the holy man in conflict will reveal the situations in Fortunatus's *Vitae* that largely define sanctity.

Three types of conflict are described throughout Fortunatus's hagiography (the first two named appearing most prominently): secular, as when the saint, on behalf of the church, confronts representatives of worldly power or physically punishes individuals for sacrilegious behavior; religious, as when the saint opposes the representatives of alternative beliefs (e.g., Arians, Jews, and pagans) or fights detractors within the church who disapprove of him; and ascetic, as when the saint battles himself in an effort to resist the alluring enticements of the flesh and the world. Of course, not every episode of conflict in a saint's Life falls neatly into one or another category; conflict occasionally appears in both secular and religious forms, as in the cases of ambitious or corrupt clerics siding with secular leaders against a saint.[66] But, on the whole, a scene of struggle usually corresponds with one of the three main divisions.[67]

The order of the categories reflects the frequency with which that type of conflict appears throughout the entire corpus of Fortunatus's prose hagiography devoted to male saints.[68] However, not every Life has all three kinds of conflict, and the proportion of the type of opposition a saint confronts varies from *Vita* to *Vita*. In one Life, ecclesiastical factionalism may frequently threaten the saint; in another, secular authorities may persistently be the source of antagonism. The historical circumstances peculiar to a particular saint account for the variation in the battles to be fought. Hilary, for instance, fiercely participated in the ecclesiastical controversies of his day, and so his *Vita* prominently reflects a religious type of conflict. Because Paternus, by contrast, spent some of his life in ascetic solitude, his biography portrays the struggles associated with an eremitical sanctity lived in the wild. One saint may most often fight heretics, another tribunes. What the holy man confronts depends on the historical setting that serves as the raw biographical material that Fortunatus conforms to the ideal of sanctity embodied in the holy warrior.

In spite of the diversity of opponents that can distinguish one Life from the next, however, all the male saints depicted by Fortunatus, at one time or another, encounter a common enemy: every *Vita* contains at least one episode in which the holy man confronts a representative of secular society.[69] Characteristic of such encounters is the saint's assertion of ecclesiastical power over secular authority. A typical scenario usually involves an obstinate secular leader refusing to grant a saint's request. As a result of this denial, the official receives a physical affliction until he yields. Such accounts occur most frequently in the *Vita sancti Germani*, which, in sometimes dramatic fashion, presents even the highest political power submitting to the demands of the holy man. For example, Fortunatus portrays Germanus entering the palace for his usual meeting with Clothar (d. 561). The saint is kept waiting at the entrance, with no announcement of his arrival made to the king. Frustrated by the long delay, the saint leaves and retaliates by keeping vigils throughout the night in his oratory.[70] In the same sentence that describes this charismatic response, Fortunatus relates that the king began suffering from pain and fever. In the morning, Clothar's high officials go to the saint's church and implore him to relieve the king's torment. The cure entails submissive gestures, accompanied by an admission of guilt. Especially important in the description of the miraculous healing is the application of ecclesiastical vestments to the ailing body of a contrite and humbled Clothar. The hagiographer presents the king's acts of homage as a surrender of secular authority to the divine power represented by the garments of the saint's church: "He [Germanus] who before was not announced enters the palace honored and beseeched. With difficulty the king rises from the bed and laments that he has been struck down by a divine scourge. He licks the *palliolum* of the holy man and he draws the priest's clothing over the painful areas. Once he confessed the fault of his crime, all pain was put to flight."[71]

To leave no doubt concerning the causal connection between behavior and illness, Fortunatus ends the account by explicitly attributing the affliction to Clothar's "contempt" for Germanus.[72] The passage follows a pattern of conflict and resolution that is consistent throughout Fortunatus's *Vitae*: Resistance to a holy man leads to physical harm in the form of a punitive miracle; to restore health, the offender must acknowledge the wrongdoing and appeal submissively to the saint for a cure; the admission of guilt followed by the miraculous cure renders the saint victorious. In the case of Clothar, the resolution of conflict asserts the supremacy of religious or ecclesiastical authority over worldly power. In fact, Fortunatus introduces the story of Clothar's punishment by proclaiming that Germanus "was accustomed to triumph over kings."[73] The accuracy of such a claim and the extent to which a representative of the church could actually wield power over royalty are matters better left for historians to decide.[74] For the immediate purpose of examining the hagiographic depiction of a saint in conflict, the passage's importance lies primarily in the literary portrayal of a holy man's confrontation with a secular ruler.

In the account of the conflict between Germanus and Clothar, the insertion of the punitive miracle into the narrative creates in the story a situation of dependence. Of course, all punitive miracles described by hagiographers have such a function because they show a punished transgressor compelled by pain to seek the mercy of the offended saint, whose miraculous healing power is needed. But in the story of Clothar's affliction, the emphasis on the king's need for the holy bishop is especially telling because the divine chastisement results precisely because the king's need for the saint's counsel went defiantly unacknowledged, as Germanus was kept waiting and unannounced at the palace. The punitive miracle then leads to a reversal of roles, with the king waiting for a cure while the royal officials "beg" the bishop to return.[75] Fortunatus thus presents a saint who, in relation to the king, is both a punisher and a healer. This dual function of the thaumaturge rhetorically accentuates the limits of secular rule. The hagiographer describes a conflict that can be resolved only when the worldly leader yields to an authority who wields greater power. The image of a sick Clothar relying on Germanus for a cure, which results from the licking and touching of ecclesiastical vestments, dramatically illustrates royal subordination to and dependence on the divine power entrusted to an episcopal representative of the church.[76]

However, in spite of Fortunatus's claim that Germanus "was accustomed to triumph over kings," the conflict described in the story of Clothar's punishment lacks the highly polarized opposition that leads ultimately to the annihilation of one of the feuding parties. Unlike the accounts of the dying martyrs, which portray an irreconcilable strife between worldly authority and church, the text of Fortunatus initially suggests an alliance between religious and secular powers.[77] After all, the saint is described as going to a meeting with the king that is planned and customary, as the phrase *ex solito* explicitly indicates.[78] Rather than an all-out attack against secular rule, the punitive miracle serves as a means of showing the conformity to the will of the bishop, not the eradication of worldly authority. The punishment does not overthrow secular power but compels it to comply with the church by honoring the bishop's role as an advisor to the king. Of course, the description of a castigated and repentant ruler receiving a miraculous cure asserts that the proper subordination of the king to the holy bishop has been restored, but the saint is not portrayed as an opponent to secular power itself. Rather, conflict arises here only when the saint is excluded from the king's circle.

This insistence on the saint's superiority can lead to a heightening of conflict, even though the saint and secular authority are described as sharing the same intentions. A king's almsgiving, for instance, cannot be depicted as surpassing that of a holy man; the generosity of Childebert (d. 558) must compete with the abundant giving of Germanus so that their harmonious activity becomes a war over charity: "Strife had to be expected between priest and ruler. They waged with each other a battle over mercy and a contest over kindness, so that they might scatter treasures and the needy might become rich from their talents."[79]

In Fortunatus's descriptions of divinely chastised rulers, the punishments lead to the reform, not the end, of secular leadership. The holy warrior is portrayed as asserting *virtus* in order to tip the balance of power back to the side of the church. The accounts of miraculously punished kings stress the conformity and subordination of temporal rule to a superior ecclesiastical power in the form of a holy bishop. One strategy Fortunatus employs to present this subordination emphatically is a comparison between animals who comply with a saint's wishes and secular leaders who foolishly resist a holy man's request.[80] In Albinus's *Vita*, for example, Fortunatus describes Childebert eagerly setting off on a hunting trip. The king is to meet the saint at a predetermined spot on the journey. Albinus, old and infirm, takes too long to arrive, and so the impatient Childebert decides to continue riding. Such a scenario obviously resembles the conflict described between Germanus and Clothar, with opposition again appearing here when the secular leader neglects to meet with the bishop. However, rather than a divine affliction for the transgression, Childebert's horse refuses to move in any direction except the one leading toward the slowly approaching saint. In addition to being a mildly amusing story, this account also portrays the ineptitude of a secular leader. The ignorant Childebert "learns from the horse" that he was "sinning."[81] In terms of the ability to reason, hagiographically measured by the capacity to comply with a holy bishop's injunction, Childebert is on a level lower than that of an animal because a "beast" is needed to "correct" the king's "human understanding."[82]

The miracle involving the horse, like those pertaining to the control of weather and the elements, shows the created world conforming to the wishes of a saint.[83] The strategy of portraying animals who act on behalf of a holy man against a king enables Fortunatus to depict an abuse of power as an act that is out of harmony with the natural order. To heighten the sense of disharmony, the hagiographer also takes advantage of the ferocity associated with beasts. A wild animal avenging a saint enables the hagiographer to show that the influence of a holy man extends to forces over which worldly claims have no authority. Beasts can thus implement the punitive miracle by viciously retaliating against transgressors, especially when the offender takes property supposedly belonging to the church. Although not specifically involving a Merovingian king, a story about a powerful Frank by the name of Chariulf illustrates such an instance. When Chariulf refuses, at the request of Germanus, to return land taken from the church, the holy warrior turns to prayer, as he did in the conflict involving Clothar. "Immediately" after this religious response to a secular affront, a bear enters the property and for two nights devours Chariulf's livestock. When the Frank finally yields, the attacks stop. Fortunatus then offers the same explanation of the event that he gives in the story of Childebert's horse: "This was done so that, with a beast castigating, the man might return to his senses and an animal might give reason to one who does not understand."[84] Besides claiming that the miraculous attack resulted in the restoration of the church's property, such an account also asserts that even the animal world respects and, if necessary, enforces the rights of ecclesiastical ownership.

Avenging animals and divine chastisements are portrayed as the miraculous forces unleashed by a holy man to oppose a transgressor. However, while the miracles in the accounts of secular conflict often occur after prayer and claim for the saint a power to which worldly leaders have no recourse, thaumaturgy itself plays only a secondary role in the confrontations so far examined. The miracle is only one of three phases in a story of secular conflict; it is placed at an intermediate stage between the initial transgression requiring retaliation and the restoration of what the hagiographer presumes to be the proper relation of power between the saint and a ruler. This last phase of restoration constitutes the resolution of conflict and always ends with the saint as the supreme power. The account of the miracle holds a subordinate position because the narrative never culminates in a thaumaturgic display but, instead, finishes with the poignant image of a secular leader complying with an episcopal authority.

Nor must the miracle be an extraordinary show of force replete with a highly supernatural content. Given the subordinate role played by the miracle, Fortunatus can actually diminish the importance of the supernatural quality of a saint's *virtus* without the final restoration being at all affected. For example, Fortunatus relates that, at the request of Saint Paternus, Childebert agreed to offer some relief for the poor. The king entrusts a royal official by the name of Crescentius to implement this plan. When Crescentius leaves without fulfilling his promise to Paternus, he is blinded on the journey and loses his way. Significantly, the hagiographer, besides using the verb *errare*, calls the sightless wandering of the deceitful official *tenebrosus error*, words not only referring to Crescentius's aimless groping in darkness but also conveying, given the other meanings of *errare/error*, a sense of going morally astray, of being in a state of mental blindness resulting from a human fault rather than from a divine affliction. Of course, as in all the other cases of secular conflict described so far, the acknowledgment of the wrongdoing leads to compliance and restoration, with the promise fulfilled, sight returned, and the saint triumphant. But, in elaborating on the significance of the healing, Fortunatus also suggests that the remedy, like the illness, is of a moral rather than a physical nature. Instead of an unusual supernatural occurrence, the cure is actually a change of heart, an enlightenment, which, insofar as it leads to conformity with the saint's wishes, serves the same purpose as even the most extraordinary punitive miracle:

> Crescentius lied about promising to fulfill this [i.e., the saint's request to assist the poor] and, having departed for the region of Burgundy without this most holy man knowing, he lost his sight and went astray for two days. Recalling his fault, for which reason the blinded wandering so suddenly befell him, he swiftly returned, and forgiveness was granted. As the fault of the heart left, light entered the eyes and, wiser after his blindness, he fulfilled the commands of God's servant so that, as a result of this, he might be thought to have received an illumination of the mind rather than of the body.[85]

Although in hagiographic literature a saint may be prominently displayed performing charitable deeds, the holy man's opposition to oppressive conditions does not normally extend to challenging the existing social order and the economic divisions of a class society.[86] The example of Paternus shows that, in this instance, the saint's *virtus* is based not so much on a miraculous ability as on a political connection to royalty and a highly placed official who, when coerced by the holy bishop, can offer the required support. The saint's power, at least as it is portrayed hagiographically, lies in the fact that he influences—not overthrows—those possessing wealth and abundant provisions.

Related to the issue of saints who do not challenge the social order are the stories of liberation from slavery, which should also be treated with caution. Hagiographic accounts describe the saint freeing slaves by buying—literally "redeeming"—them from masters. On the whole, such descriptions do not appear frequently, especially not as often as miraculous cures.[87] While those freed certainly undergo a change in social status as the result of the holy man's intervention, these reports of manumission cannot be understood as an attempt to overthrow an oppressive social system because the hagiographers never portray the saint overtly condemning the practice of bondage itself. On the contrary, hagiographers routinely depict saints owning servants. Indeed, even the most austere hermit can have a domestic on hand, without any sense of impropriety expressed by a *Vita*'s author.[88] As we might expect from sources reflecting the general acceptance of social inequality, there is no anomaly in presenting slavery alongside sanctity.[89]

Unlike poverty and slavery, however, there is one form of oppression that the saints depicted in the literature frequently attempt to eradicate: imprisonment, not simply unjust or cruel imprisonment but imprisonment altogether; indeed, the prisons themselves are sometimes destroyed.[90] We cannot here discuss in detail why this particular social condition is so unambiguously condemned in hagiographic literature.[91] Suffice it to say that, while poverty and slavery were generally regarded as acceptable and normal features of lower-class life, the fear of imprisonment extended to all levels of society; even the free or the aristocratic could suddenly become *captivi* because of an invading army or the whims of a ruler.[92] Perhaps, then, the depiction of a saint freeing the incarcerated had, as has been argued, an especially popular appeal and offered the hagiographer the opportunity to present a representative of the church actively opposing what was obviously a dreaded condition to which all were susceptible.[93] In that the topos of the miraculous prison freeing has received sufficient treatment in relation to Merovingian hagiography as a whole and Fortunatus's *Vitae* in particular, only a few observations need to be made.[94]

Stories of liberation from prison appear frequently in Fortunatus's hagiography.[95] The freeing usually occurs after an official responsible for the administration of justice—a count, tribune, or judge—refuses a saint's request that prisoners be released.[96] Although Albinus is actually depicted as miraculously killing a guard,[97] references in Germanus's *Vita* indicate that the saint makes his plea for releasing prisoners as he congenially dines with the secular officials in charge of matters pertaining to sentencing.[98] The nature of the opposition is again important in the secular conflicts involving prisoners. Given the fact that the temporal authority and the saint are otherwise on good terms, these accounts clearly show that the holy man opposes not so much the tribune or count as he does the practice of incarceration that they enforce. In support of this assertion is the fact that never is any mention made concerning the specific offense that resulted in the imprisonment. Like most hagiographers who relate such stories, Fortunatus does not discuss why the detention occurs.[99] Legal guilt and innocence are not matters for consideration in these accounts. No distinction is made between a person deservedly detained for a vicious crime or one who is cruelly jailed for failing to pay a debt.[100] Instead, the captivity itself is presented as unjust, harsh, and, as opposed to slavery, unnatural.

The prisons themselves are often subterranean enclosures holding a throng of cramped and disgruntled *incarcerati* who clamor for release. Fortunatus compares the jails to a tomb. A release from such a place is called a "salvation," a deliverance from darkness into light.[101] Unfettered, the former prisoners run to the saint; occasionally, the obstinate official becomes the one "charged."[102] Unlike a saint's encounter with the largely tolerated conditions of slavery and poverty, the holy freer of prisoners is depicted as a true liberator, a genuine inspiration urging an oppressed group to seize emancipation in a defiant escape:

> No material resisted the blessed man [Germanus], since wood, rock and iron dissolved before him. One day in Paris it happened that, after he said a prayer at the door of a prison, on the following night a light appeared to those jammed in jail. He seemed to urge them to dig so that they might come out. They said to one another that they have seen Lord Germanus, and they each told the signs. When a rib from an animal was found, the digging [prisoners] moved the rock away and they ran to meet the . . . friend of God at his church that morning, when he was returning for a rest. And so, the image of the bishop was the cause of salvation for many.[103]

Before considering the two remaining types of conflict, one other source of secular contention deserves a brief consideration. In addition to kings who exclude holy bishops, oppressive municipal administrators, and greedy usurpers of church property, Fortunatus also presents individuals who work on a Sunday or a holy day as transgressors rightfully punished. Though such anecdotes are numerous in Merovingian hagiography as a whole,[104] Fortunatus limits these accounts almost exclusively to the *Vita sancti Germani*, a work in which this type of punitive miracle appears prominently in stories involving a cross section of Merovingian society. The irreverent behavior leads to a miraculous affliction that eventually forces the offender to appeal to the saint for help. The punishments are crippling in nature and can last up to a year before a penitent receives a cure.[105] Like the miraculous freeing of prisoners, the accounts of chastised workers reflect a social circumstance that the hagiographic literature attacks. These stories of punished laborers, like the conciliar decrees addressing the problem of individuals who fail to honor liturgical feasts,[106] urge the working members of society to comply with the customs of the church or face the threat of divine punishment. These miraculous afflictions should not be regarded as a purely hagiographic invention with no historical counterpart. The bishops of this period not only denounced those who neglected to fulfill religious duties but also recommended, as the ministers of divine justice, that "slaves" and "rustics," precisely the segments of society most vulnerable to violating the ban, be severely beaten for working on Sundays or holy days.[107]

As in the other cases of secular conflict, these miracles compel violators to conform with the demands of the church by changing behavior and seeking forgiveness from a holy bishop, whose cure, besides relieving physical pain, restores offenders to the community of believers. The punishments depicted in the accounts impose a Christian order on a society pressed more by the demands of daily living than by the constraints of liturgical observances. Even individuals occupied in tasks needing urgent and immediate attention are not exempt from divine retribution.[108] The punishments themselves are psychologically compelling, coming in the form of an affliction that conforms to symptoms characteristic of what moderns would call hysteria, and the nature of the suffering fits the offense. For instance, those who perform manual labor on Sunday receive a stiffening contraction of their hands, relieved only by the holy bishop anointing the afflicted limbs with oil.[109] The hand can become so tightly closed for so long that the nails begin to grow into the palms.[110] Other punishments also suit the crime. When, on Easter Sunday, a cleric picks some nuts from a tree, he is blinded—an appropriate form of correction for one who worked "on the day of illumination."[111] Also bordering on sacrilegious behavior are those who take too great a delight in worldly pleasures. A man fond of drinking wine and eating meat finds himself unable to close his mouth. He receives a cure from Germanus, who warns him to abstain. When the warning is disregarded, the illness returns.[112]

Of course, we cannot determine with any certainty to what extent such stories were believed or how much they actually deterred what the church regarded as sacrilegious behavior. To consider the limits of belief during this period—and contrary to what some historians have argued, there certainly were limits—is a difficult matter that is beyond the scope of this discussion.[113] However, in addition to the councils and sermons concerned with the problem of disregarding the Christian sabbath, the accounts describing individuals being punished for this behavior that appear throughout Merovingian hagiography and continued to be told long after this era suggest that the practice of working on holy days could not be adequately curtailed, regardless of whether those who persisted in performing tasks during such times actually feared divine (or ecclesiastical) punishments.[114] But, putting aside the rather problematic historical issue of hagiography's efficacy in changing attitudes toward work in Merovingian society, we may say that, on the literary level, the miracles concerned with sacrilegious laborers play the same role in the narrative as the other divine punishments previously discussed. These punitive miracles depict a transgressor compelled to conform with an ecclesiastical injunction, and they heighten the dependence of a secular offender on the holy bishop, without whose help a worker remains paralyzed and powerless.

In addition to the many instances of conflict with secular society, the hagiography of Fortunatus also highlights the tension between a zealous holy man committed to Catholic orthodoxy and the representatives of other religious beliefs. A fierce *odium theologicum*, for instance, dominates the *Life of Saint Hilary*.[115] Shortly after calling the young saint a soldier destined to win "victories" for Christ, Fortunatus claims that Hilary abhorred the enemies of the Catholic religion. With an allusion to Psalm 25:5, the hagiographer attempts to justify the saint's refusal to eat with or even greet Jews and heretics.[116] Although a temporal ruler certainly plays a hostile role in the *Vita*, the main villains of the story are not secular officials but scheming Arians plotting against Hilary at church councils and eventually causing his exile. Fortunatus describes the theological turmoil with military imagery throughout the entire *Vita*. The steadfast orthodoxy of Hilary resembles a fearless soldier "bearing the standard" and bravely confronting the menace of "heretical swords."[117] Fortunatus also stylizes the saint's return from exile as a triumphal procession enthusiastically supported by the people.[118] Once back, he launches another campaign against the Arians, for which he is called a "blessed athlete of Christ," a phrase evoking the theme of contest associated with the early Christians fighting their persecutors.[119] In fact, Fortunatus stresses how Hilary, like the first martyrs, remained fearless in the face of the imperial authority that supported the Arians. Describing Hilary in this fashion naturally leads to characterizing him as a martyr. According to Fortunatus, this holy man wanted to die for Christ, and he certainly would have, if only Christians still suffered persecution.[120]

Conflict also arises when those living a religious life with the saint are forced to endure the inconveniences caused by excessive charity. Especially annoying for monks of a less generous and abstemious nature is the extraordinary beneficence of a saint giving away supplies belonging to the community. Paternus, for instance, irritates his monastic companion Scubilio when the latter finishes working and discovers that no food remains; what little there was, the saint offered to a famished traveler.[121] A far more hostile reaction occurs in the *Vita sancti Germani*. When, after being appointed abbot, the holy man gives all the monastery's food to the poor, the hungry monks revolt.[122] In both instances, the saints are vindicated when unexpected donations suddenly arrive. This replenishment of food is presented as a miraculous occurrence that chastens the saint's monastic companions. In the case of Germanus, the charismatic show of *virtus* results in a reversal of roles. After his prayers obtain gifts of food, the once frightened saint then alarms the rebellious monks, who, even though they have plenty to eat, are now themselves "terrified by the miracle."[123] Hence, as in the cases involving secular conflict, the miraculous again comes into play here to maintain or restore the superiority of the saint against all opponents, detractors, and doubters.

It is not only when lower ranking members of the church oppose a holy bishop or abbot that religious conflict occurs. Even the highest ecclesiastical authorities can appear as sources of religious contention in the life of a saint. A scene in the *Vita*

sancti Albini, reminiscent of the accounts Sulpicius Severus gives of the episcopal antagonism directed against Martin, contrasts the holy man's fidelity to the teaching
of the church with the religious and liturgical laxity of compromising bishops. Albinus insists on enforcing the decrees of the Councils of Orleans (held in 538 and
541), which excommunicated those who married within the first or second degree
of consanguinity.[124] His fellow bishops, however, unanimously insist that he absolve
those whom he has barred from communion for this offense, and the united episcopi
even compel him to bless the sacramental bread for the transgressors to receive.

Once again, the narrative presents a conflict requiring a resolution that will restore
the saint's superiority. In keeping with the previous pattern, this process of restoration naturally entails a miraculous punishment. However, Fortunatus's portrayal of
the bishops as the chief adversaries in this account raises a difficulty. Bishops are,
after all, the very class of clerics promoted by Fortunatus's hagiography. Above all
else, this author's Vitae stress the necessity of conforming with episcopal authority.
Hence, while a description of unscrupulous bishops may not appear out of place in
the writing of Sulpicius Severus, such a scene cannot be described so unambiguously
in the hagiography of Fortunatus, who, in all other instances, presents the heavy-
handed assertion of episcopal power as a mark of sanctity rather than as an abuse
of privilege. Now this power turns on the story's hero. A solution is therefore needed
that does not jeopardize the integrity of the saint's opposition but still shows his
compliance with episcopal authority. To achieve this balance between resistance and
conformity, Fortunatus portrays Albinus consenting with the bishops without actually compromising his stance against "incestuous" marriages. In the very act of
submission to his episcopal counterparts, the saint also affirms his opposition with
a prophecy of divine retribution: "Even though, according to your authority, I am
being compelled to give my blessing with the sign of the cross—while you refuse
to defend the cause of God—He Himself has the power to avenge."[125]

When Saint Martin yielded to antagonistic bishops, he experienced a "diminution
of power" as a result, and Sulpicius's hero vowed never again to participate in an
episcopal synod or be associated with any meetings in which bishops were gathered.[126] But in Albinus's Vita, no condemnation of clerical ambitio follows this story
of conflict. More important, rather than a loss of virtus, Fortunatus's holy man still
gives a display of miraculous power in spite of his reluctant concession. The show
of virtus, however, rather than directly afflicting the principal enemies of the saint,
punishes the opponents, who play only a minor role in the conflict up to this point.
After Albinus's blessing and prophecy, one of those who was formally excommunicated approaches but is struck dead before being able to receive communion.[127]
Thus, the saint remains uncompromised, the bishops, though opponents, are not
themselves the objects of divine wrath, and the punitive miracle once again leads to
the restoration of the saint's supremacy over all challengers.

Especially important in this episode of conflict is the strategy Fortunatus takes to
characterize the dilemma faced by the saint. As in the description of the religious
battles fought by Hilary, the hagiographer stylizes this ecclesiastical infighting as an
occasion of martyrdom for Albinus. According to Fortunatus, the saint endured tremendous suffering to uphold the ban against incestuous marriages. Undergoing such
trials indicates that, if necessary, he would have willingly died in his service to God:

"Condemning the detestable unions of incestuous marriages, he was blamelessly imitating blessed John the Baptist. No one will be able to explain in a worthy manner how much he endured; indeed, he would have desired to have been made a martyr if the hand of a murderer had not been absent. But he who did not hide the desires of his wish without a doubt deserved the martyr's palm."[128]

Less delicate than conflicts with feuding bishops is the unambiguous depiction of the saint's relentless warfare against individuals who refuse to accept Christianity. Hilary's hostility toward Jews has already been mentioned. Other instances in the Life of Saint Germanus portray Jews either as threatening villains who force Christians to accept Jewish law or as obstinate unbelievers whom the saint must convert.[129] Fortunatus also characterizes as demonically motivated Jews' refusal to accept Christianity. In one instance, a Jewish woman whose husband had previously converted is described as breathing fire and smoke from her nostrils while Germanus pursues her.[130] The woman's obstinacy is attributed to demonic possession so that the holy warrior fights not so much Judaism as a religious doctrine but a demon inside a potential convert who would embrace Christianity were it not for the unclean spirit. Once exorcised, not only she but "many Jews" allegedly become Christians.[131]

Unlike Gregory of Tours's Histories, which gives several instances of theological debates, albeit futile ones, between Catholics, Jews, and heretics,[132] the hagiography of Fortunatus does not even offer a distorted presentation of Jewish beliefs. In fact, his strategy for depicting Jews avoids any doctrinal consideration of their religion by presenting them as acting under demonic influences rather than as espousing a coherent system of belief. To portray an alternative form of worship as a sign of demonic possession is a strategy that enables Fortunatus to treat Judaism not so much as a rival religion whose doctrines and rites could attract Christians but as a type of illness that can be cured through a saint's virtus.[133] However, unlike the many touching scenes of sick and possessed Christians appealing to Germanus for help, this encounter involving the Jewish woman is marked by an antagonism initiated by the saint and ends only after the relentless Christian warrior has successfully coerced the conversion of one who initially did not want such a "cure" from the holy man and who actually fled his presence.

In the Lives of Hilary and Germanus, Jews represent a religious alternative which, in one case, the saint attempts to eradicate by imposing conversion.[134] Another form of belief opposed by a holy man appears in the Vita sancti Paterni, a work that portrays individuals who persist in rituals associated with a pagan cult. The militant nature of the episode resembles the description of Germanus's attempt to convert the Jewish woman. In both instances, the saint does not encounter religious foes by chance but actively seeks out non-Christians with the explicit purpose of confronting and converting them. Similar to his depiction of the Jews, Fortunatus also presents pagan opposition as demonic.[135] In addition, the conflict between the Christian saint and the venerators of the pagan cult offers the hagiographer another opportunity to associate a holy man's warfare with martyrdom.

While in a remote region of Brittany, Paternus and his monastic companion Scubilio hear of a thriving "diabolical cult," and they immediately set out to find the temple. Once at the site, Paternus demands that the practices cease, but the pagans scorn the verbal threats of the saint, who then intensifies his opposition. "Armed with the sign of the cross," the Christian warriors begin to overturn the ritual food and drink being prepared.[136] Fortunatus stylizes the scene in terms now familiar to us: "Putting aside their own danger . . . the brave soldiers were fighting for Christ, desiring martyrdom if an accursed murderer would not have dreaded to strike [them]."[137] Then, in a defiant gesture of disrespect, a pagan woman attempts to retaliate by disrobing in front of her prudish Christian attackers. This effort ends with the same result as any other attempt to oppose a saint in the hagiography of Fortunatus: Soon stricken with a debilitating illness and a bodily sore, the pagan stripper, after suffering for a year, seeks forgiveness from the holy man for her exhibitionism. Later, we are told that the venerators of the cult were expelled and their temple turned into a holding pen for livestock.[138]

The third type of conflict is the saint's ascetic battle with himself. On the whole, Fortunatus relies heavily on the conventional descriptions of saintliness in characterizing the holy man's war against the body and the passions. In spite of this fact, a few observations are in order because even the frequent, stereotypical accounts of a saint's life of prayer, vigils, and fasting reveal how Fortunatus's depiction of sanctity relates to previous hagiographic trends that will be discussed later.

As with the other types of conflict, the rhetoric of Fortunatus is again marked by military imagery that expresses the nature of ascetic battle. In addition to the usual claims that a saint "tamed" his body and "triumphed" over himself, however, Fortunatus significantly refers to the early phase in the ascetic life of Albinus and Marcellus as a tyrocinium, a term originally used to describe the first stage of a recently recruited soldier in the Roman army.[139] Besides conveying the general sense of warfare to describe the saints' battles against the self and worldly enticements, this term also has a specific clerical context: It denotes the formal admission of the saints into the lower ranks of the church so that these holy men are literally entering the army of ecclesiastical warriors. The hagiographer thus regards the acceptance of these saints into the church as analogous to entering an armed force, with the young Albinus and Marcellus at the lower ranks but destined to become, at a later stage in the respective Vitae, bishops, the commanders of the church's clerical army.[140]

The ascetic battle can also culminate with the winning of the martyr's branch. The secret devotions of Germanus, who endures sleeplessness and extreme cold, lead to a conquering of the self, a "triumph" that earns him the martyr's victory.[141] Especially important is how Fortunatus stylizes the reward Germanus deserves for his lifelong ascetic pursuits. His heavenly arrival is depicted as a triumphal adventus in which the faithful warriors of Christ, the martyrs and the apostles, greet Germanus as a "victor" worthy to be "crowned" by popular acclamation.[142] The stereotypical quality of such a description does not diminish the significance of the military overtones with which the Vita ends. On the contrary, the closing lines reaffirm the saint's militancy because the heavenly gathering itself is really a victorious army[143] welcoming another soldier to share in the triumph of Christ, the ruling commander who holds forever all "glory, honor," and—especially important given the social and political content of Fortunatus's hagiography—"power."[144]

On the whole, however, the ascetic contests of Fortunatus's saints lack the depth and detail that mark the two other major types of conflict. Unlike Antony's Life, the saints of Fortunatus's hagiography do not undergo extreme psychological torment due to a fierce ascetic detachment that leaves the mind prey to the persistent visitations of demons. With the exception of the *Vita sancti Paterni*, Fortunatus does not develop the ascetic character of a male saint beyond the ordinary sketches of pious behavior. The descriptions of Hilary, Germanus, Albinus, Paternus (though not at first), and Marcellus acting more like worldly bishops than like detached hermits correspond with a shift at this time in the perception of Saint Martin, one of the paradigmatic models of sanctity for Western hagiographers.

Martin's Image and Fortunatus's Patrons

Naturally, the immediate concerns of our discussion preclude a detailed examination of how Merovingian authors reflected and fostered this shift by modifying in their own writing Sulpicius's original depiction of Martin.[145] Generally speaking, the late-fourth-century description, offered by Martin's first biographer, of the charismatic saint living a rigorously self-disciplined monastic life even while a bishop is gradually recast. By the Merovingian age, authors whose writing, unlike the work of Sulpicius, is "ecclesiastically stamped" ignore Martin's life as a layman and monk in order to stress and extol his qualities as a model bishop.[146] In particular, Venantius Fortunatus subverts the original image of Martin in his poem based on Sulpicius's biography. Although the work is generally regarded as unoriginal,[147] Fortunatus's poetic version, besides giving scanty attention to Martin's preepiscopal life, significantly alters the saint's social class. The monkish Martin, who, according to Sulpicius, dressed like a beggar and whose father was a soldier,[148] now appears in Fortunatus's poem wearing a toga, crowned, and worthy of belonging to a *senatus*.[149] His heavenly reward explicitly entails a change in social status from a *pauper* to a senator, a title that upper-class bishops—the people about and for whom Fortunatus wrote and in whose circles he moved—appropriated for themselves.[150] Thus, as more detailed research has suggested, Fortunatus's depiction of a more socially respectable Martin helps to legitimize, during this era, the seizing of episcopal sees by members of the aristocracy, to whose tastes Fortunatus accommodates a paradigmatic model of sanctity.[151]

Of course, the *Vita sancti Martini* still remains a dominant hagiographic influence on Merovingian writers, especially on Fortunatus and Gregory,[152] but Sulpicius's eccentric saint has evolved to fit the needs of a more clerical and aristocratically controlled church, one that, at least in the West, prefers dead saints whose cults can be sanctioned and monitored rather than living holy men, who, being marginal individuals by vocation, tend to move beyond the reach of ecclesiastical authority.[153] In contrast to Martin and Antony, the saints of the Merovingian age are not "wild plants" free to grow in their own charismatic direction[154]; they are carefully cultivated, and their charisma, at least according to the hagiographic accounts, is put to work for a highly organized ecclesiastical network run by a religious and social elite. Lay sanctity is seldom the central focus of a hagiographic work, even though we can detect through the various literary sources of this era that there must have been large numbers of lay men and women leading lives of penance and *secreta conversio*.[155] It is no coincidence that these individuals' *Vitae* were rarely written. When writers do depict lay sanctity, it is often represented as subversive and in need of eradication by an ecclesiastical authority.[156]

The implications of this shift in understanding Martin are crucial for the development of Merovingian hagiography. Such a change means that holiness pertains chiefly to the episcopal rank, and, given from what class bishops were usually culled, this shift also entails, in contrast to the original portrait of Martin as a dirty, uneducated, poorly dressed soldier's son, that the ideal of holiness is "aristocratized": *sanctitas* and *nobilitas* go hand in hand.[157] A Merovingian saint is usually upper class and in a position of power, most often a bishop, sometimes an abbot, but rarely a recluse living an ascetic life detached from an urban center or some form of ecclesiastical organization.[158]

Fortunatus represents one of the period's earliest promoters of clerical sanctity. As already suggested, the use of the term *tyrocinium* to describe the careers of Marcellus and Albinus is important because it puts the context of holy warfare neither in the desert, as with Antony, nor in a private monk's cell, as with Martin, but within the boundaries of a clearly marked ecclesiastical structure. Fortunatus's hagiography leaves little room for independent holy men. In the *Vita sancti Paterni*, for instance, tension arises between a holy man roaming free in the wild and an ecclesiastical authority attempting to gain control of an unsupervised ascetic. After the saint's absence of three years, the abbot of the monastery Paternus originally left determines to find the wandering recluse. He learns of the holy man's meager diet of bread and water, supplemented only by raw vegetables. On top of this, Paternus rejects human contact, wears a hair shirt, and refuses to sleep on a bed.[159] After a reprimand from the abbot, the saint restrains his asceticism, is made a deacon, and then is ordained a priest. Paternus receives an even greater reward for moderating his fasts and fanatical reclusiveness. One night while in his cell, the saint has a vision in which the departed *episcopi* of Avranches appear and ordain him bishop. Soon afterward, his dream comes true.[160] The ascetic warrior is thus recruited into the army of clerics.

In the hagiography of Fortunatus, Paternus's *Vita* is the closest we come to an independent holy man who is cultivating a life roughly modeled on the Egyptian style of eremitical monasticism, and this *Vita* clearly shows suspicion of such behavior. As we have seen, the rugged recluse accommodates himself to the church by obeying an ecclesiastical authority. This compliance is presented in a positive light because it leads to the incorporation of an ascetically restrained holy man into the ranks of the clergy. Even the topos of a candidate refusing the episcopacy for reasons of humility is absent. As in the case of Germanus, Paternus's role as a bishop has been foreordained, with his departed predecessors' unanimous approval.[161] The saint's life as a hermit is an aberration; his life as a cleric coincides with that of the other holy men described by Fortunatus: He becomes a deacon, then a priest, and finally a bishop. Thus, his sanctity develops within an ecclesiastical setting.[162] Such sanctity is certainly gradational, but it is increased not by an interior heightening of holiness, as happens in the stories about the desert saints.[163] Rather, the sanctity described by Fortunatus progresses externally through the various clerical ranks and culminates in the episcopacy, clearly the dominant mark of holiness because every male saint described also becomes a bishop. Unlike the path of the desert fathers and even Saint Martin, the "road to paradise" on which Fortunatus sets his holy men runs straight through—and only through—a hierarchical church. By implication, the *Vitae* of Fortunatus may be regarded as a reflection of the early Merovingian church's effort to curtail the development of lay sanctity through antiascetic and proclerical hagiography.

Like his modification of Sulpicius's Martin, Fortunatus's prose *Vitae* also represent one of the era's earliest attempts to associate *nobilitas* with *sanctitas*. The prominent role played by the aristocracy in the development of the Gallican and Merovingian church has been studied in relation to hagiographic literature.[164] Perhaps just as illuminating as the scholarship concerning the impact of the rich and powerful on the Gallican church is Sulpicius's revealing remark that Martin's ascetic regimen attracted members of the upper class, who, after dabbling in the monastic life under the saint's guidance, allegedly entered the episcopacy.[165] Equally important and confirmed by the hagiographic sources is the phenomenon of Lerinian monasticism, which trained ascetically inclined aristocrats, who, in turn, also assumed more active lives as bishops.[166] However, in Fortunatus's *Vitae*, as we have already seen, there is little emphasis on rigorous monastic practices. Paternus's *Life* shows well enough that a high clerical rank is the sine qua non of sanctity. Of course, the episcopacy also happens to be a position coveted by those with a high social status.[167] Thus Fortunatus went further than previous hagiographic trends in "aristocratizing" the ideal of sanctity because he identifies holiness exclusively with the ecclesiastical aspirations of a male ruling class who fought fiercely for episcopal sees.[168] Furthermore, Fortunatus represents one of the first writers of this period who, whenever possible, stresses the high social class of his holy men.[169] Later in the era, hagiographers commonly insisted on the aristocratic origins of a saint, even if they had to invent a distinguished pedigree.[170]

Despite the claims of other researchers, the Lives of Fortunatus also indicate that the making of a hagiographic text, while it may have popular edification as one goal, occurs within a small circle of bishops, who carefully prescribe the portrayal of sanctity and decide what they want to present to "the public."[171] Fortunatus's stress on a saint's aristocratic origins and episcopal status establishes a relationship between the depiction of sanctity and the social milieu of hagiographic production. The introductory remarks attached to the Lives make this connection explicit. To almost every *Vita*, Fortunatus appends an epistolary address to the bishop who has requested an account of the saint's life.[172] The style and the content of these prefacing letters, considered in relation to the biographies that follow, reveal the close affinity between the writer's patrons and the ideal of sanctity promoted in his hagiographic works. The saints depicted in the *Vitae* reflect the aspirations, social status, and ecclesiastical rank of the elite group who commissioned Fortunatus to write. In short, as a writer whose rhetorical skills are put in the service of bishops, Fortunatus is, to paraphrase the epigraph chosen for this chapter, an "expert" in the "legitimation" of episcopal power, a kind of Merovingian "public relations specialist" for the bishops, whose ideal of sanctity his hagiography promotes.

Fortunatus uses these letters as an opportunity to link the dead holy bishop with his living successor, who requested the work. In Hilary's *Vita*, for example, Fortunatus presents the commissioner of the *Life*, Bishop Pascentius, as the spiritual heir of Hilary. The biography not only functions as a testament to the saint's life but also affirms Pascentius as the worthy episcopal successor who does not wish to "hide his affection" for Hilary.[173] Also important is how Fortunatus legitimizes the clerical status of Pascentius. Much like the saints examined so far, the religious zeal of Fortunatus's patron indicates that his episcopacy is divinely predestined: Pascentius "was born for the cultivation of ecclesiastical teaching."[174] Moreover, just as Hilary is portrayed later in the *Vita* as a defender of the church against Jews and heretics, so, too, Fortunatus in his prefacing epistle calls Pascentius a "guard" protecting "the foundation of the old order and Catholic dogma."[175]

The preface to the *Vita sancti Albini* explicitly shows the influence of an episcopal patron on a hagiographic production. Here the successor of Albinus, Bishop Domitian, actually sends to Fortunatus a cleric who serves as a kind of hagiographic research assistant.[176] This anonymous *relator* gathers information about the saint, confirms it, and, on behalf of Bishop Domitian, submits to Fortunatus his material, which is subsequently incorporated into the *Vita*. This process shows that the Bishop for whom Fortunatus writes actively oversees and participates in the creation of a hagiographic text.[177]

Given this control over hagiographic production, it is not surprising to find that the distinction between saints and Fortunatus's episcopal patrons is blurred. These bishops hold the very sees once belonging to the saints whose *Vitae* they have commissioned. Their own social, political, and ecclesiastical function is legitimized and promoted by the hagiographic glorification of their predecessors as benefactors of the poor, redeemers of prisoners, healers of the sick, and rightful punishers of the wicked, whether these be ambitious nobles encroaching on ecclesiastical property, peasants working on Sundays, or any other of the several kinds of transgressors described in the hagiographic sources. We need only recall the case of Germanus to realize how close the connection is between an episcopal patron authorizing a *Vita* and the choice of subject for a hagiographic portrait, for after his death, Germanus's own life is turned into a text by the same author he once commissioned to write Marcellus's *Vita*. Germanus becomes part of that literary corpus he fostered and patronized while alive. Fortunatus's hagiography is, then, a case in which the writer, episcopal commissioner, saint, and text are all intimately linked, and the portrait of sanctity in itself mirrors the aspirations and ambitions of that small group of men who directly assist in the production and dissemination of the *Vitae sanctorum*.[178]

Characteristic of these prefacing epistles is the attempt by Fortunatus to display his rhetorical skill. The humility topos designating the writer's inability to compose appears within long, convoluted sentences of multiple clauses with a knotted syntactical structure. The effect of such prose has been likened to "a confused drunken state" caused by "a flood of words."[179] These letters differ drastically in style from the narratives of the *Vitae* proper, which consist, for the most part, of shorter sentences and direct, consecutive accounts of the saints' miracles, much like the *De virtutibus sancti Martini* by Gregory of Tours. In these epistles, Fortunatus uses his extravagant rhetorical style to praise the literary skill of the episcopal addressees whose eloquence is favorably compared with the classical authors.[180] The writer of these prefaces places himself "beneath the feet of the learned" bishops who requested the work.

Given the literary complexity of the prefaces, the claim that these pieces are purely "masterpieces of rhetorical bombast" is difficult to refute.[181] However, while Fortunatus certainly uses the epistolary form to display his own literary talent, his excessive praise for the supposedly superior abilities of the bishops should not be seen only as overrefined rhetoric aimed at gaining admiration from episcopal patrons. Literary precedents outside hagiography show that aristocratic bishops, like Roman holders of high office before them, linked the legitimacy of their power with their eloquence as *rhetores*.[182] If rhetorical ability is a claim to power, then Fortunatus's prefaces take on a significance beyond the writer's desire to show his talent. Unlike the *Vitae* aimed at a broader and rather vaguely designated "public,"[183] the appended epistles attempt to associate the bishops with a literary style befitting their episcopal rank. Although the style of these introductions differs considerably from the actual Lives, both still affirm, in different ways, the power of the saints and the transference of this power to the episcopal patrons who authorize the biographies. In the prefaces, the bishops are presented by Fortunatus as the heirs of Roman eloquence and the divinely appointed successors of the holy men who, in the *Vitae*, engage in victorious battle against those opposing ecclesiastical authority.

Vestiges of Hagiography's Evolution

Syncretic Sanctity

The theme of the saint in conflict certainly dominates the hagiography of Fortunatus. But the variety of struggles in which the holy men engage leads to an ideal of sanctity characterized by several different attributes. As we have already noticed, the writer attempts to depict his heroes as martyrs in a contest with opposing foes. We recognize, of course, that these saints do not undergo a martyrdom in the strict sense of the word. Nevertheless, by explicitly citing their willingness to die and portraying their trials as reminiscent of martyrdom, Fortunatus obviously attempts to establish a link between his own hagiography and the highest ideal of sanctity expressed in the accounts of the early Christians, who literally imitated the suffering of Christ. The holiness of a saint is also related to biblical models so that Fortunatus's subjects represent the contemporary embodiment of a scriptural type. In addition, Fortunatus pays at least a superficial tribute to the holy man's asceticism. Besides "triumphing" over themselves, the saints in the *Vitae* of Fortunatus, after leading the life of pious monks or clerics, eventually become holy bishops. Added to these features of sanctity is a thaumaturgic element. Miracles occur throughout the career of each saint, and the holy men continue to exercise power after death by curing the sick and punishing the wicked from their tombs. These attributes, which in Fortunatus's hagiography often appear in situations of conflict, constitute syncretic sanctity. Fortunatus does not introduce any new types of holiness into his *Vitae*. Rather, he combines all the common types found in hagiography's past, and this ideal of sanctity expressed as a combination of types—that is, the one saint is, at different times, a (bloodless) martyr, ascetic monk or low-ranking cleric, bishop and thaumaturge—continues to mark Merovingian hagiography throughout its development.[184]

The amalgamation of saint types also reveals one of the chief literary concerns of Fortunatus: controlling—to some extent, even disguising—hagiographic deviancy.

The syncretic presentation of sanctity maintains a continuity with previous models of Christian heroism by incorporating into the contemporary narrative the types of sanctity represented in the earlier stages of hagiography's development. Fortunatus thus attempts to make explicit the connection between his *Vitae* and hagiography's past. The result of this strategy, however, is the absorption of hagiographic innovations—such as the glorification of a purely clerical and aristocratic sanctity—into works that assert continuity and present holy men conforming with previous exemplars, whether they are biblical figures, martyrs, or eremites. The new is presented in the context of the old. However historically different Fortunatus's saints may be from the past models, in the literature, they are still described in terms of the old prototypes—Paternus and Germanus are compared to Moses, Albinus is "like John the Baptist," Marcellus resembles Abel, and Hilary appears as a "second Adam," not to mention the explicit and veiled references to these saints as imitators of Martin. Fortunatus draws attention to the familiar and common types of sanctity—the martyr, the ascetic, the reclusive monk—even though all his saints eventually become worldly bishops, never undergo the suffering of a genuine persecution, and are hardly, except for the young Paternus, the self-mortifiers or detached monks of previous eras. Nevertheless, the strategy of stylizing a saint's conflict as an instance of martyrdom or of superficially referring to a bishop who still remained a "monk"[185] links the holy men of Fortunatus's own writing with the heroes of Christianity's past. By such a technique, Fortunatus establishes a continuity which, despite its tenuous connections to the historical martyrs and ascetics, validates on the rhetorical level the contemporary claim to sanctity.

The Problem of Martyrdom

For the hagiographic researcher, such a sensitivity to previous trends means that several traces of hagiography's evolution up to the end of the sixth century can be detected in the *Vitae sanctorum* of Venantius Fortunatus. The syncretic ideal of holiness can be fostered only by a hagiographer conscious of the genre's development and the place of his own writing within that continuing development. This awareness of hagiography as a living literature that can be adapted to new historical circumstances is reflected in the way Fortunatus carefully transfers a characteristic phase of the genre into those episodes of his narrative that lend themselves to stylization according to a previous trend. The attempt to present his saints as martyrs is one example of this technique.

Each time he utilizes the theme of martyrdom, Fortunatus acknowledges that the era of persecution has ended and that the holy warrior did not actually have to die for his faith. We may infer from such a sentiment that the historical circumstance of Christianity's toleration poses a challenge to the hagiographer's attempt to legitimize the presentation of the saint as a martyr. In fact, to make his account of martyrdom plausible, Fortunatus must diminish the importance of this historical incongruity, especially since, if his own *Vitae* are any indication, the Christians themselves are the major source of religious intolerance and persecution. To minimize the historical significance of Christianity's acceptance as the official religion, Fortunatus calls attention to a saint's desire to die, while simultaneously regarding the impossibility of such an end as a mere historical inconvenience that is subordinate to martyrdom itself. In a sense, he redefines martyrdom by stressing the role of the will[186]—and not that of blood—as the validating mark of a genuine "witnessing" (martyrium).[187]

While this technique may be rhetorically convenient, it does not entirely solve the problem. Except in the case of Germanus (which will be examined shortly), Fortunatus is clearly not glorifying his heroes as bloodless martyrs of asceticism who lived during a time of the church's peace. To make his saints pass for martyrs of the bloody rather than the ascetic type, Fortunatus employs a strategy far subtler than a rhetorical emphasis on the saint's willingness to die. The major episodes explicitly referred to as martyrdoms by Fortunatus exhibit a specific type of opposition not characteristic of the other conflicts, for which no claim to martyrdom is made. The encounters of Hilary with hostile Arians, Albinus with scheming bishops, and Paternus with angry pagans are all presented in a way that corresponds with the type of tension characteristic of authentic passiones. These older accounts heighten the polarized opposition between the Christian hero and a villainous tormentor.[188] The nature of the antagonism in the early descriptions of martyrdom is what Fortunatus attempts to capture in his own versions of a saint's persecution. It is when Hilary, Albinus, and Paternus enter into a situation of conflict analogous to the older sources that Fortunatus introduces the notion of martyrdom. In all the other cases of conflict, transgressing individuals immediately receive threats and punishments from the saint; in the episodes stylized as martyrdoms, the saints are, at first, in a position to be threatened and punished by the transgressors. More important, these conflicts associated with martyrdom are all of a religious nature. Because of a steadfast adherence to religious beliefs, the saints are in opposition to Arians, pagans, and disloyal clerics who refuse to protect the doctrines of the church. Like the depictions of the old persecutors, those who threaten the holy men in these conflicts are presented as either hostilely intolerant of or diametrically opposed to the saints' religious positions. To summarize, the accounts stylized as martyrdoms are those in which a religious issue is at stake, the saint is susceptible to suffering, and the conflict is highly polarized, even irreconcilable. Under these conditions, Fortunatus thus legitimizes the presentation of his saints as martyrs.[189]

However, the observation that Fortunatus transcends historical limitations and validates the supposed martyrdom of his saints by transposing into his text a type of opposition analogous to the early passiones does not adequately explain two episodes in the Vita sancti Germani, episodes that closely correspond to the pattern legitimizing the claim to persecution but that are not referred to as martyrdoms. We recall that the saint gives away all the monastery's food and, as a result, must retreat into his cell to avoid the retaliation of angry monks. At this moment in the narrative, we would expect to find the now familiar claim: "He was willing to have become a martyr." The same may be said of the conflict involving the fetal Germanus. Here, if anywhere, is an instance that could easily be stylized as martyrdom in that Fortunatus unambiguously portrays the mother as a potential murderer. The author, however, makes no attempt to capitalize on what seem to be ideal opportunities to present the saint as a martyr reminiscent of those who suffered bloody persecution.

As previously mentioned, a syncretic depiction of sanctity assumes the writer's awareness of earlier literary trends, and Fortunatus's stylization of a saint's conflict as a martyrdom reveals his sensitivity to the important role of religious persecution in hagiography's evolution. As is well known, another phase in the genre's development, coming shortly after the accounts of martyrdom, pertains to literature associated with the Egyptian monks, much of which was made available in the West through the translations of Evagrius and Rufinus. Hagiographers writing about these saints carefully tried to fit this new model of Christian heroism into the old one of martyrdom and persecution. The *Vita beati Antonii*, for instance, depicts the saint as his own tormentor, inflicting punishments of an ascetic nature, which are as courageously endured as those suffered by the first Christians.[190] This behavior depicted in the literature gives rise to what is known as the "bloodless martyr."[191] As we have already noticed, this martyrdom is precisely the type Fortunatus claims for Germanus. After mentioning his secret vigils, constant prayer, and ability to endure the elements, Fortunatus says that the saint "acquired" martyrdom during a time of peace.[192] Obviously, we cannot determine why Fortunatus stylizes Germanus as a bloodless martyr rather than a martyr closer to the persecuted Christians, as is the case in the "martyrdoms" of Hilary, Albinus, and Paternus. We can establish that Fortunatus avoids mixing martyr types. The saint must be presented, however superficially, as undergoing either an internal, self-inflicted agony characteristic of ascetic holy men or an externally inflicted suffering associated with the persecution of the early Christians. Both kinds of suffering correspond with two phases in hagiography, and both phases are clearly represented in the texts of Fortunatus, who obviously maintains the distinctions in the genre's development or there would have been no reason not to call Germanus a martyr in the two episodes previously discussed; indeed, the pattern of opposition almost seems to require it. Furthermore, the fact that Fortunatus does not refer to Germanus as a martyr in those cases in which such a distinction would not be out of place shows how frugal he is in applying this designation. Although every *Vita* but one contains an explicit reference to martyrdom, the word itself never appears more than once in a biography, and it is not used gratuitously, like the numerous and standard phrases denoting piety and holiness. On the contrary, the term always appears in an appropriate context, a context that corresponds with a previous hagiographic trend.

The Idea of Hagiographic Displacement

Scholars often focus on textual borrowings and the apparent sameness of hagiographic literature to fortify their conflicting arguments concerning the religious mentality or literary achievement of the Middle Ages. The homogeneity to which such borrowings attest can reveal a unified vision of sanctity expressed with such profound regularity that comparisons to icons and their religious function naturally follow.[193] Then again, the fact that, in some cases, the only difference between one *Vita* and another is the saint's name has led researchers to the conclusion that the hagiographer often lacks a literary imagination, especially when a writer must compose the life of a saint whose historical circumstances remain unknown to the author.[194] Here, I have no compulsion to accept one of these divergent conclusions reached by previous hagiographic researchers. Such arguments cannot adequately account for the hagiography of Fortunatus, not only because of their generalizing tendencies but also because the writing of this Merovingian author cannot be explained in terms of the extent to which explicit or implicit borrowings from other writers appear in his work. While we can certainly say that Sulpicius Severus and the Bible exercised enormous influence over both his poetry and prose, clearly whole hagiographic traditions—and not particular phrases from scattered texts of previous eras—are subtly insinuated into the hagiography of Fortunatus. Moreover, as we have seen in the depiction of martyrdom, these older traditions take on a new significance when they are placed in and adapted to a different historical context. A study of Fortunatus's hagiography needs to take into account how a contemporary hagiographer can rely on previous conventions and trends while creating hagiography that differs from the past, how, in other words, continuity with and adherence to hagiographic traditions also reflect change and innovation in the depiction of sanctity.

To restate the issue, Fortunatus's writing reveals a minimal amount of direct literary borrowings from other sources while also maintaining a close affinity with earlier hagiographic phases that are reflected by his *Vitae* in the form of a syncretic representation of sanctity. Previous attempts to analyze hagiography in terms of a continuous homogeneous process fail to account for the innovation that emerges from utilization of the older hagiographic models. We therefore need another way of explaining the presence of older literary traditions in this hagiographer's contemporary depiction of sanctity.

One way to address this need is to understand Fortunatus's hagiography as evolving the genre through literary displacement. In a context outside hagiography, the term *displacement* designates a strategy used by writers, especially those of romance, to incorporate myth into a story by way of simile, whether as an "analogy" or an "association" with a mythical figure. A modern critic explains the process as follows: "In a myth we can have a sun-god or a tree-god; in a romance we may have a person who is significantly associated with the sun or trees."[195] Past hagiographic trends are to Fortunatus what myth is to the writer of romance. The previous observations about martyrdom are again relevant here. The genuine martyr of hagiography's past cannot be wholeheartedly adapted by Fortunatus into his *Vitae* any more than a pure and undisguised myth can plausibly function in a modern novel. Given their historical context and distinctive style, the accounts of the martyrs are nonadaptive. In their original form, such stories cannot be placed in another hagiographic phase without obvious incongruities, and their appearance in a Merovingian *Vita* would seem entirely implausible. A major incongruity, to which Fortunatus is highly sensitive, is the saint as a martyr in a time of the church's peace. But the hagiographer still needs to link his hero with such a highly regarded type of sanctity, which can be accomplished by what may rightly be called hagiographic displacement.

Although the hagiographic genres constitute a different context from the one in which the device of displacement was originally detected, nevertheless, the application of the term to hagiographic texts refers to a kind of relationship between the *passio* and the *Vita* that is similar to the one between myth and romance. For our purposes, displacement is a basic critical term that can accurately identify the process at work in the hagiography of Fortunatus, a process that we have hitherto observed but not yet named. In such a process, the historical circumstances legitimizing the first claims to martyrdom are necessarily removed from the context of Fortunatus's hagiography and replaced by analogous situations of conflict that, as previously seen, attempt to mimic the type of opposition found in the stories of the martyrs. The displacement also occurs on the level of emphasis because the importance of the willingness to suffer, no doubt prominent in the accounts of the first martyrs and confessors, assumes virtually the total significance of martyrdom rather than a witnessing to the faith sealed with blood. Likewise, the bloodless martyr also constitutes a displacement because, in the depiction of such a saint, the internal and self-inflicted suffering characteristic of the ascetic contest is substituted for the public and externally inflicted persecution of the first Christians. In the case of the bloodless martyr, displacement is adaptation of heroic suffering to the new historical conditions in which sanctity flourishes.

The entire evolution of hagiographic literature can be understood in terms of displacement because each distinctive phase of the genre attempts to incorporate the earlier ones in such a way that the previous models of an entirely different historical setting and hagiographic context can plausibly function and continue in a contemporary portrait of a saint's life. Such a strategy facilitates the introduction of hagiographic innovation into an otherwise conservative genre by associating a new development, such as the bloodless martyr, with the older tradition. If the writing of Fortunatus is any indication, changes in portraying sanctity appear under the guise of conformity with previous hagiographic trends. The typology of sanctity must undergo such complex modifications because the martyr of one period must necessarily differ from that of another, even though the hagiographer tries to present the new type as being virtually the same as the old. Often, the very texts of Fortunatus that explicitly claim continuity with previous traditions show a high degree of displacement.

A subtle and ingenious way in which displacement functions in the hagiography of Fortunatus concerns the progression of the saint and gradational sanctity. Research on the "more obviously fictional accounts" of early hagiography suggests that the narratives correspond to a pattern found in romance literature.[196] The saint, seeking the solitude of the desert, sets out on a quest leading to greater withdrawal from worldly attachments. This quest results in a gradual heightening of holiness, corresponding to the degree of the saint's detachment and purity of life. The journey is often initiated by the young saint's dramatic flight from a spouse on the wedding night and marked by a descent in the form of an experience simulating death, which is then followed by an ascent into a life of greater and greater solitude as the saint progressively withdraws further into the desert and an interior life. In contrast to the binary opposition of the passiones, these more romantic accounts are characterized by the hero's choice of a life that is better, a life gradually increasing in holiness rather than abruptly ending in an unmediated conflict between Christian and persecutor.[197]

The differences between the stories of the desert fathers and Merovingian hagiography are significant enough to caution us against classifying the hagiography of

Fortunatus as romance. However, the *Vita sancti Paterni* offers an instance in which the pattern found in the accounts of the hermits resembles the progression of Fortunatus's saint. Let us examine this *Vita* again, this time as an instance of displaced gradational sanctity.

Like the questing recluses before him, Paternus's journey is a flight toward something increasingly better. After leaving his family and living in a monastery, the *puer-senex* "desires" a life of greater isolation. He then departs from his cenobitic community in order to embrace a more eremitical life of withdrawn *solitudo*.[198] Putting aside the reference to death in the form of martyrdom, there is still the romantic feature of descent; before battling the pagans on a mountain, the saint first enters a nearby cave, the typical tomblike dwelling of the desert hermits[199] and the place where Paternus temporarily lives before going out (or should we say up?) to destroy the "diabolical cult."[200] After the experience with the pagans, the ascent begins. The saint withdraws even from his monastic companion Scubilio. According to Fortunatus, the saint experiences no human contact. His fasting increases; he verges on becoming an omophage, like some of the more ascetically extreme monks of the earlier accounts.[201] His religious discipline, as was mentioned earlier, is rigorous and even harsh. Up to this point in the story, Paternus proceeds according to the gradational pattern of sanctity observed in the hagiography depicting the withdrawn saints of the desert. Should the pattern persist, Paternus would continue in this mode until death, just prior to which he would tell his story to a "pious traveler."[202]

Precisely when this ascetic type of sanctity heightens to the extent that it coincides with the gradational holiness characteristic of the recluses, however, Fortunatus introduces another mode of progression. Paternus still increases in holiness, but the context of the gradational pattern is displaced so that, rather than proceeding in isolated sanctity, Fortunatus's holy man enters the ranks of the church. The progression found in the earlier ascetic literature is now rechanneled by Fortunatus so that the sanctity develops according to an ascent through the ecclesiastical hierarchy. Unlike a saint such as Antony, who seeks greater and greater solitude in a search for the interior *mons*,[203] the quest of Paternus becomes external and turns outward as he mitigates his asceticism, resumes contact with people, becomes accountable to an ecclesiastical authority, and develops his sanctity within the formal structure of the church. The gradational scheme is still present in the *Vita*. Now, however, this pattern is put to use by a hagiographer sensitive to the anxiety of a highly organized *ecclesia* that needs to control independent holy men. Characteristic of the older gradational sanctity is the saint's desire for something better: The desert is better than the city, an unmarried life is better than a married one, and an eremitical monasticism is better than a cenobitic one. Certainly, this feature is still present in Paternus's *Vita*. But, when the scheme is displaced by Fortunatus, the gradational holiness is expressed in terms of a clerical life culminating in the episcopacy as better than a layman's life led in unsupervised withdrawal not just from the world but, more important, from the church.[204]

The way Fortunatus utilizes the earlier gradational pattern by displacing it in a context that reflects his church's view of holiness shows how innovation can occur in a genre that must accommodate the changing perception of contemporary sanctity and, at the same time, conservatively maintain a conscious link to the earlier literature. The writing of Fortunatus suggests that, in hagiography's evolution, one phase does not suddenly end and another begin. Rather, each stage in the genre's development is incorporated in a plausible way into the next so that the vestiges of the older literature are present in the new narratives. Displacement facilitates this evolution by allowing change without entirely breaking with the previous traditions.

Of course, displacement is not always necessary to establish continuity. A hagiographer can draw on the earlier trend without displacing it because a previous convention can plausibly function virtually unchanged in a contemporary text. The topos of the *puer-senex*, for instance, operates in the hagiography of Fortunatus in the same way as it does in the desert literature.[205] To characterize the saint as having the wisdom of an old man is a technique used at the outset of a narrative to distinguish the holy person from the ordinary lot of humankind and to put into relief the extraordinary nature of sanctity.[206] Unlike the difficulties posed by martyrdom, the topos of the *puer-senex* is not subject to historical contingencies and therefore can be wholeheartedly taken over by a contemporary hagiographer. The same may be said of the similarities in topoi, stock phrases, and conventions that continue to mark *Vitae* throughout the Middle Ages.[207] Although there are certainly short-lived and constantly changing topoi, there are also those that appear persistently with few or no modifications throughout the long development of hagiographic literature.[208] Their validity is jeopardized neither by time nor place, and they can repeatedly function in any *Vita* because they conform to what is generally known as the "horizon of expectation" in the representation of sanctity.[209]

Having examined the salient features of Fortunatus's prose biographies, let us turn now to another prolific writer of this period, Gregory of Tours. Although the two were contemporaries who knew each other well and who undoubtedly shared a similar vision of hagiography's role in the social, political, and religious spheres of sixth-century Gaul, Gregory, as we shall soon discover, consistently offers an approach to the literature that differs significantly from that of Fortunatus. Now that we have gained a sense of Fortunatus's writing, a consideration of Gregory's *Liber vitae patrum* can show us the range of hagiographic possibilities that can be exploited by another representative author of this period.

3

GREGORY OF TOURS'S
LIFE OF THE FATHERS

Gregory's religion, the condition for the masterful
hold he had on his present, is the most unsettling
phenomenon he offers to our attention, and no
one concerned with the Middle Ages can afford
to pass it casually by.
—Walter Goffart, *Narrators* (1988, p. 234)

Contextualizing the *Liber Vitae Patrum*

Among other functions suitable to a poet and writer patronized by the social and
clerical elite, Fortunatus occasionally served as the professional propagandist for his
friend and fellow hagiographer, Georgius Florentius Gregorius, a Gallo-Roman aris-
tocrat who succeeded his mother's cousin Eufronius as the bishop of Tours in 573.[1]
According to one estimate, nearly three-quarters of the extant literary works written
during the Merovingian period belong to Fortunatus and his episcopal companion,
the author known to us today as Gregory of Tours.[2] Of the two, Gregory is distinguished as "the principal hagiographic authority for the sixth century."[3] Such a claim
undoubtedly rests on the sheer bulk of his writing, which surpasses that of Fortunatus and makes Gregory one of the most prolific authors in the history of hagiographic literature. Given his remarkable literary output and the breadth of religious
life revealed by his writings, a consideration of Gregory's depiction of holiness is
essential to any study purporting to deal with the early Merovingian image of sanctity. As was the case in our examination of Fortunatus, an investigation of Gregory's
Vitae will allow us to enter one of the main hagiographic currents of sixth-century
Gaul.

Throughout his vast literary corpus, Gregory shows extraordinary versatility as a
hagiographer, far more so than Fortunatus. During the years of his episcopacy (573–
594), this guardian of Saint Martin's cult meticulously recorded miracles (DVSM, VJ),
gave rich accounts of the activities at various shrines associated with numerous saints
(GC, GM), and composed a large number of Lives (LVP), in addition to reworking
hagiographic material written by earlier authors (MA, *Seven Sleepers*).[4] Nor can we
exclude from this list his *Histories*, with their strong religious overtones and their

often explicit hagiographic accounts that glorify the triumphs of the holy and detail, perhaps in satirical fashion, the defeats of the wicked.[5]

Unfortunately, in assessing the two as writers, historians of literature tended to overlook Gregory's achievement as a consummate hagiographer, equally adept at recounting *virtutes* at a tomb or narrating the course of a saint's life. Instead, they usually attend to Fortunatus's poetry, some of which is indisputably trite, but at least two pieces in particular, his *Vexilla regis* and *Pange lingua*, arouse universal admiration and are often popularly regarded as a kind of poetic compensation for the defects, openly acknowledged or not, of his less inspired poems.[6] Naturally, the disparity scholars traditionally saw between the two authors would have diminished if researchers had examined more closely these two writers' prose *Vitae*. Then, similarities in style, content, and language would have emerged, notwithstanding Fortunatus's rhetorically elaborate prefaces.[7] But, with the exception of a few dissonant voices, the general trend in the comparisons between these contemporary writers amounted to extolling the poetry of Fortunatus as refined literature that contrasted sharply with the writing of Gregory, by whose crude prose scholars measured the depth to which learning had allegedly plunged during the Merovingian era.[8] Fortunately, we need not attempt to refute the facile comparisons earlier researchers made between Fortunatus as the great but last bright light in the history of Latin poetry and Gregory as the unrefined representative of a "barbarized Latin" that supposedly reflected the brutal realities of Frankish life.[9] Examining his work on its own terms, apart from Fortunatus, critics are gradually acknowledging the sophistication of Gregory's writing, especially the *Histories*, by far his most studied work.[10] In fact, based on some of the more innovative scholarship, we could now plausibly argue that Gregory's prose, even without considering its rhythmical quality,[11] shows by its rich presentation of life the mark of an "unconscious poet,"[12] whereas the all too often trivial verses of Fortunatus, regardless of their Vergilian or Prudentian echoes,[13] lack imaginative substance and in many cases can be considered poetry only insofar as they externally assume that literary form.[14]

Of course, the immediate aim of the present discussion is to investigate the LVP, not to redress the flawed assessment of Gregory that was commonly made on the basis of Fortunatus's poetry or, for that matter, on the basis of comparisons with Bede or Gregory the Great, which also cast the bishop of Tours in an inferior light.[15] It is also not our task to outline the complex history of scholarship on Gregory's work, especially in light of the competent treatment of this subject by previous researchers.[16] However, certain trends in the interpretation of Gregory's writings should be at least noted because these developments indicate the kinds of problems we shall confront as the discussion unfolds and also show the need for an examination of the LVP in its own right.

The unbalanced concentration on only one portion of what is unquestionably an enormous literary corpus is a chief weakness of the research on Gregory's writings.[17] Despite the abundance of purely hagiographic material, Gregory's commentators tend to focus exclusively on the *Histories*, often with little success in reaching any agreement over that work's value and meaning. Even today, it is difficult to discern precisely where the scholarly consensus lies or to determine how this episodic narrative, most of which chronicles events in Gregory's own time, can be most profitably studied.[18] As previously suggested, literary historians are gradually coming to appreciate this most discussed of all of Gregory's writings. But for such an appreciation to continue and to increase, the Histories must be treated more as a source for the study of mentalités than as a factual record of events recorded by an unassuming or, as some claim, naive reporter.[19] That it cannot be accepted as "history" in the modern sense of the word is clear from the obstacles social and political historians face when attempting to get at the "facts" of Gregory's account. Such an endeavor inevitably leads to problems of verification; much of what the author wrote cannot be "checked" against more reliable sources, given that Gregory's version of what happened is often all that survives.[20] Chief among the reasons for doubting that version is the prominent role of the supernatural.[21] Indicative of their treatment of hagiographic literature on the whole, historians of society and politics often are inept at dealing with the miraculous content and overall religious character that stamp the "ten books of histories," which helps to explain why Gregory's hagiographic productions receive such scant attention. Because virtutes are the dominant feature, Gregory's purely hagiographic works are also the most historically unreliable of his writings. Generally speaking, the methods and aims of historians are usually not conducive to treating texts that primarily record supernatural occurrences[22] (although the hagiographers themselves make no clear distinction between the natural and the supernatural[23]). So-called documents, not Vitae or miracle stories, are thought to be the best sources for uncovering reliable information about the past.[24] Even with the hagiographic elements scattered throughout the Histories, this account of the period still attempts to narrate the major events of the author's epoch chronologically and so merits at least cautious consideration. However, the numerous, repetitive stories this same writer told of the sick receiving inexplicable cures at the tombs of the holy dead can be more readily dismissed as unbridled credulity.[25]

Clearly, this disproportionate attention given to the Histories is reflected by the lack of in-depth studies on the LVP.[26] This collection of twenty Lives (literally rendered into English by the somewhat cumbersome title The Book of the Life of the Fathers) rarely receives attention beyond the superficial observations made by scholars preoccupied with Gregory's Histories but obliged to mention in passing the author's other literary productions. Moreover, whatever biographical, social, and political information the LVP may contain, the miracles still play a prominent role in the accounts and so can present the same "stumbling block to historians" as do the miraculous elements in the Histories or the purely hagiographic works devoted to recounting virtutes.[27] The original disdain for the miraculous that appears strongest in the earlier studies on the Histories can potentially carry over to the LVP and linger under a new guise and in an entirely different context.[28]

Another prominent tendency in the research devoted to the Histories has more positive repercussions on the LVP because of the observations of a literary historian who formulated an ingenious argument based on a characteristic common to both works. One aspect of the Histories, in particular, baffles those who attempt to make sense of the composition: the lack of connection between one story and the next. This aspect of Gregory's narrative creates an overall impression of incoherence. One researcher eloquently summed up the situation by referring to "the jumbled mosaic that has puzzled and exasperated historians."[29] Certainly, it was a turning point in the study of the Histories when Auerbach viewed the baffling aspects of Gregory's writing in a positive light.[30] But another historian of literature, in an attempt to argue that the Histories, even with their paratactic narrative,[31] do, indeed, contain an underlying coherence, introduced into the debate a rather innovative explanation that relies in part on a major feature of the LVP. Brunhölzl's argument hinges on the significance of the prefaces, which in the libelli of the LVP often encapsulate the meaning of the stories that follow.[32] This same feature, or so it is claimed, appears in the Histories, with the introductory material there conveying the underlying meaning behind what often appears to be an otherwise confusing narrative:

> Gregory, as he explicitly said in the introduction [to the Histories], wanted to write the history of his times, hence the first three books [which narrate the events before Gregory's era] might be regarded as "preface," definitely a preface that amounts to far more than merely organizational importance. On at least one other occasion Gregory wrote a similarly lengthy "preface," in the de cursibus ecclesiasticis. There, as also in perhaps the most accomplished work from the collection of his hagiographic writings, the Liber vitae patrum, in which he gives a kind of sermon before each Vita, the parts preceding the actual content contain Gregory's views concerning the topic for discussion, they reveal the *meaning* of the account that follows and they hold the key to understanding the whole work. This is also true of the Histories.[33]

Whether these comments accurately describe the role played by the prefaces in the Histories is of little consequence to the present study. Of great importance, however, are the observations on the function of the prefaces in the LVP, especially since a careful reading of these libelli compels us to acknowledge the partial accuracy in Brunhölzl's perception of this collection of Vitae while simultaneously recognizing the limitations of an assessment that at best offers an impressionistic summary of a carefully constructed composition.[34]

Gregory's Corpus and the Libelli of the Fathers

Before considering the obvious implications Brunhölzl's observations have for this discussion, one other difficulty touches on the very nature of the collected Vitae about to be examined. At the end of the Histories, Gregory lists the titles of his major literary productions. With the exception of allowing his writings to be versified, he requests that none of his books be "corrected" or in any way altered by any succeeding bishops of Tours, no matter how learned they might be. All his works, regardless of their rustic style, are to be kept intact. Those who ignore this warning will find themselves "condemned with the devil" on the day of judgment.[35] Gregory's insistence that his writings not be modified in any way suggests that he regards what we would categorically call his historiography, hagiography, biblical exegesis, and liturgical work as constituting a "fundamental unity," an integrity that he feared would be jeopardized by emendations, a concern which, as it turns out, is as entirely justified today as it was when he wrote.[36] However, as was briefly mentioned before, scholars have difficulty finding coherence in the Histories alone, an indication that uncovering this work's relation to the general design of Gregory's vast corpus would be especially challenging. Gregory certainly does not state the nature of this fundamental unity or elaborate on how it permeates his sentences. To discover this unity would require, therefore, a careful piecing together of all the common characteristics throughout his writings. Moreover, supposing this "unified vision" can be detected, to be compelling it would have to be present not only on the level of linguistic and stylistic parallels between one work and the next but also on the level of an underlying thought shaping Gregory's *opera*, a pervasive doctrine that is consistently and coherently, though perhaps not explicitly, expressed by his writings. Signs of such a comprehensive vision will be difficult to detect if scholars tend not to approach Gregory's writings as constituting, on the whole, a coherent teaching detailing the constant interaction between nature, human life, and divine power. Perhaps, then, the most suitable way to approach Gregory is as a kind of practical theologian, his writings constituting a theology that is, like the use of the Bible in hagiographic literature, more actualized than verbally conceptualized.[37] We can be certain that the reason his corpus is not approached in such a manner has far less to do with the obvious difficulties posed by Gregory's writings than it does with the failure of modern researchers to treat the implications of the religious ideas Gregory's work assumes or expresses.

Unfortunately, the aim of the present study does not permit addressing this broader issue concerning Gregory's writing as the unified expression of a theology reflecting and conditioning the religious beliefs and practices of late antique Gaul. But in one respect, this question pertains directly to the LVP. In that same passage summarizing his literary works at the end of the *Histories*, Gregory does not include the LVP among his "books of miracles," which the author there claims are seven in number.[38] However, in his preface to the GC, generally thought to be his last work in the collection of *Miracula*,[39] Gregory includes the LVP among what are now eight books of miracles.[40] The version that reflects Gregory's final view of the work cannot be stated with certainty.[41] Perhaps Gregory himself was not quite sure how to classify this composition and so changed his mind about how he envisaged it within the whole of his literary corpus.[42] Such an incongruity seems unlikely to be the result of an absentminded author who simply forgot what he had written elsewhere regarding the number of miracle books he had composed. Although impossible to prove, the most likely reason for the discrepancy results from the nature of the LVP itself, which is unlike any of Gregory's other hagiographic works and, for that matter, when the rich diversity of saints represented is taken into account, quite unlike anything written in the era.[43]

The uncertainty surrounding the work's place in Gregory's corpus may be due to an ambiguity in the content of the LVP itself. The "seven books of miracles" primarily record *virtutes*. These deeds of power appear in *libri* devoted to one holy man in particular (e.g., Martin or Julian, in the DVSM and VJ, respectively) or to specific groups of saints (e.g., the martyrs and confessors of the GM and GC). In either format, the focus is on postmortem miracles, which is not the case, at least not entirely, with the LVP. Here, Gregory actually attempts to tell the lives of contemporary saints and to shape the biographical material, some of which he gathered from his personal encounters with the subjects themselves, into hagiography,[44] and the content of each *Vita* pertains, at least partly, to what the holy individuals did while alive. Naturally, precisely how much content deals with the deeds of each living saint varies from *Vita* to *Vita*. However, like most Lives from this period, the accounts also relate the postmortem miracles attributed to the holy individuals, and, in that respect, the narratives assume the characteristics associated with the *septem libri miraculorum*—the emphasis on the sick appealing to the saint for a cure at the tomb, the punishments inflicted on those who offend the holy dead, and the efficacy of relics in warding off illness or danger. The *LVP* therefore holds a peculiar position between the author's more usual hagiographic format—the accounts of *virtutes*—and, insofar as there is treatment of what the holy men did while alive, the more biographical narratives characterizing saints' Lives. From the perspective of Gregory's hagiographic writings, the stories told in the *LVP* are neither pure *Vitae* nor pure miracle accounts and are thus difficult to classify within the author's corpus.

From the perspective of the other hagiography written during this period, the *LVP* also shows striking contrasts. A brief comparison with Fortunatus's *Vitae*, for instance, shows several points of departure. As was already noticed, with respect to pre-Merovingian hagiography, Fortunatus is an innovator subtly introducing change into the genre under the guise of continuity. But with respect to the *Vitae* themselves, Fortunatus's Lives show a remarkable invariability, a real lack of development or change from one Life to the next. Fortunatus is a writer who rigorously adheres to his hagiographic formulae. Considered on their own, his *Vitae* maintain a discernible regularity: With rare exceptions, every male saint is a *puer-senex*, *miles Christi*, a bishop, in some way a martyr, more powerful than secular authority during times of conflict, a defender of the downtrodden, ascetically moderate, without defects of character, and preferably aristocratic. For nearly each of these requisites of sanctity in Fortunatus's Lives, however, there is an exception in Gregory's *LVP*. Here, we encounter adult converts agonizing over what sort of life to lead, pure hermits estranged from a cenobitic community or even hostile to a slack clerical culture that a holy man eschews, a cowardly saint who avoids martyrdom, saints who are also representatives of worldly power, extreme ascetics who gruesomely mortify their bodies, a holy man with a character flaw that nearly ruins him, as well as saints who come from the lowly ranks of the impoverished and enslaved—all these in addition to saints who resemble those portrayed by Fortunatus. Even this rather superficial contrast between the two writers' hagiography suggests that in the *LVP* a rare diversity of sanctity has been represented and gathered into one work that defies analysis according to the more standard categories of sanctity into which the saints of Fortunatus's Lives fall.[45]

The Biblical Imprint

Scripture and Hagiographic Diversity

Earlier, we noticed that bishops commissioned Fortunatus to write Lives of those saints who previously held their sees and that these authorized *Vitae* express the common concerns of the author's episcopal patrons. These Lives mirror the aspirations, social and religious functions, political conflicts and ties, and the clerical rank of those who requested the work. In this way, the episcopal commissioners to whom

Fortunatus dedicates most of his Lives appear as the legitimate and worthy heirs of their holy predecessors. In addition to the usual demands made by the genre's conservative nature, these conditions of hagiographic production contribute to the "monochrome color" of Fortunatus's portraits, with each male saint described usually meeting several common criteria of sanctity.[46] But the LVP gives a quite different impression. Here, we find not only extensive diversity in the representations of sanctity but also saints with fundamentally opposite traits of holiness.[47] To account for such striking contrasts, our examination of the LVP begins where Gregory himself starts each Vita, the place Brunhölzl claims holds the key to understanding—the prefaces. Here, biblical texts appear most prominently and have a function beyond that of introduction. The sacred texts operate as the major organizing principle of the narrative since they begin the shaping of a saint's life into a scripturally based story.

This thematic function of Scripture in the LVP will be considered shortly. For now, however, let us note the most obvious hagiographic basis for the wide spectrum of sanctity that this work exhibits. Perhaps the social historian would say that the reason for such diversity lies in the fact that Gregory drew his biographical material from all walks of the religious life, thus producing an assortment of different Lives from an assortment of different subjects. Certainly, the biographical peculiarities of each saint account for differences between lives. Even Fortunatus's Lives reflect distinctions in that regard. But the argument that a variety of subjects accounts for the contrasts between one Vita and another in the LVP is not adequate or in keeping with the literary presentation of each saint, for preceding the biographical contingencies is a suprahistorical rationale accounting for the wide spectrum of saints represented. The prefaces show Gregory making full use of the rich and varied models of holiness found in the Bible. Examples from both Testaments offer abundant justifications for all manner of religious behavior. As a hagiographer anchoring the Lives of the LVP on numerous biblical texts, Gregory's vision of sanctity clearly reflects the diversity of the book on which he relies most and by which his worldview is most profoundly shaped. Scripture therefore justifies the variety of saints represented in the Life of the Fathers.

Ecclesiastes and a "Metaphorical Kernel"

Biblical quotation is, then, the starting point for these Lives, not the birth of the saint or an account of upbringing. Although these facets appear early on, they are, almost without exception, preceded by a biblically based preface on which each Vita depends and from which each one derives its distinctive coloring. In other words, each saint is filtered through the Bible. Like Fortunatus's holy men, the saints of the LVP are also portrayed as fulfillments of Scripture or as the continuators of the salvation history documented by the Bible. However, the extent and significance of Gregory's application of Scripture differ considerably from Fortunatus's incorporation of biblical texts into his narratives. Fortunatus draws directly from Scripture rather frugally; Gregory does so in abundance.[48] This difference leads to an important correlation between the depiction of sanctity and the explicit presence of the Bible in the Vitae of these two authors: Gregory relies heavily on direct citation of the

Bible and creates Lives of remarkable variety; Fortunatus inserts relatively few Scriptural texts into his prose hagiography and produces works that are fundamentally homogeneous. Such an observation does not imply that the Bible did not influence Fortunatus's writing. The difference between the two authors lies in the fact that, on the whole, Scripture plays an implicit, more indirect role in Fortunatus's Lives, notwithstanding the comparisons with Abel, John the Baptist, Moses, or Christ at the wedding feast. Even in these instances of explicit application, however, Fortunatus uses the Bible only to supplement an already well-delineated portrait of a holy person. Gregory, by contrast, actually starts his accounts with quotations from Scripture. Throughout his stories, the biblical verses appear centonically in his prose to the extent that even the modern editor and translator of these Lives do not catch every explicit citation.[49] Thus, unlike Fortunatus's hagiography, the Bible has a primary rather than supplementary function in the LVP, with the prefaces bringing a variety of scriptural verses to the thematic forefront of the accounts. Such prominence given to Holy Writ puts the telling of a saint's life almost on the level of exegesis, given that the holy person's life, as we are about to see, is really being presented by Gregory as an illustration of what a scriptural passage means in a contemporary context, as if the *Vita* itself is an exposition of the sacred text, a kind of biblical commentary in the form of hagiographic narrative.

Given the other issues that this study still needs to address, we cannot, as we were more inclined to do in the case of Fortunatus's smaller and thematically more manageable corpus, dwell on all the twenty compositions constituting the LVP.[50] We can, however, concentrate on one *Vita* that is, as far as any one *Vita* can be in such a diverse collection of Lives, representative of the whole with respect to the question of narrative structure and the clear examples it readily provides of the author's fundamental strategies in telling his stories.

The account selected for this purpose, the *Life of Saint Senoch*, appears in the fifteenth book of the LVP. We shall dwell at length on this piece, which is intimately linked to a scriptural verse. In taking into account the significance of the Bible, the scripturally based approach to this particular *Life* also suggests a basic way in which all the Lives of the LVP could be profitably studied in that the whole collection is profoundly stamped by biblical texts.

The story of Senoch is important because it offers an obvious example of how a preface relates to the following narrative of a *Vita*. In some respects, this *Life* presents nothing more unusual than Fortunatus's hagiography. There is a syncretic sanctity, with the holy man an abbot, periodically a recluse, a deacon, and then a priest. The saint is also a thaumaturge, and the *Vita* records the miracles attributed to him. Nevertheless, there is also a fundamental difference between this account and those told by Fortunatus. Rather than a saint who is portrayed as increasing in holiness as the narrative proceeds, Senoch's sanctity temporarily diminishes because of a character flaw. Initially, Gregory only hints at this blemish in the first line of the *Vita*, which begins with the familiar words "*vanitas vanitantium . . . omnia vanitas.*" This quotation from Ecclesiastes 1:2 then provides the basis for a brief commentary on one of the great perils threatening those who attempt to lead holy lives. Success at such an endeavor, often accompanied by the personal satisfaction that arises out of such purity of life, leaves saints susceptible to the sin of pride.[51] Senoch is now introduced as a contemporary case that illustrates Gregory's point. This saint's arrogance nearly ruined an otherwise unblemished existence:

> "Vanity of vanities," says the Preacher, "all is vanity." Is it true, then, that everything done in the world is vanity? Hence it happens that the saints of God, consumed by no burning lust, aroused by no enticing concupiscence, tempted by no sensual filth, not even—so to speak—in their thought, have been puffed-up by the cunning of the tempter, have regarded themselves as the most righteous, and, for this reason, inflated with the pride of high-booted boasting, they have frequently fallen. So it has happened that those whom the sword of greater crimes could not cut the light smoke of vanity easily ruined. Such [was the case with] that very man whose story we are now about to tell. Although he had been distinguished by many deeds of power, he almost fell [and would have been] buried in that pit of arrogance if the heeded exhortation of faithful brothers had not rescued him.[52]

After this introduction, Gregory proceeds to relate the course of the saint's life. The first chapter of the *Vita* appears as standard hagiography, with no mention made of vanity or arrogance. Indeed, at first it seems as if the narrator has dropped his theme entirely because he turns from the discussion on the danger of pride to focus instead on the holy man's establishing a monastery, entering the diaconate, and receiving divine favor through a miraculous response to his prayer. In an entirely positive light, the standard attributes of a holy life also appear: Senoch eats and drinks little, especially during Lent, as is typical of the more ascetically inclined saints[53]; even in winter, he goes barefoot; he mortifies himself by binding his neck, feet, and hands with chains, a practice out of place in Fortunatus's Lives of male saints but not inconsistent with stories of rigorous ascetics in the *LVP* and elsewhere[54]; he also withdraws from the other monks to live a life of solitary prayer, vigils, and fasting. Again, all of these activities are not especially unusual, given the other stories told in the *LVP* and the hagiography associated with the desert saints.[55]

But this characterization of Senoch is also part of the narrative's movement toward an intended effect anticipated by the preface. This standard depiction of Senoch's sanctity is leading toward a relatively uncommon—at least with respect to Merovingian hagiography—halt of saintly progression.

Although not mentioned disapprovingly at first, Gregory notes the charismatic appeal and popularity of Senoch. As a living holy man, the faithful flock to him. He receives money from them, which Gregory says, using Matthew 6:19 as a justification, was given to the poor or used to secure the release of numerous people from servitude and debt.[56] Then, in the second chapter, Gregory himself becomes a character in the narrative when he claims that on his arriving in Tours, presumably to assume the episcopacy,[57] Senoch left his cell, greeted the new bishop, and, significantly, returned to his family. Undoubtedly, the saint's going back to his kin precipitates an opposite movement in the development of sanctity, given that leaving or rejecting the family often marks, as previously noted, the beginning of a holy life. His return home, renowned holiness, and popularity as a healer give Senoch such great self-satisfaction that by the time he comes back to his cell he is "swollen with pride."[58] With such a description of the saint, the connection between the biblically based preface and the narrative following it is now firmly established. What emerges at this point in the *Vita* is a highly structured story organized around a central biblical text that gives coherence to the narrative or, to put it in terms of Aristotelian criticism, contributes to the story's "unity of action."[59] In fact, by the end of the second chapter, several features commonly associated with the progression of plot—exposition (preface), rising action (first chapter describing attributes of sanctity), climax (saint's arrogance and subsequent condemnation), turning point (Senoch's repentance), and denouement (the restoration of holy life lived in humility until death)—are present, although in truncated forms. We may even say that, with respect to the narrative's main theme—the danger of pride—the *Vita* structurally comes to a conclusion at the end of the second chapter. The more biographical elements of the story end here, with Senoch full of humility and settling back into the routine of a holy life. After this, with the exception of the saint's death and funeral, Gregory tells miracle stories, one after another. That this second section constitutes a different kind of story, one less oriented to telling the actual course of the saint's life, Gregory indicates with a simple transitional sentence: "Finally, having said something about the life of this saint, let us now come to the miracles, which it pleased the curing hand of the Almighty to accomplish through him."[60] Unlike the first two chapters, the accounts of *virtutes* are episodic and really constitute a subplot—a second story distinct from the previous narrative. This subplot does not develop a theme such as the peril of pride in the sanctified life. In fact, we never again hear of *arrogantia* or *iactancia coturnosa* after the second chapter. Certainly, this section has a theme—the saint's deeds of power—but not what we could call a progression of plot, such as that found in the first section. The miracle segment consists of reports, descriptions in the form of ministories that attest to the saint's thaumaturgic accomplishments and give this section of the *Vita* its episodic quality, an obvious contrast with the more structurally complex narrative of the biographical chapters. Any of the several miracle accounts could be deleted without jeopardizing the integrity of this section. Indeed, Gregory himself, like so many other hagiographers, admits here and elsewhere to leaving several miraculous incidents out of his narrative, but the story is no worse for the omissions.[61] If, however, the preface were withdrawn, with its theme-setting function, the rest of that first part of the narrative would lose its structural unity: Senoch's pride would simply be one of several other components in the story rather than the orderly fulfillment of an outcome anticipated by the opening sentence.

Obviously, the structural coherence of the *Vita*'s first plot derives from the story's adherence to a theme that, given its resurfacing quality, may be more accurately termed *leitmotif*. But the extensiveness and elasticity of this leitmotif as a shaping principle of the narrative depend on a consistent biblical recapitulation. Even though Gregory does not repeat the quote from Ecclesiastes at the point where the relation between the preface and the *Vita* proper becomes explicit, a repetition of this scriptural verse does occur, and the story does continue to maintain and develop its direct biblical orientation in keeping with the introductory remarks on pride. The recapitulation occurs thematically, with the insertion of a New Testament text corresponding with the first citation and validating Koheleth's *vanitas vanitantium* in terms of Paul's comment on the believer's need for humility:

When we arrived in Tours, he [Senoch] left his cell and went to find us. After we were greeted and kissed, he returned. For he had, as we have said, great abstinence, [and] he cured the sick. But just as sanctity came from abstinence, so too, the vanity [that comes] from sanctity began to creep up [on him]. For he left his cell and, with high-booted boastfulness, he went to find and to visit his family in the region of Poitou, which was mentioned earlier. He returned swollen with pride, and he sought only to please himself. But after he was reproached by us and the reason was understood—that the proud are far removed from the kingdom of God—he was purged of boastfulness, and he made himself so humble that no trace of arrogance remained in him at all. He confessed, saying: "Now I know the truth of the words to which the blessed apostle attests by the eloquence of his sacred mouth: 'Let him who boasts, boast in the Lord' " (1 Cor. 1:31).[62]

With respect to Fortunatus, it was mentioned earlier how the *Vitae* bear the same relation to the Bible that the New Testament does to the Old, with the saints fulfilling biblical passages much as the Gospels portray Christ fulfilling Scripture. The *LVP* also bears such a relation to the Bible. But in this work the presence of Scripture occurs on another level as well. The story of Senoch shows Gregory using different scriptural texts in one *Vita*, a practice commonly employed throughout the *LVP*. These texts, as we saw, are all thematically related so that the *Vita*, the words of the "Preacher," and Paul's remark contribute to the first plot's overall effect or unity of action. Thus, the Bible is present in this work and in the others like it throughout the *LVP*, in the same way that the Old Testament is literally present in the New.[63] Ecclesiastes 1:2 and 1 Corinthians 1:31, for instance, operate precisely as, say, the first verse of Psalm 21 functions in Christ's cry on the cross. Biblical allusion in the *LVP* appears not only in the form of comparisons along the lines of Fortunatus saying a saint is "like" (*velut*) Abel or John the Baptist. As the account of Senoch shows, the scriptural passage is literally a part of the *Vita* and inseparable from the story's theme so that the biblical verse is no more extraneous to the hagiographic narrative than the appearance of the Psalmist's "*Deus meus quare dereliquisti me*" is to the Gospels.[64] Hence, in addition to the relation between the Bible and hagiography at the level of a fulfillment or a continuation of Scripture, there is in Gregory's hagiography the wholehearted, thematic assimilation of the sacred text, which becomes so much a part of the saint's *Vita* that without it the narrative would become disjointed, lose its coherence, and, in short, cease to function as an intelligible whole.

Regarding this relationship between narrative and scriptural text, Brunhölzl observes that the theme, or what he calls "central idea" (*zentralen Gedanken*), in the Lives of the *LVP* is often "strengthened" (*bekräftigend*) by the biblical quotes at the beginning.[65] The *Vita* that follows the preface then proceeds to exemplify this initial idea or "viewpoint" (*Gesichtspunkt*) of the holy life. The story of Senoch would seem to confirm Brunhölzl's impression. With respect to the role of the Bible, however, a position opposing Brunhölzl's view may also be maintained. Rather than saying that a *Vita* is strengthened by the biblical verse, the story of Senoch suggests that the verses are strengthened by the *Vita*. The whole first plot may be regarded as an attempt to validate the scriptural passages through the telling of Senoch's life. As is the case with all miracle stories, implicitly the subplot also constitutes a validation of Scripture because the Gospels claim that Christ conferred on the apostles and will bestow on all those who believe in him the power to cure and to cast out demons—that is, to perform miracles of the sort that hagiographers record.[66] Although the appearance of Scripture lends authority to the hagiographic text and in that sense may "strengthen" the *Vita*, the saint's Life itself is really a document that supports and affirms through contemporary narratives what Scripture already proclaimed. Furthermore, the distinction Brunhölzl makes between the "central idea" and the biblical verse cannot be supported. The representative example of Senoch's *Vita* shows that the scriptural text and the story's theme are really one and the same. The verse is the *Vita*'s premise. Hence, if the narrative exemplifies the initial idea outlined in the preface and this initial idea is expressed primarily in terms of a biblical citation, then the saint's story really functions as an affirmation of the Bible and not—or at least not only—the other way around.

Brunhölzl also detects in the accounts of the *LVP* qualities resembling "short sermons" (*Kurzpredigten*) that highlight, in a manner anticipating later medieval *exempla*, essential aspects of the Christian life.[67] If we follow this line of reasoning, an account such as the *Life of Saint Senoch* represents a moralized tale intended to illustrate how pride destroys sanctity much as, say, Chaucer's "Pardoner's Tale" tells, through a story narrated by a rather greedy preacher, how avarice leads to ruin.[68] Based on our examination of the *LVP*'s fifteenth chapter, such an observation accurately describes a prominent feature in Gregory's collection of Lives. This conclusion, however, can be supported only to the extent to which the Lives of the *LVP* do, indeed, lend themselves to treatment as straightforward narratives that illustrate a particular teaching, whether that be the danger of pride, the benefit of faith, the importance of forgiveness, or the achievement of spiritual liberation through the renouncement of upper-class privilege.[69] Yet, as we are about to see, a collection of *Vitae* literally based on and thematically shaped by biblical texts introduces a more ambiguous element into the *LVP*, which initially places the story at an indeterminate stage between the Bible and pure hagiography. This element cannot be entirely accounted for in terms of rhetorical tendencies or narrative patterns exhibited by the *Vita* alone. To put it in another way, the Lives reflect, far more profoundly than Fortunatus's hagiography does, a complex biblical mentality explicitly expressed by the hagiographic texts in a manner more akin to exegetical writing than to what we commonly think of as hagiographic narrative.

For an example of this mentality's expression, let us return to the now familiar preface of Senoch's *Vita*. Immediately, we notice an assumption made on the part of the author that is not readily explainable by the story's content. Gregory obviously takes for granted the connection between "pride" (*arrogantia*) and "emptiness" (*vanitas*). But on what basis can such a connection be made? For a story that, according to Brunhölzl's general observations, resembles a moralizing sermon, the language of the preface surprisingly does not express the relation between *arrogantia* and *vanitas* in terms of an abstract morality. Contrary to what we might expect to find in a work that is supposedly a "short sermon" and to what we do actually find in the preaching of Caesarius,[70] the preface offers no explicit indications of an ethical argument formally made to explain pride as a "deadly sin" or a moral degeneration, although the notion of pride as harmful and corrupting is still conveyed. Also missing is the fiery tone of a reproach condemning "conceit." Nor is the experience of one who feels excessively proud described psychologically as an emotional state. Instead, we find some rather concrete imagery used to express the elevated self-esteem Gregory identifies as the nature of pride. Metaphor facilitates this identification in the form of metonymy and, through the author's remarkable preservation of the scriptural text's literal meaning, an element in this preface that represents a rare strain in the development of ancient and medieval exegesis on Ecclesiastes.[71]

The metonymical element appears in the phrase *cothurnosa iactancia*, literally and, for the moment, nonsensically translated as "high-booted boastfulness."[72] Used to connote pride, the word *cothurnus* and its adjectival forms also appear elsewhere in the *LVP* and throughout Gregory's writings.[73] In the first chapter of the *Life of the Fathers*, for instance, some "gourmet monks" who prefer delicacies to the plain fare befitting an austere religious life are described as *cotornosi atque elati*. When commenting on this phrase, the modern translator remarks that the word *cotornosi* is "unusual," and he adds that its association with arrogance derives from *cothurnus*, "the high-soled buskin of the tragic actor, a symbol of grandeur and majesty, and hence pride."[74] Although the word is hardly unusual—several of the major classical authors use it, as do numerous Christian writers from Tertullian to Fortunatus— the translator accurately indicates that the object known as *cothurnus* came to signify pride.[75] However, contrary to what the translator implies by distinguishing the so-called symbol from the object itself, the symbolic content of the preface cannot be so easily disentangled from the literal meaning. As the analysis proceeds, it will become clear that the reason for resisting the distinction between symbol and object is justified on the grounds that the preface's significance derives from an identification between various concrete images and the meaning of pride, an identification with an intensity not adequately appreciated by the translator's remark.

As an accoutrement of tragic costume, the *cothurnus* significantly increased the actual height of the actor, thus creating the impressive stature of a towering figure.[76] Those who wore such footwear quite literally "looked down" on those of average stature. Such a consideration is not meant to suggest that Gregory possessed any detailed knowledge of Greek dramatic costume, but it does allow us to appreciate how closely this author's writing maintains the connection between the physical appearance of the *cothurnus* and pride. When discussing the feud between the clerics Cato and Cautinus, for instance, Gregory tells how the former rejected the see of Tours in the hope of later taking the episcopacy of Clermont-Ferrand from his rival, once a new king came to power. Gregory describes this behavior of Cato as that of one who was "raised high by the arrogance of vanity."[77] Likewise, the comparative form of the adjective *altus* appears when Gregory relates how Clotild, the ringleader of the revolt at Radegund's convent, turned against her cousin and fellow rebel, Basina, whom the former "despised" with an even "higher" degree of "arrogance" than she had for the others involved in the revolt.[78] The words *elati* and *altiore* clearly preserve the sense of height that was originally associated with the wearing of the *cothurni*. The close identification between pride and the shoe is perhaps best indicated by the possibility of plausibly interchangeable translations. Although certainly not appropriate, given the context of each passage, we note, nonetheless, that when the metonymical significance is disregarded, both phrases, if isolated from the sentences in which they appear, retain their comprehensibility and convey coherent meanings;

that is, no absurdity or even solecism arises if we say that Cato was "elevated by a *cothurnus*" (*coturno elatus*) or if Clotild is described as "looking down" (*dispiceret*) from a "higher," or perhaps "very high," "*cothurnus*" (*altiore coturno*) on her cousin Basina. Obviously, the contexts of the passages make such translations inaccurate. However, it is only a matter of context by which the meaning of the phrases in question is determined. In other words, the translation that recognizes the figure of speech (metonymy) and the one that does not are both equally valid on the linguistic level, which shows how closely allied the literal meaning is with the symbolic or meta-phorical.

The sense of height associated with the shoes worn by tragic actors takes us back to the translator's original misgivings concerning the word *cothurnus*. Similar to the description of Cato found in the *Histories*, the same perfect passive participle of the verb *effero* also appears in the first chapter of the LVP. As already noted, the "gourmet monks" are called *cotornosi atque elati*, which the translator renders into English as "men vain and proud," an expression which, however much it may convey the figural meaning, loses all sense of the strong identification between the nature of arrogance and the object that physically expresses this human flaw through evoking the apt image of an artificially heightened individual. As we shall see, this evocative literalness that can be lost, easily and understandably, in translation also characterizes Senoch's *Vita*.

In addition to the association of pride with height, Gregory in this preface fur-nishes other concrete images to evoke the characteristics of *arrogantia* and *vanitas*. As the opening remarks to this *Vita* indicate, arrogance and its destructiveness evidently correspond with elements found in the natural world. Excessive pride, for instance, is literally a "deep pit" or an "abyss" (*baratro*) into which the haughty saint can easily "fall" (*occubuit*). Even more so than in cases that involve the word *cothurnus*, the identification between the object and what it may symbolize is so close that to make a distinction between a deep pit and a more metaphorical hell or "lower world"—another meaning of *barathum*—where sinners are punished would diminish greatly the concrete quality from which the preface derives its power.[79]

Likewise, what Gregory calls *vanitas* is a "thin smoke" (*levis vanitatis fumus*) that drags saints down to a similarly abysslike bottom, or so the verb "*pessumdaret*" sug-gests. Significantly, the phrase *iactantiae coturnosae*, mentioned earlier, immediately pre-cedes the words *perflati supercilio*, the former evoking again a concrete image, this time of pride having an airlike quality inflating saints, and the latter retaining a meto-nymical vestige because *supercilium*, as its prefix suggests, can refer to a prominently raised figure, whether that be an eyebrow or a summit. Thus it happens, says Greg-ory, that some saints become *iactantiae coturnosae perflati supercilio*, which may be trans-lated, perhaps somewhat cumbersomely but at least in keeping with the previously discussed significance of *cothurnus*, as "blown up with the arrogance of high-booted boastfulness." Considering all the elements, then, what emerges in the preface is something of an anatomy of pride that consists of a cluster of clear images that may be reduced to the following: elevation (*coturnosae; supercilio*), emptiness (*vanitatis; bara-tro*), air (*perflati*), and smoke (*fumus*).

Naturally, our immediate response to these locutions is to say that what Gregory *really* means is that pride *resembles* air, an empty abyss, or smoke. But presumably, had he wanted to stress similarity rather than complete identification, the author could have easily used, as he does elsewhere when making comparisons, such words or phrases as *velut, quasi, tamquam si, ac si, similiter* (a word that appears frequently throughout his writings), or *instar* to convey the sense of an analogous relation between two things.[80] Instead, we find expressions indicating a direct relation between qualities of the natural world and the attributes associated with pride. The author obviously assumes that the one can be identified with the other on the basis that both have the same characteristics. The statement of identification is a metaphor, a formal assertion that one thing is another: Arrogance is an abyss; vanity is smoke (though the author does not express this relation through predication—that is, through a form of the verb *esse*—but by placing the elements of the metaphor together by means of the genitive case as in "the light smoke of vanity" and "the abyss of arrogance").

Earlier, the discussion on metonymy and metaphor was introduced with the assertion that Gregory's preface contains an element that cannot be accounted for solely in terms of the rhetorical patterns and tendencies the *Vita* itself exhibits. We can now identify this element by considering the implications of the opening line, " '*Vanitas vanitantium*,' *dicit eclesiastes,* '*omnia vanitas*,' " a sentence with a metaphorical content that helps to explain the references to an abyss and smoke. Again, if we treat these words as we have the rest of the preface, we come face to face with an expression whose literal meaning is intensely identified with a—or we might even say the—human condition. A literal rendition of the words is the first step to bring out the metaphorical significance of the sentence. Rather than "vanity of vanities," as English translations of Ecclesiastes have it, we shall translate the sentence as " 'Emptiness of emptinesses,' says the Preacher, 'all is emptiness.' " Immediately, we notice how such a translation fits the general tone of the preface: There is the emptiness associated with an abyss or a deep pit (*baratro*), as well as with the image of figures puffed up (*perflati*) by the insubstantial air of a literally lofty "arrogance" (*supercilio*). But there is an even more remarkable correspondence between Gregory's writing and the quotation from Ecclesiastes. In discussing the meaning of this biblical text, one literary critic notes the "metaphorical kernel" of the Hebrew word "*hebel*."[81] This word, translated in the Vulgate as *vanitas*, literally denotes vapor, breath, mist, or fog, and by extension it comes to signify something that quickly passes away, something transient and lacking substance, something that can easily become nothing—in other words, emptiness, *vanitas*. Gregory thus preserves this original "metaphorical kernel" of the Hebrew text when he refers to *vanitas* as being a "light" or perhaps "thin smoke" in the phrase *levis vanitatis fumus*, the words *levis* and *fumus* obviously corresponding with the vaporous mist or fog of *hebel*.

At this point, we see how the preface, in addition to deriving its rich metaphorical content from the biblical verse, comes close to exegesis. Gregory's description of *vanitas* as a "light smoke" corresponds with a rather uncommon treatment of this biblical text in patristic commentaries. Generally speaking, writers before, during, and after Gregory's time concentrate on the "spiritual meaning" of Ecclesiastes.[82] Jerome, too, goes into lengthy allegorical interpretations of the work, which he claims he read with the woman Blesilla in the hope that the study of this biblical text would lead his female companion to renounce the prospect of remarriage and to embrace instead a celibate way of life.[83] But Jerome's training and obvious delight in philology lead him to consider first the literal meaning of the text before developing more elaborate interpretations. As he proceeds to summarize the opening lines of Ecclesiastes, he describes *vanitas* as a "vapor of smoke," a "thin mist" that quickly vanishes, words that Gregory's preface clearly echoes:

> Seeing the elements and the manifold diversity of things, I am amazed at the vastness of creation. But realizing that all things are passing away and that the world, with its limited time, is growing old and that God is the only thing that always is and always will be, I am compelled to say not once, but twice, "Vanity of vanities, all is vanity." In Hebrew, for *vanitas vanitatum, abal abalim* has been written, which, with the exception of the Septuagint translators, all have rendered similarly as Aτμοζ ατμιδων or ατμων, *which we can call a vapor of smoke or a thin mist that quickly vanishes* (emphasis added).[84]

In the context of Senoch's *Vita*, we notice that Jerome's commentary on the line "*vanitas vanitatum*" omits any reference to pride. Instead, we find a discussion that may be called, for lack of a better term, "existential." At an early stage in the treatment of the text, Jerome focuses his remarks on "man" (*homo*) and on the significance the biblical passage has as a statement epitomizing the condition of human existence. In a manner typical of patristic exegesis, he introduces another biblical passage to illuminate the one under examination.[85] He cites Psalm 36:6 as an explanation of Ecclesiastes 1:2: "Such also has been written in the Psalms: 'but utter emptiness is all human life.'"[86] The scriptural citations are then interpreted as a statement expressing not only the insignificance of human life but also the stark meaning of death: "If all human life is emptiness, death, therefore, is the emptiness of emptinesses."[87] The remarks leading into the discussion on the literal meaning of *vanitas* project the inevitability of death and the writer's understanding of mortality onto the created world so that the wonders of nature—the heavens, the earth, the sea—that in Genesis were proclaimed "good" (*bona*) are now seen as declining in the process of a gradual demise, aptly summed up by the terms *hebel*, Aτμοζ and *vanitas*.[88] According to the commentator, the only thing that will last is God: "*solumque Deum id semper esse, quod fuerit.*"

Jerome's comments and Gregory's preface indicate that the biblical text with which we are dealing cannot be reduced to a mere condemnation of pride. If we base our judgment on the representative *Vita* of Senoch, therefore, the interpretation of the LVP as a collection of moralized tales is not adequate. As the preceding remarks have attempted to show, the concrete imagery of the biblically based preface gives no hint of an abstract mentality at work to condemn pride. In fact, with the possible exception of the reference to the *temptator*, it is difficult to pinpoint specifically where in the preface any evidence can be found of a conceptualized morality that, as a matter of principle, deems pride as "bad" or "evil." All the author really provides to describe this human flaw are images drawn mostly from the natural world. By these images, pride is defined. We are left with the conclusion that Gregory regards certain appearances in nature as expressions of the human weakness that jeopardizes Senoch's holiness. To view these images as "symbolic" of pride—to make, in other words, qualifications differentiating metaphor from reality—would only introduce distinctions that the rhetorical power of the preface has actually obliterated.

However, the role of the devil in the preface appears as a challenge to an interpretation highlighting the author's blurring of the distinction between the characteristics of pride and the metaphors used to express this human flaw. After all, the
"tempter" appears as an opposing force, an agent of destruction, but not as a metaphor. Moreover, contrary to what has been said so far, the presence of a demonic
influence in Gregory's presentation of pride implies, or so it may be argued, a view
of morality, an understanding of good and evil, that derives more from the developments of Christian theology than from the author's penetrating connections between natural phenomena and the nature of pride.

To begin to address this issue, we should note that the demonic influence itself
is at least consistent with the rest of the imagery in the preface and in the other
episodes that involve pride mentioned earlier. In the same sentence containing the
phrase *iactantiae coturnosae* appears the word *elati*: Arrogant saints are said to have been
"raised high by the cunning of the tempter" (*elati aestu temptatoris*). Thus, the word
elati concretely conveys the sense of elevation that is in keeping with the image
subsequently expressed through metonymy.

But even though the imagery used to describe demonic influence corresponds
with the other elements of the preface, the appearance itself of the devil is yet to
be accounted for in terms consistent with the rest of the *Life*'s opening. How far, in
other words, is the "metaphorical kernel" of the preface consistent with the emphasis Gregory gives to a diabolical foe who is attempting to ruin holy lives? On
this point, other literary depictions of the devil outside Senoch's *Vita* are well worth
considering because there is a remarkable correspondence between the preface's
reference to the "smoke of *vanitas*" and the manner in which paradigmatic hagiographic texts portray demons.

Significantly, in the Lives of Antony and Martin, the devil is described as smoke
and, given the root of the verb *evanescere*, emptiness. In his long discourse on the
nature of demons, Antony relates the story of the enemy's coming to him in the
guise of a monk who is carrying bread and urging the saint to break his fast. When
Antony attempts to ward him off with prayer, the demon "vanishes through the
window like smoke."[89] Similarly, when the devil comes to Martin's cell dressed in
purple, wearing the diadem, and claiming that he is Christ, the saint refuses to
acknowledge him as "Lord Jesus," on the grounds that the savior would not dress
in such a manner but would come wearing the garments and bearing the wounds
of his crucifixion. After Martin says this, the devil "immediately vanished like
smoke."[90]

In both these accounts, the devil is portrayed in terms that closely correspond to
the images found in Gregory's preface. The demons described really have the characteristics associated with *hebel*. They vanish like smoke, and the verb used to describe
their disappearance is derived from the word *vanus*, from which also comes *vanitas*.
This tradition also influenced Gregory, for in another story of an arrogant saint, the
word *evanescuit* appears again in a context also associated with the "tempter."[91]

These examples suggest that the depiction of the devil in paradigmatic hagiographic texts has the same kind of metaphorical significance as the imagery Gregory
uses in the context of pride. Moreover, this portrait of a diabolical foe vanishing

like smoke once again has a biblical forerunner: The Psalms proclaim that the wicked and the enemies of the Lord will be "consumed," disappearing like fumus.[92]

The *Life of Saint Senoch* is only one example of how deeply and extensively scriptural texts can penetrate the narratives, especially the prefaces of the LVP. Let us then take this representative account as an indication of how fundamental the role of Scripture is to this collection of Lives and turn now to examining what may be, arguably, the most significant feature to arise out of a body of hagiographic texts teeming with biblical citations and scriptural resonances.

The Typological Orientation

The prominence Gregory gives to citations, figures, and events of the Bible naturally entails the typological application of Scripture.[93] To relate saints or their deeds to biblical characters or events obviously enhances the profile of a holy person and legitimizes hagiography as a contemporary and often local continuation of the Bible. We have already seen this technique at work in the writing of Fortunatus when he refers to Paternus as "another Moses." But the abundance of biblical texts directly inserted into the Lives of the LVP, the great dexterity Gregory shows in transposing scriptural themes, and the implicit influence both Testaments have on all aspects of Gregory's writing create conditions far more conducive to typological application than are normally found in the writings of an author such as Fortunatus, who uses the Bible much more sparingly. Consequently, the issue of typology in the LVP should be addressed more thoroughly and, as this collection of Lives requires, with a fuller understanding of the typological process than was called for in the examination of Fortunatus's hagiography.

However, the subject of typology is so complex that even to offer a definition of the word would be misleading and could not encompass the different contexts— hermeneutical and historical—in which typology plays a role.[94] Gregory's Lives themselves hardly offer a more simplified understanding of the concept because they, too, seem to operate on different typological levels. In spite of the difficulties of defining the term, there are also common elements in the different typological approaches to Scripture that marked the developments of biblical exegesis and also shaped the Christian understanding of history as part of a salvific plan whose meaning could quite literally be read in the Bible and, as part of the continuing documentation of that plan, in hagiographic literature.

We should start by acknowledging that typological treatment of biblical texts is not peculiar to Christianity.[95] Throughout the Hebrew Bible, people, places, and events become "types"; that is, they correspond in some essential way with later people, places, and events recorded within the Old Testament itself.[96] For example, prior to crossing the Jordan, God tells Joshua: "I am with you as I was with Moses."[97] As in Exodus, in Joshua 3:13, the waters are divided and stand upright to let Joshua and the Israelites pass.[98] Near the end of the next chapter, the typological correspondence is again reiterated: "through the dry river-bed Israel crossed that Jordan, with the Lord our God drying up its waters in your sight until you crossed, just as he had done before at the Red Sea, which he dried up until we crossed."[99]

Besides the appearance of typology within the Bible itself, Jewish exegesis, ancient and modern, offers typological interpretations of biblical passages.[100]

Christianity's debt to Jewish typological interpretations has been acknowledged by biblical scholars. Outside the realm of biblical hermeneutics, typology also appears as a theory of history.[101] Hegelian philosophy, Marxism, and liberation theology still maintain approaches to the study of history as an unfolding process progressing toward a fulfillment in a culminating event, whether that be the Second Coming or the dictatorship of the proletariat.[102] Because we are concerned with early medieval hagiographic texts in the West, the typological perspective outlined in the discussion on Gregory's *LVP* will obviously have a christological basis, both in the hermeneutical elements of the *LVP*'s typology and in the vision of history that this collection of Lives projects.

With respect to the hagiographic origins of a Christian typological presentation of a holy person, the obvious model is the Gospels' stylization of Christ as an Old Testament prophet who both commemorates and fulfills the earlier teachings. Insofar as the New Testament itself reads as an explicit fulfillment of the Old, it fosters typological interpretation. The passages in which Old Testament texts are transposed in the New and presented as fulfillments are numerous.[103] The example most often cited by biblical scholars in which the actual word *typos* appears in an explicit interpretive context that treats a figure of the New Testament in relation to another of the Old is worth quoting. In Romans 5:14, Paul speaks of Adam as a "type" (*forma*) of Christ, a statement generally thought to mean that the Incarnation marks a new creation redeemed by a second or new Adam, who undoes the sin of the first Adam: "But death reigned from Adam to Moses, even in those who had not sinned in the manner of the transgression of Adam, who is the figure of the one to come."[104]

The example from Romans and others like it show that New Testament authors handle the Old Testament in a manner that is generally considered typological.[105] Scripture itself, therefore, fosters this method of exegesis, which patristic authors in their turn adopted as an interpretive tool. Under their teaching, the Bible becomes a series of connections that link the Old Testament with the New on the basis of foreshadowing or prophecy and fulfillment. The whole of Scripture is read as a unified text.[106] The idea is most succinctly expressed in Augustine's well-known dictum: "In the Old Testament the New Testament is concealed; in the New Testament the Old Testament is revealed."[107]

We note also that the typological interpretation of the Bible involves more than simply treating Old Testament passages as fulfilled by the Gospels' account of Christ's life. In its context, Paul's statement concerning Adam as a "figure of one to come" implies—and was certainly understood by patristic commentators as showing—opposition between the "old Adam," who is described in Genesis as losing paradise, and the "new Adam," who comes to restore what was lost.[108] The typological approach to Scripture by Christian commentators thus entails an interpretive movement from semblance to contrast. Like the case of Joshua, the first aspect of this movement establishes a correspondence between two people, places, or events. There must be some link between the two subjects for the typology to work as is indicated, for instance, by the insistence on the part of Christian exegetes to find so many affinities between Christ and Adam.[109] But unlike the story of Joshua, the second aspect of this interpretive movement, the highlighting of contrast, assumes a prominent role in the Christian understanding of Scripture. We should note now, because the idea will surface again in Gregory's hagiography, that an essential feature in a typological presentation is the dialectical tension through which an original type acquires new meaning in the context of Christian revelation. The new type (i.e., Christ) is thought of as not only sharing common attributes with the old type (i.e., Adam) but also surpassing the earlier version, as being, at least according to the Christian perspective, a superior form filling out what the Old Testament type lacked. The old and new types thus maintain a relation based on affinity and opposition commonly expressed by the terms *type* and *antitype*.

Without any doubt, certain typological perspectives of the Christian biblical interpretation resurface in the context of hagiographic literature. The most influential of these are paradisiacal typology and the typological view of progress as the unfolding of God's plan in history. For our immediate purpose, we need only say now that the former is easily detected in early hagiographic texts, including the LVP, by a literary stylization of saints, usually hermits, living in an earthly paradise. This paradisiacal typology Christianity derived from the Old Testament's eschatological prophecies, which speak of the coming of a new creation, not a return to a golden age as in Greek conceptions of history, but the ushering in of a transformed human condition that represents the opposite (antitype) of the previous state of suffering and death (type).[110] Humanity is restored to paradise, described as a place where vegetation always thrives, nature provides all necessary sustenance, and man again enjoys dominion over the beasts. The natural setting and imagery of paradise found in Ezekiel, for example, will appear again in the desert literature and also in certain passages of the LVP that describe scenes of a "paradise regained" by the living of a holy life.[111]

With respect to a typological view of history, such a perspective, though admittedly not always explicitly articulated by writers of *Vitae*, is really what the very existence of hagiographic literature presupposes because the religious and social validity of saints' Lives derives from the belief that God continues to intervene and work in history through divinely appointed, predestined individuals whose wholehearted, even militant commitment to discovering and fulfilling the salvific plan is recorded for the benefit of the believing community.[112] Fortunately, in the case of the LVP, Gregory, as we shall discover, explicitly indicates that he writes within the framework of a salvation history, the developments of which he generally outlines to legitimize the contemporary expressions of the sanctity he records.

This conception of history as the unfolding of God's plan, often referred to as *Heilsgeschichte*, arises out of a typological interpretation of the Bible.[113] Unlike much of modern literary and historical criticism of Scripture, the traditional typological understanding of the Bible assumes a unity between the Old and New Testament. For patristic commentators, as well as for Gregory, the Hebrew Bible both commemorates and foretells the history of God's actions in the world. The record of the past contained in the Old Testament narrates, according to Christian typological exegesis, the stages of salvation's history and also points to its culminating fulfillment in the Incarnation, an event that gives coherence to what would otherwise have been an inexplicable course of human development. The typological understanding of history thus follows the Christian interpretation of the Bible: Just as the New Testament is thought to reveal the full meaning of what would otherwise have been an obscure collection of stories and prophecies, so, too, the Incarnation, as a historical event, makes the past intelligible in terms of a process leading to a fulfillment that explains all that previously occurred.[114]

From this brief overview, we may highlight some of the key elements in the Christian typological approach to Scripture that will relate to Gregory's application of biblical texts in the LVP. First is the correspondence between the original and the later type, as when Fortunatus, for instance, describes Paternus's feat of drawing water from a rock as the biblical type of the miracle performed by Moses.[115] The second pertinent feature of typology is the opposition between the old type and the new one, the latter excelling the former by perfecting and adding something to the original type, as when Christ is regarded as a new Adam, the antitype who restores what the first type lost through sin. This opposition is traditionally thought to lie behind Paul's actual use of typos/forma and also appears more explicitly in 1 Corinthians 15:22: "et sicut in Adam omnes moriuntur ita et in Christo omnes vivificabuntur." The third feature is the interpretation of the Jewish and Christian biblical books as constituting a unified text that records the gradual fulfillment throughout time of a divine plan revealed fully in the New Testament, confirmed by hagiographic literature's continuing documentation of postbiblical salvation history, but previously foreshadowed by the biblical figures, places, and events of the Old Testament.

This overview by no means exhausts the possible uses of typology as an interpretive tool or as a theory of history but simply points to the range of typological elements offered by the LVP.[116] Obviously, not all these features of typology are always present when we refer to a hagiographer as describing a saint or an event typologically. The example of Paternus, for instance, definitely shows the similarity with the biblical person, but the opposition, the antitype, is lacking. What we find, instead, is a use of typology to indicate congruence between a great biblical event of the past and its reenactment in the life of a contemporary saint. There is no indication that Paternus is the antitype of Moses. Hagiographers can usually indicate well enough the continuation of a type, but the subsequent antitype may not always be appropriate, especially in instances of imitatio Christi. Thus, the example of Marcellus turning water into wine is typologically limited. Fortunatus portrays the event as a reenactment of Christ's changing water into wine. While he refers to the saint's accomplishments as "nova miracula" that repeat in Gaul what happened in Galilee, he is careful not to present Marcellus as exceeding the earlier type, which would mean that the contemporary recapitulation of the miracle surpasses the original achievement of Jesus.[117] In hagiographic literature, the explicit opposition characteristic of Christian typological exegesis cannot always be present, and the same may be said of the other features associated with typological interpretation. In short, given the different aims of scriptural commentary and hagiography, we cannot always expect the hagiographer's application of biblical typology to maintain all these features of typological interpretation. However, as far as the present discussion is concerned, the fact that hagiographic literature often lacks some elements characteristic of typological treatment will not in itself be taken as a sufficient reason for not applying the term.[118]

Fortunately, we do find in the LVP a typological application carried to its full extent in the manner of patristic exegesis. The passage constitutes a complete typological sequence that explicitly shows the resemblance between the biblical type and the contemporary saint, followed by the characteristic contrast between type and antitype. In keeping with the earliest patristic motives for typological exegesis, the passage also assumes the superiority of Christianity over Judaism, the former having fulfilled and perfected what the Old Testament type lacked.[119]

Certainly, the name of the saint portrayed in the third chapter of the LVP facilitates this typological application. Abraham the Christian saint is likened to Abraham the Hebrew patriarch described in Genesis. The congruity between the Old Testament and Christian type first finds expression along general lines in the preface, which emphasizes the role of faith in the lives of saints who are able to obtain from God whatever they need simply by asking. Initially, there is no contrast between the two holy men. The first two biblical passages quoted, although taken from the New Testament, harmonize completely with the Old Testament story that highlights Abraham's steadfast trust in God, from whom, according to Matthew 21:22 and Mark 11:24, all who believe receive what they request.[120]

After these scriptural citations, Gregory gradually begins to shape the biographical details of the saint into a more specific and extensive typological context. Imitating the Old Testament account of Abraham, who at God's bidding left Ur to go to the land of Canaan, some Christian saints also leave their native soil and wander in foreign places for the sake of leading a religious life to which they believe God has called them. Saint Abraham led such a life. Born on the banks of the Euphrates, he left his home to visit the Egyptian monks and eventually, after having escaped from an unjust imprisonment, made his way to the Auvergne, where he established a monastery. As a wanderer who always kept his trust in God, the saint is, "by the greatness of his faith," comparable to "that old Abraham" to whom God had said, "egredere de terra tua . . . in terram quam monstrabo tibi" (Gen. 12:1). In name, exemplary faith, and traveling to foreign lands, the saint follows the Old Testament patriarch who is the biblical type of the Christian holy man Gregory describes.

What follows this scriptural quote that establishes similarities between the two holy men is a pure exegetical addition that carries the typological application to its fullest Christian extent in the manner of patristic commentary. Gregory introduces another text drawn from the New Testament, but, unlike the previous ones, he now inserts a line from Ephesians (4:24) to show contrast between the Abraham of Genesis and the one who lived in the light of Christian revelation. The saint Gregory describes not only left his country, as the "old Abraham" did, but also became a "new" Abraham as a consequence of the Christian teaching that the original type lacked.[121] Like the second Adam, this "new man" Gregory clearly regards as an improvement over the old one, and he thereby creates the characteristic tension between type and antitype: "Because of the greatness of his faith, he is rightly compared to that old Abraham, to whom God had once said: 'Leave your country and your kin and go into a land that I will have shown you' (Gen. 12:1). Yet [our] Abraham left not only his own country but also that way of life led by the old man, and he 'put on the new man, who was formed according to God in justice, sanctity, and truth' (Eph. 4:24)."[122]

This text is an instance in which hagiography serves the Christian interpretive approach to the Bible. Here, we cannot easily distinguish hagiography from a christological interpretation of the Old Testament that the typological treatment fosters by reading the whole of Scripture as a unified text. In fact, the most striking feature of this preface is not its hagiographic content but how closely it follows the traditional methodology of typological exegesis. The entire rhetorical structure adheres to this approach. The author initially establishes a harmony between texts of the New Testament and the story of Abraham's receiving all that is wanted, but the resemblance is followed by contrast. The citation from Ephesians highlights the difference between the old and new types. The arrangement of the presentation of the two Abrahams thus constitutes a full typological sequence, which we now see is a hermeneutical approach characterized by a movement from resemblance to contrast, from type to antitype.

Fortunatus does not carry out his typological applications to this extent, even though he assumes, as much as Gregory does, that Christianity is superior to Judaism. Instead, to validate Christianity as the preeminent religion, he portrays saints who are in conflict with Jews and who insist that they convert. But with Abraham's *Vita*, the polemic between Jew and Christian is really carried out in the realm of hermeneutics, with Gregory's juxtaposition of biblical texts used to show the saint—and hence Christianity—as the perfected type who grows out of and surpasses the old Abraham of Judaism.[123] The preface to Abraham's *Vita* is really the "mouthpiece" of Christian theology, and as such it corresponds not only rhetorically but also doctrinally with the earlier typological interpretations of the church fathers.[124]

Such a use of typology in the *LVP* suggests that the author regards sanctity as progressing by improving what preceded in time. From the Christian perspective, the emergence of the antitype affirms that the author's era continues to move toward an ever greater fulfillment of the divine plan. A new Abraham or "new hermit,"[125] like the new Adam, embodies the latest development in a history that gradually leads to the culmination of all history at the end of time. A Christian typological approach to the Bible fosters this idea of progress by treating the Old Testament from the perspective of the New, the latter marking a development so great that the validity of the first narrative derives solely from the fact that it anticipates the second and hence reveals the stages of a salvation history working in time.[126] Christianity holds that this history was fulfilled in Christ. However, until the apocalypse, the Incarnation as a historical event does not mark the end of redemptive progress. The Christian typological view of history still regards events, people, and places as signs of God's continuing action in the course of human affairs. So neither salvation history nor its narrative stops with the atoning death and resurrection. Hagiography adds to the previous documentation of redemption by continuing the Bible's account of humanity's divine progress in history.[127] The successors of the patriarchs and the apostles are the saints through whom God continues to act in the movement toward the final fulfillment of the salvific plan. Saints are indications of a further development of God's purpose. As suggested by the previous discussion of Fortunatus's utilization of Scripture, the very existence of hagiographic literature assumes that the progress of redemption does not end with the coming of Christ. Unlike the hagiography of Fortunatus, who does not elaborately articulate the implications of such an assumption, however, Gregory thematically arranges and carefully traces the workings of this salvation history to place his biographical subjects in the context of its most recent development.

The author of the LVP provides a rough sketch of where his saints fit in the various stages of salvation from biblical times to his own day. This outline of salvation history appears in the threefold pattern of the prefaces, according to which scheme the opening discourse is arranged. In nearly all the prefaces, the first phase in the development of a *Vita*'s theme is established by citations from Scripture. The biblical quotation functions as an axiom of salvation history. It not only establishes the mode of religious expression elaborated later in a Life but also legitimizes sanctity by putting it into the context of a development arising out of the biblical examples. After the biblical verses but before actually introducing the subject of the biography, Gregory usually alludes to previous holy individuals whose lives conform to the biblical passage initially cited. Then, sometimes in the last line of the preface, Gregory finally introduces the saint, who continues, in the author's own time, what the Bible proclaims and what the holy forerunners achieved by their way of life. The saint is thus put in the context of the previous developments in God's salvific plan, which the scriptures and earlier hagiographic literature record. The prefaces indicate that the author is really setting out to write an update on salvation history. As the Bible and earlier stories of saints once did, the *Vitae* are intended to record the action of God working in time through the lives of contemporary holy people, the "present signs" of a continuing redemption.[128]

Most of the prefaces conform to this threefold pattern of scriptural citation, a reference to past examples of holiness, and the introduction of the saint. When the preface contains citations from both Testaments, the verses from the Old usually precede those from the New. As we can see, each component of the pattern corresponds with a stage in salvation history. However, not all the prefaces outline the stages as distinctly as the one to the *Life of Ursus and Leobatius*. Here, Gregory develops the theme of light, which he presents as the sign, perhaps the symbolic type, of God's activity throughout time.[129] The pattern of this preface corresponds in every respect to the Christian understanding of historical progress. To illustrate the stages of redemption he starts first with a citation from the Old Testament, then proceeds to quote extensively from the New, and finally places the theme of these passages in the context of holy individuals who have carried on the teaching up to Gregory's time. The preface becomes an impressive outline of the plan of salvation from its inception up to its continuing fulfillment in contemporary saints. Rarely does a hagiographer explicitly show such an extensive view of the redemptive plan into which the subjects of the narrative are carefully placed, with their specific role in fulfilling God's purpose clearly defined. He begins with Genesis and ends by finally naming the holy men whose story he is about to tell:

> When the Legislator and Prophet began to speak of the beginning of all things . . . he added: "And God made two great lights and stars. He placed them in the firmament of heaven, so that they might rule over day and night and shine in the firmament of heaven" (Gen. 1:16–18). So now, too . . . He gave two great lights, namely, Christ and His church, which shine in the darkness of ignorance and illuminate our humble understanding, as John the Evangelist says about the Lord Himself: "This man is the light

of the world" (1:9). . . . He also put into this world stars, that is, the patriarchs, prophets and apostles. . . . Therefore, from the teaching of these ones up to our own time,
there have been men who were, like the stars in this world, not only shining by the
light of their merits but also glittering with the greatness of their doctrines, who have
lit the whole universe with the rays of their preaching, going to teach in every place,
founding monasteries for the worship of God. . . . So the story told by trustworthy
brothers concerning abbots Ursus and Leobatius shows.[130]

THE TYPOLOGY OF LIBERATION

Among the various outlines of salvific progress presented in the LVP, perhaps the
most striking and dramatic one entails an episode of class conflict, in which the
revolutionary dimension of typological application is apparent.[131] An instance of
freedom from an oppressive social structure becomes, when presented typologically,
a foreshadowing of an even greater stage of liberation to occur in the future. This
typological presentation of social transformation in the LVP adds a depth to the
meaning of liberation that the miraculous prison freeings of Fortunatus's hagiography lack. The fact that, for Gregory, God acts directly in history means that social
change can be legitimately explained as an instance of the divine justice proclaimed
by Scripture. Accordingly, God intervenes to raise the poor man from his low status
and to free those oppressed by the dominating classes. The experience of liberation
is itself a type, an adumbration of the liberation experienced by those freed from
the world and exalted in paradise, the heavenly antitype of a transformed social
status. Likewise, the divine punishment received by the oppressors on earth is a type
of the eternal punishment awaiting them after death.[132]

This outline is the typological framework of Portianus's Vita. In addition to seeing
freedom from slavery as an indication of an even greater liberation to come in the
future, the author musters an impressive collection of biblical texts from both testaments to justify social change. Like the preface to the Life of Ursus and Leobatius, the
opening remarks to Portianus's Life also trace a particular development in the course
of redemption's progress. Here, the redemptive purpose is shown working toward
fulfilling the salvation history of the poor, the progress of which the quoted lines
from the Old and New Testament record. The citations and Gregory's own remarks
highlight the possibility that the conventional social roles may be overturned, if not
in this lifetime, then certainly in the one to come. In the next life the lowly, as the
heirs of God, will also carry out the fulfillment of the salvific plan the moment they
enter the paradise from which the privileged will be justly barred:

> How much Almighty God grants to those dedicated to His name, and how much
> he rewards, with the riches of His benevolence, these same ones for their faithful
> service! For truly He promises that He is going to give them great things in heaven.
> Yet often He shows in this world what they are going to receive. For he causes slaves
> to become free and the free to become glorious, just as the Psalmist said: "He raises
> the needy from the dirt and lifts the poor man out of the dung, that he may place him
> with the princes of His people" (Ps. 113:7–8). About this, Anna, the wife of Elkanah,
> also spoke: "Those who were once full have hired themselves out for bread, and those
> who were hungry [now] have their fill" (1 Sam. 2:5). On this, the mother of our

Redeemer, the Virgin Mary herself, said: "He cast down the mighty from their seat and exalted the lowly" (Luke 1:52). In this way, the Lord Himself spoke in the Gospel: "The first [will be] last and the last [will be] first" (Matt. 20:16). Thus may divine mercy, with its love, [be] in the hearts of the poor to establish the small as great and make the lowliest the coheirs with the Only Begotten. For He has taken charge of this world's poverty in heaven, where worldly rule has not been able to ascend, so that the peasant may go to that place where the one clad in purple did not deserve to go.[133]

Following the usual pattern of the prefaces, Gregory then indicates that this particular development of the divine plan is evidently still in progress. Immediately after the last sentence of this passage, he at last introduces the saint who experiences salvation in both its typical form on earth and in its antitypical fulfillment in heaven: "Such is the case now with the blessed abbot Portianus, whom [the Lord] not only saved from the burden of worldly servitude, but also raised by great deeds of power and laid to eternal rest, after [he passed from] the world and the afflictions of this age. He placed him among the choirs of angels from which the earthly lord has been excluded."[134]

The narrative following these prefacing remarks describes the dramatic events leading to the saint's change in social status. After repeated attempts to flee from his master by running to a monastery, the holy slave is again handed over to his pursuing owner by the abbot, who insists that Portianus be pardoned. After the master, who insults the abbot by accusing him of inciting the slave to run, reluctantly agrees, he is blinded the moment he attempts to take his slave home. Part of the cure for this blindness entails the slave's manumission and hence eligibility to enter monastic life.[135] In addition, the abbot pleads with the newly freed saint to relieve the painful blindness of the now repentant owner. Portianus places his hands over his former master, makes the sign of the cross, and heals him.[136]

The holy and the wicked receive on earth a sampling of their respective rewards and punishments to come. As discussed previously, Fortunatus also gives accounts of liberation. The difference between the two is that in the *Life of Portianus* Gregory suggests how such an incident ought to be interpreted.[137] In the preface, he articulates a theology of liberation rooted in Scripture and developed typologically so that the miraculous intervention of God on behalf of a particular contemporary saint imparts a meaning beyond the event itself. In short, to be freed from servitude typifies a greater liberation to come.

THE TYPOLOGY OF PARADISE

Because earlier hagiographic literature on the desert fathers also portrays saints who fashion their own Eden out of the wilderness in contrast to the corruption of the city, it may be argued Gregory's depiction of hermits marks no new development. With respect to the actual representation of eremitical sanctity in the *LVP*, such a view is accurate. But the especially remarkable aspect of Gregory's Lives is that he often provides in the prefaces a rationale for the sanctity he sets out to portray. As we have already noticed, the introductions give Gregory the chance to put a particular expression of holiness into a biblical and salvation-historical context before the narrative assumes a purely hagiographic form. Another prominent example is in the preface to the twelfth *Vita* of the *LVP*. When introducing the story of Aemilianus and Brachio, Gregory offers his reflections on the created world and, in so doing, gradually constructs a typology of paradise far more elaborate than the conventional hagiographic stories that begin with a flight to the desert.

The dialectical movement progressing through resemblance to opposition is what appears most strikingly in the twelfth chapter of the *LVP*. The complexity of the progression of thought comes from Gregory's deep appreciation of nature, an appreciation that reveals to him a figure of paradise reflected in an alluring Mediterranean world of bright sunlight, shade, and lush vegetation.[138] But, as previously indicated, a typological mode of thought always moves forward to the future, where a better place surpasses the present one. Despite its attractiveness, the author cannot be fully satisfied with the natural setting in which he lives. The beauty of nature will not last forever, and with that realization the negation phase of the dialectic enters his discussion. The contrast between earth and paradise then becomes apparent. Once again, the opposition between the two is not diametrical but grows out of the lack of perfection the author detects in nature. The beauty of the vines offering shade from the intense sun and laden with grapes soon to yield wine will also perish in due time; the very scenery that initially suggests paradise becomes an indication of death's inevitability. The passage clearly shows an author profoundly moved by the sensual beauty of a garden setting. But in typological terms, the pleasures provided by such a lovely place can only point to something greater. By the end of the preface, Gregory's discussion has moved from acknowledging the delights of creation to articulating the realization that the comforts furnished by this world will easily and quickly vanish. Faced with the inevitability of such a pleasant spot passing away, he posits, on the basis of the beauty surrounding him, the existence of a world where the vine leaves never wither and the grapes produce a "new wine" drunk at the paradisiacal banquet of eternal life:

> The love of God raises man from earthly things, it beckons him to heaven, places him in paradise, where the blessed, with the drink of the new wine taken from that life-giving vine, are banqueting in the kingdom of God. It was necessary, therefore, that men desire to drink the mystery of this wine, so that they might be able to come to that most delightful spot of such a pleasant dwelling. Those vines that we now see spread out by their branches, the shoots sprouting, tendrils entwining, with the grapes hanging down, delight us with their lovely view, not only because they produce an abundance of fruit but also because they protect us with their shade from the heat of the fiery sun. But we know that, after the fruit is picked at the appointed time, these vines become nearly shrivelled up, with their leaves falling off. How much more ought we to desire those things that never come to an end, that do not wither from any heat of temptation, where, after hope has been lost, the very thing that was hoped for is attained and enjoyed.[139]

This view of paradise, which derives from Gregory's reflection on the natural beauty of the Mediterranean world, reveals the author's deep attachment to his environment. But to see so pleasant a setting as a foreshadowing of what will come also shows the powerful pervasiveness of a typological worldview. With such a perspective, the present, regardless of how wonderful, at best suggests something better and at worst reminds us of life's susceptibility to death. Significantly, Gregory never mentions the likelihood that another season will come again bringing wine and shade with it. He does not acknowledge the reliability of the full natural cycle.[140] This preface to the twelfth chapter also recalls the world of *hebel*, where nothing is certain and all things seem tinged with mortality. That the vines will sprout again is not definite. What is certain for Gregory is that the world will some day perish, and it is better to reject earthly corruptibility and strive to attain that paradise without end.[141]

Another aspect of this dialectic does not appear until the preface is put into the context of the narrative that follows, for in the opening remarks lie hints of what the *Vita* will later describe. If we read the preface carefully, we notice that, in spite of Gregory's awareness of the inevitable passing of earthly beauty, the attainment of paradise on earth still remains a possibility for those who love God. Gregory does not qualify this remark with "after death" but unequivocally states that "*dilectio Dei . . .* places man in paradise" (*hominem . . . paradyso locat*). Again, we are back to the biblical notion that paradise can be realized in the present by living a holy life.[142] Important, too, is the temporal and geographical context of Aemilianus's sanctity. Gregory is about to describe a holy man who withdrew like the desert saints but did so "in our own recent times."[143] Immediately following the preface, we learn that the saint went into a remote part of the Auvergne, the region of the author's ancestral origins. Thus, even as he laments the inevitable passing of the world, Gregory still hints at the possibility of attaining paradise here and now; he still acknowledges the immediacy, the "*hodie*," of everlasting life. To put it in another way, consistent with the typological significance of the preface and the proceeding narrative, the hermit Aemilianus, in Gaul and during Gregory's own time, entered paradise.

That this is the case Gregory leaves no doubt, but at this point, he provides no explicit elaboration on the thoughts outlined in the preface. Once the narrative begins, the author's reflections cease. Instead, there comes the simple description of a transformed human condition. In light of the prefacing comments, this description cannot be understood in any way other than in terms of an antitype. Instead of the withering vine, we find the saint cultivating land that provides him with all he ever needs. His garden blooms with the help of rainwater, and the vegetables are satisfying without any seasoning. The saint needs no other men for companionship; removed from human contact, he lives alone with his God. He is entirely self-sufficient. But the most obvious indication that the saint lives in the realm of paradise occurs when we see him as the companion of the birds and the beasts who gather around him. This pure paradisiacal imagery is completely in keeping with the biblical descriptions of the New Jerusalem or the literature of the desert fathers,[144] the only difference being that this paradise was created by a holy man living in Gregory's own time in an area of the world where the author himself grew up:

> Aemilianus left his family and his property and went to find solitude in the desert, in the most remote places of the forest of Pionsat in the Auvergne. Clearing the trees he made a small field, which he cultivated with a hoe and which furnished for him all the necessities of life. He also had a small garden that he watered with rainwater and from which he gathered vegetables, which he ate without any oil. He had no other consolations except the help of God, for there were no other inhabitants there except

the beasts and the birds, who gathered around him every day as around a servant of God. He gave all his time to fasting and to prayer, and for this reason no worldly cares distracted him, because he sought God alone.[145]

The portrait of the saint in nature thus becomes the antitype of the preface's withering vines. It also offers a middle stage in the dialectic of paradise, with the saint tasting eternity not in heaven but on earth while he lives in a mortal body and in a world that the author earlier claimed was in the process of decline. By his holy life, he "attains and enjoys" (*tenetur et fruitur*) a type of paradise. Nor is this attainment presented as a sudden burst of paradise into the life of a holy person, as the dramatic and miraculous liberation of Portianus is portrayed. With Aemilianus, we have, instead, a paradise sustained daily by an ascetic mode of life. His is a transformed existence. Unlike the vines described in the preface, his garden never dries up. What nature provides remains sufficient.

The saint's dominion over the beasts is further demonstrated when a pack of hunting dogs chasing a wild boar cannot enter within the boundaries of the hermit's dwelling. Such a miracle suggests that the holy man lives in sacred space that cannot be violated. Then, in attempting to convince Brachio, a servant in charge of the dogs, to leave the world, the author portrays a saint living in the peaceable kingdom, a man refreshed, free of all worldly care and quoting scriptural passages that suggest that in the life of withdrawn holiness come liberation and the taste of immortality:

> The old man came to greet Brachio, kissed him, invited him to sit down, and when they had sat he said to him: "I see that you are dressed very elegantly, my dear son, and that you follow those things that prepare the soul for damnation rather than for salvation. I beg you to abandon your worldly master and follow the true God. . . . Make yourself the subject of Him who says 'Come unto me all ye that labour and are heavy laden, and I will give you rest' (Matt. 11:28). For He is the Lord, whose burden is light, whose yoke is gentle, whose worship both offers rewards and bestows eternal life. Such are indeed His words: 'If someone renounces all that he possesses, he shall receive an hundredfold, and shall inherit everlasting life' (Matt. 19:29)." While the old man was talking vigorously in this fashion, the boar withdrew safely into the forest. The young man left the saint filled with a great admiration, having seen the boar which he had begun by hunting become, despite its natural ferocity, as gentle as a lamb in the presence of the old man.[146]

Similar stories of "paradise regained" appear throughout the *LVP*. Caluppa's life of strict enclosure is a "terrestrial prison" that paradoxically "opens the door to paradise," or so the preface suggests that this is how the *Vita* ought to be interpreted.[147] This saint occasionally enjoys fishing in a river, where he finds the fish swimming directly to him for easy catching.[148] In addition, his rocky cell holds a hidden spring discovered by the holy man. Out of the rock from which the spring burst, he carves a cistern that conveniently holds his drinking water. His solitude in the wilderness is now assured; no longer must he rely on others to fetch water for him.[149] Saint Martius sometimes enjoys sitting in the shade of his garden, which yields fruit and vegetables in abundance.[150] Like the dwelling of Aemilianus, his space is also sacred and inviolable. A thief who comes in the night to steal food from the garden remains, unable to find a way out until he is discovered the next morning, forgiven by the holy man, and permitted to leave with the produce in hand.[151] The symbiosis between transformed man and nature becomes even more remarkable in the story of Martius. This holy man quite literally lives in nature because Gregory describes him as carving out of the rock of his cave a little bench on which he sleeps and sits. Like Aemilianus, who does not season his vegetables, this example shows that the rough conditions of a natural setting—the rock is hard, and Martius has no blankets—fosters ascetic discipline and thus illustrates how fused this mode of sanctity is with the created world.[152]

Often in the LVP, Gregory speaks of how holy people are raised to heaven as a result of their conduct here on earth.[153] In such statements, he does not clearly distinguish between heaven as the reward of saintly living attained after death and this way of living itself as a means of capturing paradise while still alive. It seems, instead, that paradise is an ascending continuum extending temporally and spatially from a transient earthly type in the present to an everlasting heavenly antitype in the future. Accordingly, a redeemed humanity, even in the face of a world and flesh that are perishing, can still recover the life of paradise. Although this paradisiacal life is not experienced completely on earth and before death, it nevertheless constitutes a new creation that represents to Gregory the antithesis of fallen Adam. Perhaps this is one reason why he claims that saints are the "teachers of eternal life" (*vitae doctores aeternae*).[154] In light of the typological significance of the texts we have been examining, such a remark cannot be understood as a pious platitude or imply that saints are like gnostic metaphysicians who have acquired some special knowledge about another world, which they then reveal to their followers. Given what we have considered so far, the statement suggests something about sanctity that is much more fundamental and concrete: that a holy existence is actually the visible embodiment of paradise on earth, a sample of immortality living in the present and showing others the tangible evidence of a life to come.

This positive presentation of hermits, ascetic monks, and cave dwellers suggests an openness on Gregory's part to accepting and promoting forms of the religious life other than the clerical.[155] Scholars tend to stress that the holy man living in the wild posed a threat to urban, clerical sanctity. The antagonism between the cleric and the recluse or the wandering holy man has been detected in the hagiographic literature of the Merovingian period. The *Vitae* can become almost antieremitical propaganda, as in the case of Fortunatus's *Life of Saint Paternus*. Similarly, Gregory also indicates that Senoch's reclusiveness needed to be restrained, and he describes the compromise reached between the holy man and his clerical superiors. But stories such as those of Aemilianus, Caluppa, Martius, and Leobardus show that Gregory presents withdrawn ascetics in a far more positive light than does Fortunatus. The extreme self-mortifications of the recluse Lupicinus, for instance, are never condemned, even though the saint's penitential practices obviously contributed to his death.[156]

Something even more important than Gregory's tolerance for ascetic eccentricities emerges in the stories of the more reclusive saints, especially in light of their urban and clerical counterparts. The holy bishop cannot be easily adapted to a paradisiacal typology. In terms of literary stylization, the environmental setting of eremitical sanctity provides the natural coloring needed for a portrait of paradise regained. For the recluse in the wild, on the one hand, this natural environment becomes an extension of the holy life. The saintly bishop or cleric, on the other hand, may occasionally control the beasts and the weather or may, when needed, miraculously supply an abundance of food or wine, but it is the hermit who actually lives with the animals, sleeps in rock, and dwells beside a garden or spring. This symbiosis between the holy man and nature transforms both into a redeemed creation portrayed as a paradise on earth. As a matter of routine, the sacred space offers the necessities of water, food, shelter, and even companionship in the form of docile beasts. The saints who withdraw must be accommodated by nature in order to survive, and so the paradisiacal imagery of the "most delightful spot" (amoenissimum locum) takes on a significance that we simply cannot expect to find in the hagiography of Fortunatus, which deals almost exclusively with urban, episcopal, and aristocratic saints.[157]

Such depictions of saints attaining paradise on earth also appear prominently in those stories of the desert fathers that contain features associated with romance literature.[158] Except for an explicit reference to an experience of death, the account of Aemilianus corresponds with several characteristics of that hagiography: The saint abandons his family to set out on a religious quest; the journey leads him to a remote, pleasant spot where he lives in tranquility with animals and nature; although he subsists on little, he never wants for anything; in a miraculous context, he is discovered by someone who goes back to the world with the impression of the holy man's life fresh on his mind.[159]

Brachio, however, later returns to live with the saint and becomes the successor of Aemilianus after the holy man dies. At this point, the narrative diverges from the pattern found in the desert stories of paradise regained. Once Aemilianus is dead, Brachio begins to establish more conventional cenobitic houses, and the paradisiacal imagery never appears again, except in a rather indirect but significant way. As his death approaches, Brachio recalls a location where he once wanted to build a monastery. He now considers the area a suitable place for burial by virtue of its proximity to a river. There, his bones will lie in a "delightful spot," words not only recalling the preface's description of the place reserved for the lovers of God but also making suggestively ambiguous the distinction between the ground where the body lies buried in the earth and the heavenly abode where the saint eternally rests.[160]

REVELATION, FULFILLMENT, AND NARRATIVE STRUCTURE

These considerations concerning the role of typology in the LVP also suggest another way of treating the relation between preface and narrative. Certainly, Brunhölzl's view that the prefaces set the theme of the Lives and that they are the key to understanding the whole story is clearly beyond dispute. But if we take into account the various ways in which we have seen typology functioning in the LVP, a more penetrating explanation can be offered, one that takes into account the full extent of the biblical presence in Gregory's narratives.

When the nature of the LVP's narrative structure is taken into consideration, the prefaces to the stories do not merely set a theme. Given the explicit biblical content that dominates the opening remarks and the way the author treats scriptural texts, both exegetically and as thematic leitmotifs resurfacing later in the *Vitae*, it is far more accurate to say that the prefaces foreshadow, in precisely the way that word is understood in the context of patristic commentary, what comes later in the narratives. This foreshadowing happens throughout the *LVP*. We just saw, for instance, the subtle way in which the preface to Aemilianus's *Vita* speaks unspecifically of how the love of God places the holy in paradise. The first chapter then fulfills the opening statement; it gives a specific example of what was only generally suggested, and it also offers the antitypical response to the rest of the preface's remark about the withering vines. Not all the Lives have a connection between preface and narrative that constitutes the type-antitype relationship, but almost every *Vita* in the *LVP* has a preface that in one way or another foreshadows a later development in the narrative. We recall also that when the connection is made between these two elements of a *Vita*, as in the case of Senoch's *Life*, a unity emerges. Thus, in terms of a *Vita*'s structure, the relation between preface and proceeding narrative corresponds with the Christian approach to reading the Bible. Like the Old Testament, the prefaces are fulfilled by the accounts that follow. And the accounts that follow are presented as the new development in the salvific plan, so they assume the role that the New Testament has in light of the Old.

If we consider all the examples so far examined, there is little doubt that the telling of a saint's story really constitutes the fulfillment of the author's opening remarks. This consistent strategy is an essential feature of the typological approach to Scripture and an important aspect of the Bible itself, especially the New Testament. In fact, Gregory's abundant use and careful presentation of biblical texts in the Lives—verses from the Old Testament are, in almost every case, quoted before those of the New—makes this way of reading the *LVP* compelling.

As previously observed, Fortunatus occasionally presents his saints as fulfilling or reenacting biblical events, but Gregory's presentations are structurally different. With Fortunatus's writing, the biblical allusion occurs simultaneously with the action of the saint who is being described. But in the prefaces of the *LVP*, the biblical citation appears well before the corresponding event of the saint's life is mentioned. Again, Senoch's *Vita* offers a good example of this technique. In that work, we observed how the narrative developed to a point where the meaning of the preface became fully realized through the telling of a particular episode in the holy man's life. At that stage, a unity between the hagiographic narrative and the opening remarks appeared precisely because the story fulfilled what the preface foretold.

It seems clear, then, that the narrative structure of the *LVP* is really analogous to the Christian understanding of the Bible, in which the textual arrangement is treated in terms of prophecy and fulfillment. The examples in the *LVP* are really too numerous to illustrate, but we have already seen some of them, such as the story of Senoch, the *Life of Aemilianus*, and, more dramatically, Portianus's *Vita*, in which biblical texts legitimizing change in social status preface a story of a saint's liberation from slavery. Other instances can easily be cited. In the preface to Martius's *Life*, we find scriptural verses emphasizing the importance of loving one's enemies, later followed by stories of how the saint forgave fellow clerics who physically abused him.[161] Biblical texts that justify predestination show up in the preface to Nicetius's *Vita*, and later in the story the saint's mother urges her husband not to take the episcopacy because "she bears a bishop in her womb."[162]

These instances are only some of the more obvious connections between scripturally based prefaces that are fulfilled by later stories in the Lives. Often in a *Vita*, we could easily overlook minor incidents that are related to the preface. Introducing Saints Lupicinus and Romanus, for instance, Gregory places their lives in the context of the Gospel precept warning against storing up treasures in a hidden, deep pit where it easily corrodes (Matt. 25:18). Obviously, such a sentiment can have a general significance for two saints who set out for the rugged region of the Jura to lead monastic lives and gather followers in the religious life. But quite late in the story we learn that Lupicinus had discovered an ancient, buried treasure from which he was able to buy provisions for his monastery.[163] Moreover, the last lines of this *Life* echo the scriptural passages cited in the preface.

Likewise, in the *Life of Quintianus*, Gregory speaks of the corruptibility of the body and contrasts earthly matter with the life of the spirit, citing Galatians 5:19 as his source. Again, the remark can have a general application to the *Vita*—any *Vita*, for that matter. But this particular *Life* depicts an old and infirm saint who must be carried by aides and who holds a small bowl under his chin to catch the drool dripping from his mouth.[164] In the preface to Aemilianus's *Vita*, the author speaks early on of "discipline" (*disciplina*),[165] yet Aemilianus is portrayed as a meek man who lives the eremitical life almost effortlessly (though certainly he maintains an ascetic rigor). Only much later in the story, when the narrative turns to Brachio, do we learn how uncompromising this former master of hunting dogs is in rigidly enforcing the monastic rule. In fact, one of his great achievements is reforming a lax community.[166] Gregory even foreshadows himself when he subtly claims in the preface to Senoch's *Vita* that the saint was saved by some unspecified "faithful brothers." Only when we get to the episode of the saint's arrogance do we realize that Gregory, as the bishop rebuking the holy man for his behavior, is obviously one of the "faithful brothers"—the only one mentioned specifically—who saved the saint from *vanitas* and who thus becomes a minor hero in the story itself. Such examples can be found throughout the *LVP*. Considering how these accounts relate to the introductory remarks, we may accurately sum up this narrative strategy by paraphrasing Augustine's remark quoted earlier: In the prefaces the stories are concealed; in the stories the prefaces are revealed.

On the whole, all the examples in the present discussion show a connection to the preface based on later events described in the narrative. Sometimes the connection is obvious; at other times, we can easily miss it if the opening remarks and especially the biblical quotations are not kept in mind. In either case, the structure of the Lives derives from a preface's revelation that is fulfilled or specifically explained at a later point in the narrative. In this sense, then, we have a collection of Lives whose prefaces assume a connection to the proceeding stories that mirrors the relation between the Old and New Testament, as this was understood and fostered by the Christian typological approach to Scripture.

ALLEGORY AND TYPOLOGY

That Gregory was in touch with the two main currents of patristic approaches to Scripture is not in doubt. Perhaps one of the most striking features of the LVP from the perspective of biblical commentary is how Gregory maintains a distinction between allegory and typology. Although certainly an interpretive strategy supporting a Christian reading of the Bible, the typological approach at least stays rooted in the scriptural texts, and in this sense it is literal. When, for instance, Gregory wants to portray the Christian Abraham as a "new man," he cites a biblical text to validate his assertion rather than formulating an argument based on material extraneous to Scripture, as is the case with those interpretations involving the moral meaning of the text, an approach characteristic of allegory. Typology, as one researcher observes, legitimately extends the literal sense, whereas allegorical exegesis departs from it.[167] Often allegory reflects the peculiar psychological disposition of the interpreter, as, say, in the case of Philo, whose exegesis really serves Greek philosophy.[168] An example more pertinent to this discussion is Jerome's commentary on Ecclesiastes cited earlier, the preface to which, along with other epistolatory evidence, indicates that he wanted this biblical text to be read in a way that would promote an ascetic way of life.[169] Such interpretive approaches have little or no basis in the literal meaning of the scriptures.

One passage of the LVP in particular shows Gregory's awareness of this patristic trend in interpretation, as well as how idiosyncratic an allegorical approach can be. In this instance, the departure from the literal sense of Scripture is obvious when Gregory begins to see his own "rustic style" through the distorting lens of allegory. This interpretive approach provides the author with material to develop the humility topos. The personal significance that the allegorical interpretation has to the author's writing contrasts well enough with the typological elements of the LVP previously examined. Referring to the materials that the Israelites used to build the tabernacle (Exod. 25:1–9), he writes:

> Then they offered gifts of gold and silver, of brass and iron, of fine sparkling precious stones, double skeins of fine linen and double lengths of scarlet cloth; some brought rams' skins stained red, and goat-skins. But the doctors of the Church have said that all these things are allegorical, and that these various gifts signify various kinds of graces, and they compare the goat-skins with words of praise. And indeed we who are provided with little intelligence, are unskilled in our studies and sinful in deed, cannot offer gold or silver or precious stones or twisted and doubled skeins; but at least we can lay out goat-skins, that is to say, stories which make known the miracles of the saints.[170]

Unlike the writings of the bishop of Tours's contemporary, Gregory the Great, the influence of allegorical exegesis rarely appears in the LVP and never to the extent that we find in this passage. Even by Gregory's time, allegory had long been the favorite method of interpretation among biblical commentators.[171] Speculation on why allegorical elements play so little a role in the LVP need not detain us now. We should at least note, however, that because the typological outlook assumes that God is known through the redemptive acts of individuals in history, it is a mode of thought well suited to an author like Gregory, who explicitly treats contemporary saints and, given what the *Histories* suggests, the events of his own society as evidence of a salvific plan in the continuous process of fulfillment. Allegory, because it disconnects from the literal sense of Scripture, can easily depart from the stream of history and derive meaning from the Bible on the basis of purely conceptual—really philosophical or psychological—interpretations that not only are independent of the literal and historical significance of Scripture but also actually relegate these to the lowest level of understanding.[172] But for the hagiographer, for Gregory especially, the saint must be portrayed as carrying on the redemption, which can best be accomplished by recapitulating the Bible concretely, according to a typological pattern.[173] An allegorical perspective, because it downplays the genuine historicity of the people and events of the Bible, is simply not as easily adapted to a literature whose validity and vitality depend on the belief that God is known, not by mental abstractions, but by divine actions in time and through people whose reality is measured, as Gregory's prefaces explicitly show, in proportion to their correspondence with the biblical past.

Saint-Types and the Meaning of "Life"

Syncretic Sanctity and Its Breakdown

The variety of holiness represented in the LVP is the one aspect of these Lives that has received detailed treatment by a modern researcher.[174] Because this subject has been discussed elsewhere, we shall here make only a few observations on some of the more striking saint types found in the work.

We should begin by noting that, on the whole, a more thorough syncretism appears in the LVP than in Fortunatus's hagiography. The representative example of Senoch again offers the most obvious case. In this *Vita*, the mixing of types is so complete that the saint defies classification according to any one category of sanctity. He is a deacon and priest but also periodically a recluse. The compromise made with his superiors to prevent his arrogance from growing entails a holy life that regularly fluctuates from active to contemplative phases, depending on the cycle of the liturgical year.[175]

However, we should also acknowledge that the syncretism in the LVP occasionally strains to legitimize a contemporary saint by adapting a model of sanctity to new circumstances, much like Fortunatus's attempts to make his saints "martyrs." Such syncreticism seems heavy-handed and artificial. Given what we have previously observed in Fortunatus, it is evident that the aristocratic, episcopal holy man undergoes this kind of syncretic stylization the most because his life least of all corresponds with that of genuine martyrs and hermits. In this context, the reference to Saint Gregory of Langres as a "new hermit" is significant. By such a designation, the author implies that even as a bishop Saint Gregory accomplished all that the old hermits of the desert did, while also surpassing these monastic forerunners by achieving his sanctity "in the middle of the world" rather than in the desert.[176]

Yet Gregory of Langres lived a life that was altogether secular right up to his election as bishop. Coming from the senatorial rank, the saint is well positioned in the upper class, and his succession to the episcopacy is really a *cursus honorum*[177] marking the end of a secular career as a count of Autun, where, as the administrator of justice, the unmerciful holy man punished criminals severely.[178] Thus, there is no progression in the saint's life through the monastic or clerical ranks. With his background lacking an obvious connection with the usual modes of sanctity, Gregory introduces the convenient designation of the "new hermit" to add a depth to the subject's holiness that can—within the background of the polemics between the urban, monk-bishop style of Martinian sanctity and the eremitical, lay life of the Egyptian ascetics—lend a progressive legitimacy to an otherwise one-dimensional saint.[179] This development of the "new hermit" combines the characteristics of the old type but under different conditions, much as the persecuted Christian of the *passio* developed into the "bloodless martyr" of the desert literature and later hagiography. Of course, compared with saints stylized as martyrs, the advantage of the "new hermit" is that this designation can easily avoid betraying any deficiency in type, whereas the male "martyrs" of Fortunatus *Vitae* never fulfill a genuine martyrdom because they remain alive after their "persecution."[180] The "new hermit" can thus be presented as a superior version, while the "martyr" who does not die can, at best, only approximate the original.

Attributes of a type that seem to have no more than token significance can also be attached to a saint. The recluse Caluppa, who lives almost his entire religious life enclosed in a high, rocky crag where he has carved out a cell, is ordained deacon and priest by a visiting bishop. Yet, the saint remains in his enclosure and bears no resemblance to the syncretic saints who progress from the monastic to the clerical life of holiness. Despite his ordination, he stays a pure hermit.[181]

Caluppa's *Vita* also raises the issue concerning the tension between rival representatives of different religious lifestyles. Caluppa first starts out as a cenobitic monk. Because of his excessive fasting, the holy man becomes too weak to perform his monastic chores. His bickering religious brothers find this intolerable, and the prior rebukes the saint with Scripture: "He who does not choose to work does not deserve to eat."[182] Caluppa's religious quest then becomes a flight, not from marriage, as we often find in the eremitical hagiographic literature, but from the pettiness of cenobitic life. The departure leads to the actual breakdown of a syncretic sanctity. The holy man starts out by living a common life as an ascetic monk but ends as a pure recluse unaffected by his clerical ordination and maintaining an eremitical existence in a paradisiacal setting.

With respect to this breakdown of syncretism, the *Vita* of Patroclus is especially significant. The saint refuses to marry and, instead, enters the lower ranks of the clergy. Like Caluppa, his asceticism remains rigorous and contrasts with a laxer clerical culture in whose orbit the saint moves. His fasting, vigils, study, and prayer cut into his *convivium* with other clerics. The holy man stops eating at the communal table, an affront to his fellow clerics that leads to a chastisement from the archdeacon: "Either you take your meals with the other brothers or you leave us. It is not right that you neglect to eat with those whose ecclesiastical duties you share." The saint then departs with a "thirst for the desert."[183] He establishes monasteries and gathers followers until he finally relinquishes his cenobitic duties to live a more solitary life.[184] Moving from cleric to monk, the saint thus progresses by gradually shedding the different types of holiness acquired throughout his religious quest until he finally becomes a recluse. In both Lives, there is a flight from a particular mode of the religious life. Unlike Fortunatus, Gregory does not attempt to make an episcopal sanctity the highest level of holiness attainable, though certainly episcopal sanctity is well represented.[185] Such stories suggest a remarkable fluidity in the varieties of religious life.

Also noteworthy is the fact that Gregory does not capitalize on every opportunity to expand the syncretism in the depiction of a saint to the martyr type. Although he does speak of saints being their own persecutors during a time of peace, he also tells how Gallus actually fled from a group of angry pagans whose temple he had burned. Contrary to what we find in Fortunatus's hagiography, when the sword-wielding mob approaches Gallus, there is no "he would have been a martyr. . . ." Instead, the saint takes to his heels and runs to the king for protection. Throughout his life, Saint Gallus laments the lost opportunity of martyrdom.[186]

Gregory could have easily embellished this incident by portraying the king's unexpected intervention right before a courageous Gallus prepares to die. Unlike most hagiographers, especially Fortunatus, Gregory allows some of the less than flattering details of a saint's life to remain intact in the hagiographic account. In fact, one of the more remarkable features of the LVP is how sanctity appears alongside human failings and distinctive personality traits. A saint may be a severe secular judge, reject clerical culture, prefer only one style of holy living, know the weakness of pride, be shown a coward, or even, as in the case of Venantius, become fondly attached to his betrothed before deciding to lead a religious life.[187] In such instances, the personalities are not "absorbed" by an idealized portrait. The flaws and idiosyncrasies are the pure biographical elements that seem occasionally to spill unfiltered into the hagiographic narrative.

Literacy over Thaumaturgy

Also related to the issue of saint types is the question of the saint as miracle worker. Those who comment briefly on the saints portrayed in the LVP tend to dwell on the thaumaturgic aspect of Gregory's depictions. Similar to research on the Histories, the miracle stories are usually regarded negatively, especially by scholars who compare the holy men of the LVP to those described in the Dialogues of Gregory the Great.[188] According to this view, the sanctity of Gregory of Tours's saints is considered to be based on miraculous power rather than on a holy lifestyle, or what is called "virtue." From this perspective, thaumaturgy is indicative of a lower grade of sanctity so that the holy who attain their reputations through "virtuous" living enjoy greater legitimacy in the eyes of modern scholars.

To some extent, we have already challenged this position because the discussion on Gregory's hermits, notwithstanding their miraculous or nearly miraculous bond with nature, indicated that this mode of sanctity was a way of life maintained by ascetic discipline and withdrawal from the world. In other words, attaining paradise is a nonthaumaturgic activity, the motivation of which arises out of the saint's human desire to live a perfect life.[189] Moreover, researchers tend to overlook the fact that not all the saints portrayed in the LVP perform miracles; of the ones who do, some accomplish their *virtutes* in a rather moderate amount and with little spectacular flair.[190]

But there is another aspect to the image of sanctity in the *LVP* that also compellingly redresses the claim that Gregory's saints rely excessively on thaumaturgy. In several accounts, the ability to read or the daily practice of reading is presented as a sign of sanctity. In fact, becoming literate is portrayed as a major event, a turning point, in the lives of two saints. Gregory relates that Patroclus had to tend sheep while his brother Antonius goes to school. When they meet at home, the illiterate saint is treated as an ignoramus by his sibling, who refuses to sit next to him at table: "Sit further from me you peasant. You herd sheep while I study letters; the care of such a task ennobles me, while you are made common through your work."[191] Patroclus responds by going to school, and his education leads to a remarkable change in social status: "When Patroclus heard this he regarded the reproach as a warning from God, and he left his sheep in the field and hastened to the boys' school, born along by his agile mind and a swift pace. There he learnt so readily, thanks to his memory, all that was necessary for his age, that he surpassed his brother both in learning and in quickness of thought, assisted in all this by divine power. In the end he was recommended for employment to Nunnio, who was then very close to Childebert, king of Paris."[192] Moreover, as noted earlier, among the ascetic habits distinguishing Patroclus from the other clerics is intensive study in conjunction with prayer and fasting, a combination that will become important when we turn to Baudonivia's *Life of Saint Radegund*.

Similarly, after Brachio returns from meeting Aemilianus, he begins to rise in the night for prayer but is hampered by his inability to read. To acquire this skill, he copies out the words he sees on icons and asks a young cleric to instruct him in the meaning of the letters:

> When he was still a layman, rising at night two or three times from his bed, prostrated on the ground, he used to pour forth prayer to the Lord. But he did not know what he should sing because he was ignorant of letters. Often seeing in the oratory that letters were written over the icons of the apostles and other saints, he copied the words into a book. And since clerics and abbots constantly came to meet his master, he used to ask one of the younger ones, whom he had first been able to call over secretly, the names of the letters, and by this way he began to understand them. With the Lord inspiring, he read and wrote before he knew the [whole] series of letters. Then, when Sigivald [his master] died, he hastened to the previously mentioned old man, and [after] spending two or three years with him, he committed the psalter to memory.[193]

The sanctity of Saint Leobardus is intimately tied to his reading. When he settles into a religious life, he begins a study of Scripture and also memorizes the Psalms, which he had first learned as a child but forgot later in life. In addition to reading, this saint spends part of his time preparing parchment on which to write.[194] The description of the hermit in his cell near Marmoutier recalls a life in which asceticism and literary activity are fused: "In his cell he used to delight in fasting, praying, singing, and reading. He never ceased [from saying] the divine office and prayer. Sometimes he used to write to rid himself of harmful thoughts."[195]

Even more revealing of reading's importance to the life of sanctity is how Leobardus overcomes his desire to leave his cell. To encourage him to remain a recluse,

Gregory himself gives the saint the *Life of the Fathers* and the *Institution of the Monks*, titles that probably refer to Rufinus's *Vitae patrum* and Cassian's *De institutis coenobiorum*.[196] Reading these books inspires the saint with the necessary resolve to remain a hermit; his mastery of the material becomes one of the prominent features of his sanctity: "When I had left him I sent him books of the 'Life of the Fathers' and the 'Institution of the Monks,' in order that he might learn what hermits had to do and with what care monks had to live. He read them, and not only did he banish from his mind the evil thought that he had had, but also developed his learning so much that he astonished us by his facility in speaking of such matters."[197]

Only a small portion of this *Vita*, the last one in the collection, is devoted to *virtutes*. But most important of all, the saint's miraculous power is presented as the blessing bestowed on one who lived a long life engaged in ascetic—not thaumaturgic—activities, a life obviously spent in prayer and reading, the kind of life that those who study the *Dialogues* of Gregory the Great would call virtuous: "He remained twenty-two years occupied in this manner in his cell, and obtained so much grace from God that with his saliva alone he could banish the poison from malignant pustules."[198]

Vita or Vitae?

Finally, having gained an impression of the variety of holiness represented throughout the *libelli*, we are now in a good position to end our discussion on this work where most researchers who briefly comment on the LVP begin. What immediately strikes modern readers about the collection is its title, with its singular use of life (*vita*) rather than the plural lives (*vitae*). In the preface to the whole work, Gregory himself addresses this issue: "It is asked by some whether we ought to say life or lives of the saints. A. Gellius and several philosophers have preferred to say lives. But Pliny in the third book of the Art of Grammar says 'the ancients have said "the lives" of each of us; but grammarians did not think that [the word] life has a plural.' Hence it is clear that it is better to say 'life of the Fathers' rather than 'lives' because, although there is a diversity of merits and deeds of power, nevertheless, the one life of the body nourishes all in the world."[199]

Gregory seems to be making a purely grammatical distinction here, not a theological observation about the nature of sanctity, though the latter interpretation need not be entirely ruled out. In fact, those who do comment on the remark invariably interpret it to mean that all the holy "lived the same kind of life," the "one life in Christ" or, similarly, that "a saint reveals the same sanctity whenever God intervenes through him."[200] This interpretation leads to the conclusion that "the successful Life will contain few personal details: it is God's personality, not the saint's that counts."[201] Accordingly, Gregory's remark is used to support the view that hagiographers generally portray the same kind of miracles and manner of holy living. This interpretation of hagiography, which scholars often give on the basis of Gregory's explanation for his use of the singular form, was also elaborately articulated, probably around the year 700, by the anonymous author of Gregory the Great's *Vita*:

So let no one be disturbed even if these miracles were performed by any other of the saints, since the Holy Apostle, through the mystery of the limbs of a single body, which he compares to the living experience of the saints, concludes that we are all "members of one another." For instance, the work of the eyes and ears becomes profitable to the hands and feet as if they were for common use, and so all things are profitable to all even though they "have not the same office." Hence we know too that all saints have everything in common through the love of Christ of whose body they are members. Hence if anything we have written did not concern this man—and, remember, we did not learn about them from those who saw and heard them but only by common report—yet in his case we have little doubt on the whole that they were true of him, too. Indeed the holy man in his wisdom very clearly teaches that what one sees and admires in others always becomes one's own in turn.[202]

When we compare the statements of the two hagiographers, we notice that Gregory does not refer to all saints as members of the one body of Christ in his preface. Instead of arguing a theological position, the author of the *LVP* is attempting to justify a grammatical usage on the basis of a common, we might even say in a literal sense, existential condition of all human life—corporality. It is the "one life of the body"—*corporis* not *Christi*—that "nourishes all."

Nevertheless, given other remarks found in the *LVP* and elsewhere in the author's corpus, the theological significance usually attributed to the use of *life* instead of *lives* can find support.[203] But what most researchers fail to acknowledge is the complexity of Gregory's view regarding the unity and diversity of sanctity.[204] This issue comes to the forefront of the *LVP* right from the beginning, in the first *Vita* describing Romanus and Lupicinus, two drastically opposite, though not necessarily opposed, monastic saints. Elsewhere in the *LVP*, Gregory speaks of how the "steps" to paradise are "varied," and he even seems to understand sanctity in terms of singularity and multiplicity.[205] No attempt can be made now to explain his reasoning, but it is important at least to note how Gregory expresses himself in the preface to Venantius's *Vita* and to acknowledge that this position cannot be reduced to a simple understanding of sanctity allegedly expressed by the preference for *vita* in the title of his book: "Heavenly power bestows on the churches and on the peoples of the earth a present both unique and multiple, when it continually grants to the world not only those who can intercede for sinners but also those who can teach about eternal life. Thus what appears to be only a single gift is nevertheless multiple when it is given by the divine majesty, because all those who have wished to ask have received in abundance."[206]

This complex view of sanctity becomes especially important if we consider the form in which the *LVP* appears. It is a large collection of Lives put together, one lengthy book that consists of twenty self-contained little books, each with its own title. In this sense, the *LVP* as a collection of little books amassed into a single volume again resembles the Bible, another collection of individual *libelli* or *biblia*. But while one biblical book may explicitly refer to or transpose the text of another to carry on a theme, Gregory's *LVP* shows no signs that the author attempted to establish a specific thematic thread consistently running throughout each Life to give an impression of an overall continuity and unity that we find, for example, when the author of Revelation, the last book of the New Testament, connects his writing with Genesis, the first book of the Bible.[207]

Given the diversity of saints represented and the lack of a continuous theme explicitly expressed throughout the *LVP*, the place to look for consistency and unity is obviously in the structure of the Lives, the careful arrangement between preface and narrative that gives an account coherence. As we have seen, each *Vita* reliably follows the pattern in which the story of a saint derives its significance in light of a preface that tells precisely where that particular holy person fits within the context of a salvation history. Like the Lives themselves, the previous record of this history shows God acting through all manner of holy people. But to the author of the *LVP*, the past also indicates that a single, coherent plan is in progress and that the saints are, in all the colorful ways Gregory portrays them, interacting with one God in a concerted effort to carry out the divine purpose.

At this point, the discussion on the depiction of male saints in the *Vitae* of Fortunatus and Gregory comes to an end. This broad sample of hagiographic texts written by two very different, prolific writers of the early Merovingian period provides a solid foundation for examining the depiction of holy women. In short, a basis of comparison is now established, one that enables us to proceed by focusing on some key texts that can be considered in light of the hagiography just examined. In an attempt to have the works face each other, let us turn now to the question of how these same authors portray female saints.

PART II

Sanctae

4

"LIKE A MAN AMONG MEN"

The Female Saint in a Male Corpus

> She [amma Sarah] also said to the brothers, "It is
> I who am a man, you who are women."
> —*Apophthegmata Patrum* (1975, p. 193)

Gregory's *Life of Saint Monegund*

We have examined the common and, at least in relation to Fortunatus's hagiography, some of the distinctive features of the *LVP*. Now we turn to the nineteenth book of this collection to consider Gregory's depiction of a female saint and to see how this composition compares with the rest of the work. Similar to the *Life of Saint Radegund* in Fortunatus's corpus of prose biographies, Monegund's *Vita* is the only account in the *LVP* telling the story of a holy woman.[1]

Having gained some sense of the rhetorical strategies employed and the breadth of sanctity represented, we should now be sufficiently familiar with the more prominent characteristics of the *LVP* to be able to detect any features in the *Life of Saint Monegund* that contrast fundamentally with those found in the other Lives. There certainly are, as we have occasionally noted, significant variations in the depictions of sanctity throughout the *LVP*, which give this collection of Lives its distinctive coloring and, when considered in its entirety, set it apart from the more standard episcopal biographies written by Fortunatus and several other authors of the period. But in the present context, a "fundamental contrast" refers to a variation in the depiction of sanctity that is attributable to gender alone. So far, we have been examining texts that deal exclusively with male saints, without either Gregory or Fortunatus calling attention to this fact. If in the Lives of female saints these two authors bring the issue of gender to the forefront of their writing—and we shall see shortly that in their own different ways they do—then we should address the question of whether the hagiographers we have been studying change their approach to portraying sanctity when their subjects are holy women. In other words, given all that has preceded, we are now in an excellent position to consider what modifications the depiction and, consequently, the ideal of sanctity undergo when Gregory and Fortunatus, writers accustomed to giving accounts of holy men, narrate the lives of female saints.

The "Inferior Sex" Turned Christian Warrior

Earlier, we discovered how important a role the prefaces played in the libelli of the LVP. Monegund's Life is no exception. As with the other prefaces, Gregory introduces the Life of Saint Monegund by giving an outline of salvation history. Once again, we find a summary description of events leading toward the redemptive fulfillment of the divine plan, the familiar Heilsgeschichte that the Christian typological approach to the Bible, along with its corresponding conception of historical progress, fosters. Especially important, too, is how concrete this redemptive plan is to Gregory. The author proclaims the insignificance of words and conceptualization in grasping the reality of the Incarnation. Gregory begins by declaring the futility of attempting to comprehend by the intellect or express in writing the heavenly benefits, not necessarily because understanding and language fall short of adequately conceiving and describing divine activity in the world but because words and conceptions lack the ontological status of the "Word made flesh," the "Savior of the World" who, from the beginning of creation, was actually "seen" by the patriarchs, was "announced" by the prophets, and, finally, assumed a mortal body. Words and ideas that express the heavenly gifts bestowed on humanity are now diminished in importance by the fact that the greatest of divine gifts actually appeared on earth when God became man. Since the Savior was enclosed in the womb of Mary, the reality of salvation history supersedes rhetoric and philosophy: "The remarkable gifts of divine favors, which have been granted to the human race from heaven, could not be conceived by the understanding, spoken by words or comprehended by writing, since the Savior of the world Himself, from [the time of] the raw earth's creation, offered himself to be seen by the patriarchs, announced by the prophets and, in the end, deigned to be received in the womb of the ever virgin and undefiled Mary."[2]

As the author proceeds to elaborate on the significance of the Incarnation, he comes close to portraying his understanding of the salvific mission of Christ in terms of a warrior's conquest that led to the rescue of a defeated people: To redeem humanity, the Savior goes to death, and in doing so he conquers sin and rises victorious. Humanity itself is something of a wounded army pierced by the arrows of sin, ambushed by enemies lying in wait. Saved and now protected by Christ, the redeemed find comfort in "celestial medicine," licking their wounds with the teachings of the church: "The almighty and immortal Creator allowed himself to be clothed in the cloak of mortal flesh, to go to death as a reparation for the sin of dead humanity and to rise again victorious. [When] we were stabbed by the arrows of heavy sins and afflicted by the wounds of ambushing mercenaries, He mixed the oil with wine [and] led us to the abode of heavenly medicine, that is, the dogma of the holy church."[3]

After presenting the history of salvation as culminating in the victory of Christ, Gregory turns next to the role of saints who continue to fulfill God's purpose. The holy, armed with the teachings of the Creator and hence the doctrines of the church, continue the battle for salvation. At this point—we are now in the middle of the preface—the imagery of warfare and athletic contest begins to dominate. Saints follow the examples of other saints who previously fought. This emphasis on com-bative struggle remains consistent with other passages in the LVP and also with the hagiography of Fortunatus, who, as we have seen, often describes saints as warriors.[4] Here, however, Gregory calls attention to one segment of the fighters, and he does so for a reason we have not yet encountered. The exemplary combatants are not only men but also women, referred to collectively as *inferiorem sexum*. The "inferior sex," imitating the previous models of holiness, are not weak opponents but fight like men (*viriliter agonizantem*), attaining the heavenly kingdom after their "sweaty" (*desudantibus*) exertions in battle: "With the unceasing gift of His teaching, He exhorts us to live by the examples of the saints. He provides as an example for us not only men, but also [those of] the inferior sex itself, who fight not sluggishly but manfully. He gives a share of the starry kingdom not only to the men duly fighting, but also to the women sweating in the contest [and winning] the applause."[5]

Following the usual threefold pattern of the prefaces found throughout the LVP (i.e., biblical allusion, reference to holy forerunners, and closure with the mention of the particular saint whose life is about to be told), Gregory at last introduces Monegund as the contemporary example of the sanctity he has been describing in the introductory remarks. Significantly, as we reach the preface's end, the imagery of contest fades, and biblical typology comes into play. This holy woman, we are told, left her native soil (Chartres) and journeyed to Tours, determined to go to the church of Saint Martin. Her action resembles that of the Queen of Sheba, who went "to hear the wisdom of Solomon." The last lines of the preface conclude by intro-ducing one other important element into the typological framework, a feature with which we are now quite familiar. Gregory hints that the saint fulfilled her quest when she reached Tours and witnessed the miracles at Martin's tomb. At this saint's church, where later in the *Vita* we learn the holy woman settled, Monegund drank from the "sacerdotal font" and burst open the doors to paradise: "So it is now with the blessed Monegund, who left her native land just like that prudent queen who came to listen to the wisdom of Solomon (I Reg. 10) and came to the church of St. Martin to admire the miracles which took place there daily and to drink there as from a sacerdotal font, by which she was able to throw open the door to the grove of Paradise."[6]

Earlier, we noticed that in the outlines of salvation history Gregory aligns a saint within a particular development of the salvific plan, so that the contemporary holy person contributes to fulfilling God's purpose, first recorded in the Bible and then in the Lives of the saints, with Gregory's own documentation presented as an update on the continuing redemptive activity taking place in the world during his lifetime. The same holds true for Monegund's *Vita*. However, this preface shows a tendency, which we do not find in the other *libelli*, to highlight the role of female figures in the progress of salvation. In addition to lending support to Gregory's preference for the concrete, corporeal reality of redemption as a historical event that "dethroned" words and philosophy,[7] the reference to the Virgin also unequivocally asserts the importance of a woman in the fulfillment of God's plan.[8] Likewise, Monegund is presented as a type of Queen of Sheba who retraces the latter's steps by leaving the territory of Chartres for the city of Tours. We recall that earlier Gregory described another saint who also left his homeland to seek the wisdom of the desert monks, but in that case he likened the holy man to Abraham rather than the "prudent queen." So here we see that the typological application in the preface to Monegund's *Vita* is obviously made to suit the saint's gender.

Even so, we should be careful in assessing the significance of these variations. The great advantage of having examined a wide range of hagiographic texts before turning to the *Vita* of a holy woman is that we can now acquire a precise sense of the extent to which the modifications due to gender disrupt the usual rhetorical patterns that we found in the Lives of male saints. In our consideration of Monegund's *Life*, we should keep in mind that almost every holy man of the *LVP* undergoes an initial process of biblical assimilation to show his own special place within the framework of salvation's past and its continuation in the author's present. To put it another way, the peculiarities of sanctity's contemporary manifestations are consistently absorbed by corresponding previous developments in the salvation history outlined by the prefaces. By such a strategy, the distinctiveness of a particular saint is legitimized through association with Scripture and previous models of Christian holiness. In the preface to Monegund's *Vita*, the references to Mary and the Queen of Sheba are the particular alignments the author makes to fit his contemporary saint into the salvific plan. Although clearly these particular modifications are due to the saint's gender, these variations are minor. In most respects, the author does not alter his rhetorical approach. The structure of the preface has not changed from what we observed before, and all the other elements in the other prefaces are still here. The centrality of the Bible, the Christian view of history, the reference to past models of sanctity followed by the specific introduction of the saint by name, and the claim that the holy person by her way of life attained a type of paradise on earth—each of these elements we have seen before so that, with respect to such characteristic features, the preface shows no major points of departure from what we normally find throughout the *LVP*.

What does not fit—what we have not yet encountered and what constitutes a fundamental contrast and break with all the other *Vitae* examined so far—is the reference to the "inferior sex." In no Life does Gregory call attention to the fact that a saint is male. If we take into consideration the other prefaces previously discussed, the focus on gender and the designation of inferiority mark a significant point of departure from the usual characteristics in the *LVP*. This jarring feature at the outset of Monegund's *Life* suggests that the saint's gender is problematized in the hagiographer's approach to writing about sanctity and requires a rhetorical technique that accommodates what he clearly regards as a natural obstacle to holiness. Evidently, the author is attempting to compensate for the perception of women as weak by associating the *inferiorem sexum* with the Christian athlete and warrior, a view of sanctity that is anticipated by the description of the Savior as the resurrected victor who vanquished sin and death. With the life of Christian warfare an *imitatio Christi*, the female saint, if she is to be genuinely Christlike, must be shown as striving in the contest to attain eternal life. The traditional perception of the female as being physically and morally inferior—and here we cannot consider the various social, legal, theological, canonical, or other factors that may have contributed to such a

view[9]—obviously raises a difficulty for the author, who, in the preface, clearly identifies manliness as one of the essential attributes of sanctity. We may infer from the
fact that Gregory stresses the virile power of holy women that femininity detracts
from sanctity. Thus, at least on the rhetorical level, sanctity is expressed in terms of
physical, male power; it is the attainment of a victory in a drawn-out contest in
which the female participants assume the characteristics associated with male fighters,
an image which, as the author indicates, ultimately derives from an adherence to
the warrior as the paradigm of Christian sanctity, with the model par excellence
being the salvific assault of Christ on humanity's sin and its concomitant, continuing
call to death, either by martyrdom or asceticism, to maintain the victory of redemption originally achieved by the Savior. The preface stresses that women do,
indeed, engage in such combat, that they can follow, as much as males do, the
sacrificial example of the cross, and that they continue to take it up throughout the
history of Christianity. What remains to be seen now is whether the author continues
to problematize gender as the Vita proceeds and whether the fact that the subject of
the Life is female gives rise to changes in the depiction of sanctity.

Breaking Conjugal Bonds

Unlike the other saints whose Lives we have been examining, Monegund is at first
presented as fulfilled in family life. A positive view of marriage and especially motherhood can be detected in the opening lines of the first chapter, with the saint
depicted as gleefully enjoying the two daughters produced by her union with an
earthly—as opposed to a spiritual—spouse.[10] As we might expect in a world where
the joys of creation can easily dissipate like hebel, the two girls die.[11] At their death,
Monegund experiences unbearable grief until she resolves to lead a religious life in
the hope of assuaging her bereavement.[12] Although the emphasis on a saint's strong
attachment to offspring does not appear elsewhere in the sources we have been
examining,[13] other hagiographic texts do occasionally portray individuals deeply
fond of a relation who dies. In such cases, the death becomes such a hardship that
only a complete change of life, a conversio, can compensate for the loss.[14] After the
death of her daughters, Monegund also responds in this way, as she abandons
worldly concerns and resolves to lead an intense religious life of prayer, meditation,
and fasting.[15] Although still remaining at home, she lives enclosed in a private cell
and is accompanied in her austerities only by a slave girl, who eventually flees
because she cannot adjust to the new ascetic rigor that her mistress has imposed on
her.[16] But one impediment to conversio still looms over Monegund's life—her husband. At first, he seems to comply with the saint's desire to break off conjugal
relations, or at least no mention is made of his opposition to a wife who resolves
to remedy her sorrow by enclosing herself in the small quarters where she intends
to lead a holy life without the company of her spouse:

> Mourning and lamenting for the death of her children she did not stop weeping, day
> and night, and neither her husband nor her friends nor any of her relations could
> console her. Finally she came to herself, and said, "if I do not receive any consolation
> for the death of my daughters, I fear I may offend my Lord Jesus Christ. Thus forgetting

these laments I shall sing with the blessed Job, consoling myself thus: 'The Lord gave, and the Lord taketh away; blessed be the name of the Lord' (Job 1:21)." And saying that she took off her mourning clothes and had a small room arranged for her, which only had one small window by which she could see a little daylight. There, despising the vanities of the world and having nothing more to do with her husband, she devoted herself entirely to God.[17]

In our analysis of the preface, we noted that Gregory claims Monegund opened the door to paradise when she arrived and eventually settled at the church of Saint Martin. But she also attains a type of paradise as soon as she ceases relations with her husband and begins living a detached life while still in her household. As we might expect from what we previously observed, one indication is her relation to the environment. When her slave girl leaves, the saint, refusing to venture out for food, is ministered to by nature, which supplies her with the water, formerly fetched by the slave, needed to make bread and to break an unusually long fast. Not only does a snowfall allow her to maintain detachment and self-sufficiency, as the spring described in Caluppa's *Vita* does, but the event itself undergoes the same typological stylization found in that *Life* and in Fortunatus's story of Paternus:

> Five days passed after the departure of this girl, and her devout mistress had not taken her accustomed flour and water; she remained motionless, with Jesus Christ in her heart, in whom the one who trusts cannot be overthrown, not by any whirlwind or storm. Nor did she think to sustain her life by mortal food, but only by the word of God. . . . But as the human body cannot survive without using earthly things, she asked by a humble prayer that He who produced manna from heaven for a people when it was hungry and water from a rock when it was thirsty, might deign to give her food necessary to sustain her weak body.[18]

Another familiar indication that the saint lives in the realm of paradise comes when we learn that next to her cell Monegund has a small garden in which she occasionally strolls and enjoys looking at the plants. As with the Lives of Aemilianus and Martius, the space in which the saint lives is inviolable.[19] When a woman placing wheat to dry on the roof of a neighboring house begins to observe the saint in her natural setting, she is blinded, presumably for voyeuristic gazing, which threatens to profane the saint and her sacred ground. The contrast between the two persons and their places is aptly described by the reference to the onlooker as "filled with worldly care" as she toils with the harvest and "importunely" watches the saint, who strolls at leisure in her "little pleasure-garden": "She had, next to her cell, a small garden in which she used to walk for relaxation. She entered it one day, and walked around looking at the plants. A woman who had put wheat on the roof of her house in order to dry it, because it was a high place, began to watch the saint in an indiscreet way, filled with worldly thoughts. Soon her eyes darkened and she became blind."[20]

As the above passage implies, Monegund's rigorous life of ascetic enclosure leads to the acquisition of thaumaturgic power. She begins to attract the sick, who come to her for cures. But once her reputation as a healer grows, the saint must leave in order to avoid "vainglory." Now comes the complete rejection of and flight from all that pertains to family and married life. Leaving her home and her husband behind, she settles at the church of Saint Martin, where she again lives a life of enclosure and devotes herself to religious activities. There, too, the living holy woman gains a reputation as a healer (though her glory, as Gregory carefully stresses at later stages of the *Vita*, is kept in check by Martin's reputation as the preeminent heavenly intercessor):

> Glorified among her relations because of such prodigies, Monegund, in order to avoid the trap of vainglory, left her husband, her family, her whole house, and went, full of faith, to the basilica of the holy bishop Martin. . . . The blessed Monegund arrived at the basilica of Saint Martin, and there, on her knees in front of the tomb, she gave thanks to God for being able to see the holy tomb with her own eyes. She settled herself in a small room in which she gave herself every day to prayer, fasts, and vigils. And indeed this place was made glorious by her miracles.[21]

News of her power and way of life reach Monegund's husband, who responds by gathering his friends and setting out to fetch his wife.[22] The husband's attempt to retrieve the holy woman is one element in the *Life of Saint Monegund* that we do not find elsewhere in the *LVP* or in the Lives of male saints written by Fortunatus, even though both authors write about saints who had wives. The aristocratic Saint Gregory, for instance, had married Armentaria who bore him two sons, and Hilary also had a wife and a daughter. In both these Lives, however, the hagiographers emphasize the sexual restraint of the married holy men. At one point, Hilary's *Life* even turns into a diatribe advocating sexual renunciation,[23] and the author of Saint Gregory's story insists that sexual relations between Armentaria and her husband occurred only for the sake of having children, with mention also of how the saintly husband never "lusted after another woman."[24] The wives in these stories, unlike Monegund's spouse, never appear as impediments to the development of sanctity, though in the case of Saint Gregory there is a correlation between Armentaria's death and the widowed husband's wholehearted concentration on a religious life.[25] Moreover, other than references to the sexual moderation they share with their husbands and brief mentions of their deaths, the wives in these stories, unlike the depiction of Monegund's spouse, never receive the hagiographer's extended attention.[26]

The more important difference concerns the stories of those saints who, like Monegund, are portrayed as rejecting marriage in order to lead a religious life. In such accounts, the abandoned partner never reemerges as a threat to sanctity.[27] As far as the male saints of the *LVP* are concerned, once rejection of betrothal occurs and the holy man frees himself from family ties, an unencumbered religious life usually ensues. In the hagiography of both Fortunatus and Gregory, this rejection takes place at an early stage in a *Vita*'s narrative, and the episode is always the last we ever hear of marriage. With Fortunatus's accounts it is, like the topos of the *puer-senex*, another indication of how the saint sets himself apart from the ordinary lot of men to become a warrior of the Lord.

In Monegund's *Life*, however, even after her initial rejection of family, the interfering spouse continues to impede the saint's quest for paradise. Unlike the male saints, the holy woman is taken out of her desired religious environment by a husband who compels his wife to return home. Given what was previously observed regarding the depiction of the family in early hagiographic literature as a hindrance to sanctity, we should not be surprised to find Monegund's forced return portrayed as a frustrating diversion from the holy woman's quest toward a fulfilled sanctity. Although she is portrayed as maintaining her ascetic rigor even after being brought back, it is also clear that her holy life cannot be fully realized at home and in the shadow of her *vir*. Gregory relates that, after being taken back to Chartres, Monegund prayed for deliverance from her husband and begged Saint Martin that she be returned to Tours, where she could again lead the religious life she desired without any ties to a spouse, a request that the hagiographer claims, without any further elaboration, was granted:

> While these things [miracles] were happening, her husband, having heard of the reputation of the saint, assembled his friends and neighbours and came after her and brought her back with him and put her in that same cell in which she had lived before. But she did not cease from the work she was used to, and she gave herself over to continual prayer and fasting, so that in the end she might reach the place where she wanted to be. Again she began the path which she desired, begging for the help of Saint Martin, that he who gave her the desire might give her the means. She came to the basilica and returned to the same cell she had inhabited before; she stayed there without any trouble, without being sought for again by her husband.[28]

The Spiritual Bridegroom

What occurs, then, in Monegund's *Life* is a narrative development that is lacking in the *Vitae* of holy men. The scene of the spouse setting out to retrieve the saint takes on a prominence not yet encountered. This scene and the reference in the preface to the saint's gender are features of Monegund's story that never appear in the other *libelli* of the *LVP*.

But again, given the observations preceding this examination of Monegund's *Vita*, we can demarcate the precise lines of divergence. We already know, for instance, that the earliest hagiographic literature portrays holy individuals rejecting married life and that, insofar as such a rejection is a common sign of sanctity, it is not gender specific. Nor is spiritual marriage.[29] At least on the basis of the *LVP*, we should resist the common tendency to regard the holy women who reject their husbands as being the sole "brides of Christ" because even this designation is applicable to male and female saints alike. One of the more revealing but easily overlooked remarks concerning the relation between Christian warfare and spiritual marriage occurs in the second book of the *LVP*, where Gregory speaks of the religious instruction he received under the tutelage of Avitus, bishop of Clermont. From this instructor, Gregory came to know about the "friends" of God who took up the cross of an ascetic life. Without any reference to gender, Gregory then says that these *amici*, by their rigorous living, follow the bridegroom: "it is from him [Avitus] that I have been able to know that Jesus Christ, the Son of God, came for the salvation of the world, and to honor by worthy homage His friends who, taking the cross of an austere observance, have followed the Bridegroom."[30]

The conclusion that these remarks compel us to draw is that those men and women who imitate Christ—and this imitation entails the struggle toward perfection that the preface to Monegund's *Vita* and a host of other hagiographic texts describe in terms of warfare and athletic contest—become Christ's brides, with the path to the nuptial chamber being the way of the cross. *Imitatio Christi* is the consummation of a spiritual marriage entered into by all the saints, regardless of their gender.[31]

There are also specific examples in the *LVP* that show male saints rejecting earthly brides in favor of marriage with Christ. When the father of Patroclus dies, for example, the holy man's mother threatens to find a wife for her son. The saint, however, insists on being tonsured instead:

> When he returned home after the death of his father, he found his mother still alive. She said to him, "Now that your father is dead, my own sweet child, I live without any consolation. I am therefore going to look for a beautiful young girl, free-born, whom you can marry and help to provide some consolation for your mother in her widowhood." But he replied: "I shall never marry a worldly bride, but I shall do what my mind thinks best, with God's will." His mother did not understand, and asked what he meant. He did not explain, but went to find Arcadius, bishop of Bourges, and begged him to cut off his hair and admit him into the ranks of the clergy. And this, with God willing, the bishop did without delay.[32]

This is not an isolated example. When the father of Saint Gallus finds a woman compatible with his son's aristocratic background, the saint flees to a monastery, where he receives a tonsure and is thus saved from marriage. The abbot hesitates until he receives permission from the boy's father, whose response is worth quoting: "The abbot sent messengers to the father to see what he wanted to be done with his son. And he was saddened, and said, 'he is my first-born son, and for that reason I wanted him to marry, but if the Lord wishes to call him to His service, His will shall be done rather than mine.' "[33] Likewise, as alluded to earlier, Venantius is portrayed as being fond of his betrothed, to whom he offers the customary gifts as tokens of his affection and of his pledge to marry. But after he witnesses the miracles at Martin's tomb, he resolves to abandon the prospect of marriage and to serve Christ instead:

> Having arrived at the age of youth his parents engaged him in the bonds of betrothal. As happens with those of his age, he began to show that he was agreeable to a girl's love. He used to bring her presents of cups, and also shoes. Then it came to him, by the inspiration of God, to go to Tours. There was then a monastery near the basilica of Saint Martin, where Abbot Silvinus governed . . . a flock consecrated to the service of God. The holy man went there and, seeing Saint Martin's deeds of power, said to himself: "it seems to me that it would be better to serve Christ without blemish than to be involved through the bonds of matrimony with the pollution of the world. I shall abandon my betrothed from the land of Bourges and I shall join through faith the Catholic Church, so that I shall not sacrifice by my deeds the feelings which I have in my heart."[34]

Furthermore, with respect to marriage as an impediment to sanctity, evidence from the *LVP* suggests that men could be as vulnerable to retaliation for refusing matrimony as women and that the bonds of betrothal may have been as hard for the holy man to break as they were for his female counterpart. Lupicinus, for instance, is described as being forced into the "bonds of betrothal" against his will.[35] The case of Brachio even suggests deadly consequences for a male saint who chooses not to marry. Although mentioned only once and in passing, Gregory claims that after Brachio went to live with Aemilianus, the saint's brother often contemplated murdering the holy man for not marrying: Brachio "having spent two or three years with him [Aemilianus], learnt the psalter by heart. His brother, seeing that he did not wish to marry, often wanted to kill him."[36]

Also revealing is the conflict that arises from Leobardus's refusal to marry, described in the first chapter of that saint's *Life*. Here Gregory portrays, with unusual detail, the parents of the saint making persuasive arguments for marriage, even relying on Scripture to compel their son to conform to their wish. A vivid picture of an established bourgeois family emerges, one whose struggle to acquire property and commodities is in vain if the saint refuses to marry and provide future heirs to preserve the family's possessions.[37] In the end, the young saint is convinced. He submits to his parent's will, gives a ring to his future bride, offers the customary shoes, and celebrates with a feast. Luckily for the reluctant groom, Leobardus's father and mother die. With his parents and their insistence on marriage now gone and his brother a drunkard, the breakdown of the immediate family allows the saint to experience a burst of freedom described in one of the rare and more dramatic stories of conversion to the religious life told in Merovingian hagiography:

> When he had arrived at the age of legal majority his parents, following the custom of the world, wanted him to give to a young girl a pledge that he would take her as his wife. When he showed himself unwilling to do this his father said: "my dear son, why do you resist your father's will and do not marry, so that your seed can preserve our family for future generations? For we are just working in vain if no one comes after us to profit from it. Why fill our house with riches, if nobody from our family will use them? Why should we spend money buying so many slaves for our estates, if all of them are going to pass into the possession of a stranger? The Holy Scriptures attest that children must obey the voice of their parents, and beware if you show yourself disobedient towards your parents, lest you find yourself punished by heaven!" He spoke thus, even though there was in fact another son, thinking that since the boy was so young he would easily be able to get him to do what he wanted. Leobardus in the end gave a ring to his betrothed, offered her a kiss, bestowed shoes on her, and celebrated a feast on the day of the betrothal. After this his father and mother left this world, overtaken by the sleep of death, after having completed the course of their life. When Leobardus and his brother had finished the time of mourning, the former went to his brother's house, laden with wedding presents, and found him so drunk that he did not recognize Leobardus or let him into the house. Leobardus sighed and wept, and went away. He came to a hut filled with hay, and after tying up his horse and feeding it, he lay down on the hay to sleep. In the midst of the night he woke, got up from his bed and, stretching out his hands to heaven, gave thanks to Almighty God that he was, that he lived, and that God nourished him with his gifts, and he continued thus for a long time. He uttered long sighs, and abundant tears ran down his cheeks, and Almighty God, who foreknows and predestines men to be conformed to the image of His Son (cf. Rom. 8:29) touched his heart and inspired him to leave the world in order to serve the worship of God.[38]

All these examples suggest that both male and female saints, as Gregory portrays them in the *LVP*, are hindered by the demand to marry and that the rejection of this way of life in favor of a religious one makes the holy man as much a bride of Christ as the female saint, with both refusing an earthly spouse in order to follow the same bridegroom.

Important, too, is the setting in which the spiritual marriages in the *LVP* are consummated. After his emotional outpouring, Leobardus heads for the tomb of Saint Martin, hoping that the intercession of this patron will heal him, not with a physical cure—for he suffers from no bodily ailment—but by revealing to him the path of life he ought to take.[39] Similarly, Venantius, as we recall, refuses his betrothed after visiting Martin's tomb and settles in a monastery close to where the saint rests. Significantly, after refusing his mother's request to marry and finding clerical life unsatisfying, Patroclus builds an oratory that he consecrates with relics of Saint Martin.[40] The connection between spiritual marriage and Martin's cult is again found in the story of Monegund, with the tomb of Martin becoming the holy woman's focal point, the place where, according to Gregory, the saint attained paradise. Martin's burial spot is thus a magnet attracting the spiritually married who, in rejecting the earthly bonds of matrimony, connect themselves with Martin's tomb and relics, the physical intermediaries through which a union with the heavenly spouse is made.

Given that the author of the *LVP* regards both male and female saints as the brides of the one bridegroom, we can appreciate how slight but nonetheless significant is the change in the way Gregory tells the story of Monegund. The difference lies in how he utilizes the threat of marriage in the narrative. Male saints may be under the same coercion to establish or maintain a marital union as a female saint, but once the former manage to break off betrothment and familial obligations, an episode in a *Vita* which, when it does appear, comes always at the beginning of the story, the threat never rises again. With Monegund's *Vita*, however, the husband's pursuit after his charismatic wife adds another dimension to the story, a "chase scene," which we do not find elsewhere in the *LVP*. Yet, at the same time, the chase scene is only a development in the narrative that arises out of exactly the same circumstances in which the male saints avoiding marriage are depicted. Hence, if we speak in precise terms regarding the hindrance posed by marriage, the difference between Monegund and the other saints is really a matter of degree, and, as such, it cannot be regarded as a fundamental departure from Gregory's other narratives. Nor can this development be attributed to the peculiar embellishment of a male author because such episodes appear in hagiography produced by women.[41] In short, on the issue of marriage as an obstacle to sanctity, the contrast presented by Monegund's *Vita* consists not in the fact that she is hindered but in the extent to which she is hindered.

Furthermore, the case of Monegund as a holy person whose liberation is impeded due to her status as a married woman subject to the power of a husband also brings to light a connection that the scholarship on female saints of the Merovingian period has so far overlooked. The other group of individuals who are portrayed in the sources as subject to a dominating power are slaves. Indeed, in the *DVSM*, the female and male slaves who are liberated by Martin are as restricted, if not more so, by their social station as Monegund is by her husband. Significantly, their freedom, like Monegund's, is received at Martin's tomb.[42] Similarly, Brachio, as we recall, had to wait until his master died before he could be free to join Aemilianus in the religious life. Even more important is the similarity between Monegund and the saintly slave

Portianus, whose *Vita* we examined earlier. Although the episode with the master appears in the first chapter, where the saint is, unlike Monegund, once and for all freed from the obligation that binds him, the story also mentions that he has attempted to run away several times before and that he was always handed back to his owner rather than allowed to become a monk and remain in the monastery to which he fled. Like Monegund, he, too, is described as attempting to escape from a social bond that prohibits his religious fulfillment. While the pursuing owner does not ever reappear in the story as the husband does in the account of Monegund's life, we can still make the important observation that a slave and a married woman are both portrayed in the *LVP* as confronting oppressive and menacing social powers that attempt to remove the holy individuals from their desired religious environment. If the *LVP* is any indication, sanctity is easier to achieve if the holy person starts the quest for paradise as a freeborn man whose way of life cannot be assailed by masters and male spouses, forces of coercion from which the enslaved person and the married woman must emancipate themselves.

Monachae *and Miracles*

In the *Life of Saint Monegund*, we have discovered mostly minor alterations arising from the fact that Gregory is telling the story of a female saint. To determine whether Gregory developed the theme of the weak woman overcoming femininity with "virile fighting," let us turn to those episodes in the *Vita* describing the saint as a charismatic leader engaged in the ascetic life and in the thaumaturgic activity connected with Martin's cult at Tours.

After her enclosed life of prayer and fasting led at home, the saint also continues to maintain a rigorous ascetic routine at the church of Saint Martin, though the practices described are by no means more unusual than the behavior of the other saints described throughout the *LVP*. Regarding the transition from her life at Chartres, where she remained in the household of her husband, to her attainment of freedom at Tours, one point in particular suggests that the hagiographer is describing a consistent pattern of response to the holy person that does not change according to whether the saint is male or female. Directly following Gregory's claim that Monegund's husband never sought her again, he mentions that the holy woman began to attract followers, female followers to be precise, though Gregory mentions this fact without drawing any unusual attention to the gender of the saint's adherents.[43] This gathering of disciples after leaving secular pursuits is also consistent with those Lives in the *LVP* that describe male saints drawing to them bands of men and, in some cases, women to lead a monastic life.[44] There is, then, a kind of transference of kinship structure from the secular family and household to the religious one which, in the case of Monegund, consists of the women who look to the saint as a spiritual mother of a flock gathered at the *domus* of Martin's church, his tomb the hearth of the religious household.

After mentioning that Monegund attracted disciples, Gregory gives a description of her ascetic habits. In almost every respect, the account resembles what we have already observed in the other *Vitae*. Like the other Lives, the gender of the saint performing these activities never becomes an issue. She eats coarse bread and rarely drinks wine, and then only when diluted with water, practices mentioned in Saint Gregory's Life.[45] And like Martius, who rested on the hard surface of his carved-out cave, Monegund also refuses to sleep on a soft bed of straw. Instead, like the monks subject to the Pachomian rule, she lies only on a simple "rush mat" (mattas), which is sometimes placed on the ground.[46] Monegund herself teaches the other women how to make such mats, and their occupation in this work evidently constitutes part of their religious routine, a practice not mentioned elsewhere in the LVP but also found in the monastic literature of the desert saints:

> She gathered together a small number of nuns in that place, and stayed there, perse-vering in faith and prayer, eating only bread made of barley and not drinking any wine, except a little on feast days, and then only diluted with much water. She did not have a soft bed of hay or fresh straw, but only one of interlaced twigs, which are commonly called "mats"; she put this upon a bed frame or on the ground, and it served her as a bench, a mattress, a pillow, a bed-spread, in a word all that she needed for a bed. She taught those whom she had brought to live with her how to make these mats. And living there, praising God, she gave to many sick people, after she had prayed, healing cures.[47]

Though the reference to making and sleeping on the rush mat may suggest that Gregory is describing an Eastern influence on Monegund's life, the description of her religious routine remains in every way consistent with what we find throughout the LVP, a fact that bears directly on the issue of the reference to the inferior sexus mentioned at the beginning. Unlike the previously observed connection between the main contents of a preface and the Vita that follows, Gregory never again dwells on gender, even though he brought this issue to the forefront of the Vita by opening with remarks about how women also fight in the struggle to attain holiness. There is also no special attention given to the fact that her followers are women. Her connection to these female disciples shows no fundamental contrast with the de-scriptions of the relationships male religious leaders have with their adherents. Later on in the Life, her followers are portrayed as lamenting the passing of their teacher, referring to her as "mother."[48] But a scene that describes a group of mournful disciples who are expressing sorrow when the saint on whom they have depended is about to die occurs elsewhere in the LVP, as well as in the writing of Sulpicius Severus; the only difference is that the sad lot mourns the departure of a pater rather than a mater.[49]

All of these observations lead to the conclusion that, on the whole, the way Gregory tells the story of Monegund and the ideal of sanctity that this Vita promotes are not fundamentally altered from what we find throughout the LVP. For the most part, in the only account of a female saint found in the collection, the author main-tains a consistency with the other libelli (insofar as there is a recognizable consistency present in such a diverse assortment of Lives). Although the subject of female saints is presented problematically at the beginning of the account and the mere focus on gender is entirely out of keeping with the rest of the LVP, the narration itself never elaborates on these points, and Monegund is consistently presented throughout nei-ther as a man nor as a woman. She is, rather, the same sexless figure we find throughout this collection of Lives. We may conclusively say that the author does not problematize gender in the actual story as he does in the preface. Putting aside this stress on gender in the beginning, the narrative itself paints a picture of an ordinary saint, a holy person who is, like the others portrayed in the *LVP*, "neither male nor female."[50]

Contrary to what we would have expected from the *Vita*'s preface, there is no description of a saint struggling to overcome "feminine weakness." What we find, instead, is a depiction of a powerful, living holy woman whose charisma draws the attention of men and women alike who seek cures. In fact, so popular is Monegund as a healer that twice in the *Life* Gregory stresses how the power of this living thaumaturge did not usurp Martin's place as the supreme heavenly patron. On one occasion, the cure of a blind man is even shared between the two; the living saint illuminated one eye, and Martin secured the sight of the other from his tomb. Furthermore, judging from the words Gregory ascribes to a blind woman who sought the help of Monegund rather than Martin, criteria quite apart from gender determine the acquiring of thaumaturgic power:

> A blind woman who was brought there begged her to place her hands on her, but she replied: "what is it between you and me, men of God? Does not Saint Martin live here, who each day shines with the work of his miracles? Go to him and pray that he may deign to visit you. For I am only a sinner; what can I do?" But the woman persisted in her request, saying "God daily accomplishes remarkable deeds through those who fear His name. That is why I came to you as a suppliant, since you have received the grace of healing from God." And the servant of God, greatly moved, placed her hands on the buried eyes, and immediately the cataracts disappeared.[51]

The fact that Gregory portrays a living holy woman who shares the healing responsibilities with Martin obviously suggests that gender is not a barrier to performing *virtutes*. The fact that Monegund is a woman does not deter the throngs of the desperately ill, who are portrayed in the *Vita* as going to the church of Saint Martin to appeal to this female thaumaturge for help in a way that is reminiscent of the accounts given in the *DVSM*, with the healing power of both saints overlapping. All of her cures are signs of her holiness; none of them is presented as an example of how she compensated for being among the "inferior sex," which makes this designation in the preface out of place in light of Gregory's portrait of Monegund as a healer. In spite of the opening remarks on gender, the rest of the *Vita* does not appear to have undergone any drastic modifications in the way Gregory generally depicts holy people throughout the *LVP*. With respect to the saint's ascetic practices and her miraculous power, the depiction of Monegund conforms with the description of other monastically inclined saints in the collection.[52] Accordingly, in this instance, the ideal of sanctity embodied in the portrait of an ascetic thaumaturge is neither modified nor compromised because a male author wrote about a female saint.

At this point, rather than now attempting to explain the incongruity between the author's concern with gender in the preface and his evident indifference to this issue in the actual narrative, let us turn to Fortunatus's depiction of Radegund to consider how another prolific male writer of this period tells the story of a female saint.

Fortunatus's *Life of Saint Radegund*

Throughout this study, the prefaces again and again demand our attention, not only because they consistently exhibit important rhetorical patterns that have implications for the whole of a *Vita* but also because in the introductions the authors tend to develop ideas and express concerns not specifically addressed or directly articulated in the actual stories, so that their opening statements frequently reveal an extrahagiographic context into which the narratives fit. In a sense, the preface is where Fortunatus and Gregory suggest how the subsequent work ought to be interpreted.

In the case of the LVP, our analysis of the prefaces uncovered how a biblically oriented conception of salvation history frames this collection of *Vitae*. From our understanding of the prefaces, we also were able to pinpoint the divergences in the way Gregory approached the telling of Monegund's life and to gauge accurately the extent to which that story deviated from the other works we examined. With Fortunatus's Lives, we noticed that through the elaborate rhetoric of his openings the author strives to connect the subject of a biography with the patron and commissioner of the *Vita*, to whom the work is dedicated. The show of rhetorical force and the insistence on the addressees' eloquence serve as an impressive, if convoluted, claim to episcopal power. These *Vitae*, then, become, in turn, the narratives of that power's expression by recording the instances of conflict from which the holy heroes always emerge victorious.

But the preface to Radegund's *Vita* does not at all resemble what we observed in the other compositions of Fortunatus. To begin with, the work contains no dedication, neither to a bishop, as we usually find accompanying the other *Vitae*, nor to the abbess and nuns of Radegund's convent. No evidence exists, then, to suggest that the work was commissioned, though obviously this possibility cannot be ruled out. In addition, the preface does not show the same inflated style that we find in the other introductions. One other major difference appears in the opening remarks of Radegund's Life. Similar to what we observed Gregory do in the preface to Monegund's *Vita*, Fortunatus suddenly sees the preface as an opportunity to address the issue of the "inferior sex." As we now know from our previous examination of his work, Fortunatus's attention to a saint's gender definitely marks a change in the way he begins the story of a saint's life, and this divergence, like the one in the opening to Monegund's *Vita*, is clearly due to the fact that the author's subject is now female. Once again, then, the issue of gender comes to the fore and is problematized by the writer. As with Gregory's preface to Monegund's Life, the fact that Fortunatus is about to tell the story of a holy woman rather than a man calls for a different rhetorical strategy to compensate for the female "frailty" of his subject. Hence, the preface to Radegund's Life fundamentally contrasts with Fortunatus's Lives of male saints. And insofar as gender assumes an importance never encountered in the other *Vitae*, both Gregory and Fortunatus indicate that a female saint cannot be initially presented in the same way as that of a male saint. Another similarity between the two hagiographers is that, in the preface to Radegund's Life, the compensation strategy entails emphasizing the masculine potential of holy women. Such females can overcome their femininity, which is the mark of weakness, by their brave victories in their manly struggle toward holiness.

However, as we shall see in a moment, one important difference emerges between the ways Gregory and Fortunatus utilize the compensation strategy. With Gregory, the issue of gender certainly assumes prominence when he introduces the imagery of contest and includes women among the manly fighters. But then the concern with Monegund's femininity as an impediment to holiness quickly fades, so that the rest of the preface remains consistent with what we had previously observed. Indeed, not only did the problem of the *inferior sexus* go undeveloped in the preface but also it never again arises in the *Vita* itself; the only gender related incident has more to do with the social vulnerability of a married female saint than, as the preface at first seemed to suggest, any kind of inherent defect in Monegund due solely to her being a woman. In contrast with the opening remarks on Monegund, the preface to Radegund's *Life* dwells at length on the "womanly sex" (*sexu muliebri*). In fact, virtually the whole preface is devoted to this issue.

Moreover, not merely how much attention Fortunatus gives to the problem posed by a female saint distinguishes this preface from the one Gregory wrote to introduce Monegund. The substantial difference is where Fortunatus focuses his attention. Even though he initially claims that women overcome their physical weakness by the power of their minds, Fortunatus concentrates on the corporeal, not the mental, aspects of holy women in his preface to Radegund's *Life*. Unlike Gregory's opening remarks in Monegund's *Vita*, Fortunatus's introduction deals explicitly with the female body. In fact, the spiritual nature of women is described in physical terms and is rooted in imagery drawn from female bodily features. This focus on the body has two aspects, the first more elaborated on in the preface than the second, and the second, unlike the first, developed to its fullest extent in the actual narrative that follows.

The first aspect is the physical capacity of women to contain life within the body. Echoing 2 Corinthians 4:7, Fortunatus describes women as "earthen vessels" holding hidden heavenly treasures. He develops this view by claiming that Christ with his riches occupies the interior regions of women or, given how *visceribus* may be translated, dwells in their wombs. In addition to presenting female sanctity as a corporeal symbiosis between holy women and a womb-dwelling Christ, the emphasis on overcoming frailty leads to the other bodily aspect of female sanctity in this preface. Earlier, we noticed that suffering, "taking up the cross," is one way in which both male and female saints unite with Christ in spiritual marriage. But in Fortunatus's preface, this suffering is described not so much as a contest with an opponent, as we saw in the opening to Monegund's *Vita*, but in terms of self-mortification. Given how little Fortunatus has emphasized mortification throughout his *Vitae* and that the subject is never addressed in the other prefaces, we should treat the reference to women *mortificantes se* as another fundamental contrast with what we previously observed in his prose biographies. Considering Fortunatus's introductory remarks as a whole and in light of the unusual punishments that are described later in Radegund's *Vita*, the preface implies that for women the battle is not merely against sensuality, as is the case for all saints, but against the female body itself:

So rich is the bounty of our Redeemer that in the womanly sex he celebrates brave victories, and those very women who are more frail in body he renders glorious by the power of their illustrious mind. Christ makes those who are weak in birth strong with faith, so that, when they are crowned with merits, those who seem feeble accumulate the praise of the Creator by whom they are made productive through having the hidden treasures of heaven in their "earthen vessels" (2 Cor. 4:7). The king dwelling inside of them with his treasures is Christ. These women who mortify themselves in this world . . . seeking to live for God, have been joined to paradise for the glory of the Redeemer.[53]

The "Tortrix"

Although a stress on bodily mortification appears as a regular feature throughout much of hagiographic literature, such an emphasis, as we know, never figures prominently in the other prefaces written by Fortunatus. In this particular case, the writer's view of the saint's gender has led to a shift in emphasis from an ideal of sanctity in which asceticism was largely curtailed to one in which physical mortification assumes a primary place. While asceticism remains restrained and controlled in his depiction of male saints, self-inflicted suffering, graphically detailed, is the distinguishing feature of Radegund's holiness. The main conflict in this Vita is between the saint and her body. The heightening of such a struggle contrasts not only with Fortunatus's other Lives but also with Gregory's depiction of a female saint (though the author of the LVP does, indeed, as previously indicated, portray male saints engaging in severe ascetic behavior). Furthermore, what is especially striking in Radegund's Vita and resembles none of the other narratives examined so far is the development of mortification as a dominant theme rather than simply a stock element in the saint's profile, which is what we normally find in Fortunatus's hagiography.

At the initial stage of the Vita, this emphasis on mortification takes the form of the familiar claim that the saint desired and earned martyrdom. Early on, Fortunatus relates that the young saint endured persecution in the form of her domestic chores and her indefatigable care for other children, whom she feeds and washes. This initial description follows the same pattern of the other Lives previously discussed. The young Radegund is a puella-senex whose activities as a young girl will be the very ones performed as an adult, just as each male saint in Fortunatus's corpus is a puer-senex, who also leads a sanctified life from the beginning.[54] At this point, too, the association of the saint with the achievement of martyrdom during the time of the church's peace has as little supporting evidence behind it as do the other instances in which Fortunatus attempts to portray his male saints as martyrs. Thus, at least at the narrative's beginning, nothing substantially deviates from Fortunatus's usual practice in delineating childhood and attempting on the rhetorical level to link the austerities endured by the holy person with the experience of martyrdom.[55]

However, unlike his other Vitae, Fortunatus proceeds to record physical austerities that gradually increase in the degree of suffering and exceed all ascetic norms so that the claim to martyrdom is no longer a rhetorical token, as in the other accounts, but is substantiated by meticulous descriptions unprecedented in the rest of his hagiographic corpus. In the fifth chapter, for instance, the concern with Radegund's body leads to a description of how the saint conducted herself as the wife in the bed of a Merovingian king. Fortunatus relates that when Radegund reclined at night with Clothar, she used to ask to leave his bed on the pretense of relieving herself. Once at the privy, she presses her body on the cold surface of the floor while praying. According to Fortunatus, she experienced the death of her flesh at such moments. By the time she returns to the royal chambers, neither the fire from the hearth nor, as Fortunatus carefully notes, the heat of the bed can warm the now numb spouse of King Clothar:

> While reclining with the ruler at night, she asked to get up on account of human necessity. Rising, she went out of the bedroom and for a long time, with her hair shirt thrown off, she leaned down in prayer in front of the privy so that, warmed by the spirit alone, she would lie pierced by the cold, completely dead with regard to the flesh. Not caring about the torments of the body, she, [with her] mind intent on paradise, regarded what was being endured as a trifle, so that she might not be considered worthless to Christ. Then she returned to the bedroom and was scarcely able to become warm, either by the fire-place or the bed. Concerning her, it was said to the king that he had a monk as a wife rather than a queen. The king was angered by this.[56]

The tortures increase, especially in Lent and after Radegund has left Clothar to found the monastery of the Holy Cross. According to Fortunatus, one of the forty-day periods she spends bound in chains so tightly wrapped around her body that they become embedded in her skin. Unable to take off the irons at the end of Lent, she must cut her flesh and bleed her body until the fetters become loose enough to remove:

> But I shudder to speak of the pain she inflicted on herself after all these labors. Once, for the forty day period, she bound herself on the neck and arms with three broad chains. While putting them on, she had tied the chains so tightly around her body [that] her tender skin grew over them and enclosed the hard iron. When the fast finished and she wanted to remove the chains that were enclosed under the skin, she was not able. The flesh was cut by the circulet through her back and chest over the iron of the chains, so that the flow of blood nearly drained her little body to the last drop.[57]

As the more biographical section of the *Vita* comes to a close, the extreme self-tortures also culminate. At the twenty-sixth chapter, Fortunatus details how Radegund once heated a brass plate with the image of Christ on it and then applied this object to her skin. On another occasion, she ordered a wash basin to be filled with burning coals and brought to her cell, where she again privately burns her flesh, the culminating act of self-mortification. Fortunatus now refers to Radegund as a *tortrix*, who, although not living during the period of persecution, became a martyr through her own initiative:

> On another occasion, she ordered that a brass plate be made in the sign of Christ. When this plate was heated, she pressed it very deeply onto two places of her body. The flesh was scorched completely. Thus, with her spirit on fire, she caused her limbs to burn. During one Lent, that *tortrix* devised something more severe beyond the harsh

fasting and torment of a parched thirst. While the hair shirt, a file with rough bristles, is still ravaging her tender body, she orders a wash-basin full of burning coals to be brought [into her cell]. Then, after the others leave, with her limbs trembling, her mind is armed for punishment, [as] she thought [that] because these were not times of persecution, she might become a martyr by her own [doing]. At this time, so that she might cool her inflamed mind, she decides to burn her body. She applies the glowing hot brass. The burning limbs sizzle. The skin is consumed, dug out deepest where the heat touched it. Quietly, she covers the holes, but the putrefying blood shows what the voice did not utter in punishment. Thus the woman willingly received so many bitter [torments] for the sweetness of Christ. Then it happened that what she herself concealed, the miracles would not keep silent.[58]

Quite clearly, Radegund's martyrdom differs from all the others described throughout Fortunatus's Lives. The holy men in the other *Vitae* are never portrayed as suffering brutal physical torments, self-inflicted or otherwise. More to the point, the previous instances of martyrdom are specially crafted rhetorical pieces that attempt to fit the male saints into a category of sanctity to which they have only a dubious claim. As we recall, to compensate for the historical circumstances of the church's peace, Fortunatus attempts to create on the rhetorical level the polarized opposition of the *passiones*, by stylizing his saints as martyrs when they encounter a threatening antagonist whom the saint must combat. In this way, the holy man earned martyrdom purely by the desire to suffer. With the exception of what we may infer from the comparison between Abel and Marcellus, the only other bloodless martyr was Germanus, whose ascetic practices were more moderate than what we find in the passages that detail Radegund's mortifications and even some of the saints mentioned in the LVP. The fact that the account of Radegund's suffering is a description of actualized rather than potential torments makes her the only holy person in Fortunatus's corpus whose wish for martyrdom is genuinely fulfilled. As an indication, we need only recall that, in the culminating act of self-torture, Fortunatus does not claim that the saint "would have become a martyr if only a persecutor were at hand," as he invariably does in the other *Vitae*, but claims that she actually "became a martyr" (*fieret martyra*). The detailed descriptions of this achievement substantiate what is normally only a topos in Fortunatus's biographies.

Furthermore, in the case of Radegund, the distinction between the martyr of persecution and the bloodless one of asceticism is no longer maintained. Her own ascetic feats are presented as inducing a death experience and the physical pain normally associated with persecution. This point is clear not only from the author's reference to Radegund's being physically dead (*tota carne praemortua*) after chilling her body but also from the accounts that describe the shedding of blood and the burning of flesh. Thus, Radegund's *Vita* is the only instance we find in Fortunatus's corpus in which the private torments of an ascetic entail the punishments normally associated with the public martyrdoms of early Christianity. This type of martyr corresponds with nothing previously observed in Fortunatus's *Vitae*, and it remains unusual even within the broader context of early hagiographic literature.[59] With respect to the author's account of how the saint treats her body, the *Vita sanctae Radegundis* is unquestionably an anomaly within Fortunatus's hagiographic corpus.

There is also some indication that the punishments of Radegund are directly related to the problem of attaining sanctity in a female body, an issue that the prefaces of Fortunatus and Gregory both address, though the latter does not dwell on gender the way Fortunatus does or ever develop his remarks concerning the "inferior sex." We noticed earlier that Fortunatus named mortification in the preface as one of the attributes of female sanctity. Obviously, the incidents in the *Vitae* just mentioned substantiate this claim, but there may also be grounds for regarding the methods of mortification as gender specific. In all the instances of torment discussed by Fortunatus, the upper body appears to bear the brunt of pain, and the scenes necessarily assume the bare exposure of flesh. For example, the incident at the privy suggests, depending on how *iactato cilicio* may be best translated, that either the bare chest of the saint was exposed to the frigid floor, or else the holy woman placed the hair shirt between her upper body and the ground, so that this region of her body suffered both the cold and the pricks of the garment.[60] In either case, the description implies that some form of pectoral nakedness is involved because, immediately following the phrase *iactato cilicio*, Fortunatus suggestively adds that Radegund was warm "in spirit alone" (*iactato cilicio, ut solo calens spiritu, iaceret*). Again, in the description of her bondage during Lent, it is clear not only that the irons were applied directly to the bare skin but also that the upper body, specifically the back and chest (*caro per dorsum atque pectus . . . est incisa*), was the area that had to be cut and bled for the fetters to be removed.[61]

Most significant of all is the account of Radegund's burning herself with the brass plate. In his description of the mortification, Fortunatus specifically refers to Radegund's pressing the heated plate onto two places of her body: *laminam in signo Christi oricalcam, quam accensam in cellula locis duobus corporis altius sibi inpressit.*[62] The figure on the plate is also important. Fortunatus mentions only that the brass object is made *in signo Christi*, without drawing the necessary connection between the image and the method of mortification: If the plate is heated, then the "sign of Christ" would be branded onto the skin.[63] The obvious implication is that Fortunatus is describing Radegund as scorching her breasts with the image of Christ. On the whole, then, the methods of self-torture described by the author seem designed to afflict that region of the saint's body that is most ostensibly female.

Fortunatus also gives one other clue to suggest that the suffering of the saint is related to gender. When he ends chapter 26, he does not say that a saint suffered these mortifications but that a "woman willingly received so many bitter [torments] for the sweetness of Christ" (*sic femina pro Christi dulcedine tot amara libenter excepit*). In its context, the implication of the remark is that the ability to devise and endure self-inflicted suffering, which entails, as we have seen, the mutilation of the female body, verifies Radegund's sanctity. Fortunatus explicitly makes a connection between self-mortification and thaumaturgic power. Immediately following the reference to a *femina* enduring these torments, the author ends his account of Radegund's tortures by saying: *hinc actum est, quod ipsa abdiderit, hoc miracula non tacerent.* Thus, unlike Gregory, Fortunatus has developed to the fullest extent the theme of "frail" women overcoming their weakness. Radegund bears the marks of Christ rather than femininity. Evidently, she is a saint because she is no longer hindered by being a woman.[64] Having conquered what was female, she has earned her thaumaturgic power, as the last line of chapter 26 just quoted indicates. At this point, the course of the *Vita* changes, with Fortunatus's focus exclusively on the saint's miracles.

So far, we have been treating the graphic descriptions of Radegund's self-torture purely as Fortunatus's literary presentation of a female saint. This approach assumes that the portrait of the holy woman's eccentric mortifications is the literary creation of a hagiographer who is consciously altering his approach to telling a saint's life because his subject is a holy person whose gender is perceived as a mark of weakness, a "frailty" that must be compensated for by descriptions of unusual ascetic feats. By the time the narration of *virtutes* comes, the female saint is the physical equivalent of a man, or what modern researchers call a *virago*.

One challenge to this understanding of Fortunatus's presentation comes from the historian who treats the relevant texts of this *Vita* as the work of a contemporary observer who is simply recording the extreme mortifications in which his historical subject engaged.[65] In this view, Fortunatus is regarded as the accurate reporter of events, a reliable writer relating what he saw or heard while in the saint's company and religious community. The argument may be made that the difference between his *Life of Saint Radegund* and his other *Vitae* is due to the peculiar behavior of his subject rather than the biographer's strategy for portraying female sanctity.

In dealing with the question of Fortunatus as an accurate reporter, we should first of all acknowledge the impossibility of verifying his descriptions of self-torture, especially since they are not corroborated by the other contemporaries who wrote about Radegund.[66] Nevertheless, we may even concede to the view that Fortunatus simply related the saint's mortifications and still be able to show how this understanding of the author as a historically reliable narrator of Radegund's punishments cannot be accurate. The most damaging evidence against Fortunatus as a trustworthy reporter comes not from what he says but from what he leaves out. In his version of her life, Fortunatus fails to mention some of the most important and controversial events involving not only Radegund but also the city of Poitiers, where she established her convent. Both Gregory of Tours and Baudonivia relate the scandal surrounding the arrival of the true cross, which Radegund obtained from Emperor Justin II in 569. According to these authors, Maroveus, the bishop of the city, refused to accept the cross and departed when it arrived, leaving its official reception to be carried out by another bishop, who, after some royal persuasion, agreed to perform the rites befitting the arrival of such a relic.[67] This glaring omission is made all the more noticeable by the fact that Fortunatus himself was involved in the ceremony. It was, after all, for this occasion that he composed his famous *Vexilla regis*, the processional hymn honoring the relic's arrival. Moreover, Gregory of Tours comments on how this same bishop repeatedly refused to support Radegund's monastic foundation, despite appeals to do so from the saint.[68] In addition, both Gregory and Baudonivia suggest that Maroveus unnecessarily delayed his arrival at the saint's funeral, where a crowd of nuns and mourners were kept waiting for days until Gregory himself consented to preside over her burial.[69] Fortunatus therefore omits the very affairs that most aroused the animosity of the bishop and were crucial events in the life of the holy woman, her convent, and the people of Poitiers, at least according to the testimony of Gregory and Baudonivia.[70] In light of these omissions, the obvious conclusion is that even if Fortunatus is relating exactly how Radegund mortified herself, he is still consciously choosing what to include and what to exclude from his account. He has left out all evidence that is damaging to episcopal authority. At the same time, he has accentuated the *tortrix* features of the saint's profile. Therefore, in the case of Radegund, the inclusion and exclusion of material, even if what is included accurately describes the saint's behavior, is clearly subject to the writer's conscious choice of how he wishes to portray this holy woman. Given what information we do have from the other hagiographers about Radegund, we are compelled to conclude that Fortunatus deliberately stylized his saint as a tamer of the flesh rather than as an episcopal antagonist and that this stylization arises from a literary predisposition regarding the depiction of holy women, as we might well expect from what the prefaces to the Lives of Radegund and, to a less extent, Monegund reveal about the problem of presenting a woman as a saint. Because of these striking omissions, we cannot say that Fortunatus is a detached observer whose commitment to historical accuracy entailed recording the extreme mortifications endured by one of his contemporaries. On the contrary, he evidently chose to leave out what others regarded as important in the saint's history. This is not to say that Fortunatus's self-mortifying saint is purely a literary fabrication. Radegund could very well have been a *tortrix*; however, other authors as intimately connected with the saint as Fortunatus suggest that she was much more. As we shall see in greater detail later, by comparison with the other descriptions of Radegund's holiness, it may be argued that Fortunatus's portrait of the mortifier offers only a partial picture, an unbalanced distortion of a more complex biographical subject.

The Episcopal Image and Radegund's Vita

Besides their unusual nature, another reason that the mortifications stand out so strikingly is that they appear in a Life which, in most other respects, coincides with what we previously observed in our discussion on Fortunatus's depiction of holy men. One important similarity is that, even though the saint is a woman, she still has, at least nominally, clerical status. When she leaves King Clothar after that ruler murdered her brother, Radegund succeeds in having Bishop Medard of Noyon consecrate her a deaconess, though precisely what this clerical rank signifies at this time and why it was preferable to becoming a nun are matters that have yet to be adequately resolved.[71]

Even if we cannot ascertain the function of a *diaconissa* in the Merovingian church,[72] the miracles attributed to Radegund in Fortunatus's *Vita* reveal how closely she resembles the clerical sanctity represented in the other Lives. The nun Animia, for instance, on the verge of dying from dropsy, dreams that Radegund and her abbess come to pour oil over her head and cover her in new clothes.[73] On another occasion, a nun suffering from chills and a fever is immersed in water, after which she is brought wine to drink and is then completely restored.[74] Cures that involve oil, water, and wine clearly show the sacramental significance behind Radegund's thaumaturgic power.[75] Those who are ill receive a cure by symbolically participating in liturgical services.

Also significant is how Radegund's Vita shows the same concern with the saint's social function that we find in Fortunatus's other Lives. Like the bishops he wrote about, Radegund is also portrayed as engaged in a variety of charitable activities on behalf of the disadvantaged classes in Merovingian society. She washes and feeds the poor and extracts their lice and worms before preparing them a meal.[76] She turns no one away, even embracing and kissing lepers.[77] In addition, her thaumaturgic power extends to a social cause commonly associated with the exercise of episcopal power. Besides her entreaties to Clothar to act mercifully toward the condemned, Fortunatus's account also features the freeing of prisoners, one of the chief concerns of holy bishops.[78] Like the other Vitae in his corpus, these prison freeings again show the holy person as the opponent of a cruel secular authority and the champion of those who are presented as being subjected to an oppressive form of punishment by a political power. In one instance, he shows a group of prisoners who demand to be set free when Radegund walks near their place of confinement. After inquiring about the commotion, the holy queen's attendants claim that the noise comes from a throng of beggars seeking alms. But later that night, after a prison official attempts to quiet the jailed men, Radegund's prayers cause the chains to be broken, and the condemned burst out of the prison and run immediately to their holy liberator. The passage shows the same kind of overt political message found in the other accounts of freeing that were earlier discussed. She gains the allegiance of those whom the Vita presented as oppressed, and those who supported this oppression become, in turn, the condemned: "when the chains were broken, those who were freed ran from the prison to the holy woman. Once this was known, those who lied to the blessed lady saw that they were the condemned, while the ones who had been condemned were free from their chains."[79]

The last miracle recorded in the Life also shows Radegund encountering a political figure, from whom she demands the release of prisoners. In a dream, she appears to the tribune Domolenus, and, very much like a bishop, on behalf of the "people" (plebs) she requests that a church be built. After securing the establishment of a new church, the saint is portrayed curing the tribune, who is slowly suffocating from a contracted throat. The cure is given, however, only on condition that he free those incarcerated at a prison under his jurisdiction.[80] Once again, illness and health are dependent on a secular power's willingness to comply with the demands of a saint. Such a scene resembles the encounters between bishops and secular rulers described throughout Fortunatus's hagiography, instances in which secular authority is portrayed as succumbing to episcopal power. In fact, just prior to the account involving Domolenus, Radegund's thaumaturgic power is compared to the greatest of bishops, at least in the view of Merovingian hagiographers, Saint Martin. Thus, as far as the depiction of the saint's social function is concerned, the portrait of Radegund is very much in the mold of the episcopal biographies. In the Vita of this female saint, Fortunatus again paints a dismal picture of the conditions under which people live, and he presents the holy woman as offering the remedy for social ills. His saint is the alternative to disease, hunger, and the brutality of imprisonment. Like the holy bishops, this saintly queen and monastic founder offers food, cures, and protection from oppressive secular leaders so that the image of Radegund, like the other saints in his corpus, reflects the needs of the oppressed segments of the population, whose only solace, at least according to the hagiographic evidence, comes from the leadership of powerful ecclesiastical representatives.

Becoming Male

In the writings of both Gregory and Fortunatus, we have detected changes arising when the subject of a *Vita* is a holy woman. If the saint is female, then both authors attempt to compensate for the gender by stressing the masculine qualities that holy women can acquire through the living of an ascetic life. In the case of Monegund's *Vita*, on one hand, the alteration remains confined to the preface, and the Life itself shows no fundamental contrasts with the other *Vitae* of the LVP. Fortunatus, on the other hand, heightened the role of mortification in his *Vita sanctae Radegundis* to an unprecedented level, with a quasi-pornographic focus on the saint's body and a narrative development that leads gradually toward a climax of pain.[81] With respect to mortification, this *Vita* resembles none of the others in Fortunatus's corpus, and its detailing of torments cannot be attributed solely to the eccentric self-abuse of the historical Radegund. Furthermore, after an examination of certain key passages, we discovered textual evidence suggesting that the aim of these mortifications is the eradication of femininity, with self-tortures culminating in the acquisition of thaumaturgic power or, to use the term that explicitly indicates the close connection between manliness and the ability to perform miracles, *virtus*.

However, rather than accounting for these divergences historically by attributing them only to the misogyny of the hagiographers and their patriarchal church, we can, instead, attempt to offer a literary explanation based on the depiction of women in the hagiography written before the Merovingian era. Naturally, we cannot discuss this subject in the detail it deserves, but we can, at least, highlight a few fundamental texts whose overall importance, in the history of hagiographic literature and in the development of the ideal of sanctity, no one disputes. These sources can reveal the larger literary and, to an extent, religious context behind the Lives of Monegund and Radegund. By proceeding in this way, an explanation may be offered for what we have observed in these *Vitae*, an explanation based on an understanding of a literary tradition whose continuity with the writings of Gregory and Fortunatus has been largely unexplored by researchers of female sanctity in the Merovingian period.[82]

From Maccabees to the Desert

The most suitable starting point is 2 Maccabees 7, one of the key scriptural texts on which the ideal of Christian martyrdom is founded.[83] What makes the seventh chapter of the second book of Maccabees so appropriate is that it not only provides a biblical foundation for heroic behavior in the face of religious persecution but also prominently portrays a woman and so offers the chance to see how a text fundamental to the first stage in hagiography's evolution presents female sanctity.

The chapter recounts a particular instance of persecution carried out by King Antiochus IV (d. 163 B.C.) against a Jewish mother and her seven sons, all of whom refuse to violate their dietary laws by eating pork. The mother is forced to watch the torture of her children, who are, starting with the oldest and ending with the youngest, mutilated in various ways before being burned.

The mother, who is the central figure in the account, can hardly be called a *virago*—that is, a woman with the attributes of a man. The references to the female body are positive, and, in one instance, the mother even recalls how she bore her youngest son in the womb and breast fed him for three years after his birth.[84] But in the description of the mother as she urges her sons to be brave while enduring the tortures, one important feature has special significance in light of what we have seen in the accounts of Monegund and Radegund. Just before relating the words of encouragement that she gave each child, the author claims that in bravely exhorting her sons the mother replaces a feminine mentality with masculine fortitude: "she was urging on each of them in the language of their forefathers, bravely filled with wisdom and inserting manly courage into her womanly mind."[85]

Thus, in one of the most important scriptural passages depicting martyrdom, the exemplary behavior of a religious woman entails the ability to assume what the author regards as a masculine disposition, which here represents the breakthrough of courage at a decisive moment when the power to endure intense suffering for the sake of keeping the faith is required for the attainment of sanctity. Let us note, then, that at the beginning of hagiography's development in the Christian West, we find an association of martyrial sanctity with masculinity. In addition, given the context of the phrase *masculinum animum inserens*, we can already begin to formulate an idea of sanctity based on the way the author of Maccabees has implicated gender into the meaning of martyrdom. If the steadfast commitment to a religious way of life in spite of persecution is regarded as a mark of masculinity, then the female who attains sanctity through a form of martyrdom has thus crossed a threshold and passed from what the author evidently regards as an inherent weakness to a state of newly acquired power, a change evidently thought of as the transformation from femininity to masculinity.

What we have inferred from a few words found in 2 Maccabees 7 can be substantiated by numerous examples from every major stage in the early evolution of hagiographic literature. The most striking instance of all is the well-known contest episode in the *Passio sanctarum Perpetuae et Felicitatis*, which marks the full expansion of everything that the author of Maccabees implies by the words *masculinum animum inserens*.

The day before she is to die, Perpetua has a vision (her fourth one), in which she is taken into the amphitheater, where she finds, to her surprise, not beasts but an Egyptian accompanied by attendants and prepared to fight her.[86] Perpetua, too, has her assistants, who "rub her down with oil." However, an important change occurs directly before her rubdown. When her clothes are taken off, the female martyr discovers that she has become a man:

> The day before we were to fight with the beasts I saw the following vision. Pomponius the deacon came to the prison gates and began to knock violently. I went out and

opened the gate for him. . . . And he said to me: "Perpetua, come, we are waiting for you." Then he took my hand and we began to walk through rough and broken country. At last we came to the amphitheatre out of breath, and he led me into the center of the arena. . . . I looked at the enormous crowd who watched in astonishment. I was surprised that no beasts were let loose on me; for I knew that I was condemned to die by the beasts. Then out came an Egyptian against me, of vicious appearance, together with his seconds, to fight with me. There also came up to me some handsome young men to be my seconds and assistants. My clothes were stripped off, and suddenly I was a man. My seconds began to rub me down with oil, as they are wont to do before a contest. Then I saw the Egyptian on the other side rolling in the dust. Next there came forth a man of marvellous stature, such that he rose above the top of the amphitheatre. He was clad in a beltless purple tunic with two stripes, one on either side, running down the middle of his chest. He wore sandals that were wondrously made of gold and silver, and he carried a wand like an athletic trainer and a green branch on which there were golden apples. And he asked for silence and said: "If this Egyptian defeats her he will slay her with the sword. But if she defeats him, she will receive this branch." Then he withdrew.[87]

There then follows a description of the fight with the Egyptian. The martyr is portrayed as a skillful opponent who receives the branch of victory after her struggles as a male contestant. Such a scene obviously has resonances in Gregory's preface to Monegund's *Vita*, which also invokes the imagery of the amphitheater by referring to women engaging in manly contest (*viriliter agonizantem*), "sweating" (*desudantibus*) in the struggle for salvation, and winning the applause (*faborabiliter*) of the crowd:

We drew close to one another and began to let our fists fly. My opponent tried to get hold of my feet, but I kept striking him in the face with the heels of my feet. Then I was raised up into the air and I began to pummel him without as it were touching the ground. Then when I noticed there was a lull, I put my two hands together linking the fingers of one hand with those of the other and thus I got hold of his head. He fell flat on his face and I stepped on his head. The crowd began to shout and my assistant started to sing psalms. Then I walked up to the trainer and took the branch. He kissed me and said to me: "Peace be with you, my daughter." I began to walk in triumph towards the Gate of Life. Then I awoke. I realized that it was not with wild animals that I would fight but with the devil, but I knew that I would win the victory.[88]

As is the case with the mother of Maccabees, a woman's courage is again presented as an acquired masculinity that charges the saint with power to endure suffering and maintain an unflinching commitment to the faith. But unlike the woman of the biblical passage, Perpetua's attainment of power is portrayed as a more substantial transformation from an already strong female to a more powerful male, whose masculinity is signified not by a change of mentality (such as going from *femineae cogitationi* to *masculinum animum*) but by sheer phallic empowerment (*facta sum masculus*) that vividly marks the breakthrough of a new identity.[89]

Although not in as dramatic a fashion as Perpetua's *Passio*, this masculinization of the female saint continues in the martyr romances and the apocryphal acts, with the latter having, according to some scholars, a special appeal to a female audience.[90] Thecla, for instance, speaks of her desire to cut her hair and follow Paul wherever he goes.[91] After having escaped unscathed from her persecutors, she longs to be with the holy man who had separated from her during the course of her trials.[92] Having baptized herself, she then dresses in the clothes of a man and sets out to find Paul.[93] Her new masculine identity is obviously a mark of a changed religious status. When she does finally find Paul, he is stunned by her appearance, which she explains by saying: "Paul, I have received baptism, for He who has acted on you in preaching has acted on me in baptizing."[94]

Thecla's story is not unusual in the apocryphal acts. In the strongest terms possible, the necessity of masculinity for the attainment of holiness is expressed in the Gospel of Thomas, when Jesus says: "Look, I will lead her [Mary Magdalene] that I may make her male, in order that she too may become a living spirit resembling males. For every woman who makes herself male will enter the kingdom of heaven."[95]

In the desert literature, we find so many accounts of female monks disguising themselves as men that one researcher has regarded such stories as a literary cycle.[96] The tendency to portray female hermits as male can be traced, in part, to what we have already said about the stress on masculinity in the depiction of female martyrs. If the life of the ascetic is a form of bloodless martyrdom, then we should expect to find the same kind of agon imagery that we encountered in Perpetua's Passio. In fact, references to female saints struggling in spiritual warfare and athletic contest with the devil appear frequently.[97] But unlike the account of Perpetua, the explicit indication of a woman transformed into a man occurs not with a phallic recognition upon the removal of clothing but, similar to Thecla's case, with wearing clothes that match the dress of male monks.[98] Like the accounts of male saints, the narrative pattern of such stories is a flight from the world, followed by seclusion or entrance into a monastic community. Such accounts thus adhere to the familiar romance structure, with the major difference that, in the Lives of holy women, a male disguise is maintained and gender is undetected until the moment of death, at which time the female identity is recognized by male monks or is revealed by the saint herself, whose body can then be washed by women rather than men after her passing.[99]

The "motif" of the so-called transvestite saint in early hagiographic literature has been studied by previous researchers, so here we need look at only a few features of the depiction of holy women in the desert literature that bear directly on what we have observed in the Lives of Monegund and Radegund.[100]

With the stories of the Egyptian saints, we can begin to find narratives that bear a greater likeness to the Merovingian Vitae than what we encounter in the martyr acts. One point of convergence that is of great significance to our study is how a pre-Merovingian author begins his work when he turns to the subject of female saints. Appearing prominently in this earlier presentation of holy women is the very rhetoric that characterizes the prefaces to the Lives of Monegund and Radegund.

Coinciding with both the thought and the language that our Merovingian authors express and use in the Lives of Monegund and Radegund is a passage from Palladius's Lausiac History, a work probably written around 420 and translated from the Greek into several Latin versions. Shortly after its translation, it became one of the libelli in the Vitae patrum collection, through which so much of the desert literature came to be known in the West.[101] Here, we find a version of Melania the Elder's Life, in which the author begins by stressing the need to recall the "manly and honorable women" who have pleased God. In addition to the now familiar emphasis on the masculinity of female saints, the opening remarks also show the same compensation strategy at work that we find in the Merovingian authors. Moreover, in this particular passage, the hagiographer expresses the dichotomy between the weakness of femininity and the strength of religious women who engage in ascetic battle in words and phrases that Fortunatus's preface to Radegund's *Life* parallels: "Necessarium autem existimavi, virilium quoque et honestarum mulierum meminisse in hoc libro, quibus Deus aequalia donavit praemia viris qui ex virtute vitam egere, et ipsis reddidit coronam eorum qui ipsi placuerunt, ne molles teneraeque reddantur quae sunt socordiores, et praetextum quaerant et excusationem, tanquam quae sint imbecilliores ad certamina virtutis, et ad honestam vitam agendam."[102]

Similar remarks are found in a work on the desert saints that was sometimes appended to the *Historia Lausiaca*, entitled *Heraclidis paradisus*.[103] Again, when the author comes to a section in which he intends to write about several holy women, he begins by referring to the "manly character" of these saints, while also contending with the issue of their perceived weakness. Significant in light of Monegund's *Vita* is that, while grappling with the problem of gender in the prefacing remarks, the author mentions the "inferior sex." In one of the more rhetorically innovative attempts to compensate for female saints, the writer initially plays on how the two words are normally associated, by claiming that God would not grant to women rewards and battles that are "inferior" to those of the "virile sex": "Necessarium autem valde et hoc puto, ut mulieribus quoque, sicut praefati sumus, viriles mores habentibus atque honestos, ad memoriam sempiternam libelli nostri paginam praebeamus, quibus Deus noster non inferiora sexu virili certamina donavit et praemia, ut demeret aliis negligentibus omnem excusationis occasionem. Quae quia sexus inferioris videntur, non posse se dicunt ad commendandam virtutis gloriam pervenire."[104]

We may quite rightly ask to what extent such stories of manly female saints actually penetrated Merovingian hagiography beyond the standard prefacing remarks that seem consistent whenever male hagiographers discuss holy women. An account told by Gregory in the *Liber in gloria confessorum* shows how the earlier tradition could remain virtually unchanged in Merovingian hagiography. The existence of the story of Papula indicates that the similarities we have observed between the desert literature and our Merovingian authors cannot be coincidental and, at least in this instance, are at a much deeper level than simply a rhetorical strategy for portraying holy women. As is easily noticed, the short narrative on Papula, closely following accounts of disguised women in the stories of the desert and also showing a continuity with the apocryphal acts of Thecla, has all the resonances of the earlier literature. But in addition to showing similarities with the narrative pattern of hagiographic romance and its portrayal of female saints, the passage also articulates what the experience of becoming a man signifies. Like the stories of freedom from slavery and, in a way, even similar to the saints who are described in the *LVP* as learning how to read, the masculinization of Papula is presented as an experience of liberation that empowers the saint, as becoming a man empowered Perpetua, to make a breakthrough into the full life of sanctity. Given how well it addresses the issues with which we have been concerned in this stage of our discussion, the passage is worth quoting in full:

> Papula was very holy. Since she often demanded of her parents that she be placed in a monastery of girls—because at her parent's house, with worldly cares impeding, she is not able to serve God—and they, on account of their love, will not want her to be separated from them, she cut the hair of her head and, dressed in male clothing, went to the diocese of Tours, offering herself to a congregation of monks. Spending her life there in fasts and prayers, she then shone by many deeds of power. For she was like a man among men; her sex was not known to anyone. Her searching parents were never able to find her. When the abbot of the monastery to which she had come died, the monks, not knowing her sex, chose her as abbot because of her constant deeds of power. This [post] she refused with all her might. For thirty years she was in the monastery, known by no one what she was. But on the third day before she departed from this world, she revealed it to the monks. And so, when she died, she was washed by other women, was buried and, from that time on, by many deeds of power she shows that she is the maidservant of God. For those who have chills or are seized with other illnesses are often restored to health at her tomb.[105]

Here, the rejection of family, the cutting of hair, the donning of male attire, and the flight to the monastery represent not so much the rejection of femininity as the assertion of spiritual freedom—for there is, after all, not one mention of womanly weakness in this account. And what this freedom leads to tells us much about the ideal of sanctity in relation to gender. The way Gregory describes it, Papula's becoming a man leads to power. In this respect, her story is not any different from the others we have encountered, for in all the texts of Fortunatus and Gregory examined so far, the point most consistently and emphatically made is that sanctity is the attainment of power. This idea of the attainment of power appears at every stage in the narrative that describes Papula. First, there is the power to break the ties of family and the social barriers defining male and female. Second, there is the power over the self exhibited by fasting and the diligence needed to maintain a life of prayer, behavior that makes her the equal of male ascetics or, as Gregory puts it, "like a man among men." Third, she obtains power over the other monks when she is chosen abbot.[106] Fourth, as the last sentence of the story states, there is the thaumaturgic power granted to the heavenly intercessor, who, after leading a holy life, now cures the sick at her tomb.

This overview of the hagiographic background to the depiction of holy women enables us to gain a sense of the extent to which Gregory and Fortunatus attempted to maintain a continuity with the earlier literature, from the book of Maccabees to the stories of the desert saints.[107] At the end of the section on Monegund, we noted what appeared to be an incongruity between the author's concern with gender in the preface and his indifference to this issue in the actual narrative. But having seen what an author such as Palladius does when he comes to the subject of female saints, we may now regard Gregory's opening remark as a common strategy for introducing a discussion on holy women that has its origins in the stories of martyrdom, in which accounts women assume what is evidently regarded as male behavior and the characteristics of a masculine identity. Hence, what we find in his preface to Monegund's Life is really similar to what Fortunatus does when he calls his male saints martyrs. It is an attempt to make a connection with an earlier ideal of sanctity. Once the rhetoric of a rationale for depicting holy women is presented according to the previous pattern, continuity is established, and the author is at liberty to tell his story without any regard for gender. Thus, the *Life of Saint Monegund* resembles a situation very similar to the one Gregory claims existed in Papula's monastery. The story shows no visible signs that it is significantly different from the other *Vitae* of the *LVP*. Although pertaining to a female saint, it fits in with the rest of the corpus.

Our overview of the literature also allows us to confirm our initial impression of Fortunatus's *Life of Saint Radegund*. We are certainly able to link his preface, with its attempt to compensate for the saint's gender, with previous hagiographic trends. But the earlier literature does not show the extended attention to the body that Fortunatus gives to a female saint. Moreover, the whole ascetic tone differs considerably from what we find in the accounts of the holy women of the desert. The contest imagery does not appear in Radegund's *Vita*, as it does in Gregory's preface to Monegund's *Life* and the other prefaces that deal with female hermits previously mentioned. In addition, Radegund's battle is not with demonic forces. Instead, the *Life* portrays ascetic struggle carried out in a masochistic conflict with the female body.

Contrary to the recent scholarship, then, we can make three observations about the depiction of female saints in the corpus of Gregory and Fortunatus. First, regardless of the misogynistic tendencies the authors may have had, to varying extents they both consciously attempted to follow literary trends established prior to the Merovingian Age. Second, Fortunatus and Gregory cannot be regarded as being of the same mind with respect to the depiction of holy women. Hence, generalizations that claim a uniformity in the male depiction of female saints during the early Merovingian period cannot be substantiated. Third—and this is a problem that has yet to be considered by scholars studying the role of women in Merovingian hagiography, religion, and history—certain writings pertaining to female saints and authors portray in a positive light the shedding of femininity in order to obtain the power associated with sanctity.

Interpretive Difficulties

The last observation relates to what we found in the story of Papula. In the current state of scholarship on Merovingian female saints, such an account would be regarded as another instance in which a holy woman was turned into a man by a male author. But what is striking about the story is how closely it resembles what we find in sources that are now considered to be of female authorship. Researchers studying the early Christian and Merovingian sources have made great advances in reclaiming literature once neglected or thought to be the work of male authors. A difficulty arises, however, when the very literature thought to express an authentic female voice shows the same stress on masculinity that we find in male works. The visions of Perpetua, for instance, are treated as her own description that was recorded by a redactor.[108] Yet, one of these visions, as previously seen, shows a rather explicit gender transformation that stresses the martyr's attainment of a power obviously thought of in terms of masculinity.

In an analogous case, scholars emphatically assert the authenticity of Aldegund's visions, the account of which is regarded as the saint's own narrative on her religious experiences.[109] This assertion is motivated by a much needed challenge to Wilhelm Levison, who actually purged the section of Aldegund's visions in his edition of that saint's *Vita*.[110] But in redressing Levison's dismissal of Aldegund's visions, another problem arises that has still not been addressed. If this section of the *Life* offers the actual female voice of the saint, then scholars will first have to acknowledge and then attempt to explain the resoundingly manly tone of the holy woman's speech.[111]

Similarly, the letter of Caesaria II to Saint Radegund is now being treated as an authentic Merovingian text produced by a female writer.[112] Here, too, the woman who is speaking assumes a male persona. The letter not only is filled with the familiar imagery of warfare and contest but also explicitly exhorts Radegund to act *viriliter*. Indeed, the very wording of the text conforms exactly to what male authors have written elsewhere about female saints: " 'Act like a man! May your heart be strengthened' (Ps. 30:25). Just as if you were men who were about to fight your enemies bravely and manfully, so that your body might not be struck, so too firmly and manfully fight against the devil, so that he may not ruin your souls through deception and wicked thoughts."[113]

Texts such as these raise a perplexing problem that scholars now dealing with these sources have largely failed to address. There is no doubt that, in the works just cited, the female voice is unambiguously male. Rather than distinctiveness due to the feminine influence of a female writer, we find, at least on the literal level, women—not male hagiographers—assimilating themselves to the masculine ideal of holiness. And this assimilation is presented in an entirely positive light. Hence, the presentation of the holy woman as a *virago* can pertain as much to the female depiction of *sanctae* as it does to the male one; at least, this seems to be the obvious impression, albeit a rather superficial one, that these texts make when a woman describes her own religious experience or that of another female saint.[114]

In light of such evidence, we can discern a continuity not only between the male hagiographers of the early Christian era and the most prolific Merovingian authors but also between the voice of Christian women recorded in the earlier sources and that expressed by female saints of the Merovingian age. Indeed, Amma Sara saying that she is the one who is "the man" coincides exactly with what we find in Aldegund's visions and Caesaria's letter. In short, there is sufficient textual evidence which, when taken at face value, suggests, completely contrary to what the current scholarship claims, that women who attained sanctity regarded themselves positively as male.

Certainly, such passages attest to the pervasiveness of the masculine ideal of holiness. But that observation by itself is hardly an adequate explanation for what we find in such texts as the account of Aldegund's visions, Caesaria's epistolatory exhortations to Radegund, or earlier sources such as Perpetua's *Passio* and the stories of women in the desert.[115] The very difficulties raised by such accounts suggest the presence of a *mentalité* that cannot be sufficiently accounted for merely in terms of an oppressive misogyny that undermines the reports of women's religious experiences. Indeed, even to refer to these passages as evidence of "phallocentric discourse" or, more to the point, the "sadistic sexual politics of hagiography" will not make it possible to explain the complexity arising from the testimony of women whose transformation of gender is positively associated with the attainment of sanctity and spiritual liberation.[116]

In support of the assertion regarding the literature's complexity, another text may be offered that poses an even greater challenge to the present scholarly trend dealing with the issue of gender and sanctity in the early Middle Ages. Although the passage is the work of an author writing during the time in which Gregory and Fortunatus flourished, he is not a Merovingian hagiographer situated within the *regnum Francorum*. Even so, given that this writer is a contemporary of the Merovingian authors considered here and is also a major hagiographer of the early Middle Ages, introducing a passage from his work that pertains directly to the issue of gender and sanctity is appropriate, especially because the text in question has never before been considered in the recent scholarship on the role played by masculinity and femininity in the depiction of holy individuals.

Earlier, a reference was made to the so-called transvestite saints. Significantly, all the cases of disguise in the sources pertain to women who dress like men rather than men who dress like women.[117] The account of Papula, of course, offers the most notable example found in the Merovingian sources of a woman who disguises herself as a man to gain entrance into a male monastery, where she earns such great respect that she is asked to be the abbot. Although there is no account of a male saint who dresses as a woman to enter a convent, Gregory the Great (ca. 540–604), in his *Dialogues*, tells an intriguing story about Equitius, who was abbot over several male monasteries. Despite this saint's pious living, his holiness is not entirely secure. He is engaged in a struggle with sexual temptation. Then one night, after much prayer, he has a dream. Not unlike Perpetua's dream, Equitius undergoes a transformation of his sexual identity. He is castrated, and this newly acquired status leads to a spiritual liberation in exactly the same way that becoming male led to newfound freedom and empowerment for the holy women we have been discussing. Once he becomes a eunuch (*eunuchizari*), he is able to associate with female monastic communities, which he then directs without any of his original fear of yielding to lust. Hence, the losing of the phallus brings him the same status that Papula achieved by, figuratively speaking, gaining one:

> One night, when he was seeking, with constant prayer, a remedy [for lust] . . . from almighty God, he saw himself being castrated with the help of an angel, and in his vision it appeared that he was cutting off all the drive from his genitals. From that time on he was removed from temptation, as if he did not have a sexual body.
>
> Afterwards, supported by that power from the help of almighty God, he began, just as he had done before with men, to take charge also of women.[118]

This account certainly raises questions regarding the legitimacy of thinking about sanctity in terms of male and female, at least in any conventional way that those terms are commonly used. Equitius, for instance, may be symbolically castrated by having defeated lust, but is he still male insofar as he gains a new power that he would not otherwise have had if he had remained unchanged? And if the sources indicate that the attainment of some kind of spiritual or religious power corresponds with masculinity, then even the losing of the phallus could qualify as an example of becoming male.[119] In short, the story of Equitius and the other accounts of transformation mentioned here suggest that the traditional categories of gender no longer apply to the experience of attaining sanctity.

In light of that last point, it may be helpful to contrast the depiction of Equitius with the cross-dresser at Radegund's convent, whom Gregory of Tours describes in his *Histories*.[120] In the aftermath of the revolt at Sainte-Croix, a tribunal hears the accusations of Clotild, one of the ringleaders of the uprising.[121] She accuses the abbess of keeping and sleeping with a man in the monastery who dresses like a woman. After questioning this man, the tribunal learns that he is impotent. As a sign of his impotency, he wears female attire: "Clotild claimed that the abbess kept a man in the monastery, who dressed in female clothing and was taken for a woman, although it was quite evident that he was a man and that he was constantly sleeping with the abbess. Pointing to him with her finger, [she said]: 'Look at him.' He stood before us all, dressed, as was mentioned, in female clothing. He said that, with respect to virile activity, he was able to do nothing and, for this reason, he had changed his clothing."[122]

Here, the loss of phallic power is associated with femininity. But when Equitius has his dream of becoming a eunuch, that same loss leads to the acquiring of new "power" (*qua uirtute fretus*), to an experience from which he was previously barred precisely because of his virility. Thus, the symbolic castration in the context of sanctity in no way corresponds with the story of the impotent man described in the *Histories*. In the latter case, wearing a dress obviously signifies loss and what was undoubtedly regarded as feminine weakness. In the former instance, by contrast, the removal of the most obvious physical characteristic of masculinity occurs after an experience of heightened religious activity and leads to a new mode of existence by lending a much needed power to an individual whose abilities were previously limited because of human weakness. Unlike the individual described by Gregory of Tours, Equitius's loss is presented as the means by which something greater is gained. By contrast, the cross-dresser is portrayed as an unfortunate freak of nature, a diminished man at whom the members of the tribunal stare. Significantly, he is not reprimanded for his practice of dressing like a woman.[123] In fact, his explanation for wearing female clothing is presented as a legitimate excuse, one that the tribunal obviously finds entirely acceptable under the circumstances. But the eunuch Equitius, rather than being presented as having suffered some misfortune, is depicted as an example of how the supernatural can transform human nature. In light of the account from the *Histories*, the story of Equitius, like that of Papula, suggests that the conventional roles of gender as socially defined do not necessarily or even normally apply to what can only be described as the liminal experience of sanctification.

At this point, the texts cited in this section of the study should be sufficient to highlight some of the perplexities that modern scholarship must face to treat sources pertaining to sanctity and gender, sources that even this brief overview has shown to be of far greater complexity than the heavy-handed and rather simplistic misogyny that, according to the current research, supposedly taints the literature male authors write about female saints.

Having considered the hagiography produced by the prolific male authors, along with some key sources that present an obvious difficulty to the current trend in the study of the Merovingian *Vitae sanctarum*, we can turn now to the question of how a female writer of this period portrays a holy woman.

5

BAUDONIVIA'S
LIFE OF SAINT RADEGUND

Sainte Radegonde, priez pour nous,
Fille de race royale,
Fille du Dieu Très-Haut
Fille d'une vraie et grande pénitence,
Miroir d'humilité,
Modèle de la vie religieuse,
Vous qui avez toutes les vertus réunies,
Reine possédant la beauté du corps et de l'âme,
Reine qui avez méprisé les royaumes de ce monde,
Reine proposée à l'imitation de toutes les reines,
Diamant très précieux de la France,
Perle très riche du diadème de Jésus-Christ,
Amante passionnée de la Croix très sainte de Jésus-Christ,
Vous si attachée au culte des saintes reliques,
Observatrice très scrupuleuse de la règle,
Vous si empressée de pourvoir aux besoins des pauvres,
Très clémente libératrice des prisonniers,
Épouse très pure de l'Époux céleste,
Vous que le Christ votre époux honora parfois de ses visites,
Très noble habitante d'une humble cellule,
Patronne très sûre des Poitevins. . . .
> —*Litany of Saint Radegund*, in F. Brittain,
> *Saint Radegund* (1925, p. 82)

Not too long after Fortunatus composed his *Vita sanctae Radegundis*, and probably after he had died, a nun at the convent Radegund founded, who also knew the saint personally, wrote another biography of this holy woman.[1] That two contemporary authors well acquainted with the same holy person both wrote biographies is relatively rare in Merovingian hagiography.[2] If her reason for undertaking this task is taken, at least for the moment, at face value, the author of the second *Vita*, Baudonivia, intends to fill out Fortunatus's incomplete portrait of the saint. To put it in her own words:

We are not going to repeat what the apostolic man, Bishop Fortunatus, wrote concerning the life of the blessed woman. Instead, we are going to discuss the things he overlooked [for the sake of avoiding] prolixity, since in his own book on Radegund, Fortunatus himself referred to the shortness of his work when he said: "Let the scantiness concerning the powers of the blessed woman suffice, lest an abundance of writing be disliked, and where the full extent of a few things is known, may it not be considered too short." Therefore, with that divine power inspiring us, whom blessed Radegund in her lifetime desired to please and with whom, after her lifetime, she rules, we will try to grasp, not through refined language but in plain words, the things she did and we will attempt to describe a few of her miracles.[3]

Baudonivia's initial remark does not suggest that she writes to supplant Fortunatus's version of Radegund's life. Rather, she expresses the need to supplement the original narrative[4] and claims that she will attempt to fulfill this need by adding material that Fortunatus neglected to mention for fear of the "dislike" (*fastidium*) that a long-winded story would arouse in his readers. The implication of Baudonivia's reason for writing is that the two works taken together will constitute a whole; her version will contain what is missing in Fortunatus's account while also leaving out those episodes of the saint's life elaborated on in the first *Vita*. In her view, each narrative is dependent on the other because what his version lacks hers will supply and what his includes she will exclude.

The Medieval Integrity of Radegund's Dossier

If later versions of Radegund's life are any indication, Baudonivia's understanding of her composition in relation to Fortunatus's account served as the guiding principle by which later writers and compilers of hagiographic material related information about the holy woman and determined how the story of Radegund was to be arranged and circulated. Those hagiographers in the later Middle Ages who compiled material on Radegund treated the two works together, usually drawing equally from Fortunatus and Baudonivia, as if the two versions together made a more complete picture of the saint and complemented each other, an integrating interpretation that Baudonivia's preface seems to foster.[5] The manuscript tradition of the two Lives also indicates that medieval readers tended to approach the biographies as constituting a hagiographic whole because both *Vitae* usually appear together, with Fortunatus's earlier account always preceding Baudonivia's later version.[6] Moreover, there is also iconographic evidence showing that the presence of both *Vitae* can be detected in the pictorial representation of the saint, even in scenes depicting an event recorded by only one of the authors.[7]

Recently, however, the two versions of Radegund's life have come to be considered to display fundamental variations because of the difference in the authors' gender.[8] This approach to the narratives as representing opposing views of Radegund's sanctity has now become the dominant trend in the scholarship on the *Vitae*. The tendency to accord to Baudonivia a distinctive place as a female author who highlighted the feminine aspects of Radegund's sanctity arises as a reaction against earlier scholarship that allegedly gave one-sided attention to Fortunatus and routinely dismissed Baudonivia as an inferior writer. The current perception is to see the earlier researchers as forming an alliance with Fortunatus and his male perception of Radegund's sanctity.

The history of the modern debate concerning the two Lives of Radegund has already been adequately outlined elsewhere and need not detain us now.[9] But two important points, which the current scholarship related to this debate does not acknowledge, ought to be made before proceeding any further in our discussion. The first, just alluded to but not sufficiently elaborated and emphasized, is the medieval perception of the two Lives as a unity. The second, which will be discussed at length in the next section, is the failure of the current research to acknowledge the full range of opinions that past scholars have given on Baudonivia's text.

The significance of the first point needs to be at least recognized because it highlights the gulf between medieval and modern readers and so offers an intriguing challenge to the legitimacy of the current approach to the Lives. As previously mentioned, the unambiguous evidence of such a unified view appears in the later medieval redactions, which present the two works as a harmonious whole rather than as divergent accounts divided along the lines of gender. Indeed, the seventeenth-century litany that serves as the epigraph to this chapter remarkably reflects the extent to which both versions eventually came to be fused, with these liturgical verses themselves forming what is undoubtedly the most extensively integrated perception of the saint to grow out of the medieval interpretation of the two accounts. The prayer invokes the socially active saint of the first *Life* and, as we shall see, the monastic model of the second. The "liberator of prisoners" (*libératrice des prisonniers*) and the nun who dwells in her "humble cell" (*humble cellule*), the active saint who tends to the "needs of the poor" (*besoins des pauvres*) and the contemplative who is told in a vision that she is the most precious jewel in Christ's crown (*perle très riche du diadème de Jésus-Christ*) are thus thoroughly blended in the liturgical text.[10] In contrast with modern scholars, who tend to disjoint the accounts, these medieval compilers turned the two narratives into one *Vita*.

The later hagiographic evidence is not being cited now as a rebuttal against the current approach or mentioned as part of an attempt to invalidate research based on gender analysis. What Vincent of Beavais and Henry Bradshaw suggest by their work is that both Lives were previously regarded as a unity. Not to acknowledge that fact by, instead, starting with the assumption that both works are mutually opposed is to deny the validity of what amounts to the later medieval interpretation of the Lives given by hagiographers who followed Fortunatus and Baudonivia. Those of us who do study the Lives for evidence of the connection among sanctity, its depiction, and gender should at least acknowledge that historically this approach may not only be interesting and innovative but also aberrant and alien in its treatment of hagiographic texts. If the medieval approach to the Lives no longer has merit, if it is severely flawed or insignificant to the modern debate, then arguments must be brought forth that can convincingly make such a case. A gendered reading of the Lives can bring to light aspects of the narratives of which the Merovingian and later medieval authors and audiences were not aware. By the same token, however, it may be equally true that we ourselves are not conscious of how the two narratives fit together and may be as blind to their coherence as we are perceptive to the differences arising from male and female authors.[11]

"Commending the Woman's History"

Less difficult to assess than the merits of the current approach to the *Vitae* is the second point, concerning the way in which contemporary researchers either selectively present the earlier scholarship on the Lives or else are unaware of the full range of criticism on Baudonivia's narrative.[12] Of course, one prominent example supports the claim that Fortunatus's *Life of Saint Radegund* was undeservedly favored at the expense of discrediting Baudonivia's account. In his introductory comments on the two *Vitae*, Bruno Krusch not only reveals the limitations of his narrow philological approach when dealing with Baudonivia's prose[13] but also shows how easily Fortunatus as a Latin stylist has won over scholars with his elaborate rhetoric, which can be as flawed, at least by Krusch's standards, as Baudonivia's writing but does not receive the same disapproval as does the female author of the second *Vita*.[14]

However, what all the recent scholarship on this issue fails to acknowledge is that Krusch is of two minds when assessing Baudonivia's narrative. If as a philologist he finds her writing flawed, as a historian he values Baudonivia's account far above Fortunatus's. Modern researchers invariably cite his negative criticism in his introduction to the two *Vitae* printed in the *Scriptores Rerum Merovingicarum* series of the *Monumenta Germaniae Historica*. There, taking exception to what he considers to be Baudonivia's barbarized speech and anacoluthic constructions, Krusch claims that the nun does not know how to write and cites her heavy reliance on other Lives as proof of her incompetence.[15] But what scholars neglect to recall or are not aware of is his assessment of Baudonivia in the slightly earlier edition of the first *Life of Saint Radegund*, a text that appears along with the other poetical and prose works in Fortunatus's literary corpus. In this collection of poems and *Vitae*, published in the fourth volume of the *Auctores Antiquissimi* series of the *Monumenta*, Krusch expresses a very different view while introducing Fortunatus's version of Radegund's life. Here, in very strong terms, the poet from Ravenna is considered deficient, and the nun Baudonivia is regarded as having authored a work of greater historical value: "Within a short time after Fortunatus wrote, his *Life* hardly seemed sufficient to the nuns at Poitiers since they demanded that it be re-done by Baudonivia. For truly there are many things which commend the history of the woman rather than the miracles of the poet."[16]

René Aigrain took a similar view of Baudonivia in two major studies. Like Krusch, he noted what he considered to be stylistic inadequacies but praised the nun for giving a fuller picture of Radegund. Again, the account of Fortunatus is deemed an inadequate source for the saint's history, with Aigrain calling attention to the "strange lacunae" of the first biography.[17] Even in the manner of literary competence, Fortunatus was not always regarded by earlier researchers as superior to Baudonivia. In their preface to Radegund's dossier in the *Acta Sanctorum*, the Bollandists show no preference to either author. According to their view, both hagiographers wrote "in a rough and difficult style," which the editors of the *Acta* politely refrain from correcting out of "respect for antiquity," unlike the twelfth-century redactor Hildebert, who took the liberty of providing a more polished version of the two Lives.[18]

Furthermore, in comparison with Gregory of Tours and with the literary productions of the period as a whole, Baudonivia's *Vita* received favorable criticism. Max Bonnet, although acknowledging the role copyists, editors, and other correctors from the ninth century to our own day played in altering Merovingian literature to suit their stylistic standards, states that Baudonivia writes "more correctly" than Gregory of Tours.[19] And not long before the gender approach to the two Lives became fashionable, Riché had also commented favorably on Baudonivia's Latinity and, without qualifications, praised her hagiography.[20] Considering the various views of the earlier scholarship, it is difficult to substantiate the claim that Krusch's negative assessment of Baudonivia influenced other researchers, "who tended to disparage her work as mere compilation, especially in comparison to Fortunatus's . . . *Vita*."[21] Hence, in all fairness, the unfavorable remarks of Krusch cannot be legitimately cited as the last word on the subject of the early scholarly assessment of Baudonivia's composition. His own view of her work is, as we have seen, clearly divided. And if he did influence later scholars, as the researcher just quoted claims, that influence was not limited to philological considerations but extended to regarding the second *Vita* as a valuable document precisely because it was not "a compilation" but a *historia* filling in the first author's "strange lacunae."

Moreover, on the basis of the various assessments outlined here, one can hardly conclude that there was a concerted effort among prominent male scholars of the past to discredit Baudonivia. On the whole, either researchers were of two opinions when assessing Baudonivia's work and comparing it with the first *Vita* (Krusch and Aigrain), or they treated it neutrally in relation to Fortunatus (the view of the Bollandists who edited the Lives in the *Acta*), or else they expressed, with little or no qualification, a positive view of her writing (Bonnet and Riché). But among none of the early researchers can there be found a critique that consistently dismisses Baudonivia's composition as being categorically inferior to Fortunatus's first biography. In addition, there is also the overwhelmingly positive assessment of Baudonivia's writing given in 1914 by Goyau, whose unbridled praise of the second *Vita* sounds remarkably like the recent scholarship.[22] These considerations are important when we recall that the justification for the present scholarly trend rests in part on the assumption that Baudonivia's *Life of Saint Radegund* has been unequivocally "disparaged" because of a bias favoring Fortunatus's version.

Using Convention

Some of the recent scholarship on Baudonivia's *Vita sanctae Radegundis* argues that this piece, along with two other works of female authorship, introduces new "female values and ideals" into the depiction of sanctity, so that the second biography of Radegund represents an innovation in the evolution of hagiographic literature.[23] The originality of Baudonivia's work is thought to derive from her perspective as a female author who is able to highlight aspects of Radegund's sanctity that the first male biographer sought to efface. We shall deal directly with the accuracy of this assessment later in the chapter and in the concluding remarks, after we have taken the opportunity to examine more closely the salient features of Baudonivia's narrative and to observe how it compares with Fortunatus's. But, for the moment, let us note that the current approach to Baudonivia's *Vita* tends to ignore the textual elements that pose the most obvious and direct challenges to the argument in support of the view that Baudonivia has produced a highly distinctive portrait of Radegund. By way of contrast, then, we shall turn first to what appears to be that very aspect of Baudonivia's text that is literally not her own—namely, the portions of the preface drawn extensively and explicitly from Fortunatus's hagiography. Moreover, rather than attempting to find what distinctive features Baudonivia added to Radegund's profile, we shall first concentrate on the significance of what is omitted from her narrative. Given the variety of hagiographic works previously examined, we are now in an excellent position to detect divergences arising not only from explicit textual content but also from what is noticeably missing in her rhetorical strategy.

Throughout this study, prefaces have been especially important for discovering an author's conception about a *Vita's* meaning. Baudonivia's opening remarks are also crucial for understanding the significance of her writing in light of what we have seen in the introductory statements of Fortunatus and Gregory. As there are several different aspects of the preface worth calling attention to, it will be best to quote the opening remarks at length now, leaving off where the previously cited reference to Fortunatus's work begins:

> You impose on me a task that is no less impossible to do "than it would be for a finger to touch heaven." You put this burden on me so that we may venture to say something about the life of that holy woman, Lady Radegund, whom you knew best. But this task ought to be imposed on those "who have a font of eloquence within them, from which whatever is imposed on them is explained more richly in poetry flowing like water. However, there are those of limited understanding who do not have flowing eloquence through which they can refresh others or assuage the drought of their own dryness. Such people not only have no desire to say anything on their own, but also become terrified if something be imposed on them." And I, being timid and having little understanding, realize that "it is as proper for the learned to speak as for the unlearned to remain silent. For in their discussions, the learned can make a mountain out of a molehill but when the unlearned speak, they do not know how to make even a molehill out of a mountain. And so, what is sought by some is dreaded by others." Since I am the humblest of all the humblest women and was "nursed from the cradle at her feet as her adopted little servant girl," I obediently submit to your most benign wish that . . . I, "if not completely at least in part, tell the story of her renowned work." For I am the heraldess proclaiming her glorious life "to the ears of her flock." Although the way in which I speak is unworthy, it is, nevertheless, devout. So I who am less learned but more devout ask you to help me by your prayers.[24]

In light of how Gregory and Fortunatus begin their Lives of female saints, we are able to notice a paradox in Baudonivia's preface to the *Life of Saint Radegund*. What makes Baudonivia's opening so distinctive is how it conforms in one fundamental respect with the way male saints are introduced by Fortunatus and Gregory. Like her male counterparts writing about men, Baudonivia shows an utter indifference to the saint's gender in the *Vita*'s opening. As we will recall, neither Fortunatus nor Gregory ever call attention to the fact that they are writing about a saint who is male. That the indifference to gender constitutes the norm was verified earlier by the way the accounts of holy women could be seen to deviate predictably. Only when the subject was female would the issue of gender arise as a special problem for the writer. Before such narratives could proceed, the male authors first had to assimilate the holy women into a masculine ideal of sanctity. As previously discussed, this technique of compensation for the "inferior sex" attributes to female saints masculine qualities by stressing the worthiness of holy women through the imagery of athletic contest, warfare, or physical mortifications, in which activities the male authors claim that the female saints are as much participants as the holy men in struggling to attain paradise. From a brief examination of the pre-Merovingian hagiography depicting *sanctae*, we also learned that this compensation strategy has a long tradition, whose continuity Gregory and Fortunatus, in their own different ways, maintained.

Thus, given all that has been considered regarding the various strategies Fortunatus, Gregory, and their hagiographic predecessors employ when treating male and female saints, Baudonivia's introduction to the life of a holy woman, which appears without any attempt to assimilate her to a male model of sanctity, marks a break not only with the two most prolific Merovingian writers but also with an entire literary tradition that treated the female saint as a problematic figure. Instead of compensating for Radegund's femininity, we find in Baudonivia's opening the standard disregard for gender exhibited in the *Vitae* of male saints composed by Fortunatus and Gregory. Where these authors deviate from their ordinary practice, Baudonivia adheres to the hagiographic standard. Herein lies the paradox: Her preface is different by the very fact that it remains typical when introducing a female saint, precisely the situation in which male authors alter their rhetorical strategies. Thus, Baudonivia's maintenance of a convention in the very situation in which male authors normally suspend their usual practice because their discourse concerns a woman is a strategy that turns the convention against itself. In its context, this standard indifference to gender constitutes a real distinctiveness, perhaps an instance in which the norm is subverted.

To view the preface as distinctive because of its very adherence to convention also has implications on how to regard the numerous lines that Baudonivia has borrowed from Fortunatus's Lives of Hilary and Marcellus.[25] Again, in an effort to stress Baudonivia's originality, recent scholars have chosen either to ignore or to downplay the borrowings from Fortunatus's hagiography, thus leaving Krusch's earlier assessment substantially unchallenged. Yet, when repeated in Baudonivia's text, Fortunatus's words can no longer retain their original meaning, with his phrases now appearing in a context that normally would have required a change in a male writer's strategy. Fortunatus's words are inserted into a text in which his usual introductory rhetoric would not be applicable since the subject of the discourse is now a female saint. If we recall Fortunatus's prefaces, we remember that, by his use of elaborately constructed sentences, he went to great length to develop the humility topos.[26] His elevated style suited his episcopal patrons and highlighted his own talent, even while he protested that his inadequacies as a *rhetor* made him unsuitable to compose biographies about and for bishops. However, in his preface to Radegund's *Vita*, there is only one token phrase referring to his literary deficiencies, and the inflated style characteristic of his epistolatory addresses is diminished greatly when introducing the only biography he wrote about a holy woman.[27] Instead of developing the humility topos, the whole preface, as we have seen, focuses on the female body and emphasizes the importance of mortification in the lives of female saints.

Baudonivia, by contrast, begins her preface with a citation from Fortunatus's *Life of Saint Hilary*, words used to express her inability to perform the task of writing the life of her illustrious, monastic founder. In Baudonivia's text, there appears, then, not only the standard humility topos but also the very words of a major Merovingian hagiographer whose usual rhetoric is now being assimilated into a work in which his normal strategy would have been considered out of place. This adherence to his style and language appears in the very context that was characterized by their absence. Fortunatus is thus speaking in his own usual manner in the one place where he would have deviated from his regular practice—that is, the Life of a female saint. In this sense, Fortunatus's prose appears in Baudonivia's preface in such a way that "the master's words are no longer his own."[28]

As is well known, the identification of direct borrowings in hagiographic texts can lead to more perplexing problems than it solves on the issue of how to interpret such unaltered material in *Vitae* that purport to be authentic accounts.[29] For this reason, the view of Baudonivia's borrowings from Fortunatus's hagiography as a subversive use of his writings can be offered only tentatively and as a partial explanation, one without due consideration to the broader issue involving the rationale behind this not uncommon hagiographic practice. The interpretation that Baudonivia undermines the standard, by quoting the customary remarks of Fortunatus in a context which he himself, as is indicated from his own *Life of Saint Radegund*, regarded as an occasion to deviate from the norm, merely suggests one possible way of approaching an important aspect of her writing that modern scholars either overlook, if they wish to present her work favorably, or highlight if, like Krusch, they wish to expose its literary deficiencies. Obviously, to those who attribute to Baudonivia's account so much distinctiveness, the extensive quotations from Fortunatus's Lives pose a problem that has yet to be adequately addressed. To argue that, in light of an examination of Fortunatus's and Gregory's hagiography, such borrowings as we find in Baudonivia's text take on a different valence there and are not necessarily, or at least not only, instances in which she "plundered" (*spoliavit*) whatever *Vitae* were at her disposal squarely faces one of the most obvious arguments against the originality of her work, while also opening up the possibility that what passes as conventional in one context can, when transposed to another, convey a quite unconventional meaning. In the case of Baudonivia's insertion of Fortunatus's texts into her preface, the meaning may well be that the standard hagiographic introduction need not be altered to accommodate a perception of saintly women as weak or inferior. Hence, Baudonivia's use of texts drawn entirely from Fortunatus's Lives of male saints can be seen as an assertion of equality.

The Mirror of Sanctity

Regardless of how the appearances of Fortunatus's texts in Baudonivia's *Life* are interpreted, there is still the undeniable impression of the second *Vita* as a document that contains more than simply an accumulation of textual fragments taken from various saints' Lives. Later medieval hagiographers, to Krusch's discredit, surely realized this, or else her version of Radegund's life would never have continued to be copied and circulated as another account to be used along with Fortunatus's original work. Rather than subsumed into Fortunatus's narrative, as, say, anonymous miracle accounts are sometimes indiscriminately added on to earlier ones so that the latest material is virtually indistinguishable from the earliest, Baudonivia's composition, although dependent on the first *Vita* when considered in light of the fullest possible portrait of the saint that can be gained, is by itself a hagiographic whole, a full narrative structurally as complete as any other *Vita* we find from the period, albeit one that is not as tightly structured as several of the Lives found in the *LVP*.

Thus, as the preface indicates, Baudonivia sets out to tell a new story, one that is separate from the original. At the same time, the original version is literally present, not only in the preface but also throughout the work, and the author of the second *Life* repeatedly shows her awareness of this earlier narrative. Her consciousness of Fortunatus's first story is initially expressed when she claims that her account "will not repeat" what the previous hagiographer wrote. Her awareness of the role Fortunatus's account has on the shaping of her story persists when she moves from the preface to the narrative proper and explicitly refers to the contents of the first *Vita*. Sometimes this mentioning of the earlier account merely alerts the reader to the nature of the material being excluded, so that the reference to the "first book" functions as a modern parenthetical note, a citation indicating that the pertinent information has already been adequately discussed by the previous author. At other times, however, her own text appears to engage Fortunatus's original portrait so that the author of the second *Vita* seems to be contending with the presence of the first narrative in her writing, as if the original has left a strong impression still lingering and capable of impinging on her own story. For instance, twice in the same chapter, Baudonivia refers to one feature in particular of Fortunatus's depiction of Radegund. Significantly, it is precisely the aspect of his narrative that also deviates, with respect to its extended graphic detail, from his own and Gregory's hagiography examined earlier. Judging from her references to this aspect of Fortunatus's writing and the way she positions her own account in relation to it, Baudonivia especially engages the way Fortunatus describes the saint's treatment of the body.

With regard to her discussion of Radegund's ascetic practices, Baudonivia is obviously going over ground already covered in the original *Vita*, a revealing observation in light of her claim that she "will not repeat what the apostolic man" previously said. In mentioning Radegund's treatment of her body, Baudonivia touches on an aspect of the first narrative that Fortunatus extensively developed, an indication that the second version cannot be considered only as an addendum to Fortunatus's account but must also be treated as a recasting of the original portrait, the articulation of another point of view on a dimension of the saint's life already handled by the first biographer.

As her own account explicitly shows, she is well aware of the previous hagiographer's emphasis on the *tortrix*. But in the very place Baudonivia refers to this emphasis, the role of extreme mortification in her version of the saint's life is never heightened. Instead, alternatives to self-torture appear prominently. That she positions her own text as an alternative to Fortunatus's *tortrix* episodes is clear from the structure of the sentence following the most striking reference to the "first book." Significantly, the adversative conjunction *tamen* and the comparative adjective *fortioribus* appear immediately after she refers to the sections of Fortunatus's narrative that detail the incidents of mortification. Instead of a hot brass plate and tight fitting chains covering her body, the sentence emphasizes the "stronger arms" girding Radegund—continual prayer, vigils, and reading:

> Et cum esset aliis misericors, sibi iudex effecta est, reliquis pia, in se abstinendo severa, omnibus larga, sibi restricta, ut madefecta ieiuniis non sufficeret, nisi et de suo corpore triumpharet.
> His igitur studiis occupata per omnem modum, sicut est in libro primo intimatum, meruit soli Deo prompte vacare. Quo tamen tempore fortioribus armis induta, sine cessatione orationibus, vigiliis, lectione propensa.[30]

Thus, after mentioning Fortunatus's depiction of the saint "triumphing over her body,"[31] Baudonivia introduces the ascetic aspects of the saint that were eclipsed by the graphic scenes of bloodletting and burning flesh described in the "first book." At the point where those striking episodes of Fortunatus's account begin to impinge on Baudonivia's narrative, a countering strategy can be detected that keeps the first portrait from coloring the new image of the saint. Here, the syntactical elements of her remarks offer the surest guide for interpretation. The word *tamen*, unlike so many other particles in the Latin of this period, often retains its "classical force" as an adversative conjunction.[32] In this passage, *tamen* clearly signifies the introduction of material that contrasts with what came immediately before it—namely, the reference to the episodes of mutilation found in Fortunatus's text and recounted in the general description culminating with the claim that the saint triumphed over the flesh. That Baudonivia's narrative is now engaging the earlier one is further indicated by the comparative adjective modifying *armis*. For this sentence to make sense, Fortunatus's version must be seen as providing a point of reference against which Baudonivia's text is positioned (as the use of *tamen* reveals) and with which her own depiction of the saint is being compared (as the word *fortioribus* indicates). The weapons of prayers, vigils and, reading are, in other words, the "stronger" or more powerful displays of sanctity than those of brutal self-mortifications. These aspects of the holy woman were lost sight of in a narrative that climaxed with the graphic exposure of "auto-torture."[33] Indeed, other than a brief reference to Radegund having been educated, the first *Vita* never mentions, as the second one frequently does, that Radegund constantly read.[34]

What eludes most of the more recent scholars, however, is that this engaging of Fortunatus is not diametrical opposition to the first *Life* but a subtle contrast that complements the original portrait so that there is again a kind of dialectic present, though a quite different one than what is at work in the *LVP*. Despite Baudonivia's recasting of Radegund's ascetic profile, she still insists on interpreting the saint's life as a martyrdom, and in doing so she aligns her text with a salient feature of Fortunatus's *Vitae*, in which the holy men are presented as martyrs.[35]

Thus, with respect to the saint's treatment of her body, what appears in the second *Vita* is a narrative strategy characterized by considerably more restraint than is displayed by Fortunatus. The second hagiographer mentions the fasts, the hair shirt, the tireless helping of the poor, and the care of the sick, without providing extensive details. For instance, the social commentary implicit in Fortunatus's moving accounts of a former queen extracting lice and worms from pus-infected flesh is present in Baudonivia's narrative only on the most superficial level. It becomes apparent from what immediately follows the last passage cited that the events lavishly illustrated in Fortunatus's account are tempered by Baudonivia's lighter rhetorical touch: "she served food to strangers at the table. With her own hands she washed and wiped the feet of the sick. She did not allow a servant girl to give her comfort. Instead, the devout woman rushed about to fulfill her service. She confined herself in so arduous a restriction of abstinence that, insofar as weakness allowed, the mind that strained for God no longer required earthly food."[36]

Instead of the lavish, bibulous, and bountiful banquets described in the first *Vita*,[37] Baudonivia simply mentions that the saint served food to the needy. She washes the poor, but no mention is made of their infections. She dutifully performs her chores but is not the frantic housekeeper, the "new Martha," of the first *Vita*, who took out dung, brought in firewood, cooked, washed dishes and swept every corner of the monastery.[38] She fasts, but only to the extent that health allows. She does wear a hair shirt that "tames her tender limbs," but it cannot be regarded as an unusual ascetic practice.[39] Most important of all, there is not the tremendous emphasis on Radegund's body that appears in Fortunatus's account. And, in addition to their diminished intensity, the ascetic rigors that do appear lack the gratuitous quality found in Fortunatus's version. Fasting and vigils increase either when the saint especially needs divine intervention, as when Clothar comes to take her away, or when she is thankful for having received it, as when the dejected king returns home without his spouse.[40]

These contrasts take us to the heart of understanding the differences of the two Lives. So many scholars stress that Baudonivia's Radegund even as a nun still behaves like the queen she once was.[41] The evidence cited for this comes from the accounts describing the diplomatic activities the saint has with the Frankish kings and her connections to the ecclesiastical and political powers of eastern Christendom. But Fortunatus's Radegund is no less active. Her activity, however, occurs in a different, less glamorous sphere of human life than the one described by Baudonivia. The first hagiographer detailed the social function of the living saint in her community. Fortunatus heightened her role as an indefatigable servant of the poor, a lover of lepers, and a bold intercessor on behalf of the imprisoned. As we noticed from our examination of Fortunatus's prose biographies, the care of the weak and oppressed is also associated with the holy bishops, whose acts of social justice are prominently portrayed as part of an effort to promote and legitimize the ecclesiastical hierarchy's exercise of power. Significantly, Baudonivia's Radegund, when compared with the portrait of her and of the other saints in Fortunatus's hagiography, is a less socially charged figure within Merovingian society. In the second *Life*, the saint's interaction with society's downtrodden lacks the depth and intensity found in the first. Perhaps the most obvious evidence is the absence of any miraculous prison freeings recounted in Baudonivia's narrative, the most dramatic expression of the Merovingian church's intervention on the part of an oppressed social group and hence an opportunity to highlight saintly power over secular authority. We may argue, of course, that Baudonivia in this regard is only keeping her word about not repeating what Fortunatus already said. But we now know from the way Radegund's self-mortification was handled that Baudonivia does indeed cover already familiar territory as part of an attempt to recast the image of sanctity in a way that contrasts with Fortunatus's portrait. Hence, the lack of content dealing with contemporary social conditions should be regarded as an indication that a different kind of sanctity altogether is being described in Baudonivia's account.

In light of what we have observed in Fortunatus's hagiography, we are in an excellent position to pinpoint where this difference lies. The episcopal sanctity portrayed by Fortunatus appears most limited in terms of its viability to be imitated. In fact, even to consider Fortunatus's hagiography as edification literature, the way saints' Lives are usually regarded, makes little sense. After all, with the exception of how it depicts Jews, pagans, and those who engage in what is regarded as sacrilegious behavior, Fortunatus's narratives are less overtly concerned with the laity and providing a model of sanctity for the faithful to live by than they are with illustrating the deeds of one particular ecclesiastical rank. The connection of his hagiography with the people is really based on securing their submission to and support for episcopal power. As previously seen in the discussion on Fortunatus's *Vitae*, the conditions of hagiographic production hardly reflect the romantic notion of a *Reinkultur* giving inspiration to this literature, as if it were the "poetry of the people."[42] Instead, based on what is revealed from Fortunatus's own comments on his function as a writer, his hagiography reflects the product of a small group of clerics' carefully overseeing the compositions and connecting the Lives to their own episcopal ambitions. For the most part, the literature's mimetic function appears rather limited, restricted primarily to an identification of dead saints and their glorious deeds with the vision that the episcopal commissioners have of themselves as community leaders, whose own actions can find justification and support in the narratives on their predecessors. On the face of it, this kind of hagiography leaves little room for imitation, given that its aim is to make the heroes fundamentally indistinguishable from the cadres of the ecclesiastical hierarchy.

With the first *Life of Saint Radegund*, another element is introduced that further diminishes the edificative function of the narrative and its potential as a model of saintly behavior. Now, there appear not only the usual features associated with an episcopal sanctity, evidenced by the emphasis on Radegund as a force who alleviates wretched social conditions, but also a heightening of ascetic practices, an aspect that shares nothing with the accounts of the male saints, all of whom who were portrayed as moderate in that regard or at least, as in the case of Paternus, shown not to become extreme, perhaps the best indication of how this hagiography reflects the episcopal milieu in which it was produced. But with Radegund's *Life*, there is not only a zealous asceticism of the sort Paternus once displayed; there are acts of self-torture presented in an unprecedented manner. The image of sanctity emerging from this account is thus a strange amalgamation of episcopal elements and exotic asceticism that corresponds to none of the forms of syncreticism characterizing the saint types previously encountered.

Ultimately, this example of sanctity considered in its entirety is obsolete. Here, it is interesting to note that more than one researcher has claimed, usually with no or little substantiation, that Fortunatus's *Vita sanctae Radegundis* became a literary model followed by later hagiographers. To be sure, the explicit influence of his narrative can be detected in several Lives.[43] But one important fact emerges after we sift through the texts that relied on Fortunatus's account of Radegund. Nowhere does there appear the extreme mortifying activity that so characterizes Fortunatus's narrative. Certainly, the authors borrow phrases describing Radegund's asceticism, such as her habit of eating coarse bread, wearing a hair shirt, or performing the most demeaning chores in the monastery.[44] But nowhere do we encounter a repetition of extreme, self-inflicted mutilation, even when the subject of a biography is a female saint, as in the case of Balthild's *Vita*, whose author in other respects depended on Fortunatus's narrative. What we do find inserted into the Lives of Balthild, Arnulf, and Eligius are the texts describing Radegund's care of the poor, as well as words borrowed to facilitate the humility topos and other prefacing material.[45] But an account relying on the depiction of Radegund as a *tortrix* is not likely to be found.[46] Hence, in spite of the influence his composition exercised over other hagiographers, if the selection of borrowed texts in these other narratives is any indication, the model of the extreme mortifier could not be adopted as a preferred example of the sanctified life. And this observation regarding what image of sanctity can function successfully as an imitable example of holiness brings us back to Baudonivia's text.

We have already examined one instance in which she engages the "first book." In the same chapter, shortly after this reference to Fortunatus, Baudonivia once more mentions the first book and again calls attention to how this account emphasizes the saint's self-imposed hardships. Then, significantly, Baudonivia immediately claims that Radegund "made herself poor . . . in order to be an example to others." Here, there is no adversative conjunction or use of the comparative adjective to indicate that the text is positioning itself against Fortunatus's narrative. What we do find is a succession of saintly vignettes, all of which are related to monastic life. The nature of the activity described contrasts with the content of the "earlier book" mentioned immediately before because Baudonivia recounts small, almost unnoticed practices of the saint, practices that any nun in the convent can obviously imitate:

> The first book taught many things about her rigorous abstinence and servitude. She made herself poor for God to such an extent that she provided an example to others. The only time she had a glove to wear on her hand was when she made two of them from the leather of her worn-out shoes. But she led the life of a poor person in such a way that the abbess did not detect what she was doing. Who can explain her patience, charity, fervor of spirit, discretion, benevolence, holy zeal and continual reflection day and night on the law of the Lord? Since she herself did not cease preaching or meditating on the Psalms, the lectoress,[47] along with the other nuns, never stopped reading

in her presence. The praise of God did not leave her heart or mouth, so much so that when she had by chance seen the monastery doorkeeper, Eodegund, passing by and wanted to call her, instead of saying the nun's name, she shouted "alleluia." She did this sort of thing a thousand times. Never did a slander, never did a lie, never did a harsh word against anyone come from her lips. Not only did she not speak against anyone, she did not tolerate listening to someone who did.[48]

All of these little episodes culminate in a scene that has no parallel in Fortunatus's version. The second biographer includes extended, direct speech of the saint speaking intimately to the community of women. Thus, in contrast to the "first book," Baudonivia, by inserting the simple but powerful discourse of her founder into the narrative, penetrates the character of a monastic saint who leads by imitable examples and heartfelt preaching rather than by the inimitable mortifications or even the kind of intense activity in society associated with the episcopal sanctity beyond the conventual walls:

> She always prayed for those persecuting her and taught us to pray. She loved the congregation gathered in the name of the Lord and full of the desire for God so much that she did not even remember having parents or a royal husband. Often when she was preaching to us, she used to say: "You, I have chosen as my daughters; you, my eyes; you, my life; you, my total rest and happiness; you, the new plantation. Come with me in this world so that we may rejoice in the next. Let us serve the Lord with full faith and full affection of the heart. Let us seek him in the fear and simplicity of the heart so that with confidence we can say to him: 'Grant, Lord, what you have promised, because we have done what you have ordered.' "[49]

Fortunatus does not offer any glimpse of the saint in an extended dialogue with the community, although he does occasionally record brief, sometimes jocular remarks.[50] The strategy of recording Radegund's preaching gives an intimacy to the second *Vita* that the first one lacks, and it is a technique that Baudonivia turns to again. The insertion of direct address, as that quoted here, not only adds a greater spiritual depth to Radegund's portrait than what is found in the first narrative, it also reveals the psychological world of an enclosed monastic community. Although Fortunatus lived for a time in this religious milieu, he does not normally penetrate its psychological nature in his poems to Radegund and Agnes, with his verses all too often expressing the poet's appreciation of food and wine rather than the spiritual life of the convent.[51]

The most obvious evidence that this rich psychological and spiritual world found expression in Baudonivia's writing is the recounting of dreams and visions, an aspect of Radegund's religious experience that never appears in the first *Vita*.[52] Besides reporting these events, Baudonivia also relates how they became part of the hagiographer's material, by claiming that Radegund confidentially entrusted her personal religious experiences to a few intimate associates, another indication of how the second narrative provides a glimpse into the intimate spiritual life shared within the monastic community.

But the role that reading plays in the second story shows how the psychological depth and spirituality of the saint affect the members of her religious community in a way that the personal experiences of dreams and visions do not. As previously mentioned, Fortunatus's depiction of Radegund's monastic life consists largely of the saint's performing humble chores, duties also described in Caesarius's *Rule for Nuns*, which Radegund's convent had adopted.[53] If the depiction of the self-mortifying Radegund can hardly be implemented as a model of asceticism, this utilization of the rule's directives concerning manual labor may perhaps be in Fortunatus's narrative the only prominent aspect of Radegund's sanctity that would bear directly on the daily life of ordinary nuns. Significantly, however, there is another noteworthy feature of Caesarius's rule, one that Baudonivia emphasizes—the importance of reading.[54]

We have already observed how hagiographic literature can capture the important role of reading in the monastic life. Gregory's account of Saint Leobardus, as was previously discussed, especially highlights the textual orientation of monastic sanctity. Similarly, Baudonivia's depiction of Radegund's religious life and that of her nuns repeatedly focuses on the reading of texts. Radegund is shown constantly reading and involving others in this activity. The reading is obviously associated with the meditation on and the interpretation of the literature being studied or recited, as much of the content in the ninth chapter of the second *Life* richly illustrates. Here, we glimpse how reading texts works internally on the saint and her community, something quite different from what is found in the story of a hermit such as Leobardus or in Fortunatus's account, the latter making no mention of such occurrences. As described by Baudonivia, the meditation required by reading causes those listening to reflect on themselves. Rather than the first *Life*'s detailed description of chores, this ninth chapter subtly reveals behavior at conventual reading sessions and highlights not only the reflective nature of Radegund's sanctity but also how the other nuns are drawn into her spiritual world by her preaching and example, and we once more find a connection between the saint and her followers that is based on the possibility of the latter imitating the former, a possibility not offered by the example of the *tortrix*. After mentioning how her founder worked as an example within the community, Baudonivia reveals, again through the use of the saint's direct speech, the concentrated gaze of Radegund and the community, initially on a text, then at each other, and finally into themselves individually:

> Whenever a servant of God came, she would anxiously inquire how to serve the Lord. If she learned from him anything that she was not doing, with all eagerness she immediately imposed it first on herself. Afterward she would teach it to the congregation by word as well as show it to them by example. If, by chance, the reciting of a Psalm had ceased in her presence, she would start reading and never stop reading day and night, even while she refreshed her body a little. When a text was being read, she, bearing the care of our souls with pious solicitude, used to say: "If you do not understand what is being read, why is it that you do not solicitously search the mirror of your souls?" And even though the nuns presumed not to ask too many questions out of respect for her, she, for the salvation of souls, did not cease expounding what the reading contained. . . . At night, when she seemed to be taking an hour's nap, there was always a text being read. Just from feeling the languor of sleep coming over her while she read, she thought she was already getting a little rest. When the mind that yearned for Christ ceased reading, she used to ask, as if to say, "I sleep but my heart is awake" (Ct. 5:2): "Why are you silent? Read and do not stop reading."[55]

The generally acknowledged function of saints' Lives in the Gallican liturgy,[56] the frequency with which the two accounts of Radegund were copied, and the fact that both *Vitae* usually appear together should caution us against arguing too emphatically that the differences in the stories told by Fortunatus and Baudonivia are indicative of how the authors tailored their narratives to suit different audiences. Yet, the way in which each author addresses readers lends support to the claim that the divergences between the two biographies of Saint Radegund arise, at least in part, from differences among each author's readers or, as is more likely the case, listeners.[57] Baudonivia, for instance, dedicates her *Vita* to the "holy ladies and abbess of Radegund's congregation,"[58] and she allegedly undertakes her task at the request of her monastic superior, someone—and here we can only be speculating—who may have been as responsible for and intimately connected with the final product and the image of sanctity it aimed to promote as Fortunatus's episcopal patrons were when they commissioned him to write hagiography reflecting and legitimizing the claims of episcopal power. Out of Baudonivia's initial expressions of humility, her "linguistic helplessness," emerges a certainty in her role as a writer.[59] She refers to herself confidently as a "heraldess" (*praeconia*), a female crier proclaiming the "glorious life" of Radegund specifically to the "ears" of her founder's "flock." Obviously, Fortunatus's audience for Radegund's *Life*, like the rest of his hagiography read by Baudonivia, also included the monastic community of Sainte-Croix. However, in his own preface, he does not single out Radegund's sisters as an audience or even dedicate his composition to her monastic community. Instead, like his other Lives, he explicitly states that he intends to proclaim his *Vita* to the "public." As he expresses it, his aim is to have the memory of the former queen and wife of King Clothar "celebrated in the world."[60]

Such considerations help to confirm the impression that, contrary to much of the present scholarship that insists on seeing in Baudonivia's portrait a still active queen, the second *Vita* promotes primarily a monastic sanctity and leaves an image of a more deeply spiritual woman than the one Fortunatus first describes. If this is the case, then Baudonivia's narrative also becomes, indirectly, a critique of Fortunatus's hagiography as a whole, because, in extensively delineating a monastic type of sanctity, she has capitalized on the very feature of the holy life that Fortunatus's writing never comes close to penetrating, given its emphasis on an episcopal sanctity which, though tenuously connected with a monastic holiness through a usually superficial syncreticism, really finds its fullest expression in manipulating social and political conditions rather than in the development of an interior life.

Reading and contemplation, dreams and visions, all taking place within an enclosed environment where intimate, verbal exchanges occur, are not the features that come prominently to mind when we recall Fortunatus's *Life of Saint Radegund* and the rest of his prose hagiography devoted to holy bishops. This is not to say that Baudonivia ignores the social dimension of sanctity emphasized by Fortunatus. The virtue of her narrative is that she does not let it dominate, and so she recaptures the original ideal of Martinian sanctity, where the power of holiness is displayed not only in the social and political spheres of life but also by a genuine monastic detachment.[61]

If there is any validity to these conclusions on the differences between the two Lives, then an episode such as the conventual reading session assumes an added, mimetic significance. The passage gives a description of Radegund as the "solicitous" caretaker of "souls" immediately before recounting how she used to tell the nuns who did not understand the meaning of the passage to "search the mirror" of their own "souls" for an answer. The text itself at this point becomes a kind of rhetorical mirror, where Radegund's advice to the nuns given in the clause containing the words *sollicitudine animarum vestrarum* echoes or, better, reflects what immediately preceded it, the description of the saint as "*sollicitudine . . . animarum nostrarum curam gerens.*"

The use of language here calls to mind what would have been the most obvious function of Baudonivia's narrative. The creation of a rhetorical mirror occurs precisely in a description that corresponds with the very setting in which her own work would have been read.[62] Given that *Vitae* probably constituted much of the monastic reading at Sainte-Croix, as is evident from Baudonivia's own use of hagiographic texts in her narrative, the context of the passage describing the reading session is exactly that in which her own *Life of Saint Radegund* would have been read.[63] In other words, those who listen to a reading of Baudonivia's *Vita* are doing what the text itself describes, and there is an explicit connection between the saint's activity of the past and the nuns' continuation of that same activity in the present. The very act of reading and listening to the story constitutes a sharing in the life of sanctity because such activity directly imitates what the saint did while alive. The reading scene thus acquires a functional power as a mimetic device that reinforces the possibility of saintly behavior in the ordinary routine of monastic life.

The *Virago*

Although usually not discussed in detail, scenes such as the one just examined have rightly been cited as examples of how Baudonivia presents Radegund as a spiritual mother.[64] Her devotion to the women is further demonstrated by her ability to obtain numerous, precious relics, including a piece of the cross. The acquiring of such objects thus assures a steady stream of pilgrims whose benefactions will provide for the community after the founder dies.[65]

In concentrating on such episodes, however, we should not lose sight of the fact that they represent only a portion of what is a larger, more complex portrait. So far, we have tended to examine most closely the differences between the two Lives. Yet, even a brief glimpse at where Baudonivia's hagiography coincides with that of Fortunatus can show that the current trend, which finds in the Radegund of the second *Vita* a nurturing spiritual mother, fails to acknowledge the dissonance in the second Life, the very aspect of Radegund's sanctity that is undoubtedly the least attractive to modern sensibilities and to scholarship that tends to highlight primarily the charity of holy women.

One episode not adequately addressed by the current research is Radegund's burning of a pagan temple. It is the fanatical, religiously intolerant sanctity so characteristic of Fortunatus's holy warriors. The scene is especially reminiscent of the behavior attributed to Paternus and his monastic companion, when the two, as previously discussed, are said to have bravely risked their lives in an attempt to disrupt what was regarded as diabolical rituals. Prior to Fortunatus, Sulpicius Severus also describes

Saint Martin's antagonism toward pagan ceremonies and prominently displays, as Baudonivia does Radegund, the militant holy man who sets pagan temples ablaze.[66] In this instance, then, a female writer attributes a deed to a holy woman that conforms with what is generally regarded as a masculine ideal of sanctity. Here, not Fortunatus, but Baudonivia presents a saint who is what modern scholars call a *virago*:

> In the course of her journey, as a train of worldly followers accompanied her and with a long distance still left to travel, there was a temple worshipped by the Franks within one mile of the blessed queen's route. Hearing that the Franks worshipped there, she ordered her servants to set the temple on fire, thinking it unjust that the God of heaven is being despised and that diabolical schemes are being carried out with veneration. When the Franks and the whole crowd heard this, they began to defend the temple with swords, clubs and all sorts of diabolical ranting and raving. But the holy queen, unmoved and steadfast, bearing Christ in her heart, sat on her horse which did not move until the temple was consumed by flames.[67]

Within the community, too, the female saint can inflict punitive miracles as harshly as any of the holy bishops who are displayed by Fortunatus as protecting church property or punishing sacrilegious behavior.[68] In an example that is again reminiscent of a story told by Sulpicius about Martin, for instance, a slave of the monastery, who insolently sits in Radegund's chair, is fittingly punished by her heavenly master:

> Vinoberga, one of the maidservants, with reckless daring presumed to sit on the chair of the blessed queen after she had passed away. When this happened, Vinoberga was struck by the judgement of God: she caught on fire and everyone saw the smoke billowing up from her. In public she proclaimed to everyone what she had done and confessed that she had sinned, saying that she was burning because she had sat on the chair of the blessed woman. For three days and three nights she endured the burning until she screamed and shouted: "Lady Radegund, I have sinned and acted badly. Cool off that part of my body which is inflamed and in terrible pain! . . ." Seeing her in so much pain, all the people prayed for her as if Radegund were present, saying that whenever she is invoked out of faith she is present: "Good Lady," they cried, "spare her so that she does not expire from so much suffering." So the blessed woman kindly indulged everyone's prayers and extinguished the burning flame.[69]

Such scenes obviously pose a challenge to those who tend to see in Baudonivia's portrait of Radegund the innovative introduction of a feminine ideal of sanctity into Merovingian hagiography. We can and have found sharp contrasts in Baudonivia's account and observed how she engages the first narrative in a way that significantly recasts the image of Radegund's sanctity that Fortunatus's writing projects. Whether these divergences in her narrative reflect the vision of a female writer or that of a less gender-conscious nun cannot be as easily determined as much of the current scholarship would have us believe. One point we can be sure of: the richness of Baudonivia's writing cannot be reduced to either of these alternatives. To disentangle the female writer from her monastic outlook is impossible, especially if this outlook is predominantly shaped by a religious rule that differs only in minor ways from the *regulae* of men.[70] Also difficult is the task of understanding how her psychological portrait of the spiritual mother interacting with a community of women meshes with the image of the masculine warrior, the *belligator*, doing the deeds of holy destruction that we find in the pages of Fortunatus and Sulpicius Severus.

Martha and Mary

Another important feature of Baudonivia's rhetorical strategy also coincides with Fortunatus's hagiography. Scriptural texts are inserted into her narrative with a similar moderation and purpose that we saw displayed throughout Fortunatus's *Vitae*. Hence, a miracle involving the everlasting abundance of wine is likened to the feeding of the five thousand, much as a similar deed in the story of Marcellus was compared with the other obvious biblical precedent, the wedding feast at Cana.[71] And scriptural resonances can be detected when the behavior of the saint during a time of conflict needs to be justified, a technique also employed by Fortunatus and, of course, countless other hagiographers. Thus, in relating the controversy surrounding the arrival of the true cross, which Radegund requested and received from Justin II, Baudonivia associates Bishop Maroveus's refusal to honor the relic with the events leading to Christ's crucifixion: "No less harm did the holy cross suffer through envy than the Lord who . . . after he was called and recalled before the chiefs and judges, patiently endured every evil so that what he had created would not perish."[72]

With respect to her use of Scripture, Baudonivia clearly has far more in common with Fortunatus than with the author of the *LVP*. The limited application of biblical texts at a few points in the narrative, rather than a pervasive and explicit scriptural orientation operating throughout the story, is characteristic of Radegund's *Lives* and differentiates Fortunatus and Baudonivia from Gregory of Tours.

However, as is the case with the explicit borrowings in Baudonivia's text, the very quality her writing shares with Fortunatus's in the matter of scriptural allusion can also reveal an intriguing divergency. The author of the first *Life* emphasizes the saint's constant activity as a monastic housekeeper. As will be recalled, her devotion to chores is mentioned early on, when the *puella-senex* is described as washing the heads of her little companions and cleaning around the altar of the church she visits. These tasks anticipate the activity of the saint in her monastery, where she performs a variety of chores, from sweeping to "removing the dung." This emphasis on Radegund's work in her community naturally leads to a comparison to the biblical figure who, in allegorical interpretation, is commonly regarded as the model of the active life. Thus the saint constantly feeding, bathing, clothing, and cleaning is called the "new Martha."[73]

Significantly, Baudonivia associates Radegund with a biblical prototype commonly regarded as typifying the contemplative life. By likening the saint to Mary of Bethany, she chooses to compare Radegund to a biblical model that stands for the exact opposite of what Martha represents.[74] Admittedly, the context of the reference does not concern the contemplative life but highlights parallel acts of love, a similarity between Mary's wiping the feet of Jesus with her hair and Radegund's own practice of washing feet with her hands.[75] However, the Mary in John 12:1–8, to which Baudonivia alludes, is thought to be the same Mary who sat at Christ's feet while her sister Martha busily attended to the "service" of hospitality.[76] As a type of the contemplative life, her significance obviously extends beyond the context in which she is referred to in Baudonivia's text. The name itself represents a particular religious mode, one that also happens to contrast with Fortunatus's depiction. With the exception of Christ, Martha and Mary are the only biblical persons mentioned by name in the two Lives of Radegund. For this reason, the names stand out as unique elements in both versions.

Because Fortunatus compares Radegund with Martha and Baudonivia associates her with Mary, two different images of sanctity are conveyed. And these two different images derived from the contrasting biblical models correspond, as can be readily seen from our examination of these Lives, with the depiction of the active Radegund that generally characterizes the first account and the more interiorly spiritual saint described in the second narrative. In addition, the implicit connotations that the mere names of Mary and Martha can convey in the context of the two different *Vitae* may also indicate a subtle preference justified by Christ's arresting words to Martha when she protests her sister's idleness. Of the two versions of Radegund's biography, it is the portrait given by Baudonivia that is thus associated with the "better portion."[77]

Let us conclude this chapter by iterating that Baudonivia's resistance to male hagiographers' tendency to try to compensate for a perceived womanly weakness marks her most significant and identifiable departure from the whole history of the literature. In fact, by understanding the significance of a female author who adheres to a prominent convention in an instance when that convention itself is normally suspended, we can establish grounds for arguing that Baudonivia's preface undermines the dominant rhetorical strategy that male authors consistently employ to approach the subject of female saints. But let us also add that in one important respect the *Life* also conforms to what we have observed in the depictions by male authors of holy women. Indeed, no more convincing a *virago* could be imagined than the fanatical holy warrior intolerantly and fearlessly razing a pagan temple. This and the texts previously mentioned, in which women describe themselves as acting "manly" (*viriliter*), suggest that the nurturing image of a spiritual mother cannot adequately account for the more comprehensive and problematic image of female sanctity that we have discovered.

6

CONCLUSION

A World Turned Upside-Down

The possibility that Frankish nuns may also have
made a contribution to the meager literary production predating the Carolingian Renaissance and
that their writings may be buried among the anonymous hymns, chronicles, and saints' lives in early
medieval manuscripts has not been seriously considered.
— Susan Wemple, *Women* (1981, p. 182)

The closing remarks in the previous chapter anticipate a few final observations that
we can now make after having considered a significant body of hagiographic texts.
Let us begin by summarizing the findings related to Gregory's account of Monegund's life because, of all the sources considered, this story offers the most unambiguous evidence.

Certainly, there is a tendency among male writers to problematize gender when
the subject of a biography is female. But a reference such as the one made by Gregory
of Tours in his *Life of Saint Monegund* to women taking part in the manly contest for
salvation is hardly out of keeping with what is now regarded as the "authentic voice"
of some prominent holy women. If Gregory is negatively viewed on that count,
then we shall also have to offer a similar assessment of sources such as those describing Perpetua's vision or Caesaria's letter to Radegund, texts highly regarded in
the current research as documents that record the religious *mentalité* of early Christian
women. However, the explicit reference to the "inferior sex" is something that we
do not encounter even in those instances when women speak like men. Certainly,
this attention to gender and the negative view of women as inferior mark a fundamental change in his rhetorical strategy. But aside from that phrase and initial
focus, we cannot find other evidence that Gregory's approach to the genre was
significantly altered when he wrote about a female saint.

Hence, although we can speak of a noticeable modification in the preface to
Monegund's *Vita*, one that undoubtedly marks a break with all the other Lives in the
collection and arises from the author's perception of the saint's gender as a mark of
weakness, this feature, significant as it is, never appears again in the narrative. With
the exception of a few lines at the beginning, nothing stands out on the basis of
gender as the narrative proceeds to its conclusion. Nor can we cite the episode of

Monegund's attempt to free herself from her husband as being the peculiar interest of a male author because a similar scene is described by Baudonivia. Furthermore, ample textual evidence in the LVP shows that the coercion of a saint's family to marry could be as great for some male saints described in the collection as it was for Monegund. And those who choose to lead holy lives, regardless of whether they are male or female, become the brides of Christ. On the whole, when the text of Monegund's *Vita* faces the others in the LVP, the level of dissonance that can be detected is minimal. Therefore, in almost every respect, this *Life* is consistent with what we find throughout the LVP.

As an example of a striking contrast with Gregory's depiction of a holy woman, we can cite Fortunatus's *Life of Saint Radegund*. The author's focus on the saint's self-mutilation is highly unusual, not only from the perspective of his own corpus but also in light of all the other texts examined in this study. Again, it can only be repeated that Fortunatus goes beyond Gregory's depiction of Monegund and any of the earlier hagiographic literature describing the asceticism or heroics of women. His female *tortrix*, who also shares several common characteristics with the profile of holy bishops, makes for the strangest kind of syncretism encountered in our sources. Obviously, generalizations about the male depiction of female saints should not be made on the basis of Fortunatus's account, especially in that this text can hardly be said to be representative of his hagiography as a whole. With respect to how it displays the saint treating her body, it is a hagiographic anomaly, as Aigrain had previously suggested. But in noting this irregular feature, we must also keep in mind that other aspects of his narrative, especially the episodes describing Radegund's charity, were influential and became, as other scholars have observed, paradigmatic.

In addition, both writers appear to draw on a common tradition when they turn to the subject of female saints. This fact is not meant to serve as an excuse for their misogyny, but it does highlight how strong and long-lasting a literary trend can be, with some of the same phrases and themes found in the oldest Christian sources appearing virtually unchanged up to the time Gregory and Fortunatus composed their works. Even more important than establishing the textual continuity between the major Merovingian writers and their male hagiographic predecessors, the brief overview of the older sources allowed us to begin to appreciate how complex the relation between gender and sanctity can become when this issue is explicitly raised by authors. At this point in the discussion, we were compelled to acknowledge that some of the texts now thought to be representative of a female perspective offer a conception of sanctity that, at least on the superficial level, appears to be male. Making such an observation enables us to highlight an important oversight in the current scholarship on Merovingian female saints: The image of the *virago* can be as much the product of a woman's perception of female sanctity as it is that of a man's.

Hence, we can see a line of continuity from Perpetua's vision of herself as a man to Gregory's story of Papula putting on male clothes and living in a monastery *tamquam vir inter viros*. Needless to say, such a connection is not one that the current research is in a position to make, not only because of its limited treatment of sources but also because this feature of the literature forces scholars to rethink the assumption that a feminine perspective somehow leads to a different ideal of sanctity based on "female values." Indeed, the more perplexing texts suggest that the experience of sanctity really occurs in a kind of world turned upside-down, where a man can gain power by dreaming of castration and a woman by acquiring a phallus.

Of course, it is this attainment of power in a variety of forms that is the sine qua non of sanctity. As we have seen throughout this study, seizing power leads to saints who control various critical spheres of human life, or at least this outcome is what the hagiographic literature attempts to demonstrate. A holy person may exercise power over kin by breaking familial or conjugal ties, over the enticements of the world by rejecting the privileges associated with high social status; over the body through sexual abstinence and a meager intake of food, over political leaders responsible for maintaining oppressive social conditions by liberating the imprisoned, over non-Christians by coercing them to convert and persecuting them, over rival representatives within the saint's own church by creating factionalism, and over the natural world by miraculously manipulating it. Indeed, the holy person acquires the ability to perform miracles of all sorts, an aspect of sanctity described by a word that reveals just how closely the ideal of sanctity is entwined with the attainment of power—virtus. From what we have seen, a female hagiographer is as inclined to present a holy woman as an imposing, manly figure of power as any of her male counterparts. Whether it is the militant Martin or Radegund who is burning down a pagan temple or the quietly sustained and disciplined rigor that comes from living in the hollowed-out rock of a cave, the sources indicate that there can be no claim to holiness without some demonstration of power. This is the common mark of sanctity, and it is not gender-bound.

In addition to highlighting this common ideal of sanctity as the attainment of power, the focus on the basic features of the hagiographic literature produced by male writers also leads to sound conclusions about Baudonivia's narrative. Obviously, coordinating the study on the basis of prefaces, textual borrowings, and Scripture allows us to recognize the context in which certain strategies normally appear. Hence, the words borrowed from Fortunatus's writing on male saints can be interpreted as having another meaning altogether when they appear in a context in which that author himself would have resorted to a different strategy. And the comparison of Radegund with Mary of Bethany offers an intriguing contrast between the two Lives, especially when we take into account that the mention of Martha in Fortunatus's text is the only other reference to a biblical figure, with the exception of Christ, to appear in the *Vitae*.

With respect to the similarities Baudonivia's text has with Fortunatus's hagiography, the story of Radegund's burning the pagan temple undoubtedly resembles the depiction of holy warriors discussed in the second chapter, as well as Sulpicius Severus's description of the militant Martin.[1] Baudonivia's *Vita* is the one commonly cited for the way it presents Radegund as a nurturing spiritual mother, so the emphasis on this episode in the later part of the study is meant to balance the one-sided attention on the "female values" that supposedly characterize the work. Indeed, this portrait of Radegund by Baudonivia is another instance in which a woman proudly describes what would be considered, if a male author had told the story, behavior characteristic of a *virago*. Here again, we can identify a continuity that persistently resists the conventional gender roles, so that the fervor of Radegund's religious commitment resembles the phallically endowed and fighting Perpetua or the defiant mother recorded in Maccabees rather than what really amounts to a bourgeois nun nicely settled in her cultured convent, which is the image that the current scholarship regularly presents as the feminine ideal of sanctity.

Undoubtedly, these considerations make it more difficult to determine what in Baudonivia's portrait might be attributable to a female perspective and what are simply part of the less gender-conscious operations of an early medieval hagiographer or, more precisely, a religious writer who encountered sanctity. In the Life of Rusticula, for instance, the narrator gives an account that in several respects reflects the same concerns of an enclosed women's community recorded in Baudonivia's narrative, with a monastic model of sanctity emerging that is strikingly similar to Radegund's second Vita. And this correspondence occurs despite the fact that the author of Rusticula's Life is male.[2]

Moreover, the same difficulties encountered in Baudonivia's text arise when we turn to the Vita sanctae Balthildis. It is quite true that the female author of this work did not, as male writers do, make any reference to "womanly weakness" when prefacing the Life and that there is not a trace of the virago motif in the story. Yet we have another instance of a female—not a male—writer's relating how the saint avoided her first prospect of marriage, another indication that this tendency to portray women fleeing from husbands cannot be attributed only to male hagiographers.[3] What is even more perplexing for the current trend in the scholarship on the Merovingian Vitae sanctarum is the fact that the woman who wrote Balthild's Vita, when seeking a model for the depiction of female sanctity, turned not to Baudonivia's but to Fortunatus's Life of Saint Radegund.

Also similar to one of the problems raised by Baudonivia's text is the difficulty of dealing with the conventional aspects of hagiographic narrative shaped by a woman's discourse. For instance, despite whatever distinctiveness may be detected in the visions of Aldegund, the relation of this saint's personal religious experiences occurs in a Vita so conventional that Delehaye quotes it at length as one of the generic examples of a saint's Life.[4] Hence, one of the key texts that the current scholarship turns to for finding evidence of a special female spirituality appears in a narrative of standard hagiography, though Delehaye remains the only one who acknowledges it as such. Certainly this aspect of the Life needs to be addressed in relation to the visions, which are now treated in isolation from the very text in which they are recorded.

The fact that female writers seem to use the same strategies as male hagiographers suggests where the focus of scholarship should turn. Clearly, it is the male writer who makes the jarring adjustment to a female saint when he begins to tell the story. The most explicit dissonance and obvious distinctiveness lie here, and hence attention initially ought to focus here, given that the male authors are the ones who assume in their opening remarks that femininity and sanctity do not easily match. Baudonivia does, indeed, give us a glimpse of the militant, manly woman but she does so without any sense of its being incompatible with the saint's gender, whereas the male authors must first note the possibility of overcoming femininity at the outset of their stories.

This assertion, of course, takes us back to where we started this investigation— that is, to the question of methodology. In the epigraph chosen for this concluding chapter, Wemple suggests the possibility that much more literary material produced by women may exist in anonymous form. To be sure, this is an intriguing prospect—a body of literature still extant that was written by women and yet never acknowledged or studied as such. But Wemple's suggestion raises problems beyond the hope of actually uncovering a female, Frankish literature. Clearly, the problem is a methodological one. What criteria can be established to determine whether an anonymous life was produced by a woman, especially if, as we have discovered, there is no clear-cut correlation between the depiction of sanctity and an author's gender?[5] Moreover, the fact of anonymity itself could reveal something about the nature of hagiography and the culture in which it flourished. In the production and reception of the anonymous pre-Carolingian literature to which Wemple's remark refers, an author's name, and hence the question of gender, obviously had little significance in the dissemination of the literature, given that the writers themselves, or later scribes who copied their works, evidently felt no compulsion to reveal authorial identity. At the risk of promoting Bernoulli's highly romanticized treatment of Merovingian hagiography, it should be at least mentioned that the existence of a large body of texts circulating anonymously might be more profitably considered as evidence of a collective understanding of sanctity rather than as the individual expressions of female authors.[6]

Wemple's tempting suggestion, along with the difficulty in carrying it out, also brings to mind another view about the recovery of women's literature and history. In a well-known passage from Virginia Woolf's *A Room of One's Own*, the indifference scholars used to show toward the history of women is expressed by the lament that "nothing is known about women before the eighteenth century."[7] Certainly, the work of recent scholars in bringing to light the roles played by women during the Middle Ages has increased our awareness and advanced our knowledge to the point that Woolf's words are no longer as compelling as they were when first written.[8] But in another way, her comment does speak to the major problem raised but not acknowledged by Wemple's speculation. There may very well be a still unrecognized body of literature produced by women. Now, however, the difficulty encountered in uncovering it arises not from an indifference to this subject but from the lack of a sound methodology. Unless the texts themselves explicitly call attention to their distinction, it will be difficult to detect with certainty what may be female concerns expressed in works produced by anonymous women. In short, given all that needs to be considered, methodologically speaking, when we attempt to study adequately a text in which we know for certain that the author is female, such as in the case of Baudonivia's work, the challenges facing researchers trying to discover female authorship through a textual examination based on style and content alone, without any empirical evidence to go by, seem almost insurmountable at this time.

Obviously, Wemple's sensitivity to the possibility of more texts belonging to women than has hitherto been realized arises from her argument that female authors represent a thriving countermovement in hagiography's evolution, one that revealed the nature of feminine sanctity and spirituality in a way male writers could not. Of course, the alternative to the view that the literature produced by and about women reveals a different perspective from that written by and about men is the position that the attainment of sanctity described in the sources reflects a circumstance in which male and female transcend gender differences and achieve equality.[9] This study has highlighted some of the similarities in the texts pertaining to holy men and women that could lend support to the claim of equality. But this claim cannot be made without reservations. If sanctity is an attainment that puts holy individuals on equal footing, we should also note that the opportunity to achieve such a status was not as readily available to all classes of society. If the relative uniformity of biographical subjects is any indication, those in charge of hagiographic production evidently succeeded in carefully controlling what image of sanctity was to be most prominently promoted. As we can easily tell from the texts in the corpus of Gregory and Fortunatus, our sources do not record as many women as they do men who attain such a status, and this silence itself may say more about the prominence of gender inequality than the surviving works of male authors who wrote accounts of female saints. If this is true, however, women must be viewed as part of a larger group of holy people whose social and lay status made them largely unsuitable subjects for biographies, in spite of the fact that, as Waldron has so carefully and conclusively shown with exhaustive documentation from the sources, such "saints" obviously existed throughout the religious landscape of Merovingian Gaul.[10]

Undoubtedly, the consequence of a highly organized, clerical, and patriarchal church is the promotion of saints who reflect the concerns of the ecclesiastical hierarchy, a development that evidently marginalized the more free-spirited women and men whose biographies would never be written. This fact makes some of the independent saints of the LVP, including the charismatic Monegund dwelling at Martin's tomb, all the more extraordinary simply because their lives were recorded. And they were recorded not by a writer antagonistic toward the growing ambitio of a clerical culture, an attitude expressed by Sulpicius Severus, but by an author who himself claims to come from a long line of aristocratic bishops and who took his see uncanonically as the result of his connection with royal power.

This realization of Gregory's achievement as a hagiographer leads to the most important concluding observation that we can make after having examined the hagiography of Fortunatus, Gregory, and Baudonivia. The present search for a distinctiveness that is determined purely on the basis of gender is undoubtedly a misguided approach to the study of the Merovingian Vitae. If we consider all the major texts that have been discussed throughout this investigation, then we notice that Fortunatus and Baudonivia have far more in common with each other as hagiographers than they do with Gregory of Tours. The restrained use of Scripture, the dedication to the writer's patron, and the selection of texts she draws on make Baudonivia an author who still maintains, despite the differences in her version of Radegund's Life, a close affinity to the kind of hagiography Fortunatus writes. Putting aside the elaborate epistolary addresses to episcopal patrons, her work resembles Fortunatus's way of telling the life of a saint far more than it does Gregory's.

The author of the LVP is a hagiographer of an entirely different stock. In terms of the rhetorical strategies employed, his collection of Lives is undoubtedly the work that stands out as the distinctive document of the early Merovingian period. The carefully structured connection between preface and narrative, the innovative use of Scripture, the wide range of sanctity represented, and his ability to place his saints into the stream of a progressing salvation history make the claims to a flourishing distinctive female literature during this period less persuasive. In short, there does not seem to be anything in Merovingian hagiography that compares to the LVP, with its comprehensive vision that spans the biblical world and the author's contemporary society in a way that gives an elaborate coherence to both.

The fact that this work is never even mentioned when the current scholarship grapples with the issue of distinctive hagiography is a serious oversight. But should the high assessment of the LVP given here be regarded as excessive, even so, no one can legitimately refute the obvious implication that our discussion of this collection has in general on the study of female saints and writers of the early Middle Ages. Any claims of a distinctive, female literary movement during or shortly after the Merovingian period that do not take into consideration what the LVP offers cannot be well founded. That assertion may be made with confidence because the literature was treated here for what it intrinsically offers as hagiography before it was considered as an expression of male or female views of sanctity. In coming to such a conclusion, this investigation, despite its limitations, compels those who study the sources on early medieval women to reconsider the validity of attributing distinctiveness to hagiographic documents on the basis of gender alone. More significant, however out of fashion it may be, a comparative approach, philologically oriented and entailing extensive treatment of material not directly concerned with women, opens up a sure way to advance the study of female saints and writers to another level of understanding, one that reflects the depth of complexity, the dissonance, and the perplexing difficulties that these rich sources pose to the modern reader.

APPENDIX

Tabular Comparison of Miracle Stories
in the Lives of Radegund

The following tables are useful for comparing the two accounts of Radegund's *virtus*. In several places I have filled in what may be inferred from the texts. Fortunatus, for instance, often does not name the specific place where a miracle occurs. Hence, I have assumed that miracles pertaining to nuns took place at the convent of Sainte-Croix. On some occasions, I have also tentatively supplied a source of transmission that is not in the text. With regard to the healing miracles, only the specific accounts are noted, not the general remarks made by both authors on Radegund's cures or remedies. The categories by which the miracle stories are classified are based almost entirely on the scheme offered by Claire Stancliffe, *Saint Martin and His Hagiographer*, pp. 363–71.

The following abbreviations are used in the tables:

Ref = Reference to Text
Wit/Trans = Witness/Transmission
R = Radegund
Time wrt R = Time of Miracle's Occurrence with respect to Radegund's Life (a category that also states whether the saint herself is reported to have been present when the miracle took place)
S-C = Sainte-Croix

Nature Miracles

Ref	Description	Place	Wit/Trans	Time wrt R
Baudonivia				
10	R's wine barrel never empties	S-C	S-C nuns	R alive & present
12	Vinoberga burned when she sits on R's chair[1]	S-C	She repents in public	R dead
14	Finger of Mammetis offers itself to Patriarch	Jerusalem	Reovalis and people assembled at tomb	R alive but not present
17	Envoys saved from drowning at sea through invocation of R's name	En route to Constantinople	Reovalis and others (*supradictum presbiterum cum aliis*)	R alive but not present
19	Disruptive night bird is expelled by nun through sign of cross and invocation of R's name	S-C	S-C nuns	R alive & present
25	Candle leaps up at R's funeral & lands in coffin	R's oratory (Basilica of Saint Mary where nuns were buried)	Gregory of Tours; Mourners at R's funeral	R dead but present
Fortunatus				
11	Prison freeing while R prays	Pérrone	?	R alive but not present
30	Shrew mouse dies when it tries to eat R's thread	S-C?	?	R alive but not present
31	Ship of Floreius saved from sinking when name of R invoked	Somewhere near S-C (he is a fisherman for R)	?	R alive but not present
33	Dried laurel blooms after R prays	S-C	Agnes	R alive & present
38	Domolenus told in dream where relics of Martin are and to release prisoners	House of Domolenus	Domolenus tells his wife & prison officials	Occurs on day of R's death

1. A miracle also classified as a cure because the burning stops after R is repentantly invoked.

Healing Miracles

Ref	Disease	Procedure	Place	Wit/Trans	Time wrt R
Baudonivia					
11	Mammezo blinded	She prostrates herself & invokes R's name	R's basilica	She tells S-C nuns	R dead
12	Vinoberga on fire for sitting on R's chair	She repents & invokes R's name	S-C	She repents in public	R dead
15	Leo's eye clouded by blood clot	He prays & prostrates himself on R's hair shirt; he invokes R's name	R's basilica	Leo tells synod & S-C nuns	R dead
24	Blind man cured during R's funeral	He is led to R's bier as procession pauses	Tower outside monastery walls	Mourners at funeral	R dead
26	Abbo suffers from toothache	He prostrates himself in front of R's tomb & bites her robe draped over it	R's basilica	Abbo tells many people	R dead
Fortunatus					
27	Bella is blind	She prostrates herself at R's knees; R makes the sign of the cross over Bella's eyes	Poitiers (S-C)	?	R is alive
29	Nun with chills & fever	She is brought to R's cell & put in water; R tells all to leave; R touches her for two hours & gives her wine	S-C	Nun shows herself in public	R alive & present
32	Goda has feverish chills	She gets candle made according to R's stature; lit candle wards off illness at times chills usually occur	?	?	R alive but not present

(continued)

Healing Miracles (continued)

Ref	Disease	Procedure	Place	Wit/Trans	Time wrt R
Fortunatus					
34	(Clotted?) blood blinds eye of nun	R puts absinthe on nun's eyes	S-C	S-C nuns?	R alive and present
34	Stillborn child	Child revived when touched by R's cloak	?	Anderedus, R's servant who digs grave	R alive and present
35	Animia, swollen with dropsy, is close to death	She dreams R and abbess pour oil over her head and cover her in new clothes	S-C	S-C nuns	R alive but not present
37	R hears weeping and learns of young nun's death	The body is taken into her cell; R tells all to leave, then touches her for seven hours and prays until life restored	S-C	S-C nuns	R alive and present
38	Domolenus suffocates from constricted throat	R appears in a dream and puts hand down his throat	Domolenus's house	He tells his wife	Occurs on day of R's death

Demoniacs and Exorcisms

Ref	Description	Place	Wit/Trans	Time wrt R
Baudonivia				
26	Two female demoniacs rave at Hilary's basilica	After leaving Church of St. Hilary, they are cured in R's basilica	Arnegisselus and his monks	R dead
Fortunatus				
28	Fraifledis is tormented by a demon	Saix[1]	?	R alive but not present
28	R prays for Leubila; the demon is expelled in the form of a worm, which departs through her shoulder; Leubila then crushes worm with her feet	In the country (in rure)	She is cured in public	R alive but not present

Ref	Description	Place	Wit/Trans	Time wrt R
30	R steps on demoniac's neck & expels demon "*fluxu ventris*"	?	?	R alive & present
33	Abbess jokingly tells R she will be excommunicated if she does not free a demoniac; next day, as R prays, demon departs through the ear	S-C	?	R alive; may or may not be present

1. Place of Clothar's estate in Poitou; see A. Longnon, *Geographie de la Gaule au VIe Siècle* (Paris, 1878), p. 116, n. 2.

Encounters with Supernatural Beings: Baudonivia[1]

Ref	Description	Place	Wit/Trans	Time wrt R
18	Thousands of demons in the form of she-goats are put to flight by R's making sign of the cross	Monastery walls	S-C nuns	R alive & present
22	Stonecutters hear angels talking as R is taken to heaven	On a mountain	?	R dead
23	Gregory of Tours sees angel at the death of R	S-C	Gregory tells nuns	R dead

1. Nothing appears to fall directly into the above category in Fortunatus's account.

Dreams and Visions: Baudonivia[1]

Ref	Description	Place	Wit/Trans
3	R sees a man in the form of a ship	Saix	R secretly tells trustworthy followers
13	In sleep, R is told that all her relics will be put in one place; she opens her eyes and sees a *splendissimum virum*	Saix	?
20	A year before her death, R sees a beautiful young man	S-C	Two trustworthy nuns

1. Regarding dreams and visions in Fortunatus's account: for dreams, see section on healing and nature miracles; no visions are related in his *Vita*.

NOTES

CHAPTER I

1. In expressing his reservation, Bellarmine writes: "Addo etiam alia duo, unum ne forte originalibus historiis multa sint inepta, levia, improbabilia, quae risum potius quam aedificationem pariant. . . ." Bellarmine also discouraged such work because of the great effort and expense that would be required to prepare a critical edition of the Lives of the saints. The full text of the letter, dated March 7, 1608, appears in *AASS* 55 (Pars Prior), October, vol. 7, p. 1.

2. See Charles De Smedt, "Les fondateurs du Bollandisme," in *Mélanges Godefroid Kurth*, vol. 1: *Mémoires historiques* (Liège, 1908), pp. 295–303; Hippolyte Delehaye, *The Work of the Bollandists through Three Centuries* (Princeton, 1922); David Knowles, *Great Historical Enterprises: Problems in Monastic History* (London, 1963), pp. 4–32; Paul Peeters, *Figures Bollandiennes contemporaines* (Brussels, 1948).

3. See, for instance, William McCready's illuminating remarks, with extensive references to the modern scholarship, in *Signs of Sanctity: Miracles in the Thought of Gregory the Great* (Toronto, 1989), pp. 154–75; see also Caroline Bynum, *Holy Feast and Holy Fast: The Religious Significance of Food to Medieval Women* (Berkeley, 1978), p. 310, n. 21.

4. Some notable examples of approaches developed in this century vary from folkloric, sociological, or psychological to quantitative, geographical, or temporal: C. G. Loomis, *White Magic: An Introduction to the Folklore of Christian Legends* (Cambridge, Mass., 1948); Pierre Delooz, *Sociologie et canonisations* (Liège, 1969); Rudolph Bell, *Holy Anorexia* (Chicago, 1985); Michael Goodich, *Vita Perfecta: The Ideal of Sainthood in the Thirteenth Century* (Stuttgart, 1982); Stephen Wilson, ed., *Saints and Their Cults: Studies in Religious Sociology, Folklore and History* (New York, 1983); Richard Kieckhefer, *Unquiet Souls: Fourteenth-Century Saints in Their Religious Milieu* (Chicago, 1984); Pierre-André Sigal, *L'Homme et le miracle dans la France médiévale, XI–XIIe Siècles* (Paris, 1985); André Vauchez, *La Sainteté en occident aux derniers siècles du moyen âge: d'après les procès de canonisation et les documents hagiographiques* (Rome, 1988); Thomas Head, *Hagiography and the Cult of Saints: The Diocese of Orléans, 800–1200* (Cambridge, 1990).

5. On the intellectual trends that influenced modern approaches to historical and hagiographic sources, Thomas Heffernan offers valuable insights in *Sacred Biography: Saints and Their Biographers in the Middle Ages* (New York, 1988), pp. 38–71; see also John Finnis, "Historical Consciousness" and Theological Foundations, The Etienne Gilson Series 14 (Toronto, 1992), pp. 20–22.

6. The poetic quality of Brown's writing is noted by Alexander Murray, "Peter Brown and the Shadow of Constantine," *JRS* 73 (1983): 202.

7. Delehaye, *Cinq leçons sur la méthode hagiographique* (Brussels, 1934), p. 13: "Ceci nous amène à définir ce que nous voudrions appeler, d'un term emprunté à la géométrie, les coordonnées hagiographiques, éléments simples mais nécessaires et suffisants pour identifier un saint." For a more extensive discussion and application of the hagiographic coordinates, see René Aigrain, *L'hagiographie: ses sources, ses méthodes, son histoire* (Paris, 1953), pp. 247–72.

8. Bertrand Russell, *A History of Western Philosophy* (New York, 1945), p. 524: "they taught Descartes more mathematics than he would have learnt elsewhere." Before pursuing hagiographic research, Delehaye studied philosophy and taught mathematics and the natural sciences; see Paul Peeters, "Father Hippolyte Delehaye: A Memoir," in *The Legends of the Saints*, trans. Donald Attwater (New York, 1962), p. 188.

9. Delehaye, *Cinq leçons*, p. 28: "Il en résulte des ensembles d'un aspect assez particulier, qui prend parfois une teinte de paganisme à peine déguisé. Ceux qui savent que la légende n'est pour le saint qu'un vêtement d'emprunt ne sont pas déconcertés par ces apparences." Frantisek Graus offers a critique in *Volk, Herrscher und Heiliger im Reich der Merowinger* (Prague, 1965), p. 31. Carl Bernoulli, *Die Heiligen der Merowinger* (Tübingen, 1900), pp. 151, 169, 204, 208, had claimed to have identified several Merovingian saints as "disguised gods" (*verkappten Götter*); his position has been conclusively refuted by Graus, *Volk*, pp. 192–96; see also Yitzhak Hen, *Culture and Religion in Merovingian Gaul*, A.D. 481–751 (Leiden, 1995), pp. 154–207.

10. Delehaye, *Sanctus: Essai sur le culte des saints dans l'antiquité* (Brussels, 1927), p. 240: "L'ideal de la sainteté consiste donc dans un ensemble harmonieux des vertus chrétiennes."

11. Murray, "Peter Brown," p. 194.

12. Delehaye, *The Legends of the Saints*, trans. V. M. Crawford (London, 1961), p. 229: "And yet, who can deny that in spite of all the ignorance of technique and the clumsiness of execution, there is exhaled . . . something of that mysterious and sublime poetry which pervades the walls of our ancient cathedrals?" For comments on this view, see McCready, *Signs*, p. 162. Henceforth, all citations of Delehaye's *Legends* refer to Crawford's rather than Attwater's translation.

13. For a point-by-point critique that modifies and challenges Brown's approach, see Raymond Van Dam, *Saints and Their Miracles in Late Antique Gaul* (Princeton, 1994), pp. 5–6.

14. Here, I am assuming that Delehaye has an approach more Cartesian in spirit than simply taking over the idea of the geometrical coordinates. One significant fact is Descartes's concern with developing a single method for investigating all issues with a sound systematic approach, whether the object of inquiry be human anatomy or the question of God's existence; see F. E. Sutcliffe, trans., *René Descartes: Discourse on Method and the Meditations* (London, 1968), pp. 7–8. Like Descartes, Delehaye is also especially occupied with the task of developing and expounding an all-encompassing method for the study of hagiography, with two of his major works (*Cinq leçons, Legends*) devoted exclusively to this subject.

15. For a critique of Delehaye's scientific approach, see Heffernan, *Sacred Biography*, p. 57.

16. Brown, "The Saint as Exemplar in Late Antiquity," *Representations* 1.2 (1983): 15; for a brief critique of Delehaye, whom Brown compares with Hume and Newman, proponents of the "two-tiered" model that distinguished the religion of the enlightened few from the un-

refined "vulgar," see idem, *The Cult of the Saints: Its Rise and Function in Latin Christianity* (Chicago, 1981), p. 17.

17. Van Dam, *Saints*, p. 4; Edward James, trans., *Gregory of Tours: Life of the Fathers* (Liverpool, 1985), p. 9.

18. Alexandra Hennessey Olsen gives a shallow critique of Delehaye and the Bollandists: " 'De Historiis Sanctorum': A Generic Study of Hagiography," *Genre* 13.4 (1980): 407–29. Olsen offers (at pp. 407–8) a very different presentation than the one given here regarding the influence of the Bollandists on modern hagiographic researchers, specifically literary critics, whom she sees as having been duped by Delehaye.

19. See Julia M. H. Smith, "Review Article: Early Medieval Hagiography in the Late Twentieth Century," *Early Medieval Europe* 1.1 (1992): 69–76.

20. See John Corbett, "*Praesentium signorum munera*: The Cult of the Saints in the World of Gregory of Tours," *Florilegium* 5 (1983): 45–46; idem, "The Saint as Patron in the Work of Gregory of Tours," *Journal of Medieval History* 7 (1981): 1; more recently, Gisselle de Nie, " 'Consciousness Fecund through God': From Male Fighter to Spiritual Bride-Mother in Late Antique Female Sanctity," in *Sanctity and Motherhood: Essays on Holy Mothers in the Middle Ages*, ed. Anneke Mulder-Bakker (New York, 1995), p. 103; Brown himself, *Cult*, p. xv, acknowledges that he does not intend his work to be exhaustive but "to open up a way" for other approaches.

21. Nostalgic admiration: Lancelot Sheppard, *The Saints Who Never Were* (Dayton, 1969), pp. 14–27; pointed criticism: Graus, *Volk*, pp. 27, 30–32.

22. See Jacques Fontaine, "Le culte des saintes et ses implications sociologiques. Réflexions sur un récent essai de Peter Brown," *AB* 100 (1982): 17–41. Identifying the "soft areas in B.'s argument" is Murray's "Peter Brown," pp. 191–203; for other critiques, see Van Dam, *Saints*, p. 4.

23. See the illuminating discussion on the scholarly trends and problems in hagiographic research outlined by Patrick Geary, *Living with the Dead in the Middle Ages* (Ithaca, 1994), pp. 9–29.

24. See Edmund Kern, "Counter-Reformation Sanctity: The Bollandists' Vita of Blessed Hemma of Gurk," *JEH* 45.3 (1994): 415.

25. See Donald Weinstein and Rudolph Bell, *Saints and Society: The Two Worlds of Western Christendom, 1000–1700* (Chicago, 1982), pp. 1–15, with an "Appendix on Method," pp. 277–90. For a critique, see Aviad Kleinberg, *Prophets in Their Own Country: Living Saints and the Making of Sainthood in the Later Middle Ages* (Chicago, 1992), pp. 13–16.

26. Graus, *Volk*, p. 31; see also Olsen, "De Historiis," pp. 407–8.

27. An exception is Kern's excellent article, "Counter-Reformation Sanctity," pp. 412–34.

28. Delehaye, *Work*, pp. 91–94, 209. Note the strong language he uses as he continues his critique: "In this way, documents of much interest have been suppressed. . . . This was, in the main, a dangerous tendency. The editors were obliged to publish certain Acts the general tone of which did not excite any real suspicion but of which the historical accuracy was no greater than that of the most fantastic compositions. . . . The rule laid down by Papebroch was far better, viz.: not to make any distinction between the texts, but to explain clearly in the introduction what consideration was due to each." When discussing a later phase of Bollandism, he welcomes an important change to the *Acta Sanctorum*: "The first volume appeared in 1887. To the eye of the layman nothing distinguishes it from those that preceded. . . . Yet it is marked by two important changes. The first consists in giving the Acts of the saints under all the forms in which they are found in the manuscripts, without regard to their historical value. Interpolated, apocryphal or fabulous Acts are in no wise excluded. The literary point of view is the one resolutely adopted, and we now see, methodically applied, the principle

accepted by the former Bollandists, but to which they often hesitated to adhere rigidly in practice."

29. Problems such as the difficulties imposed by two world wars and the suppression of the Jesuits; see Delehaye, Work, pp. 157–75; Knowles, Enterprises, pp. 18–21, 26–27.

30. "Enabl[ing]" researchers "to follow the evolution of the saint's biography": Delehaye, Work, p. 209.

31. Officium b. Monegundis, AASS 28, July, vol. 1, p. 281.

32. Delehaye, Cinq leçons, p. 7: "L'hagiographie critique est une branche de la science historique."

33. Delehaye, Work, pp. 38, 32, 41, 47, 50, 68–69, 73, 84, 107–9, 112, 125, 163, 165, 172, 181, 192.

34. Ibid., p. 226, n. 7; Knowles, Enterprises, pp. 11–12, 24, 28, notes the obvious literary talents of certain Bollandists.

35. Delehaye, Legends, pp. 60–61.

36. Edith Wyschogrod, Saints and Postmodernism: Revisioning Moral Philosophy (Chicago, 1990).

37. See Van Dam, Saints, p. 151.

38. Graus, Volk, p. 41, gives perhaps the harshest assessment: "Hier möchte ich nur betonen, dass die Arbeitsweise der Verfechter dieser Schule [i.e., the historical-critical school] bei der Untersuchung einzelner Quellen erfolgreich sein kann, jedoch bei einer Analyse der eigentlichen Legenden versagen muss. Dieses Versagen ist nicht zufällig; es ist die logische Konsequenz der Suche nach dem 'historischen Kern.' " On the contrasting historical approaches to hagiography, with extensive references to the modern studies on this issue, see Paul Fouracre, "Merovingian History and Merovingian Hagiography," Past and Present 127 (1990): 3–38.

39. Fouracre, "Merovingian History," pp. 4–5, n. 5, mentions O. Holder-Egger as one "who literally edited the 'non-historically useful' material out of the Miracula and Translatio texts he published." He states that Krusch and Levison at least "published the whole of the works they edited." But this is not entirely accurate; regarding the visions in the Vita Fursei abbatis Latiniacensis 2 (MGH SRM 4, p. 435, n. 2), Krusch states: "Visiones omissae sunt." Levison also excluded the visiones in his edition of Aldegund's Life (ibid., 6, p. 80). Omitting texts is far more common than Fouracre's remark suggests; Karl Morrisson, I Am You: The Hermeneutics of Empathy in Western Literature (Princeton, 1988), p. 195, complains that the works of Gerhoh of Reichersberg have been "mutilated" by the Monumentist editor Sakur, who purged the theological sections from the modern edition.

40. Graus, Volk, p. 28.

41. Ibid., p. 39.

42. On the Bollandists as a Catholic apologetical movement, see Graus, Volk, pp. 26–27, 32. The crudeness of popular piety is a veritable leitmotif in Delehaye's Legends, pp. 49, 53, 56–57.

43. Fouracre, "Merovingian History," p. 3.

44. Marc Van Uytfanghe, "Les avatars contemporains de l''hagiologie,' " Francia 5 (1977): 647, notes Krusch's frustrated disqualification of hagiographic texts as "ecclesiastical swindling-literature" (kirchliche Schwindelliteratur); see also Fouracre, "Merovingian History," p. 5, n. 5.

45. Here, it is important to note that the fascinating discussion of Fouracre, "Merovingian History," p. 13, depends on the unfounded assumption that an atheistic outlook enables the modern researcher to discover the historicity of hagiographic texts.

46. Ibid., pp. 5–8, for a useful critique of the modern, literary-critical approach to hagiography.

47. Régis Boyer, "An Attempt to Define the Typology of Medieval Hagiography," in *Hagiography and Medieval Literature*, ed. Hans Bekker-Nielsen, et al. (Odense, 1981), pp. 27–36.

48. Alison Elliott, *Roads to Paradise: Reading the Lives of the Early Saints* (Hanover, Pa., 1987), offers one of the most successful structural approaches.

49. Olsen, "De Historiis," p. 425: "A successful hagiographic work has a controlled narrative structure, makes appropriate use of traditional imagery and themes, and enmeshes its polemical arguments within its narrative structure. Although a work can fail in one of these areas and still possess literary merit, if it fails in all three—no matter how historically accurate it may be—it will presumably have little literary value." Of course, the obvious question to ask, among others raised by these criteria, is: What happens if a work "fails" in two areas? It is also interesting to note here that Olsen's approach leads to an assessment of the text on the basis of its literary value that is similar in its reductionism to what she claims is the flaw of Delehaye's assessment on the basis of its historical value; in either case, we are left with what Graus would call a "sacrifice" (*Opferung*): Olsen sacrifices history for literature, Delehaye literature for history.

50. See Graus, *Volk*, p. 35, who also gives (at pp. 25–59) an overview of all the main approaches to the literature.

51. The article of Mary Lefkowitz is often illuminating and intriguing, but her conclusions regarding Saint Perpetua's "unconscious incest" remain unconvincing: "The Motivations for St. Perpetua's Martyrdom," *Journal of the American Academy of Religion* 44.3 (1976): 417–21.

52. See J. L. Derouet, "Les possibilités d'interprétation sémiologique des textes hagiographiques," *RHEF* 62 (1976): 153–62, who is favorable to applying the latest techniques to the literature and offers a "deconstructionist" interpretation of the seventh-century *De virtutibus beatae Geretrudis*. Fouracre, "Merovingian History," p. 8, maintains that literary-critical techniques alone are not adequate. For a Marxist approach, see Graus, "Die Gewalt bei den Anfängen des Feudalismus und die 'Gefangenenbefreiung' der merowingischen Hagiographie," *Jahrbuch für Wirtschaftsgeschichte* 1 (1961): 61–156.

53. Werner Affeldt, et al., eds. *Frauen im Frühmittelalter: Eine ausgewählte kommentierte Bibliographie* (Frankfurt am Main, 1990).

54. "Not only German, by any means," as stated by Walter Goffart, "Two Notes on Germanic Antiquity Today," *Traditio* 50 (1995): 16. For racist trends in modern intellectual history, see, in general, Robert Eriksen, *Theologians under Hitler: Gerhard Kittel, Paul Althaus and Emmanuel Hirsch* (New Haven, 1985).

55. Wyschogrod, *Saints and Postmodernism*, p. xviii: "It is not possible, it could be argued, to renew interest in hagiography because as a literary form such narratives have become kitsch. This criticism is not without merit." In light of such a comment, see Graus, *Volk*, p. 43; Brown, *Society and the Holy in Late Antiquity* (Berkeley, 1982), p. 230.

56. See Van Uytfanghe, "L'hagiographie et son public à l'époque mérovingienne," *SP* 16, ed. Elizabeth Livingstone (Berlin, 1985), p. 54.

57. Notable exceptions: Benedicta Ward, *Miracles and the Medieval Mind: Theory, Record and Event, 1000–1215* (London, 1982); Heffernan, *Sacred Biography*, especially pp. 123–84; Claire Stancliffe, *St. Martin and His Hagiographer* (Oxford, 1983); Martin Heinzelmann, *Gregor von Tours (538–594): "Zehn Bucher Geschichte": Historiographie und Gesellschaftskonzept im 6. Jahrhundert* (Darmstadt, 1994). I did not become aware of Heinzelmann's book on the *Histories* until after the present study was nearly finished; unfortunately, his findings were not utilized in my treatment of Gregory's *LVP*.

58. See Wyschogrod, *Saints and Postmodernism*, p. 261.

59. Ibid., p. xiv.

60. Although Van Uytfanghe's earlier articles are regularly cited by scholars, it is important to note that the latest North American studies on the Merovingian texts do not even acknowledge the existence of his fundamental work concerning the influence of the Bible on the hagiographic literature of this period, *Stylisation biblique et condition humaine dans l'hagiographie mérovingienne (600–750)* (Brussels, 1987).

61. Graus, *Volk*, p. 409 (with reference to Etienne Delaruelle, "Saint Radegonde, son type de sainteté et la chrétienté de son temps," *EM* [Paris, 1953]: 65–74): "Eine etwa verschiedene Einstellung Fortunats und der Nonne Baudonivia ist schon verschiedentlich aufgefallen und wurde sogar stark übertrieben."

62. See C. Erickson and K. Casey, "Women in the Middle Ages: A Working Bibliography," *Medieval Studies* 37 (1975): 340–59; for more recent studies on medieval women, see the literature cited by Bynum, *Holy Feast*, pp. 311–12, n. 7; see also, in general, Jane Chance, ed., *Gender and Text in the Later Middle Ages* (Gainesville, Fla., 1996).

63. See, for instance, Andrée Lehmann, *Le rôle de la femme dans l'histoire de France au Moyen Age* (Paris, 1952). Although evidently not known to modern researchers, the earlier work of Lucie Félix-Faure Goyau is important for its exclusive focus on Christian women, including Radegund and Baudonivia: *Christianisme et culture féminine* (Paris, 1914), pp. 3–45. With respect to scholarship written in English, the study of Lina Eckenstein also anticipates the current trend in research: *Women under Monasticism: Chapters on Saint-Lore and Convent Life between A.D. 500 and A.D. 1500* (Cambridge, 1896).

64. See Janet Nelson, "Commentary on the Papers of J. Verdon, S. F. Wemple and M. Parisse," in *Frauen in Spätantike und Frühmittelalter*, ed. Werner Affeldt (Sigmaringen, 1990), p. 328; Van Uytfanghe, *Stylisation biblique*, p. 256, n. 397; Bynum, *Holy Feast*, p. 29, n. 73; Patricia Wasyliw, review of *Sainted Women of the Dark Ages*, ed. and trans. Jo Ann McNamara and John Halborg, with E. Gordon Whatley, *Speculum* 71.2 (1996): 467–68. Especially through reviews in widely circulated publications McNamara's important contributions to the study of women are now generally known; see Lawrence Cunningham, "Religious Booknotes," *Commonweal* 120.3 (February 12, 1993): 26; Fiona MacCarthy, "The Power of Chastity," *The New York Review of Books* 43.20 (December 19, 1996): 31–33.

65. A sporadic and superficial critical response has recently started: Nelson, "Women and the Word in the Earlier Middle Ages," in *Women in the Church*, ed. W. J. Sheils and Diana Wood (Oxford, 1990), pp. 53–78; Hen, *Culture*, p. 123, n. 5; Smith, "Early Medieval Hagiography," p. 74. Yet in her recent review of *Sainted Women*, pp. 467–68, Patricia Wasyliw gives an assessment that is entirely positive; Penny Gill's review of *Sainted Women*, *Church History* 63.3 (1994): 437, offers no negative criticism; similarly, MacCarthy's review ("The Power of Charity") of McNamara's *Sisters in Arms: Catholic Nuns through Two Millennia* (Cambridge, Mass., 1996), is strongly favorable, especially regarding the author's treatment of early Christian women.

66. Suzanne Wemple, *Women in Frankish Society: Marriage and the Cloister 500 to 900* (Philadelphia, 1981), p. 183; see also Jane Schulenburg, "Saints' Lives as a Source for the History of Women, 500–1100," in *Medieval Women and the Sources of Medieval History*, ed. Joel Rosenthal (Athens, Ga., 1990), p. 300.

67. Wemple, "Female Spirituality and Mysticism in Frankish Monasteries: Radegund, Balthild, and Aldegund," *MRW PW*, pp. 48–49; Wemple also claims that "the importance of charity in spiritual life . . . was not a literary *topos* in early medieval hagiography" and that the "ideal of charity" was "introduced by women in female and double monasteries of the Merovingian kingdom."

68. McNamara et al., *Sainted Women*, p. 8; McNamara, "The Need to Give: Suffering and Female Sanctity in Medieval Europe," in *Images of Sainthood in Medieval Europe*, ed. Renate Blumenfeld-Kosinski and Timea Szell (Ithaca, 1991), pp. 199–221. Similar to the connection seen

between female sanctity and charity, McNamara evidently associates certain attributes of the Christian life as being gender-specific, so that men can become like women by engaging in particular kinds of holy activity: "Cornelia's Daughters: Paula and Eustochium," *Women's Studies* 11 (1984): 22.

69. Benedicta Ward, trans., *The Wisdom of the Desert Fathers: Apophthegmata Patrum (The Anonymous Series)* (Oxford, 1975), pp. xv–xvi. According to Ward (who provides examples substantiating her claim): "The aim of the monks' lives was not asceticism, but God, and the way to God was charity. The gentle charity of the desert was the pivot of all their work and the test of their way of life. Charity was to be total and complete." Among the manifestations of charity Ward discusses are the "innumerable stories about desert hospitality." Similarly, Thomas Merton, trans., *The Wisdom of the Desert: Sayings from the Desert Fathers of the Fourth Century* (New York, 1960), pp. 16–17: "There is sometimes question in the *Verba* of matters relating to the work and to the commerce involved. Charity and hospitality were matters of top priority, and took precedence over fasting and personal ascetic routines. The countless sayings which bear witness to this warm-hearted friendliness should be sufficient to take care of accusations that these men hated their own kind. Indeed there was more real love, understanding and kindliness in the desert than in the cities, where, then as now, it was every man for himself."

70. *VM* 3 (CSEL 1, pp. 113–14).

71. On the relationship between motherhood and sanctity in early hagiography, see Nie's excellent discussion, "Consciousness," pp. 100–161. On the *virago* (a word that to the best of my knowledge does not appear in the Merovingian *vitae*, though it does in the Vulgate's reference to Eve, Gen. 2:23), see Marie-Louise Portmann, *Die Darstellung der Frau in der Geschichtschreibung des früheren Mittelalters* (Basel, 1958), pp. 19–24; Barbara Newman, *From Virile Women to WomanChrist: Studies in Medieval Religion and Literature* (Philadelphia, 1995), pp. 3–11.

72. Wemple, "Female Spirituality," pp. 39–53 (mostly repeats what she had previously said about Radegund, Balthild, and Aldegund in chapter 8 of her book, *Women in Frankish Society*, pp. 181–87); McNamara, "A Legacy of Miracles: Hagiography and Nunneries in Merovingian Gaul," in *Women of the Medieval World*, ed. Julius Kirschner and Wemple (New York, 1985), pp. 36–52 (concerned primarily with Radegund and her Lives as a reflection of female monasticism); idem, "The Ordeal of Community: Hagiography and Discipline in Merovingian Convents," *Vox Benedictina* 3.4 (1986): 293–326 (discusses the role of the Caesarian *Rule* in Radegund's *Vitae*). Although the book is still focused on holy women, McNamara's recent work, *Sisters in Arms*, is a broad treatment extending from the early Christian period to modern times. This latest study appeared when the present work was being prepared for press.

73. Though other scholars, whose research is not as well known, have surveyed a wider selection of early Christian, Merovingian and Carolingian hagiographic sources on women: Susanne Wittern, *Frauen, Heiligkeit und Macht: Lateinische Frauenviten aus dem 4. bis 7. Jahrhundert* (Stuttgart, 1994); Marta Cristiani, "La sainteté féminine du haut Moyen Âge: Biographie et valeurs," in *Les fonctions des saints dans le monde occidental (IIIe–XIIIe siècle)* (Rome, 1991), pp. 385–434; Portmann, *Die Darstellung der Frau*; Maria Stoeckle, *Studien über Ideale in Frauenviten des VII–X Jahrhunderts* (Munich, 1957).

74. Though Nelson more than once expresses reservations about using *Vitae* as a source for women's history: "Women and the Word," pp. 58–59, 66; idem, "Commentary," p. 327.

75. Graus, *Volk*, pp. 23–24, 210; Goffart, *Barbarians and Romans, A.D. 418–584: The Techniques of Accommodation* (Princeton, 1980), pp. 24–25.

76. Graus, *Volk*, pp. 37–38: "Nur ein Werk muss noch besonders erwähnt werden, die Arbeit von L. Van der Essen, die zwar nur den merowingischen Heiligen des alten Belgien gewidmet ist, aber einen neuen Weg aufzeigte. Zum Unterschied von den vorgenannten Untersuchungen [i.e., the work of Bernoulli and Marignan], ging Van der Essen nicht von den

Heiligen, sondern von ihren Legenden aus. Durch die Untersuchung der einzelnen Legenden-umkreise gewann der Verfasser Ergebnisse von dauerndem Wert und vervollkommnete so die historisch-kritische Methode, die schon Krusch und Levison verwendet hatten. Neuere Fort-setzungen haben jedoch diese Arbeiten nicht gefunden; mit den Legenden befassten sich Forscher im Rahmen der Kirchengeschichte und Hagiographen beim Studium einzelner Hei-liger. Die Legende dieses Zeitabschnittes wurde als Ganzes nicht näher erforscht." By contrast, in speaking of Van der Essen's work, J. M. Wallace-Hadrill, The Frankish Church (Oxford, 1983), p. 424, merely states that it was "confined to saints of Belgium."

77. Van der Essen, Étude critique et littéraire sur les Vitae des saints mérovingiens de l'ancienne Belgique (Louvain, 1907), p. xi.

78. Ibid., p. ix.

79. Ibid., p. x.

80. Ibid., p. xvii.

81. See now Fouracre and Richard Gerberding, Late Merovingian France: History and Hagiography, 640–720 (Manchester, 1996). This work appeared shortly before the present study went to press.

82. Namely: Max Bonnet, Le Latin de Grégoire de Tours (Paris, 1890); Louis Sas, "Changing Linguistic Attitudes in the Merovingian Period," Word 5 (1949): 131–35; Erich Auerbach, Literary Language and Its Public in Late Latin Antiquity and in the Middle Ages, trans. Ralph Manheim (New York, 1965), pp. 85–179; Van Uytfanghe, "Latin mérovingien, latin carolingien et rustica romana lingua: Continuité ou discontinuité?" Revue de l'Université de Bruxelles 1 (1977): 65–89; idem, "Histoire du latin, protohistoire des langues romances et histoire de la communication," Francia 11 (1983): 579–619; Richard Collins, "Observations on the Form, Language and Public of the Prose Biographies of Venantius Fortunatus in the Hagiography of Merovingian Gaul," in Columbanus and Merovingian Monasticism, ed. H. B. Clark and M. Brennan (Oxford, 1981), pp. 105–31; Carl Rice, "The Phonology of Gallic Clerical Latin after the Sixth Century" (Ph.D. diss., Harvard University, 1902); see especially Hen, Culture, pp. 21–42, who also gives an exhaustive citation of the relevant studies.

83. See Magdalena Carrasco, "Sanctity and Experience in Pictorial Hagiography: Two Il-lustrated Lives of Saints from Romanesque France," in Images of Sanctity in Medieval Europe, ed. Renate Blumenfield-Kosinski and Timea Szell (Ithaca, 1991), pp. 64–65.

84. Van Dam, Saints, p. 151: "Many important authors . . . in particular, Fortunatus, would benefit from comprehensive and up-to-date studies"; see also Nie, review of Venantius Fortunatus: A Latin Poet in Merovingian Gaul, by Judith George, in Speculum 70.1 (1995): 143, 146.

85. Collins, "Observations," pp. 105–31, provides an excellent overview of Fortunatus's prose Lives, and I frequently rely on him. I am also greatly indebted to Van Dam's important discussion concerning Fortunatus's poem on Saint Martin; his remarks are used for the way they help to shed light on the Vitae: "Images of Saint Martin in Late Roman and Early Mero-vingian Gaul," Viator 19 (1988): 1–27. For other scholarship on Fortunatus, especially his poetry, see the studies cited in Brian Brennan's recent article, "Deathless Marriage and Spiritual Fecundity in Venantius Fortunatus's De Virginitate," Traditio 51 (1996): 73–97.

86. Ian Wood discusses the dating problems at length in "Forgery in Merovingian Hagi-ography," in MGH Schriften, vol. 33 (Hannover, 1988), pp. 369–84. On the current project of redating and critically examining the early hagiographic sources, see François Dolbeau, Martin Heinzelmann, and Joseph-Claude Poulin, "Les sources hagiographiques narratives composées en Gaule avant l'an mil (SHG), Francia 15 (1987): 701–31.

87. Collins, "Observations," p. 120, n. 26; on the approximate dates and authenticity of the Lives attributed to Fortunatus, see Wilhelm Meyer, Der Gelegenheitsdichter Venantius Fortunatus (Berlin, 1901), p. 23.

88. Vita Severini episcopi Burdeglensis (MGH SRM 7.1, pp. 206–24).

89. See Wood, "Forgery," p. 369. Harry Waldron, "Expressions of Religious Conversion among Laymen Remaining within Secular Society in Gaul, 400–800 A. D.," (Ph.D. diss., Ohio State University, 1976), pp. 370–75, provides the dates that various researchers have given for the composition of several Merovingian Lives; Van Uytfanghe, *Stylisation biblique*, pp. 8–11, gives more recent findings based on the research still in progress of Poulin, Heinzelmann, and Dolbeau. Opinions on the dating of Radegund's Lives are given at the beginning of chapter 5.

90. See Peter Dronke, *Women Writers of the Middle Ages: A Critical Study of Texts from Perpetua (d. 203) to Marguerite Porete (d. 1310)* (Cambridge, 1984), pp. 26–29; Hen, *Culture*, pp. 39–40.

91. See Nelson, "Queens as Jezebels: The Careers of Brunhild and Balthild in Merovingian History," in *Politics and Ritual in Early Medieval Europe* (London, 1986), p. 46, n. 33; Wemple, *Women*, p. 182. Ian Wood suggests that Gertrude's *Life* could also have been authored by a woman: "Administration, Law and Culture in Merovingian Gaul," in *The Uses of Literacy in Early Medieval Europe*, ed. R. McKitterick (Cambridge, 1991), p. 70, n. 50. But McNamara, following Krusch and Van der Essen, attributes it to a "monk of Fosse" in *Sainted Women*, p. 220; on the question of Merovingian female authors, see also McKitterick, "Frauen und Schriftlichkeit im Frühen Mittelalter," in *Weibliche Lebensgestaltung im frühen Mittelalter*, ed. H. W. Goetz (Cologne, 1991), pp. 65–118; Hen, *Culture*, pp. 38–40.

92. See McNamara, *Sainted Women*, p. 235, who uses three different editions: Joseph Ghesquière and Cornelius Smet, *Acta sanctorum Belgii selecta*, vol. 4 (Brussels, 1787), pp. 315–324; Levison, *Vita Aldegundis abbatissae Malbodiensis* (MGH SRM 6, pp. 79–90); and the *Acta Sanctorum* version (*AASS* 3, January, vol. 3, pp. 649–70). Wemple, *Women*, p. 314, supplements Levison's inadequate edition with Ghesquière's text.

93. For the various positions regarding its authorship, see Karen Cherewatuk and Ulrike Wiethaus, eds., *Dear Sister: Medieval Women and the Epistolary Genre* (Philadelphia, 1993), pp. 41–42, n. 3; McNamara, *Sainted Women*, p. 65, n. 22; Charles Nisard, "Des poésies de Sainte Radégonde attribuées jusqu'ici à Fortunat," *RH* 37.2 (1888): 56.

94. Hugeburc wrote an account of Willibald's travels, entitled *Hodoeporicon* and a *Life of Winnibald*, both edited by O. Holder-Egger, MGH SS 15, pp. 80–117; see also C. H. Talbot, trans., "The Hodoeporicon of Saint Willibald," in *Soldiers of Christ: Saints and Saints' Lives from Late Antiquity and the Early Middle Ages*, ed. Thomas F. X. Noble and Thomas Head (University Park, Pa., 1995), pp. 141–64; on the epistolary sources, consult Hen, *Culture*, p. 39.

95. However, the connection between one epistolary text and a common hagiographic theme in the depiction of women was too striking to ignore; the material is discussed briefly in chapter 4.

96. *Aristotle's Metaphysics*, trans. Hippocrates Apostle (Grinnel, Iowa, 1979), pp. 39–53. On the *disputatio*, see Knowles, *The Evolution of Medieval Thought* (New York, 1962), p. 175; Jean Leclerq, *The Love of Learning and the Desire for God*, trans. Catharine Misrahi (New York, 1977), pp. 201–3.

97. Kerstin Aspegren's study, *The Male Woman: A Feminine Ideal in the Early Church* (Stockholm, 1990), provides a good overview that addresses the main problems within the context of ancient and patristic thought on women. Her discussion also treats key hagiographic texts in which early Christian female saints are depicted as "manly." Highlighting some of the modern interpretive difficulties regarding the role of gender in medieval sources, including a passage from Gregory of Tours's *Histories*, is Nancy Partner, "No Sex, No Gender," *Speculum* 68.2 (1993): 419–43. On the late antique hagiographic sources, including Radegund's Lives, and the question of gender, the insights offered by Nie, "Consciousness," pp. 101–61, are also valuable; on the later medieval *Vitae* and the significance of gender, see the general observations made by Bynum, *Holy Feast*, pp. 23–30.

98. On "old-fashioned" methodology as a viable approach, see Bynum, *The Resurrection of the Body in Western Christianity, 200–1336* (New York, 1995), p. xvi.

99. On Bolland, see the most recent work by Donald Sullivan, "Jean Bolland (1596–1665) and the Early Bollandists," in *Medieval Scholarship: Biographical Studies on the Formation of a Discipline*, vol. 1: *History*, ed. Helen Damico and Joseph B. Zavadil (New York, 1995), pp. 3–14.

CHAPTER 2

1. Normally, the biographical subject is portrayed as a saint from the beginning of a *Vita*. The era's rare conversion stories are the exceptions: Gregory, *LVP* 12.2 (*MGH SRM* 1.2, p. 712); *Vita Richarii sacerdotis* 3 (*MGH SRM* 7.2, pp. 445–46), with Graus, *Volk*, pp. 70, 102–4. It should not be inferred from the hagiographer's insistence on a "born saint" that there is otherwise no correspondence between historical biography and hagiography. Waldron, "Expressions," pp. 358–60, cites instances in which the literary formulae could substantiate the actual practices of holy people whose lives are consciously modeled on religious conventions that the topoi reflect. More recent scholarship supports this position: Georg Scheibelreiter, "Der frühfrankische Episkopat: Bild und Wirklichkeit," *Frühmittelalterliche Studien* 17 (1983): 136; Van Dam, "Images," p. 18; Van Uytfanghe, "Modèles bibliques dans l'hagiographie," in *Le Moyen Âge et la Bible*, BT 4, ed. Pierre Riché and G. Lobrichon (Paris, 1984), p. 453; Brown, "Saint as Exemplar," p. 18; see also the study on the remarkable Neophytos, who literally conformed his life to the hagiographic formulae: Catia Galatariotou, *The Making of a Saint: The Life, Times and Sanctification of Neophytos the Recluse* (Cambridge, 1991). Furthermore, the fact that hagiographic writing is formulaic and that the descriptions of holiness attributed to one saint can be virtually the same as those of another are not in themselves sufficient reasons for dismissing hagiographic accounts as unreliable; see Graus, *Volk*, p. 74; Aigrain, *L'hagiographie*, pp. 168–69, 203–5, 243–44.

2. The indifference toward age has been cited as one of the literature's chief shortcomings: John Henry Newman, *Historical Sketches*, vol. 2 (New York, 1917), pp. 230–31.

3. See Gregory, *DVSM* 1, pref. (*MGH SRM* 1.2, p. 585); idem, *DVSM* 2.43 (ibid., p. 624); idem, *GC* 6 (ibid., p. 752); Fortunatus, *VP* 1, 29 (*MGH AA* 4.2, pp. 33, 37); idem, *VMarc* 2 (ibid., p. 50).

4. Gregory, *LVP* 17.1 (*MGH SRM* 1.2, p. 728), with James, *Life*, pp. 153–54, n. 3.

5. Profligates: see Brown, *The World of Late Antiquity* (London, 1971), p. 101; for prostitutes, the Lives of the desert harlots in the *Vitae patrum* collection are the obvious examples: PL 73, pp. 651–90, with Ward, *Harlots of the Desert: A Study of Repentance in Early Monastic Sources* (Oxford, 1987); murderer: before living a life of repentance, Abbot Apollo cruelly cut open a pregnant woman to see what a fetus looked like: *Apophthegmata patrum* 69.2 (PG 65, p. 134), with Ward, *Harlots*, p. 5. For evidence of the knowledge and circulation of such stories in the Latin West by the sixth century, see the remarks of Paschasius in his letter to Martin of Braga: *Vitae patrum* 7 (PL 73, p. 1025); Helen Waddell, trans., *The Desert Fathers* (London, 1936), pp. 211–13; *LVP* 20.2 (*MGH SRM* 1.2, p. 742), where Gregory gives Rufinus's translations of desert literature to a hermit; *Vita Eligii episcopi, prol.* (ibid., 4, p. 664), also shows evidence of Rufinus's influence.

6. Jerome, *Vita Malchi monachi captivi* (PL 23, pp. 53–60). Compare the tenth-century *Vita Landelini abbatis* (*MGH SRM* 6, pp. 438–44). On Jerome's hagiography, see Herbert Kech, *Hagiographie als christliche Unterhaltungsliteratur: Studien zum Phänomen des Erbaulichen anhand der Mönchenviten des hl. Hieronymous* (Göppingen, 1977); J. N. D. Kelly, *Jerome: His Life, Writings and Controversies* (London, 1975), p. 172; Edward Gibbon, *The History of the Decline and Fall of the Roman Empire*, vol. 4, ed. J. B. Bury (London, 1925), p. 60.

7. Augustine's influence on early Latin hagiography was indirect and came by way of later authors (e.g., Cassiodorus, Caesarius of Arles, Gregory the Great) who utilized his scriptural commentaries; see Van Uytfanghe, *Stylisation biblique*, p. 44.

8. Delehaye, *Cinq leçons*, p. 10: "Cette absorption de la personnalité par la figure idéale du 'saint' dépourvue de toute caractéristique n'empêchait point la pratique du culte dès que la coutume s'en était établie."

9. Of course, modern biographies exhibit hagiographic tendencies; see Graus, *Volk*, p. 62. With respect to describing character flaws, see Bede, *Vita sancti Cuthberti*, ed. Bertram Colgrave, in *Two Lives of Saint Cuthbert: A Life by an Anonymous Monk of Lindisfarne and Bede's Prose Life* (Cambridge, 1940). While Bede claims (1, p. 154) that Cuthbert submitted himself to monastic discipline *ab ineunte adolescentia*, he also says that the process of the saint's introduction into the religious life was gradual (*paulatim*); in fact, unlike Fortunatus's saints, Cuthbert's boyhood is marked by a rambunctious enthusiasm for sport that must be stopped (1, p. 158). Gregory the Great's Benedict is more like Fortunatus's young saints than Bede's Cuthbert: *Dial.* 2, prol., ed. Adalbert de Vogüé (SC 260, p. 126): "Fuit uir uitae uenerabilis, gratia Benedictus et nomine, ab ipso pueritiae suae tempore cor gerens senile."

10. In light of this quality, I think Stoeckle's generic scheme of hagiographic narrative, *Studien*, p. 1, is misleading. Also problematic but useful is the "typical scheme" offered by Boyer, "Typology," pp. 27—36.

11. Though, occasionally, Fortunatus's saints predict their deaths not long before they die, as is common in hagiographic literature: *VG* 76 (MGH SRM 7.1, p. 418); *VP* 18 (MGH AA 4.2, p. 37).

12. As will be discussed shortly, Germanus's mother tries to abort him by taking an unspecified "potion." Such practices were condemned at this time by Caesarius of Arles, *Sermon* 1.12 (SC 175, pp. 246—48); 19.5 (ibid., p. 492); 44.2 (SC 243, pp. 328—30, where aristocratic women are warned that abortion among the lower classes could lead to a shortage of slaves); 51.4 (ibid., pp. 428—30); 52.4 (ibid., pp. 436—38). On Caesarius and abortion, see Wemple, *Women*, p. 24.

13. Graus, *Volk*, pp. 68—69; though see Laurent Theis who, despite the scanty information hagiographers normally give on a saint's kin, addresses the question of family structure presented in the Merovingian *Vitae*: "Saints sans familles? Quelques remarques sur la famille dans le monde franc à travers les sources hagiographiques," *RH* 255 (1976): 3—20.

14. Fortunatus, *VG* 3 (MGH SRM 7.1, pp. 373—74); *VP* 3 (MGH AA 4.2, p. 34). See also *VBA* 3 (PL 73, p. 128), where the saint, after the death of his parents, entrusts his sister to a community of religious women before embarking on an ascetic life.

15. According to Sulpicius, *VM* 6.3 (CSEL 1, p. 116), Martin converted his mother but not his father. Aridius's mother is also "converted" (to an ascetic life) by her son's influence: *Vita Aridii abbatis et Confessoris* 5 (MGH SRM 3, p. 583).

16. There is support for the rejection of the family in Scripture: Matt. 10:34—38; 19:29; Mark 3:33—35; Luke 14:26. Instances of rejecting the family or a member of the family are found throughout early hagiographic literature: *Passio sanctarum Perpetuae et Felicitatis* 3 (ACM, pp. 108—9); *Acts of Paul* 20, 21 (NTA 2, p. 332). For Latin versions of Thecla's *Vita*, see Bonino Mombrizio, *Sanctuarium seu vitae sanctorum*, vol. 2 (Paris, 1910), pp. 599—64 and Oskar Leopold von Gebhardt, *Die Lateinisch Übersetzungen der Acta Pauli et Theclae*, TU, NF 7.2 (Leipzig, 1902). Cases involving desert saints rejecting the family, specifically marriage, are numerous; see Elliott, *Roads*, pp. 81—102; for the Merovingian and Carolingian examples, see Graus, *Volk*, pp. 472—77.

17. I am not aware of any other instances in which a hagiographer actually describes an abortion attempt; see Van Uytfanghe, *Stylisation biblique*, p. 64; though there are hagiographic

texts suggesting the practice of infanticide: *Vita sanctae Balthildis* 6 (*MGH SRM* 2, p. 488); *Vita Odiliae abbatissae* 2–3 (ibid., 6, pp. 38–39).

18. *VG* 1 (*MGH SRM* 7.1, p. 372): "Cuius genetrix, pro eo quod hunc post alterum intra breve spatium concepisset in utero, pudore mota muliebri, cupiebat ante partum infantem extinguere."

19. Ibid.: "Cuius genetrix . . . cupiebat ante partum infantem extinguere, et accepta potione, ut abortivum proiceret, nec noceret, incubabat in ventre, ut pondere praefocaret, quem veneno non laederet. Certabatur mater cum parvulo, renitebat infans ab utero: erat ergo pugna inter mulierem et viscera. Laedebatur matrona nec nocebatur infantia; obluctabatur sarcina, ne genetrix fieret parricida. Id actum est, ut servatus incolomis ipse inlaesus procederet et matrem redderet innocentem. Erat hinc futura praenoscere ante fecisse virtutem, quam nasci contingerit." On *parricidium* used in the context of abortion, see I. L. S. Balfour, "The Fate of the Soul in Induced Abortion in the Writings of Tertullian," *SP* 16, ed. Elizabeth Livingstone (Berlin, 1985), pp. 127–31.

20. *VG* 47 (*MGH SRM* 7.1, p. 402): "mox ad militiae suae belliger arma covertitur"; similarly, *VH* 5 (*MGH AA* 4.2, p. 2); *VMarc* 1 (ibid., p. 49). Martin, too, is portrayed as a warrior "armed" with prayers and the sign of the cross: Sulpicius, *VM* 4.5 (*CSEL* 1, p. 114); idem, *Ep.* 1.15 (ibid., p. 141); idem, *Dial.* 1.24 (ibid., p. 177); Gregory, *DVSM* 4.26 (*MGH SRM* 1.2, p. 656); Edmond Le Blant, *Inscriptions chrétiennes de la Gaule anterieures au VIIIe siecle*, vol. 1 (Paris, 1856), nos. 166–167, 228; Van Dam, "Images," pp. 4, 15. On the warfare of the desert saints, see Ward, trans., *The Sayings of the Desert Fathers* (London, 1975), p. 75; *VBA* 8, 15 (*PL* 73, pp. 131–32, 137); Graus, *Volk*, p. 66, 455–62. For the biblical sources on the idea of holy warfare and of life itself being a battle, see Job 7:1; Luke 22:36–38; Rom. 6:13–14; 13:12; 2 Cor. 6:7; 10:3–8; Eph. 6:10–18; 1 Thess. 5.8; Phil. 2:25; 1 Tim. 1:18; 2 Tim. 2: 3–4. Plato and the Stoics also used the notion of *militia spiritualis* to describe the philosopher's life; see David Gracie's introduction to his translation of Adolf Harnack's *Militia Christi: The Christian Religion and the Military in the First Three Centuries* (Philadelphia, 1981), p. 19. Harnack establishes (at pp. 53–55) that Christian warfare, by the time of Tertullian, cannot be regarded as being purely metaphorical; similarly, John Bugge, *Virginitas: An Essay in the History of an Ideal* (The Hague, 1975), pp. 47–58; see also James Russell, *The Germanization of Early Medieval Christianity: A Sociohistorical Approach to Religious Transformation* (New York, 1994), p. 170.

21. Heffernan discusses the various meanings of *virtus* (perhaps best translated literally as "power") throughout *Sacred Biography*; see especially pp. 151–57; on the word's significance in Merovingian hagiography, see Wittern, *Frauen*, pp. 75–78.

22. *VG* 2 (*MGH SRM* 7.1, p. 373).

23. Again, there are biblical precedents, not only the Gospel accounts of Christ's birth but also the story of John the Baptist (Luke 1:5) and passages in the Old Testament: Judg. 13:2; Jer. 1:5; see Boyer, "Typology," p. 32; Graus, *Volk*, pp. 68, 102, who discusses the theological difficulties raised by the notion of a predestined saint; see also Van Uytfanghe, "L'empreinte biblique sur la plus ancienne hagiographie occidentale," in *Le monde latin antique et la Bible*, BT 2, ed. Jacques Fontain and Charles Pietri (Paris, 1985), p. 595.

24. On the *puer-senex*, see Elliott, *Roads*, pp. 71–81, who cites the relevant studies.

25. *VH* 3 (*MGH AA* 4.2, p. 2): "Cuius a cunabulis tanta sapientia primitiva lactabatur infantia, ut iam tunc potuisset intellegi, Christum in suis causis pro obtinenda victoria necessarium sibi iussisse militem propagari."

26. *VA* 5 (ibid., p. 29): "parentes ad quorum desiderium solet infantia festinanter recurrere pro karitate Christi magis iste voluntarie reliquisset et velut hostes animae carnales affectus effugisset."

27. Ibid., "ut salva morum honestate nihil sibi de ingenuitatis privilegio vindicaret, ubi quem origo liberum genuit famulum voluntas addixit, intellegens magis esse laudabile, ut amore Christi nobilitas inclinaret."

28. VMarc 4 (ibid., p. 50): "he surrendered himself completely to heavenly discipline so that from infancy itself he grew up as an adult." Similarly, VP 3 (ibid., p. 34): "ab ipsis annis infantiae maturae vitae frena suscepit."

29. See AASS 62, November, vol. 1, p. 263.

30. VMarc 4 (MGH AA 4.2, p. 51): "cum divinis armis initiatus accingeretur ad spem felicem palmam de hoste publico relaturus, in militia Christi exercitando lector effectus est ac se ipsum templo Christi pro primitiis offerens velut Abelis sacrificium hostia victae carnis et purae mentis exceptus est."

31. On the early ascetics, see, in general, Philip Rousseau, Ascetics, Authority, and the Church in the Age of Jerome and Cassian (Oxford, 1978).

32. VMarc 4 (MGH AA 4.2, p. 50): "et positus in corpore quasi nihil de carne portaret."

33. Compare the interpretation Perpetua gives to the dream in which she fights an Egyptian opponent and wins the branch: Passio sanctarum Perpetuae et Felicitatis 10 (ACM, pp. 118–19). The theme of a saint's self-sacrificing life leading to the defeat of demonic forces also appears throughout Antony's Vita.

34. Although, apparently, age was not of great importance, inscriptional and literary evidence indicates that there was a tendency in the post-Constantinian church to admit young children into the rank of lector. This admission usually marked the beginning of a long ecclesiastical career; see DACL 8.2, pp. 2247–49. Significant in light of Marcellus's "warfare" and his appointment as lector is the remark of Remigius of Reims (written sometime between 500 and 533) to Bishop Falco of Tongres, Epistulae Avstrasicae 4 (CCSL 117, p. 411): "primicerium scole dares militiaeque lectorum."

35. On the various types and their presence in Merovingian hagiography, see Graus, Volk, pp. 88–120.

36. On the "justificative use" of the Bible by Merovingian hagiographers, see Van Uytfanghe, Stylisation biblique, pp. 36–40.

37. Regarding Fortunatus's knowledge of Christian exegesis, it is worth recalling Abbé Tardi's summation on the author's familiarity with patristic literature, Fortunat: Étude sur un dernier représentant de la poésie Latine dans la Gaule mérovingienne (Paris, 1927), pp. 42–44: "Conclouons donc qu'il avait des Peres de l'Eglise une connaissance, superficielle peut-être, mais réelle et suffisamment étendue pour son epoque." On the use of biblical typology by hagiographers, see Van Uytfanghe, "Modèls bibliques," pp. 455–56; idem, Stylisation biblique, pp. 17–21. With respect to the exegetical quality of early hagiography, Van Uytfanaghe's remarks, "L'empreinte biblique," p. 572, are applicable to Fortunatus's Vitae: "Officiellement, la littérature relative à ces 'hommes—et femmes—de Dieu' n'est pas devenue une 'Bible supplémentaire' comme le voulait l'auteur de la Passio Perpetuae . . . mais officieusement elle se présente comme une exégèse pratique de la Bible, comme une Bible 'actualisée.' Elle 'médiatise' pour ainsi dire l'Ecriture comme ses héros eux-mêmes font office de 'médiateurs' pour les fidèles, auprès du Médiateur par excellence qu'est le Christ."

38. On the early Christian theme of an ascetic life, especially the practice of sexual abstinence, reflecting the resurrected state, see Brown, The Body and Society: Men, Women and Sexual Renunciation in Early Christianity (New York, 1988), pp. 47, 87, 111, 222–24.

39. Augustine, De civitate Dei 15.15 (CCSL 48, p. 475): "Hunc [Cain] secutus Abel, quem maior frater occidit, praefigurationem quandam peregrinantis ciuitatis Dei, quod ab impiis et quodam modo terrigenis, id est terrenam originem diligentibus et terrenae ciuitatis terrena felicitate gaudentibus, persecutiones iniquas passura fuerat, primus ostendit." Cyprian, Ep. 56.5

(*PL* 4, p. 353): "Imitemur, fratres dilectissimi, Abel justum, qui initiavit martyria dum propter justitiam primus occiditur."

40. See, for example, *VBA* 23 (*PL* 73, p. 147). On the "bloodless martyrdom" (*sine cruore martyrium*; *blutlose Märtyrertum*) in Merovingian hagiography, see Graus, *Volk*, p. 64, 101–2; see also Ernst Lucius, *Die Anfänge des Heiligenkults in der christlichen Kirche* (Tübingen, 1904), pp. 396–404, who gives an exhaustive citation of the patristic and hagiographic sources; Delehaye, *Sanctus*, pp. 109–14; on the ascetic life as a form of martyrdom, see, in general, Edward Malone, *The Monk and the Martyr: The Monk as Successor of the Martyr* (Washington, D.C., 1950).

41. In describing patristic exegesis, Beryl Smalley, *The Study of the Bible in the Middle Ages* (New York, 1952), p. 2, says: "We are invited to look not at the text, but through it."

42. Among other biblical figures, Gregory mentions Abel in connection with the martyrs and "his patron" Julian, also a martyr: *VJ* 1 (*MGH SRM* 1.2, p. 563).

43. See Matt. 23:29–39, where the persecution of the prophets, the sacrifice of Abel and the foreshadowing of Christ's death are linked in the tirade against the scribes and Pharisees.

44. Augustine, *De civitate Dei* 15.18 (*CCSL* 48, p. 480): "Ex duobus namque illis hominibus, Abel, quod interpretatur luctus, et eius fratre Seth, quod interpretatur resurrectio, mors Christi et uita eius ex mortuis figuratur." If Abel is Christ, then Cain signifies the Jews in Augustine's view; 15.7 (ibid., p. 462): "[Cain] significauerit etiam Iudaeos, a quibus Christus occisus est pastor ouium hominum, quem pastor ouium pecorum praefigurabat Abel, quia in allegoria prophetica res est." Similarly, Ambrose, *De Cain et Abel* 1.2 (*CSEL* 32.1, p. 341): "per Cain parricidalis populus intellegitur Iudaeorum, qui domini et auctoris sui . . . sanguinem persecutus est, per Abel autem intellegitur Christianus adhaerens deo."

45. See Van Uytfanghe, *Stylisation biblique*, pp. 25–28.

46. Van Uytfanghe, "L'empreinte biblique," p. 573.

47. Ibid., pp. 572–73; perhaps this process of "actualizing" Scripture was not limited to hagiography; Wallace-Hadrill, *The Frankish Church*, pp. 50–53, suggests that the Old Testament provided Merovingians with a national ethos.

48. Tardi, *Fortunat*, pp. 40–42, considers Fortunatus's application of the Bible but does not come to any definite conclusions concerning what Latin versions, besides the so-called Vulgate, were used. Related to this subject, and able to shed light on Fortunatus, is the discussion by Max Bonnet, *Latin*, pp. 53–59, who indicates that Gregory of Tours used versions of the Latin Bible earlier than the Vulgate; see also Wallace-Hadrill, *Frankish Church*, p. 51.

49. The comparison may also suggest a liturgical influence: the portrayal of Marcellus resonates with the *canon missae*'s description of the biblical figures preceding Christ's sacrifice; *Missale Romanum*, vol. 1, ed. Robert Lippe (London, 1899), 209: "habere dignatus es munera pueri tui iusti abel. et sacrificium patriarce nostri abrae. et quod tibi obtulit summus sacerdos tuus melchisedech sanctum sacrificium immaculatam hostiam."

50. With respect to Marcellus as a lector and the association of Christ with martyrdom, it is interesting to note how Cyprian, *Ep.* 33 (*PL* 4, p. 319), characterizes the function of a recently ordained lector (referred to earlier in the letter as a "*fortissimus miles*"): "Sed interim placuit ut ab officio lectionis incipiat, quia et nihil magis congruit voci quae Dominum gloriosa praedicatione confessa est, quam celebrandis divinis lectionibus personare; post verba sublimia quae Christi martyrium prolocuta sunt, Evangelium Christi legere, unde martyres fiunt."

51. Van Uyfanghe, "L'empreinte biblique," p. 573.

52. Ibid., pp. 567–70.

53. See Graus, *Volk*, p. 49; Baudouin de Gaiffier, *Études critiques d'hagiographie et d'iconologie* (Brussels, 1967), pp. 50–61. For literary influences outside the Bible and Christianity, see Graus, *Volk*, p. 129; Delehaye, *Legends*, pp. 33–39, 153–59.

54. In Merovingian hagiography, the beverage is usually wine: *Vita Vedastis episcopi* 4 (*MGH SRM* 3, p. 408); *VR* 2.10 (ibid., 2, p. 384); *Vita Eligii episcopi* 1.18 (ibid., 4, p. 709); for an exception see Gregory, *GC* 1 (ibid., 1.2, pp. 748–49); the Irish saints are more associated with beer: *Liber primus de vita sancti ac beatissimi Columbani* 16 (ibid., 4, p. 82); see Charles Plummer, *Vitae sanctorum Hiberniae*, vol. 1 (Oxford, 1910), ci.

55. See also *Passio Sanctarum Perpetuae et Felicitatis* 1 (*ACM*, p. 105), with Heffernan, "Philology and Authorship in the *Passio Sanctarum Perpetuae et Felicitatis*," *Traditio* 50 (1995): 315.

56. *VMarc* 6 (*MGH AA* 4.2, p. 51): "Sed unde tam nova miracula, ut dum portaret aquam, quodam modo quasi uvas exprimeret, nasceretur illi palmes in palma?"

57. Ibid.: "Videmus non uno in loco beneficia divina concludi, dum quod praecessit in Galilaea successit in Gallia. Ibi ad nuptialem mensam Christus aquas vertit in vina, hic quae ad mensam Christi sufficerent nova vina sumpsit altare. Illud praecessit tempore hoc honore, nam quod tunc dederunt sex hydriae hic unum et modicum vas explevit, sed tunc effecit ut se dominus proderet, nunc ut famulum non celaret." Text in *AASS* 62, November, vol. 1, p. 264, offers more helpful punctuation.

58. See Van Uytfanghe, "L'empreinte biblique," pp. 605–6.

59. Jacques Fontaine, ed., *Sulpice Sévère: Vie de saint Martin*, vol. 1 (SC 133, p. 68), speaks of hagiographic texts being a "biographie continuée du Christ."

60. On the *imitatio Christi* in hagiographic literature, see Heffernan, *Sacred Biography*, pp. 5, 20, 69, 203, especially 216–21. On the problems that the *imitatio Christi* posed to the church and hagiographers, see Graus, *Volk*, p. 67.

61. Van Uytfanghe, "Modèles bibliques," p. 456.

62. Corbett, "Changing Perceptions in Late Antiquity: Martin of Tours," *Toronto Journal of Theology* 3.2 (1987): 240.

63. *VMarc* 8 (*MGH AA* 4.2, p. 35): "ubi beatus Paternus tetigit de baculo humum fons erupit ab abysso et ita replens exilivit, ac si Moyses alter virga perforante aquas traxisset de lapide."

64. See Van Uytfanghe, "L'empreinte biblique," p. 580; idem, "Modèles bibliques," p. 455.

65. Disease: *VG* 47 (*MGH SRM* 7.1, p. 402); *VA* 11 (*MGH AA* 4.2, p. 30). In these two cases involving illness, the saint is explicitly described as turning to "weapons" (*arma*, i.e., prayer and the sign of the cross) for obtaining cures. Likewise, Gregory, *DVSM* 1.24 (*MGH SRM* 1.2, p. 601), describes Martin coming to heal a sick man as "consueta deferens arma." Sulpicius, *Ep.* 1.15 (*CSEL* 1, p. 141), also says that Martin "uero uexillum crucis et orationis arma repetisset." Concerning poverty and cruel enslavement, in *VG* 22, 10 (*MGH SRM* 7.1, pp. 385–86, 379–80), explicit military language is not used, but the description is that of a retaliating saint inflicting harm against the offenders.

66. *VH* 2 (*MGH AA* 4.2, pp. 2–3); *VA* 18 (ibid., p. 32). This theme also appears prominently in Sulpicius, *Dial.* 3.11–14 (*CSEL* 1, pp. 208–12).

67. There are also minor battles with snakes, *VH* 10 (*MGH AA* 4.2, p. 5), *VMarc* 10 (ibid., pp. 53–54), and demons, *VG* 70, 71 (*MGH SRM* 7.1, pp. 413–14). Because these conflicts play such a small role, I have excluded them from the discussion.

68. Though the numbers are at best a close approximation and the scheme itself overlooks textual nuances, the numerical breakdown of conflicts based on explicit textual references is: fifteen secular, nine religious, and five ascetic.

69. Almost every secular conflict involves an official representative of worldly power (king, tribune, count, etc.). The only exception is Marcellus's *Vita*, in which the secular conflict, if we can call it that, occurs when the saint goes to a workshop, probably a smithy, and encounters an *artifex* who despises the monk and forces him to remove some hot iron from a furnace: *VMarc* 5 (*MGH AA* 4.2, p. 51).

70. VG 23 (MGH SRM 7.1, p. 386). On the location of the oratory, the *domus ecclesiae* and Clothar's palace mentioned in this chapter of the *Vita*, see May Vieillard-Troie-kouroff, *Les monuments religieux de la Gaule d'après les oeuvres de Gregoire de Tours* (Paris, 1976), pp. 201–5.

71. VG 23 (MGH SRM 7.1, p. 386): "ante nec nuntiabatur, intrat honoratus et exoratus palatium. Rex vix adsurgit de lectulo, caesum se divino flagello conquiritur; adlambit sancti palliolum, vestem sacerdotis deducit per loca doloris. Culpam confessus criminis, mox dolor omnis fugatus est." Whether *palliolum* simply designates the same garment usually referred to as a *pallium* or is actually a smaller version of that vestment, as the diminutive form would literally indicate, I cannot ascertain. That *palliolum* denotes clerical clothing there can be no doubt; Saint Leobinus, also a bishop, is described as curing individuals with his *palliolo*: *Vita sancti Leobini* 21 (MGH AA 4.2, p. 80). In addition, Gregory, GM 65 (MGH SRM 1.2, p. 532), uses the word to describe the garments stolen by robbers from a church. But *palliolum* also has a wide variety of meanings, among which is the cloth covering a tomb: GC 29 (ibid., p. 766). If the *palliolum* mentioned here by Fortunatus is the equivalent of *pallium*, there is no reason to assume that it is the special *pallium* given by a pope to a metropolitan. A Merovingian example of this garment that signifyies a special papal honor (*pallii privilegium*) is found in the *Vita Caesarii episcopi* 1.42 (ibid., 3, p. 473).

72. VG 23 (MGH SRM 7.1, p. 386): "Id actum est, ut cuius incurrerat de contemptu periculum, sentiret tactu remedium."

73. Ibid.: "sacerdos Christi solitus erat de ipsis quoque regibus triumphare."

74. On the historical issues pertaining to the boundaries of royal and ecclesiastical power, see Ian Wood, *The Merovingian Kingdoms 450–751* (London, 1994), pp. 71–87; Patrick Geary, *Before France and Germany: The Creation and Transformation of the Merovingian World* (New York, 1988), pp. 123–39; James, *The Origins of France: From Clovis to the Capetians 500–1000* (London, 1982), pp. 49–63; Scheibelreiter, *Der Bischof in merowingischer Zeit* (Vienna, 1983), pp. 177–78; Van Dam, *Saints*, pp. 99–103. On the attitude hagiography shows toward kings and worldly power, see Graus, *Volk*, pp. 353–90; idem, "Gewalt," pp. 69–70, for other important observations concerning the limits of royal power.

75. VG 23 (MGH AA 4.2, p. 386) "ut sua visitatione regi doloris vim mitiget, obtimates deprecantur."

76. For understanding the political significance of such miracles, I am indebted to the insights offered by Collins throughout his discussion, "Observations," pp. 105–31.

77. Graus, *Volk*, p. 390 and "Gewalt," pp. 86–88, claims that kings and worldly power are generally presented in a positive light throughout Merovingian hagiography; against Graus's view, see Friedrich Prinz, *Frühes Mönchtum im Frankenreich* (Munich, 1965), p. 496.

78. VG 23 (MGH SRM 7.1, p. 386): "Igitur cum glorioso Chlodchario regi occurrisset ex solito."

79. VG 13 (ibid., p. 382): "Erat ergo expectanda contentio inter sacerdotem et principem. Faciebant apud se de misericordia pugnam et de pietate certamen, thesauros ut spargerent, et de suis talentis egeni ditiscerent." When comparing Frankish kings to their charitable wives, McNamara, "The Need to Give," p. 201, seems to suggest that it was socially unacceptable for Frankish leaders to behave generously toward the poor: "Secular lords of the sixth and seventh centuries could not risk compromising their warlike qualities. Women, on the other side, used the saintly role to participate in the dialectic of taking and giving. In this way, they became innovators of a new brand of lay sanctity." This passage from Germanus's *Vita* does not lend support to McNamara's view.

80. For other instances involving animals in the hagiographic literature, see A. Marignan, *Le culte des Saints sous les Mérovingiens* (Paris, 1899), pp. xxiii–xxiv, xxvi–xxvii.

81. *VA* 14 (*MGH AA* 4.2, p. 31): "coepit ab equo discere quod homo peccaret." Likewise, according to Sulpicius, *Dial.* 2.3 (*CSEL* 1, pp. 183–84), after Martin was beaten by some soldiers, their mules refused to move until the saint "ueniam . . . clementer indulsit." Gregory gives similar "horse stories": *DVSM* 1.29 (*MGH SRM* 1.2, p. 602); *GC* 8 (ibid., p. 753); *GM* 60 (ibid., pp. 529–30); see also *VBA* 54 (*PL* 73, pp. 164–65). Perhaps the source for such accounts is the story of Balaam's ass: Num. 22:22–35.

82. *VA* 14 (*MGH AA* 4.2, p. 31): "humanus intellectus haberet quod pecus corrigeret."

83. See *VA* 7 (ibid., p. 29); *VG* 4 (*MGH SRM* 7.1, p. 375); *Vita Audoini episcopi* 8 (ibid., 5, p. 558).

84. *VG* 5 (*MGH SRM* 7.1, p. 376): "Id actum est, ut, bestia castigante, homo sensum acciperet et daret non intellegenti belua rationem."

85. *VP* 15 (*MGH AA* 4.2, p. 36): "Quod ipse inplere promittens mentitus est, profectusque ad partes Burgundiae praedicto sanctissimo nesciente, per biduum Crescentius excaecatus erravit. Qui culpam reminiscens unde illum tam repente tenebrosus error invaserit, regressus velociter, inpetrata venia, ut culpa cordis exiit oculis lux intravit et doctior post caecitatem servi dei iussa conplevit, ut ex hoc crederetur recepisse luminaria magis mentis quam corporis."

86. Graus, "Gewalt," p. 88.

87. In fact, Gregory usually depicts freedom from slavery by associating the liberation with a preceding miraculous cure of an ailment, so that the restoration of health and a change in social status are directly related; see Corbett, "Saint as Patron," p. 10; Van Dam, *Saints*, pp. 103–5.

88. *LVP* 19.1 (*MGH SRM* 1.2, p. 737); other examples: *Vita Bertuini episcopi* 4 (ibid., 7.1, p. 179): "Nihil secum retinuit nisi tantum libros canonicos et reliquias sanctorum et pueros, qui in eius aderant obsequium"; *Vita Landiberti episcopi* 5 (ibid., 6, p. 358): "nec amplius in obsequium eius remanserunt quam duo pueri"; see also *Vita Sadalbergae abbatissae* 12 (ibid., 5, pp. 56–57); *Passio Thrudperti* 5 (ibid., 4, pp. 359–60); *VR* 2.12 (ibid., 2, pp. 385–86). Yet out of all the "captivi" Saint Richarius redeemed, *Vita Richarii sacerdotis* 7 (ibid., 7.2, p. 448), "nullum, de quo sua fuit potestas, in servitio reliquit." On the hagiographic depiction of saints with slaves, see Graus, "Gewalt," pp. 90–91.

89. On the church's acceptance of slavery, often viewed as the inevitable result of a fallen world, see R. W. and E. J. Carlyle, *A History of Medieval Political Theory in the West*, vol. 1: *The Second Century to the Ninth* (London, 1903), pp. 111–24; for the Merovingian period, see Emile Lesne, *Histoire de la propriété ecclésiastique en France*, vol. 1: *Epoques romaine et merovingienne* (Paris, 1910), pp. 227–51; Charles Verlinden, *L'esclavage dans l'Europe médiévale*, vol. 1: *Péninsule ibérique-France* (Bruges, 1955), pp. 665–89; see also Marc Bloch, *Slavery and Serfdom in the Middle Ages*, trans. William Beer (Berkeley, 1975), pp. 13–14; Orlando Patterson, *Slavery and Social Death: A Comparative Study* (London, 1982), p. 275. The study of Paul Allard is too biased in favor of the church to be of use: *Les esclaves chrétien depuis les premiers temps de l'Église jusqú à la fin de la domination romaine en occident* (Paris, 1914).

90. *VG* 61 (*MGH SRM* 7.1, p. 409) "ibique tempore nocturno catenae discussae sunt, validus tormenti rigor ad fragmenta redigitur, serra gravis inliditur, postes cardine vellitur, feralis carcer recluditur." See also *VA* 16 (*MGH AA* 4.2, p. 31).

91. The subject is treated from various perspectives throughout the first sections of Graus's article, "Gewalt," pp. 61–106.

92. *LH* 6.45 (*MGH SRM* 1.1, pp. 317–19), with Graus, "Gewalt," pp. 69, 91.

93. Graus, "Gewalt," p. 99.

94. The lengthiest discussion on the subject is Graus's informative article, which considers the historical issues and the literary influences and also provides a typology of the freeings. See also James, "Beati Pacifici: Bishops and the Law in Sixth-Century Gaul," in *Disputes and Settle-*

ments: Law and Human Relations in the West, ed. J. A. Bossy (Cambridge, 1983), pp. 33–36. For comments on Fortunatus's portrayal of prison-freeings, see Collins, "Observations," pp. 116–18.

95. *VG* 30 (MGH SRM 7.1, p. 390); 61 (ibid., p. 409); 66 (ibid., p. 412); 67 (ibid., p. 412); 22 (ibid., p. 385); 64 (ibid., p. 411); 72 (ibid., p. 415); *VA* 16 (MGH AA 4.2, p. 31); 12 (ibid., p. 30); *VR* 1.11, 38 (MGH SRM 2, pp. 368, 376).

96. Count: *VG* 30 (MGH SRM 7.1, p. 390); tribune: *VG* 61, 66 (ibid., pp. 409, 412); judge: *VA* 16 (MGH AA 4.2, p. 31).

97. *VA* 12 (MGH AA 4.2, p. 30): "Tunc illo insufflante in eius faciem temerator sacerdotis celeri morte multatus est."

98. *VG* 30 (MGH SRM 7.1, p. 390): "Hinc a Nicasio comite invitatus ad prandium, vir Dei coepit de misericordia habere conloquium." Similarly, *VG* 66 (ibid., p. 412).

99. See Graus, "Gewalt," pp. 93, 95.

100. Nor is any such distinction found in the scriptural exhortation (Luke 4:18–19, with Isa. 58:6–7) "to preach freedom to captives" (*praedicare captivis remissionem*).

101. *VG* 30 (MGH SRM 7.1, p. 390): "dies in carcerem reducitur, damnati de tenebris in lucem procedunt." *VA* 16 (MGH AA 4.2, p. 31): "Hinc egressi quasi de sepulchro viventes, in basilica sancti Maurilii domno Albino gratias referentes, se ad vestigia eius prostraverunt, eo quod suspectos de funere redire fecerat ad salutem."

102. *VG* 61 (MGH SRM 7.1, p. 409): "tribunus reus effectus est."

103. *VG* 66 (ibid., p. 412): "Et quia beato viro nullum obstitit metallum, cum ligna, saxa, ferramenta ante ipsum soluta sunt, accidit una dierum Parisius orationem cum daret ad ostium carceris, sequenti nocte trusis apparet lumen in carcere. Visus est eis, ut admoneret, quod foderent, ut foris procederent. Qui dicentes ad invicem domnum Germanum vidisse, et signa singuli referent. Inventa costa de pecude, fodientes amovent lapidem et praedicto amico Dei occurrunt ad ecclesiam matutino tempore, cum rediret ad requiem. Sic multis causa salutis fuit imago pontificis."

104. They are especially prominent in the hagiography of Gregory; see I. N. Wood, "Early Merovingian Devotion in Town and Country," in *The Church in Town and Countryside*, Studies in Church History 16, ed. Derek Baker (Oxford, 1979), pp. 61–76.

105. *VG* 51 (MGH SRM 7.1, p. 404).

106. Concilivm Agathense 506, 47 (CCSL 148, p. 212); Concilivm Aurelianense 538, 31 (ibid., 148A, p. 125); Concilivm Matisconense 585, 1 (ibid., p. 239); Concilivm Cabilonense 647–653, 18 (ibid., p. 307); Sinodvs Dioecesana Avtissiodorensis 561–605, 16 (ibid., p. 267). The various Merovingian councils are discussed by Odette Pontal, *Histoire des conciles mérovingiens* (Paris, 1989).

107. The *servi* do not fare as well as lawyers and clerics; Concilivm Matisconense 585, 1 (CCSL 148A, p. 239): "Si quis itaque uestrum hanc salubrem exortationem parui penderit aut contemtui tradiderit, sciat se pro qualitatis merito principaliter a Deo punire et deinceps sacerdotali quoque irae implacabiliter subiacere; si causedecus fuerit, irreparabiliter causam amittat; si rusticus aut seruus, grauioribus fustium ictibus uerberabitur; si clericus aut monachus, mensibus sex a consortio supendetur fratrum." Yet, as Wood notes, "Merovingian Devotion," p. 65, secular law (i.e., *Pactus legis salicae*) demanded the opposite: "From a rural point of view . . . the canons could be destructive; a man had to make sure that his fences were effective, even on a Sunday; this was not just a matter of common sense, it was a point of secular law. Thus at one level the promotion of the *dies dominica* in sixth-century Gaul was a reflection of urban and perhaps upper-class interests, so that a peasant farmer might have objected with some justice that the sabbath was made for man, not man for the sabbath." Graus, *Volk*, pp. 87, 481–84, also suggests that the "Sunday-punitive-miracle" (*Sonntagsstrafwunder*) is directed at the lower classes.

108. *VG* 49 (*MGH SRM* 7.1, p. 403), where Cusinus tends to his sick horse; 50 (ibid.), where Libanius tries to fix a fence; see also *DVSM* 2.13 (ibid., 1.2, p. 613), where a slave, ordered by his master to check the grounds, discovers livestock leaving through a hole in the fence and is blinded when he attempts to fix it.

109. *VG* 14, 16 (ibid., 7.1, pp. 382–83).

110. *VG* 14 (ibid., p. 382): "cum [quidam] die dominico quiddam operatus sit, ita contrahitur digitus, ut unguium acumen partem transiret in alteram."

111. *VG* 51 (ibid., p. 404): "pro eo quod operatus est in die inluminationis, caecitate percussus est."

112. *VG* 18 (ibid., p. 383): "Quem signum crucis inpresso et sanitati reddito vetuit, ne acciperet vini potum aut carnis edulium. Qui praecepto postposito, ad normam sui langoris statim reductus est."

113. On the view that the period was marked by unbridled superstition, see Graus, *Volk*, pp. 40–47.

114. For examples of later punitive miracles that resemble the Merovingian accounts, see H. Bodenstaff, "Miracles de Sainte Radegonde: XIII et XIV siècle," *AB* 23 (1904): 433–77, especially 439.

115. On Hilary's theological disputes, see in general: C. F. A. Borchardt, *Hilary of Poitiers' Role in the Arian Struggle* (The Hague, 1966); Jean Doignon, *Hilaire de Poitiers avant l'exil: Recherches sur la naissance, l'enseignement et l'épreuve d'une foi épiscopale en Gaul au milieu du IV siècle* (Paris, 1971); see also the articles by Jean-Remy Palanque, Michel Meslin, Yves-Marie Duval, and Roger Gazeau (who discusses the spread of Hilary's cult) in *Hilaire et son temps: Actes du Colloque de Poitiers 29 septembre-3 octobre 1968 à l'occasion du XVI centenaire de la mort de saint Hilaire.*

116. *VH* 3 (*MGH AA* 4.2, p. 2): "Nam quod inter mortales valde videtur difficile, tam cautum esse, qui se a Iudaeis vel haereticis cibo suspendat, adeo vir sanctissimus hostes catholicae religionis abhorruit, ut non dicam convivium sed neque salutatio fuerit cum his praetereunti communis. Vitabat haec Davitico suffultus exemplo, ne cum haereticis mensae participando fieret illi in scandalum."

117. *VH* 5 (ibid.): "tunc vir sanctissimus timore nudus fidei fervore vestitus quasi signifer belligerator per medias acies inter hostiles fremitus inter haereticos gladios se ingerebat."

118. *VH* 8 (ibid., p. 4): "Cum vero Seleuciam pervenisset, magno favore a cunctis exceptus est"; likewise, 11 (ibid., p. 5): "Cum de exilio regressus introivit Pictavis, summo favore plaudebant omnes pariter, eo quod ecclesia recepisset pontificem, grex pastorem: et ac si omnes cum ipso tunc redissent ad patriam, ita sine illo se exules fuisse deflebant."

119. Ibid.: "beatus athleta Christi Hilarius." Some examples of martyrdom associated with contest: *Passio sanctarum Perpetuae et Felicitatis* 10 (*ACM*, pp. 116–19); *Passio sanctorum Mariani et Iacobi* 1 (ibid., pp. 194–95); 10 (ibid., pp. 208–9); *Passio sanctorum Montani et Lucii* 4 (ibid., pp. 216–17); 14 (ibid., pp. 226–27); *Passio sancti Irenaei episcopi Sirmiensis* 1 (ibid., pp. 294–95).

120. *VH* 8 (*MGH AA* 4.2, pp. 4–5): "Nam quod se pro domino sic ingerebat aperto periculo, optabat martyrium, si non defuisset percussor: et tamen animus sumpsit gloriam, etsi tempus non intulit poenam. . . . Quid autem sibi interest, vel pro vita aeterna factum fuisse martyrem, vel amplius vixisse, ne reliqui perirent? Igitur sanctissimam animam etsi gladius persecutoris non abstulit, palmam tamen martyris non amisit."

121. *VP* 7 (ibid., pp. 34–35).

122. *VG* 3 (*MGH SRM* 7.1, p. 374): "quibus elemosinis profusus extiterit, illa res una testis est, cum iam, rebus reliquis pauperibus erogatis, nec panis ipse resideret, quatenus fratres reficerent, qua de re insurgentibus adversum se monachis, retrudens se in cellula, amare flevit et doluit."

123. *VG* 3 (ibid., p. 375): "ut exinde monachi cum saturarentur cibo, terrerentur miraculo."

124. See Pontal, *Histoire des conciles*, p. 109.

125. *VA* 18 (*MGH AA* 4.2, p. 32): " 'Etsi ad imperium vestrum ego signare conpellor, dum vos causam dei recusatis defendere, ipse potens est vindicare.' "

126. See *Dial.* 3.13 (*CSEL* 1, p. 211); Gregory *LH* 10.31 (*MGH SRM* 1.1, p. 527), suggests that Martin experienced a loss of *virtus* simply by becoming a bishop: "fecitque multa signa in populo, ita ut ante episcopatum duos suscitaret mortuos, post episcopatum autem unum tantummodo suscitavit."

127. *VA* 18 (*MGH AA* 4.2, p. 32): "antequam eulogias excommunicata persona in ore susciperet, expiravit, et priusquam portitor perveniret, sermo sacerdotis obtinuit."

128. Ibid.: "incestarum nuptiarum execrabiles copulationes iure condempnans, beatum Iohannem inreprehensibiliter imitabatur. Quanta vero inde sustinuerit, nullus digne poterit explicare: siquidem martyr effici cuperet, si non defuisset dextera percussoris, sed procul dubio palmam martyii meruit qui voti desideria non abscondit."

129. *VG* 64 (*MGH SRM* 7.1, p. 411): "[Germanus] adiungit itinere quendam Amantium iuvenem, quem deprehendit a Iudaeis duci nexum in ferreis. Requiritur, quid fecerit. Puer respondit veraciter ob hoc duci in vinculis, quia se recusaret legibus subdi Iudaicis. Tunc dissimulabant cum clave Iudaei vincula ferri reserare. Facto a sancto viro desuper crucis signaculo, mox ferri serra revellitur." Fortunatus does not state if Amantius is a slave owned by Jews. To prevent conversions, Merovingian councils condemned the practice of Jews or pagans owning Christian slaves; see Verlinden, *L'esclavage*, pp. 672–79, 707–16; on related issues, see Bloch, *Slavery*, p. 3; Patterson, *Slavery and Social Death*, pp. 275–76.

130. *VG* 62 (*MGH SRM* 7.1, p. 410): "Statim a circumstantibus de mulieris naribus, scintillante igne, fumus egredi visus est."

131. Ibid.: "Qua petente ac precante, effici christianam propria domo promeruit, et quasi capite subdito, exemplo eius multi Iudaeorum conversi sunt."

132. *LH* 5.44 (*MGH SRM* 1.1, pp. 252–56); 5.43 (ibid., pp. 249–52); 6.40 (ibid., pp. 310–13); 6.5 (ibid., pp. 268–72); 10.13 (ibid., pp. 497–500). On the futility of Gregory's theological debates, see Goffart, *The Narrators of Barbarian History* (*A.D. 550–800*): *Jordanes, Gregory of Tours, Bede, and Paul the Deacon* (Princeton, 1988), pp. 143, 196.

133. According to James, *Origins*, p. 102: "In general the relations between Christian and Jew seem to have been good, hence the constant efforts of ecclesiastical legislators to sever or control those relations. The danger of conversion to Judaism was increased by the strong emphasis the Church in the early Middle Ages itself placed upon the Old Testament (the legal and political structure of ancient Israel was close enough to that of Frankish Gaul to make it an obvious inspiration), and also by the proximity and frequency of Jewish communities."

134. For the accounts Fortunatus and Gregory give of the forced conversion of Jews at Clermont, see Goffart, *Narrators*, pp. 163–64. Goffart indicates that Gregory knew that the conversions were forced, even though the *Histories* present a more peaceful picture. For a discussion on the forced conversion of pagans, see Graus, *Volk*, pp. 145–49.

135. *VP* 4 (*MGH AA* 4.2, p. 34): "diabolica cultura quae gentili sub errore male veneratur."

136. *VP* 5 (ibid.): "Tunc sanctus cum collega suo tam fervore fidei quam vexillo crucis armati accedentes ad vasa ubi pulmentaria decoquebant, singula suis baculis everterunt: potum vero per cupellas dispositum deorsum evellere voluerunt."

137. Ibid.: "postponentes suum periculum, dummodo fortes milites pugnarent pro Christo desiderantes martyrium, si devotus ferire non reformidasset percussor."

138. *VP* 10 (ibid., p. 35).

139. *VA* 6 (ibid., p. 29): "Erat enim ad oboediendum promptus, ad vitia calcanda maturus, ita ut in ipso iuvenili tyrocinio iam senibus esset exemplum." *VMarc* 5 (ibid., p. 51): "Denique cum adhuc clericali tyrocinio celaretur, miraculis proditur et signis caelestibus inlustratur." See also Tertullian, *De paenitentia* 6.14 (*SC* 316, p. 168).

140. Compare Fortunatus, *carm.* 2.9, 27–30, 42–43, 71–72 (MGH AA 4.1, pp. 38–39), where Bishop Germanus is described as the "commander" (*dux*) in charge of a clerical army; for comments on the poem's "military overtones," see Judith George, *Venantius Fortunatus* (Oxford, 1992), pp. 71–72.

141. *VG* 75 (MGH SRM 7.1, p. 417): "Qui cum suis visceribus dimicaret et vinceret, paene se ipsum obliviscens, ut, domestico tormento superato corpore, de se triumphatum in pace factus martyr adquireret."

142. *VG* 76 (ibid., p. 418): "per orbem mirandis actibus adipiscendus martyribus, apostolis adgregandus, glorificandus meritis, coronandus in populis, raptus corporeo vinculo, immaculato spiritu, beatis fidei dotibus perpetualiter victurus, victor evolavit ad caelos, regnante domino nostro Iesu Christo, cui est gloria, honor et potestas in saecula saeculorum."

143. Fortunatus, *Vita sancti Martini* 2.446–50 (MGH AA 4.1, p. 328), also describes Martin in the ranks of the heavenly hosts with the "invincible king" flanked by the apostles, prophets, and martyrs, who constitute an army.

144. For contemporary iconographic depictions of Christ dressed as a warrior and armed with weapons, see Edouard Salin, *La civilisation mérovingienne*, vol. 4 (Paris, 1959), pp. 396–403, especially plate 1, where Christ is bearing weapons and has, as Salin puts it (at p. 399), "chose étrange, un long phallus."

145. See Corbett, "Changing Perceptions," pp. 236–51; idem, *Praesentium signorum munera*, pp. 44–61; Van Dam, "Images," pp. 1–27; Alston Hurd Chase, "The Metrical Lives of St. Martin of Tours by Paulinus and Fortunatus and the Prose Life by Sulpicius Severus," HS 43 (1932): 51–76; Graus, *Volk*, pp. 113–14; Fontaine, "Hagiographie et politique, de Sulpice Sévère à Venance Fortunat," RHEF 62 (1976): 113–40. For a tabular comparison of Fortunatus's poem on Martin with the *Vitae* written by Paulinus and Sulpicius, see Gerald Malsbary, "The Epic Hagiography of Paulinus of Perigueux" (Ph.D. diss., University of Toronto, 1987), pp. 334–46.

146. Graus, *Volk*, pp. 120, 196: "Die Legende war in der Merowingerzeit stark kirchlich geprägt"; see Van Dam, "Images," p. 10.

147. Van Dam, "Images," pp. 9–10; Corbett, "Changing Perceptions," p. 248.

148. *VM* 9.3–4; 1.2 (CSEL 1, pp. 119, 111). Other references to Martin's shabby clothing: *Dial.* 2.1 (ibid., pp. 180–81), where the saint wears a rough garment originally intended for a beggar; in *Dial.* 2.3 (ibid., p. 183), the mules are frightened when they see Martin "*in veste hispida.*"

149. *Vita sancti Martini* 2.451–58 (MGH AA 4.1, p. 329): "nec videt hoc oculus quod habet super astra senatus:/ his frueris, Martine, bonis sub principe caeli"; similarly, *Vita sancti Martini* 3.52 (ibid., p. 522). On Martin being depicted as a senator by Fortunatus, see Van Dam, "Images," pp. 11–12.

150. Heinzelmann, *Bischofsherrschaft in Gallien* (Munich, 1976), p. 237, calls attention to this upper-class milieu on the basis of ten episcopal epitaphs composed by Fortunatus: "Daneben bleibt allerdings zu berücksichtigen, dass der Hofdicter Fortunat, der immerhin zehn der 27 Texte geschrieben hat, sich mit Vorliebe mit Personen der höchsten sozialen Ebene befasste"; see Van Dam, "Images," p. 11; compare Hen, *Culture*, p. 27. In the capacity of a poet seeking patronage, Fortunatus's association with the rich and powerful was not limited to bishops but embraced the secular aristocracy as well; see George, *Venantius Fortunatus*, pp. 106–79.

151. Van Dam, "Images," pp. 11–12.

152. See especially Hilary's *Vita*, in which Fortunatus relies throughout on Sulpicius's *VM* and his *Chronica*. For Gregory, see Krusch's remarks, MGH SRM 1.2, p. 460.

153. According to Brown, *Society and the Holy*, p. 185, "there is the obvious feature of a marked shortage of living holy men. A society which knew all about Symeon Stylites somehow did not want one of its own. . . . The appearances of itinerant holy men in Tours are recounted

by Gregory in tones of 'While the cat's away, the mice do play. . . . ' I would like to posit a climate of opinion that actively withheld enthusiasm from all but the most well-tried bearers of the holy. 'Call no man holy until he is dead' is the motto of Gregory's writings." Perhaps the best known example of the Merovingian church attempting to control a holy man is that of Vulfolaic, LH 8.15 (MGH SRM 1.1, p. 381), who in frigid Trier, with icicles on his beard, sat on a column as Symeon Stylites once did. The local bishops ordered him down; he complied because "sacerdotes non obaudire adscribitur crimini." Some other accounts in which the behavior of holy men is regarded with suspicion or hostility: GC 37 (ibid., 1.2, p. 771); Vita sancti Goaris confessoris 6 (ibid., 4, pp. 416–17); Vita sancti Romani abbatis 12 (ibid., 3, pp. 137–38). The Council of Orleans in 511 also took measures to control independent holy men (CCSL 148A, 11): "Nullus monachus congregatione monasterii derelicta ambitionis et uanitatis inpulso cella construere sene [i.e., sine] episcopi permissione uel abbatis sui uoluntate praesumat." See Graus, Volk, pp. 108–10.

154. Graus, Volk, p. 114: "Der Held der Hagiographie ist kein wild wachsendes Gewächs, das vom Legendisten abgebildet worden ist; er ist eine liebevoll gezüchtete und gehegte Zierpflanze."

155. Of course, it is impossible to give an exact figure. However, in discussing this matter, Waldron, "Expressions," p. 338, states: "In brief, the safest conclusion to be made about the numbers of lay converts in Gaul throughout our period is that they were not uncommon. No contemporary author betrays puzzlement over encountering the tradition. Probably everyone knew of at least a convert or two in his local community." (Here, convert refers to one who leads a life of "heightened religiosity," not, as we commonly use the term, one who has decided to adopt the teachings of a particular religion.)

156. See Graus, Volk, pp. 108–15.

157. Ibid., p. 117: "Das Hervortreten dieses Heiligentypus [i.e., the holy bishop] und sein Vorherrschen in der merowingischen Hagiographie hatte aber zur Folge, dass sich das Heiligenideal aristokratisierte." On sanctitas and nobilitas, see Scheibelreiter, Bischof, pp. 16–28.

158. Graus, Volk, pp. 114–17.

159. VP 9 (MGH AA, 4.2, p. 35).

160. VP 16 (ibid., pp. 36–37): "Quadam nocte visus est ei ipse locus mira claritate perfusus et ad eum venientes in visione sancti qui ad deum migraverant, Melanius, Leontianus et Vigor episcopi, per revelationem eum ordinaverunt antestitem. Tum ipse stupefactus sed apud se retinens, quamvis tunc tractaverit, post probavit."

161. Before becoming bishop Germanus, VG 12 (MGH SRM 7.1, p. 380), dreams that an old man comes to give him the "claves portae Parisiacae."

162. Fortunatus's male saints proceed through the clerical/monastic ranks thus: Hilary: priest, bishop; Germanus: deacon, priest, monk, abbot, bishop; Albinus: monk, abbot, bishop; Paternus: monk, cellarer (then temporary recluse), deacon, priest, bishop; Marcellus: lector, subdeacon, priest, bishop.

163. See Elliott, Roads, pp. 136, 42, 83.

164. On the so-called Adelsheiligen, see Russell, Germanization, pp. 168–69; Franz Irsigler, "On the Aristocratic Character of Early Frankish Society," in The Medieval Nobility: Studies on the Ruling Classes of France and Germany from the Sixth to the Twelfth Century, ed. and trans. Timothy Reuter (Amsterdam, 1978), p. 112–22; Prinz, "Aristocracy and Christianity in Merovingian Gaul," in Monographien zur Geschichte des Mittelater 11, ed. Karl Bosl (Stuttgart, 1975), pp. 153–65; idem, Frühes Mönchtum im Frankenreich, pp. 489–504; idem, "Heiligenkult und Adelsherrschaft im Spiegel merowingisher Hagiographie," Historische Zeitschrift 204 (1967): 529–44; idem, "Gesellschaftsgeschichtliche Aspekte frühmittelalterlicher Hagiographie," Zeitschrift für Literaturwissenschaft und Linguistik 3 (1973): 20–27; Karl Bosl, "Der 'Adelsheilige': Idealtypus und Wirklichkeit, Gesellschaft und Kultur im merowingerzeitlichen Bayern des 7. und 8. Jahrhunderts," in Mön-

chtum und Gesellschaft im Frühmittelalter, ed. Friedrich Prinz (Darmstadt, 1976), pp. 354–86; Hein-zelmann, "Neue Aspekte der biographischen und hagiographischen Literatur in lateinischen Welt (1.-6. Jahrhundert)," Francia 1 (1973): 40–42; Graus, "Sozialgeschichtliche Aspekte der Hagiographie der Merowinger- und Karolingerzeit: Die Viten der Heiligen des südaleman-nischen Raumes und die sogenannten Adelsheiligen," in Mönchtum, Episkopat und Adel zur Grün-dungszeit des Klosters Reichenau, ed. Arno Borst (Sigmaringen, 1974), pp. 131–76; Scheibelreiter, "Der Frühfrankische Episkopat," p. 136. For further references and ample examples drawn from the sources, see Van Uytfanghe, Stylisation biblique, pp. 166–70.

165. VM 10. 8–9 (CSEL 1, p. 120): "quod eo magis sit mirum necesse est, quod multi inter eos nobiles habebantur, qui longe aliter educati ad hanc se humilitatem et patientiam coegerant: pluresque ex eis postea episcopos uidimus. quae enim esset ciuitas aut ecclesia, quae non sibi de Martini monasterio cuperet sacerdotem?" However, Van Dam, Saints, p. 15, n. 22, observes that "it is difficult to identify any monks from Marmoutier who became bishops."

166. Prinz, Frühes Mönchtum, pp. 47–87, 452–61.

167. See Collins, "Observations," p. 114.

168. Ibid.

169. Ibid.: "He [Fortunatus] is the first of a long succession of hagiographers to make nobilitas the veritable foundation of an episcopal career."

170. On inventing a genealogy, see Alexander Bergengruen, Adel und Grundherrschaft im Mer-owingerreich (Wiesbaden, 1958), pp. 25–26.

171. As we shall see shortly, there is evidence suggesting that Fortunatus's episcopal pa-trons largely control the production of hagiographic texts. They determine what "saints" will have biographies written and they provide the information they want included in the Lives. The process moves from the bishops to the people, not vice versa, which is especially clear when, as in the case of Marcellus, VMarc 2 (MGH AA 4.2, p. 50), the saint's miracles could be forgotten (and hence the cult disappear) if they are not recorded by the hagiographer: "tem-porum vetustate subrepta, nec facile memoria recolit quod annositas numerosa fraudavit, quoniam quidquid in libris non figitur vento oblivionis aufertur." On the basis of Fortunatus's Vitae, the romantic conception of hagiography as being purely the product of the people cannot be compelling, though such a view is advocated by Delehaye, Legends, pp. 16–39, 49–59 (perhaps for Catholic apologetical reasons; see Graus, Volk, pp. 26–37) and Bernoulli, Die Heiligen der Merowinger, p. vii.

172. Germanus's Vita is missing a preface. Whether it was lost or never written cannot be determined; see Richard Koebner, Venantius Fortunatus: Seine Persönlichkeit und seine Stellung in der geistigen Kultur des Merowingerreiches (Leipzig and Berlin, 1915), p. 107, n. 1. The other Vita lacking a prefacing letter is Radegund's, the only work of Fortunatus's prose hagiography not commis-sioned by high-ranking clerics.

173. VH 1 (MGH AA 4.2, p. 1): "Cuius [i.e., Hilary] operis amore praeventus eo usque me dignatus es [Pascentius] perurguere, quo de actibus sacratissimi viri Hilarii confessoris . . . ut impensi muneris vel verba rependeres, ideo etsi non plena vel ex parte complexa perstrin-gerem: quatinus dum sui gregis auribus vox quodam modo et vita pastoris antiquissimi re-sonaret, et ille probaret ministerium et ipse non celares affectum." For comments on this passage, see Collins, "Observations," p. 108.

174. VH 1 (MGH AA 4.2, p. 1): "ut facile sit perspicuum ad culturam ecclesiasticae dis-ciplinae et fuisse te genitum et esse provectum."

175. Ibid.: "inrefragabiliter veteris dispositionis ac catholici dogmatis fundamentum custos observans."

176. I quote the passage in full because it explicitly shows the process of a hagiographic production and the measures a bishop took to keep the memory of the saint's life from slipping

into oblivion by commissioning the writing of a *Vita*. Note also that the *Life* is not the result of "popular imagination" overflowing but entirely the initiative of a clerical culture, with "the people" (*populum*) playing only a secondary role; *VA* 2 (ibid., p. 28): "Intellegitis sane velociter fugientes a saeculo memoriae subripi, et si de vita sanctissimi neglegantur aliqua cito lapsura litteris alligari, non facile rursus in animum recipi quod semel inceperit oblivione temporis invadente subduci. Huius rei inpulsor quidam postmodum mandata vestrae beatitudinis exequens a me si quidem annuerem inconperendinatim id fieri flagitavit. Illud vero adiciens, ut quae ipse de gestis sancti viri Albini iuxta fidem conpererat eo insinuante indubitabiliter propalarem, in hoc se magis querimoniarum mole conficiens, eo quod quae praedictus vir occulte quidem sed digna relatu gesserat per veritatis indaginem nec ad ea singula meruerit pervenire et aliqua se de cognitis memoraret a memoria abolevisse. In his autem qui meminit sine ambiguitate suo testimonio populum nobis attulit assentantem, cum certe de eius praeteritis dubitare non liceat qui operatur in singulis cotidie clariora.

Congratulatus sum relatori, eo quod de vestris nutrimentis talis vir adoleverit, qui iniuncta sibi tam strenue peroraret et de proprio aliquid causa venustatis non inconpetenter offerret, immo dilucide ipse per se quod aliunde poposcerat explicaret. Si quidem quidquid de illo elicitur, vestris hoc praeconiis deputatur, quoniam est meritum magistri laus discipuli et ministri solatia sunt pontifici ornamento."

177. See Collins, "Observations," pp. 109–10.

178. Ibid. Provided hagiographic elements are substituted for jousts and the like, Fortunatus's aristocratic episcopal patrons who promote the deeds of saints may be related to the *Vitae* they commissioned in precisely the way Frye, *The Secular Scripture: A Study of the Structure of Romance* (Cambridge, 1976), pp. 56–57, claims a horse-riding aristocracy is related to chivalric romance: "In a medieval chivalric romance the jousts and tournaments, the centripetal movement of knights to Arthur's or Charlemagne's court and their dispersal out from it into separate quests, the rescued damsels and beloved ladies, the giants and helpful or perilous beasts, all form a ritualized action expressing the ascendancy of a horse-riding aristocracy. *They also express that aristocracy's dreams of its own social function, and the idealized acts of protection and responsibility that it involves to justify that function*" (emphasis added).

179. Koebner, *Fortunatus*, p. 78: "Er will in seiner Briefprosa sich und den Empfänger durch den Wortschwall in einem verwirrten Rauschzustand versetzeln"; similarly, Wattenbach and Levison, *Deutschlands Geschichtsquellen im Mittelalter. Vorzeit und Karolinger*, vol. 1: *Die Vorzeit von den Anfängen bis zur Herrschaft der Karolinger* (Weimar, 1952), p. 97: "unerträglich ist seine Prosa, schwülstig, geziert, kaum verständlich"; Van Dam, *Saints*, p. 155: "Even with this [i.e., Krusch's] fine edition it is still sometimes a struggle to make sense of Fortunatus's ornate Latin."

180. *VA* 3 (*MGH AA* 4.2, p. 28): "cum ante vestram peritiam ipsa Ciceronis ut suspicor eloquia currerent vix secura, et cui apud Caesarem Roma aliquid deliberans Aquitanico iudice forsitan Galliam formidaret, incongruum esse persensi, quod a me infra doctorum vestigia latitante res alta requireretur."

181. Koebner, *Fortunatus*, p. 116: "Meisterwerke rhetorischen Schwulstes sollten . . . seine Prosaepisteln sein."

182. Collins, "Observations," pp. 109–10, applies the findings of Heinzelmann and argues convincingly that Fortunatus's prose prefaces that emphasize the bishops' rhetorical proficiency ought to be seen in light of a similar emphasis in the episcopal epitaphs of the Gallo-Roman aristocracy.

183. Ibid., pp. 110–11, for remarks on the relation between Fortunatus's language and his "public"; on the question of audience in general, see Van Uytfanghe, "L'hagiographie et son public," pp. 54–62, who concludes by stressing "un public diversifié, à toute la *plebs christiana*"; similarly, Hen, *Culture*, p. 27.

184. Graus, *Volk*, pp. 119–20.

185. *VG* 12 (MGH SRM 7.1, p. 381): "Denique adeptus gradum curae pastoralis episcopus, de reliquo vero monachus persistebat."

186. Caesarius also claims that imitation of the martyrs is possible if one is willing; *Sermo* 223.2 (CCSL 104, pp. 882–83): "Sed dicit aliquis: Et quis est qui possit beatorum martyrum vestigia sequi? Huic ego respondeo, quia non solum martyres, sed etiam ipsum dominum cum ipsius adiutorio, si volumus, possumus imitari." According to Owen Chadwick, *Western Asceticism* (Philadelphia, 1958), p. 20: "Long before the age of persecution was past, the word *martyr* is applied to anyone who lives a truly self-sacrificing life. Tertullian could write of a martyrdom of will 'perfect without suffering.' "

187. On the literal meaning and use of the word *martyrium*, see Elliott, *Roads*, pp. 22–24, 36.

188. Charles Altman, "Two Types of Opposition and the Structure of Latin Saints' Lives," in *Medievalia et Humanistica*, vol. 6, ed. Paul Clogan (Cambridge, 1975), p. 1, attempts to distinguish hagiographic texts on the basis of opposition in plot structures. The *passiones* "operate according to the principles of diametric opposition . . . the *vitae* grew slowly away from the diametrical configuration of the *passio*, eventually adapting fully the gradational form of romance." For a critique, see Olsen, "De Historiis," p. 407.

189. Compare Sulpicius's characterization of Martin, *Ep.* 2.9–12 (CSEL 1, pp. 143–44).

190. *VBA* 23 (PL 73, p. 147): "ad pristinum monasterium regressus, quotidianum fidei ac conscientiae martyrium merebatur"; in more dramatic fashion, Jerome, *Vita Malchi monachi captivi* 6 (PL 23, p. 56): "Habet et servata pudicitia suum martyrium. Jaceat insepultus Christi testis in eremo, ipse mihi ero et persecutor et martyr."

191. Graus, *Volk*, p. 64, 101–2; Lucius, *Die Anfänge*, pp. 396–404; Delehaye, *Sanctus*, pp. 109–14.

192. *VG* 75 (MGH SRM 7.1, p. 417): "Qui cum suis visceribus dimicaret et vinceret, paene se ipsum obliviscens, ut, domestico tormento superato corpore, de se triumphatum in pace factus martyr adquireret."

193. James Earl, "Literary Problems in Early Medieval Hagiography" (Ph.D diss., Cornell University, 1971), pp. 54–98, considers the relation between icons and *Vitae*. Whatever shortcomings this work may have, Earl's discussion is in no way as simplistic as Olsen, "De Historiis," pp. 407, 410, 420, presents it in her argument against his views.

194. Delehaye, *Legends*, pp. 26–39, 91–106; idem, *Cinq Leçons*, p. 11; idem, *Les passions des martyrs et les genres littéraires* (Brussels, 1921), p. 223. Ferdinand Lot, *The End of the Ancient World and the Beginnings of the Middle Ages* (New York, 1931), pp. 162–63, had an especially harsh view of hagiography based on the prominence of literary borrowings: "At an early date, it is admitted that no blame attaches to a writer, if in recounting the life of a saintly man, he borrows a fact from another life, for the purpose of edification. The study of the lives of saints . . . has in store for us . . . painful literary disappointments. Very few of these *Vitae* are sincere and have real emotion. The vast majority of them are abominable trash. Hagiography is a low form of literature like the serial novel in our own days."

195. Frye, *Anatomy of Criticism: Four Essays* (Princeton, 1957), pp. 136–37.

196. Elliott, *Roads*, pp. 10, 13–14, 42.

197. Ibid., pp. 16–17, 45, 83–85; Altman, "Two Types," pp. 1–11.

198. *VP* 4 (MGH AA 4.2, p. 34): "Qui [i.e., Paternus and his companion] dum in quadam insula propter solitudinem desiderarent accedere."

199. General references to caves and caves functioning as tombs are numerous in the desert literature; for examples, see Elliott, *Roads*, pp. 104–16, 238.

200. *VP* 5 (MGH AA 4.2, p. 34): "Tunc circa sinum montis in receptaculo cavernae . . . heremita ingressus est." The text does not indicate if the temple was located at the top of the

mountain. If so, then Paternus would have literally ascended. For instances of pagan worship on mountains or hilltops, see Wallace-Hadrill, *Frankish Church*, p. 30.

201. On omophagy ("eating raw"), see Elliott, *Roads*, pp. 138–39.

202. Ibid., pp. 71, 74.

203. *VBA* 51 (PL 73, p. 162).

204. See Max Weber's comments concerning the "routinization" of charisma and bureaucratic authority: *On Charisma and Institution Building: Selected Papers*, ed. S. N. Eisenstadt (Chicago, 1968), pp. 48–65; idem, *The Sociology of Religion*, trans. Ephraim Fischoff, (Boston, 1964), pp. 180–83.

205. There is also the scriptural parallel to the *puer-senex* in the story of the young Christ teaching in the temple: Luke 2:46–52.

206. Elliott, *Roads*, p. 81.

207. In fact, the conservativism of the genre and the persistent reliance on models has added another dimension to the debate over the discovery of the individual, which allegedly took place during the twelfth century. Note how Bynum, "Did the Twelfth Century Discover the Individual?" *JEH* 31.1 (1980): 9, uses hagiography to support her argument: "Despite their new interest in the self or the inner landscape of the individual, twelfth-century people tended to write about themselves and about others as types. . . . Twelfth-century biographers . . . see their subjects as following models. In a fine example . . . the biographer of Gerald of Salles describes Gerald (d. 1120) as follows: 'In all his deeds, he was redolent of Hilarion, resembled Anthony, Christ really lived in him. He was totally on fire and he put others on fire; he acted and spoke now [like] John in the desert, now [like] Paul in public.' " A reply to Bynum is given by Colin Morris, "Individualism in Twelfth-Century Religion. Some Further Reflections," *JEH* 31.2 (1980): 195–206.

208. See Graus, *Volk*, pp. 74–86.

209. Elliot, *Roads*, pp. 8, 184.

CHAPTER 3

1. Gregory's uncanonical episcopal election and the ecclesiastical factionalism that probably arose from it were smoothed over by Fortunatus's *adventus* poem acclaiming the popularity of the royally appointed bishop: "*Ad cives Turonicos de Gregorio episcopo*," carm. 5.4 (MGH AA 4.1, pp. 106–7). On the poem, see George, *Venantius Fortunatus*, pp. 74–77. According to Brennan, "The Career of Venantius Fortunatus," *Traditio* 41 (1985): 77, Fortunatus's function as a poet "acted in concert with his patron, Gregory, in a highly controlled exercise of diplomacy to achieve specific ends." For his rhetorical services, Gregory handsomely rewarded Fortunatus with the gift of a villa that is commemorated in the poem "*Ad eundem pro villa praestita*," carm. 8.19 (MGH AA 4.1, p. 199). On all other matters pertaining to Gregory, including his association with Fortunatus, his ancestry, writings, life, and episcopal career alluded to here, consult the following recent studies, which provide extended bibliographies: Heinzelmann, *Gregor von Tours*; Wood, *The Merovingian Kingdoms*; Van Dam, *Saints*; Goffart, *Narrators*; Nie, *Views from a Many-Windowed Tower: Studies of Imagination in the Works of Gregory of Tours* (Amsterdam, 1987).

2. Collins, "Observations," p. 105. For the significance of Gregory's full name as an expression of kinship structure, see James, *Origins*, p. 76.

3. Erik Kemp, *Canonization and Authority in the Western Church* (Oxford, 1948), p. 31; Wallace-Hadrill, *The Long-Haired Kings and Other Studies in Frankish History* (London, 1962), p. 54.

4. For an overview of Gregory's whole corpus, see Goffart, *Narrators*, pp. 127–53. Gregory composed his works simultaneously over several years. For the approximate dates of each composition, see Bonnet, *Latin*, p. 12, whose own estimates appear alongside the sometimes slightly different assessments of Gabriel Monod, *Études critiques sur les sources de l'histoire mérovingienne*,

1ère partie, Introduction, *Grégoire de Tours, Marius d'Avenches* (Paris, 1872), p. 44; see also Krusch, MGH SRM 1.2, pp. 451–58. James, *Life*, p. 4, concludes (based on Krusch's research) that the Lives of the LVP did not reach their final form as a whole book until 592 or later.

5. Goffart, *Narrators*, p. 152: "It makes little sense, then, to distinguish the *Wonders* as hagiography from the *Histories*. Both multibook works incorporate the same mode of storytelling and affirmations of stylistic rusticity, along with the same premises and pastoral concerns." For the relevant studies on the hagiographic features of the *Histories*, see ibid., p. 152, n. 8; Nie, *Views* 12–13. Goffart also argues, *Narrators*, pp. 197–203, that the *Histories* is a work of satire; Van Dam, *Saints*, p. 148, rejects this view.

6. After mentioning the "emptiness of thought" in Fortunatus's "occasional poems," Maurice Hélin, *A History of Medieval Latin Literature*, trans. Jean Snow (New York, 1949), pp. 15–16, remarks: "In contrast, a breath of lyric inspiration permeates the *Vexilla regis prodeunt* . . . and the *Pange lingua*"; similarly, Helen Waddell, *The Wandering Scholars* (Boston, 1929), p. 26: "the coming of the relics to the church at Poitiers . . . gave him the inspiration of the greatest Processional of the Middle Ages, the *Vexilla regis*. . . . Both this and the other *Pange lingua gloriosi* are a mystic's Dream of the Rood"; see also Frederick Raby, *A History of Christian-Latin Poetry from the Beginnings to the Close of the Middle Ages* (Oxford, 1927), pp. 89–91. On the textual history and liturgical significance of the "*Pange lingua*," see C. H. Kneepkens, " 'Nil in ecclesia confusius quam ymni isti cantantur': A Note on the Hymn *Pange, lingua gloriosi*," in *Frvctus Centesimvs*, ed. A. A. R. Bastiaensen et al. (Dordrecht, 1989), pp. 193–205. For the state of criticism on Fortunatus's poetry in general, see George, *Venantius Fortunatus*, pp. 1–3, who cites the relevant studies.

7. Franz Brunhölzl, *Geschichte der lateinischen Literatur des Mittelalters*, vol. 1: *Von Cassiodor bis zum Ausklang der karolingischen Erneuerung* (Munich, 1975), p. 134, notices that in the LVP Gregory's style switches from elevated in the prefaces to plain in the narratives that follow. This pattern was observed in Fortunatus's Lives; with Gregory, however, the stylistic difference between preface and hagiographic narrative is not nearly as pronounced.

8. Collins, "Observations," p. 105, who cites the relevant scholarship on this issue, states: "The work of these two writers differs formally to such an extent that historians have hesitated to consider them as representatives of the same past." On the state of learning in Merovingian Gaul and its assessment by modern scholars, see Pierre Richè, *Education and Culture in the Barbarian West: Sixth through Eighth Centuries*, trans. John Contreni (Columbia, S.C., 1976), pp. 193–246; see also Wood, *Merovingian Kingdoms*, pp. 20–32, 239–50.

9. "Barbarized Latin": Wallace-Hadrill, *Long-Haired Kings*, p. 54. Still the most thorough study of Gregory's language is Bonnet's *Latin*. There is a tendency in the scholarship on the *Histories* to see Gregory's language as a mirror of the turbulent and harsh period in which he lived; see Nie, *Views*, pp. 8–22; Goffart, *Narrators*, pp. 114–15, 146–53, who offers important insights into Gregory's language; the connection made (ibid., p. 150) between Gregory's prose and a christological worldview marks one of the more significant advances in understanding Gregory's writings.

10. Its popularity owes much to being one of the first of Gregory's writings to be translated into several modern languages: Goffart, *Narrators*, p. 120, n. 37.

11. Ibid., p. 118.

12. Nie, *Views*, p. 23, 131, 75, 84; Max Manitius, "Zur Frankengeschichte Gregors von Tours," *Neues Archiv* 21 (1986): 549–57. Goffart, *Narrators*, p. 155, compares Gregory to an "epic poet."

13. On Fortunatus's familiarity with the Latin poets, see George, *Venantius Fortunatus*, p. 21. A verse-by-verse comparison showing Fortunatus's borrowings from Vergil's poetry is given by Stephan Zwierlein, *Venantius Fortunatus in seiner Abhängigkeit von Vergil* (Würzburg, 1926). Blomgren's extensive studies on Fortunatus's literary borrowings were not available to me.

14. See Charles Nisard, "Des poésies de Sainte Radégonde attribuées jusqu'ici à Fortunat," RH 37.2 (1888): 56, who refers to the "bad taste" (mauvais goût) pervading Fortunatus's poetry.

15. See Goffart, Narrators, pp. 116–17, 231.

16. Nie, Views, pp. 1–26, gives a clear overview; throughout the section on Gregory in Narrators, pp. 112–234, Goffart also succinctly summarizes and engages the previous scholarship.

17. See Van Dam, Saints, p. 51.

18. Nie, Views, pp. 13–14, summarizes with great precision the points of disagreement and consensus.

19. Mentalités: Nie, Views, p. 14; naive reporter: Goffart, Narrators, pp. 114–19.

20. See James, The Franks (Oxford, 1988), p. 17; Nie, Views, p. 14. Yet the massive accumulation of data gathered from Gregory's writings by Margarete Weidemann is remarkable: Kulturgeschichte der Merowingerzeit nach den Werken Gregors von Tours, 2 vols. (Mainz, 1982).

21. On this point, Fortunatus fared no better than Gregory; see Collins, "Observations," p. 1, with Aigrain, L'hagiographie, p. 159, and G. Strunk, Kunst und Glaube in der lateinischen Heiligenlegende: Zu Ihrem Selbstverständnis in den Prologen (Munich, 1970), p. 43.

22. See Van Dam, Saints, p. 84; Fouracre, "Merovingian History," pp. 4–5; Graus, Volk, p. 41; Geary, Living with the Dead, pp. 9–29; Felice Lifshitz, "Beyond Positivism and Genre: 'Hagiographical' Texts as Historical Narrative," Viator 25 (1994): 95–113.

23. As G. Kurth says so succinctly when referring to Gregory, "De l'autorité de Grègoire de Tours," in Études Franques, vol. 2 (Paris, 1919), p. 122, "ne connat rien de plus natural que le supernatural." Graus, Volk, pp. 44–46, offers further insights into Gregory's view of the miraculous. On the medieval understanding of the miraculous as natural, see Ward, Miracles, pp. 3–19.

24. Graus, Volk, p. 28: "so konnte der Historiker eigentlich nur bedauern, dass der Hagiograph eben Hagiograph war, und nicht lieber nur Urkunden abschrieb"; e.g., Wilhelm Levison's introduction to the Vita Nivardi episcopi Remensis (MGH SRM 5, p. 159): "Pauca autem utilia quae Vitae insunt e chartis Remensibus et Altivillarensibus pendent, e quibus Almannus nonnula exerpsit. . . . Quare gratia ei habenda est, quae certe maior esset, si chartas integras descripsissent pro fabulis et verbis inanibus, quibus opusculum produxit" (emphasis added). Similarly, in the introduction to the Vita sanctae Aldegundis (MGH SRM 6, p. 80), he states: "Atque longe maxima pars opusculi e visionibus miraculisque constat, qualia ut sunt vix ullius momenti cuilibet et personae et aevo attribui possint. Primis capitibus ultimoque exceptis, de cursu vitae nihil fere narratur, atque Aldegundem 'matrem coenobitarum' fuisse obiter tantum comperimus" ; hence the sections describing the visions (chapters 5–17) are purged from the edition (ibid., p. 88, n. 5): "Visiones Aldegundis quae sequuntur omissae sunt." However, Collins, "Observations," p. 1, notes a change in Levison's attitude toward the historical value of the Lives: "Taking issue with a 'wrong or misguided rationalism' that sought only to challenge the truth of such accounts, W. Levison had affirmed as early as 1921 that 'the facts that are at the base of a so-called miracle are of less concern than the belief that made some events appear as a miracle' "; see Van Uytfanghe, "Avatars contemporains," p. 647. Regarding the use of the term document: I occasionally refer to hagiographic sources as documents and regard the Lives as having as much claim to that title as do charters, legal texts, etc. The modern historian's insistence to consider only the latter as documents may be rightly regarded as a misappropriation, given the early use of the word to designate religious and hagiographic literature; Passio sanctarum Perpetuae et Felicitatis 1 (ACM, p. 106): "Si uetera fidei exempla et Dei gratiam testificantia et aedificationem hominis operantia propterea in litteris sunt digesta ut lectione eorum quasi repraesentatione rerum et Deus honoretur et homo confortetur, cur non et nova documenta [emphasis added] aeque utrique causae conuenientia et digerantur?"

25. Van Dam, *Saints*, p. 150: "Many modern historians remain distinctly uneasy in the presence of stories about miracles, and in the case of Gregory they have often minimized or outright ignored his 'books of miracles' in favor of his 'books of histories.' "

26. As far as I am aware, only one article exists that is devoted exclusively to the LVP: Adele Castagno, "Il vescovo, l'abate e l'eremita: tipologia della santità nel Liber Vitae Patrum di Gregorio di Tours," in *L'agiographia latina nei secoli IV–VII*, Augustinianum 24 (Rome, 1984), pp. 235–64. Castagno gives an excellent overview of the types of sanctity represented throughout the LVP, and she amply cites the modern studies related to issues raised by this collection of Lives. There is also the English translation of the LVP by James, who gives a brief introduction and useful notes providing new information that has come to light, including archaeological findings, since Krusch's edition of the work first appeared. Although several of my own renditions of passages taken from the LVP appear throughout the discussion, I have also consulted and relied often on James's translation.

27. James, *Life*, p. 9, suggests that historians are now less put off by the miraculous content of hagiographic literature, thanks to such researchers as Brown, Graus, and Stancliffe. Similarly, Geary, *Living with the Dead*, pp. 9–10, claims that hagiographic texts are no longer subject to the "positivist concern to separate 'fact' from 'fiction.' " Such views may be overly optimistic. Historians still tend to see the literature—not their methodologies—as severely limited. Consider, for example, the recent remarks of Joan Petersen, "The Spirituality and Miracles of St. Radegund," in *Monastic Studies: The Continuity of Tradition*, ed. Judith Loades (Bangor, 1990), p. 34: "Both lives [of Radegund], though based on personal recollections, suffer from the limitations of medieval hagiography. As they were written to edify what was probably a largely monastic audience rather than promote historical truth, the authors pay little attention to the chronological order of events and to dating, they make abundant use of *topoi*, and they attribute to their subject deeds and personal characteristics that earlier writers have already attributed to other holy persons." Similarly, Nelson, whose work certainly reflects "the positivist concern," continues to express reservations about using hagiographic material as a historical source (though she frequently relies on *Vitae* in her research; e.g., "Queens," pp. 1–48); see idem, "Women and the Word," pp. 58–59, 66; idem, "Commentary," p. 327. Moreover, even as historians claim to have overcome their reservations with the miraculous and religious content of the literature, the same attitude that always characterized historical research on hagiographic texts is still present, though it is not as obvious as it once was. For instance, Van Dam, whose recent work, *Saints*, marks one of the most up-to-date approaches to Gregory's miracle stories, well into his work states (at pp. 114–15) that his attempt to account for miracles with the help of comparative anthropology and other modern, interpretive tools is meant "to relieve our uneasiness" arising from the stories of *virtutes*. Similar tendencies are found among church historians; speaking of "the major nineteenth-century historians of dogma" who regarded the cults of saints as "second class Christianity," Goffart, *Narrators*, p. 130, n. 7, observes: "That opinion has markedly improved since then seems doubtful."

28. See McCready, *Signs*, pp. 91–92; the position represented by McCready is addressed later in this chapter.

29. Nie, *Views*, p. 9.

30. *Mimesis: The Representation of Reality in Western Literature*, trans. Willard Trask (Princeton, 1953), pp. 67–83.

31. See J. T. Roberts, "Gregory of Tours and the Monk of St Gall: The Paratactic Style of Medieval Latin," *Latomus* 39 (1980): 173–90.

32. Compare James, *Life*, p. 6.

33. Brunhölzl, *Geschichte*, p. 137. On Brunhölzl as regarding only books 1–3 as introduction, see Goffart, *Narrators*, p. 124, n. 54.

34. Though Brunhölzl, *Geschichte*, pp. 133–34, does give a more detailed summary of the *LVP* than is generally found. His assessment of the work is high: "Literarisch bemerkenswert sind sie, abgesehen von der auch in ihnen zutage tretenden Erzählungskunst des Autors, vor allem wegen ihrer Form, die sich Gregor vermutlich selbst geschaffen hat"; see also Goffart, *Narrators*, p. 130.

35. LH 10.31 (MGH SRM 1.1, pp. 535–36): "Decem libros Historiarum, septem Miraculorum, unum de Vita Patrum scripsi; in Psalterii tractatu librum unum commentatus sum; de Cursibus etiam ecclesiasticis unum librum condidi. Quos libros licet stilo rusticiori conscripserim, tamen conjuro omnes sacerdotes Domini, qui post me humilem ecclesiam Turonicam sunt recturi, per adventum domini nostri Jesu Christi ac terribilem reis omnibus iudicii diem, si numquam confusi de ipso iudicio discedentes cum diabolo condempnemini, ut numquam libros hos aboleri faciatis aut rescribi, quasi quaedam eligentes et quaedam praetermittentes, sed ita omnia vobiscum integra inlibataque permaneant, sicut a nobis relicta sunt." Regarding the list of works, Goffart, *Narrators*, p. 128, states: "Gregory had more minor writings to his credit than he chose to list. No trace survives of the collection he once says he made of the Masses of Sidonius Apollinaris and introduced with a special preface."

36. Van Dam, *Saints*, pp. 147–48, n. 153, following Boesch Gajano, states: "Gregory's insistence [on keeping his writings intact] suggested that he imagined all his writings within a unified vision, and that he may have used similar literary devices throughout them." Gregory's request not to alter his work went unheeded as early as the seventh century, when an editor supplied an abridged "History of the Franks." Modern translators continued to offer abridged versions of his writings: Ernst Brehaut, trans., *History of the Franks by Gregory Bishop of Tours* (New York, 1969); translations by W. C. McDermott of *DVSM* 1, *LVP* 6 and 7, *The Seven Sleepers of Ephesus* and *Seven Wonders of the World*, in E. Peters, ed., *Monks, Bishops and Pagans: Christian Culture in Gaul and Italy, 500–700* (Philadelphia, 1975). On the whole textual history of the *Histories*, see Goffart, *Narrators*, pp. 119–27; a fuller account is given in his "From *Historiae* to *Historia Francorum* and Back Again: Aspects of the Textual History of Gregory of Tours," in *Religion, Culture, and Society in the Early Middle Ages*, ed. T. F. X. Noble and J. J. Contreni (Kalamazoo, 1987), pp. 55–77.

37. Nie, *Views*, p. 129: "For Gregory, miracles were symbolic expressions of spiritual truths in concrete, visible reality. He intended his collections of stories to be a lively kind of practical theology"; Goffart, *Narrators*, p. 152: "Perhaps no other Christian thinker has come nearer than he to placing *res gestae*—present events no less than those of the past, at the center of his theology"; see also Van Dam, *Saints*, pp. 105–14.

38. LH 10.31 (MGH SRM 1.1, pp. 535–36): "Decem libros Historiarum, septem Miraculorum, unum de Vita Patrum scripsi."

39. Goffart, *Narrators*, p. 127; Van Dam, trans., *Gregory of Tours: Glory of the Confessors* (Liverpool, 1988), p. 4.

40. GC, pref. (MGH SRM 1.2, p. 748): "Igitur in primo libello inseruimus aliqua de miraculis Domini ac sanctorum apostolorum reliquorumque martyrum, quae actenus latuerunt, quae Deus ad corroborandam fidelium fidem cotidie dignatur augere; quia valde molestum erat, ut traderentur oblivioni. In secundo posuimus de virtutibus sancti Iuliani. Quattuor vero libellos de virtutibus sancti Martini. Septimum de quorundam feliciosorum vita [i.e., *LVP*]. Octavum hunc scribimus de miraculis confessorum."

41. I take Goffart's statement, *Narrators*, p. 128, as speculative: "Since the 'fathers' of the *Vita patrum* were comparatively recent saints, Gregory's decision, recorded in the *Histories*, to treat this tract as separate from a seven-book *Wonders* may be a later and more final idea than the eight-book order described in the *Confessors* and maintained in the text tradition."

42. Ibid., p. 127; James, *Life*, pp. 3–4; Krusch, MGH SRM 1.2, p. 451.

43. See Brunhölzl, *Geschichte*, p. 134; Goffart, *Narrators*, pp. 129–30; Graus, *Volk*, p. 111.

44. See Heffernan, *Sacred Biography*, p. 4; Goffart, *Narrators*, p. 128, n. 70. Gregory claims to have had personal encounters with several of the saints he describes: *LVP* 2.2 (*MGH SRM* 1.2, p. 670); 8.2 (ibid., p. 692); 11.3 (ibid., p. 711); 15.2 (ibid., p. 722); 20.3 (ibid., p. 742). James, *Life*, pp. 5–6, notes the author's personal ties to the subject matter of the Lives: the *LVP* "is a collection of twenty saints' lives, of varying lengths, all being the lives of Gallic saints and all of them (except those dealt with in VP I and X) connected in some way either with Gregory's own family or with the two dioceses in which he spent most of his life, Clermont and Tours. VP is thus a celebration of the saints of his own family . . . it is a celebration of those saints whose miraculous powers had aided his family . . . and it is a glorification of the two cities or dioceses most closely associated with his family and its secular and ecclesiastical power."

45. Yet Prinz, "Aspekte Frühmittelalterlicher Hagiographie," in *Mönchtum, Kultur und Gesellschaft: Beitrage zum Mittelalter*, ed. Alfred Haverkamp and Alfred Heil (Munich, 1989), p. 184, seems to think that all 20 compositions of the *LVP* are episcopal biographies: "allein Gregor von Tours hat in seinem "liber vitae patrum" 20 bischöfliche Kurzbiographien beigesteuert."

46. Delehaye, *Les passions*, p. 223.

47. *LVP* 1 (*MGH SRM* 1.2, pp. 663–68) tells the lives of two saints, Romanus and Lupicinus; the latter is a stern disciplinarian (*severus valde in districtione fratrum*) who sets himself up as abbot and punishes infractions of the rule; he performs no miracles (though his ability to ward off thirst by dipping his hands in water perhaps may be interpreted as such); he avoids all contact with women (*mulierum quoque vel colloquia vel occursus valde vitabat*), and when he dies he is buried within the monastic walls. The former was an easygoing thaumaturge, sharing none of the severity of Lupicinus (*ita erat simplex, ut nihil de his penitus ad animum duceret*) and bestowing blessings on men and women alike (*tam viris quam mulieribus*); at the end of his life, he requests to be buried outside the monastery so that women will have access to his tomb. In addition, the two companions briefly clash over their different approaches to the religious life; see Graus, *Volk*, p. 91.

48. The *LVP* contains approximately 75 direct citations from Scripture (about 50 from the New Testament and 25 from the Old); the Pauline Epistles are most frequently quoted (roughly 23 times), with Matthew (19 times) coming second. Of the Old Testament, the Psalms are most frequently mentioned (25 times).

49. See, for instance, *LVP* 3, pref. (*MGH SRM* 1.2, p. 672); the citation and passage are discussed later in the section on typology.

50. Of the twenty *libelli*, three are double Lives: *LVP* 1 (*MGH SRM* 1.2, pp. 663–68); 12 (ibid., pp. 711–15); 18 (ibid., pp. 733–35).

51. Compare Sulpicius, *Dial.* 1.21 (*CSEL* 1, p. 173).

52. *LVP* 15, pref. (*MGH SRM* 1.2, pp. 720–21): " '*Vanitas vanitantium*,' dicit eclesiastes, '*omnia vanitas*.' Verumne est ergo, quia omnia quae geruntur in mundo cuncta sint vanitas? Unde agitur, ut sanctos Dei, quos nullus libidinum aestus exussit, nullus concupiscentiae exagitavit stimulus, quos nullum luxoriae caenum nec in ipsa, ut ita dicam, cogitatione temptavit, aestu temptatoris elati, visi sunt sibi esse iustissimi, et ob hoc iactantiae coturnosae perflati supercilio, saepius corruerunt. Factumque est ita, ut, quos non valuit maiorum criminum gladius trucidare, levis vanitatis fumus addictos facile pessumdaret, sicut et ipse ille de quo nunc nobis sermo futurus est, cum multis virtutibus floruisset, pene in illo arrogantiae baratro obrutus occubuit, si eum non exhortatio fratrum fidelium attenta recuperasset." The text of the Vulgate gives *vanitatum* rather than *vanitantium*, although the latter reading is represented in some manuscripts and also appears in Augustine's quotations of Eccles. 1:2 (see the *apparatus criticus* in the editions of Weber and Krusch for the variations and usage); see also Bonnet, *Latin*, p. 362, n. 3. The variant reading (*MGH SRM* 1.2, p. 721) given for *aestu* is *astu* ("cunning"), which

makes better sense than "heat," and appears throughout Gregory's writings when the devil is described.

53. Radegund's Lenten austerities being the most striking example: VR 1.22 (MGH SRM 2, p. 371).

54. Lupicinus, LVP 13.1 (ibid., 1.2, p. 715), is also severe, wearing a stone around his neck that causes him to vomit blood; he prevents sleep by carving two sharp points at the end of his staff which he places under his chin; other instances of ascetic rigor: 5.1 (ibid., p. 676); 11.1 (ibid., p. 709); Radegund also wears chains: VR 1.25 (ibid., 2, p. 372–73).

55. Antony also left his monks to find greater solitude: VBA 24 (PL 73, p. 148).

56. LVP 15.1 (MGH SRM 1.2, pp. 721–22).

57. See James, Life, p. 153, n. 5; Krusch, MGH SRM 1.2, pp. 608–9, n. 1.

58. LVP 15.2 (MGH SRM 1.2, p. 722): "Nam egressus de cellula, iactantia coturnosa ad requerendos visitandosque parentes in pago Pectavensi, cui supra meminimus, abiit. Regressusque, tumidus arrogantia sibi soli placere nitebatur."

59. Poetics 8 (1451a), trans. Richard McKeon, The Basic Works of Aristotle (New York, 1941), p. 1463.

60. LVP 15.3 (MGH SRM 1.2, p. 722): "Denique, quia de conversatione eius pauca prolocuti sumus, ad virtutes, quas per illum medicabilis divinae potentiae dextera operari dignata est, accedamus."

61. LVP 15.4 (ibid., p. 724): "Sed et multa alia ibi gesta conperi, de quibus haec tantum memoriae habenda mandavit"; similarly, 2.5 (ibid., pp. 671–72); 7.5 (ibid., p. 690); 16.4 (ibid., p. 725); 17.5 (ibid., pp. 732–33). At the end of a Vita, Merovingian hagiographers sometimes switch from a perfect or imperfect tense to a present tense to indicate that miracles are continuing to take place at a tomb. Theoretically, the virtutes need never end; hence, updated accounts can be appended to previous ones as a continuatio: Virtutum sanctae Geretrudis continuatio (ibid., 2, pp. 471–74).

62. LVP 15.2 (ibid., 1.2, p. 722): "Cum autem nos in Toronico venissemus, [Senoch] egressus est de cellula, venitque ad inquirendos nos, salutatisque ac deosculatis, regressus est iterum. Erat enim, ut diximus, valde abstenens, sanans infimitantum languores; sed ut de abstenentia sanctitas, ita de sanctitate vanitas coepit obrepere. Nam egressus de cellula, iactantia corturnosa ad requerendos visitandosque parentes in pago Pectavensi, cui supra meminimus, abiit. Regressusque, tumidus arrogantia sibi soli placere nitebatur; sed obiurgatus a nobis, et accepta ratione, quod superbi longe fiant a regno Dei, ita se purgatus iactantia humilem reddidit, ut nulla in eum penitus radix superbiae remansisset; ita ut ipse profiteretur, dicens: 'Vera nunc esse cognovi, quae beatus apostolus sacri oris contestatur eloquio: Qui gloriatur in Domino glorietur.' " Translation relies slightly on James, Life, p. 105.

63. See Frye, The Great Code: The Bible and Literature (San Diego, 1982), p. 79.

64. Matt. 27:46; Mark 15:34.

65. Brunhölzl, Geschichte, p. 134; see also James, Life, p. 6; Krusch, MGH SRM 1.2, p. 454.

66. Ward, Miracles, p. 170: "The cures of diseases in the Lives of the saints reflect the list given in the Gospel: 'The blind receive their sight, the lame walk, the lepers are cleansed, the deaf hear, the dead are raised up' (Luke 7:22)."

67. Brunhölzl, Geschichte, p. 134.

68. "The Pardoner's Tale," in The Works of Geoffrey Chaucer, ed. F. N. Robinson (Cambridge, 1957), p. 148, is chosen here since it also starts with a biblical text introduced at the beginning and repeated again: "My theme is alwey oon, and evere was—/ Radix malorum est Cupiditas."

69. Faith: LVP 17, pref. (MGH SRM 1.2, p. 727); forgiveness: 14, pref. (ibid., pp. 717–18); privilege renounced: 6, pref. (ibid., pp. 679–80).

70. Sermo 48 (SC 243, pp. 390–405), entitled: "Ammonitio quae ostendit quod ab initio saeculi omnes scripturae humiles benedixerint, et eos qui perseverant in superbia maledixerint."

71. This will be discussed shortly in the context of Jerome's commentary.

72. On the use of metonymy in Gregory's writings, see Bonnet, Latin, pp. 281–84.

73. For the Histories, see the useful work of Denise St-Michel, Concordance de l'Histoire Francorum de Grégoire de Tours, vol. 1 (Montreal, 1979), p. 186.

74. James, Life, p. 130, n. 8.

75. Fortunatus, VMarc 2 (MGH AA 4.2, p. 50); Sulpicius also uses it: Dial. 1.27 (CSEL 1, p. 179); for the various uses of the word throughout Latin literature, consult the Thesaurus Linguae Latinae, vol. 4 (Leipzig, 1906–1909), pp. 1086–88.

76. Margarete Bieber, The History of the Greek and Roman Theater (Princeton, 1961), pp. 22, 26–27, 242–43; see especially figs. 798 and 799 for the surviving evidence (statuettes) of the cothurni as "high blocks" and "lofty stilts" that "lengthen the body immensely." There is the possibility that the soles could reach as high as ten inches, though Kendall Smith argues against this: "The Use of the High-Soled Shoe or Buskin in Greek Tragedy of the Fifth and Fourth Centuries B.C.," HS 16 (1905): 123–64. This heightening from the buskin was intensified by a "high hairdress" (onkos) that helped to maintain a sense of proportion from head to toe. Moreover, the considerable increase in height that resulted from wearing the cothurnus was due not simply to a single high sole attached to the bottom of a soft buskin, as the translator mentioned here seems to imply. As the Greek theater developed over the centuries, more soles continued to be added so that the boots began to look and function almost like short, thick stilts that elevate actors to a height originally unprecedented.

77. LH 4.11 (MGH SRM 1.1, p. 142): "Erat enim vanitatis coturno elatus, nullum sibi putans in sanctitate haberi praestantiorem."

78. LH 10.15 (ibid., p. 502): "atque ita haec quae iactantia tumuisset, ut consubrinam suam Basinam altiore coturno dispiceret."

79. There is an indication that Gregory saw hell manifested in nature, particularly in Mount Etna: Nie, Views, p. 147.

80. Bonnet, Latin, pp. 462, 320, 322–23.

81. Frye, Code, p. 123: "This word (hebel) has a metaphorical kernel of fog, mist, or vapor, a metaphor that recurs in the New Testament (James 4:14). It thus acquires a derived sense of 'emptiness,' the root meaning of the Vulgate's vanitas. To put Koheleth's central intuition into the form of its essential paradox: all things are full of emptiness. We should not apply a ready-made disapproving moral ambience to this word 'vanity,' much less associate it with conceit. It is a conception more like the shunyata or 'void' of Buddhist thought: the world as everything within nothingness."

82. Augustino Bea, ed. Liber Ecclesiastae qui ab Hebraeis appelatur Qohelet (Rome, 1950), xii: "Inter veteres Ecclesiastae interpretes vix ullus est qui sensum litteralem libri invenire quaesierit, sed plerique . . . sensum spiritualem (moralem, allegoricum) proponunt." For an overview of the patristic and medieval interpretations in the West, see Christian Gingsburg, Coheleth, Commonly Called the Book of Ecclesiastes (London, 1861), pp. 101–12.

83. Jerome, Commentarivs in Ecclesiasten, pref. (CCSL 72, p. 249).

84. Jerome, Commentarivs 2 (ibid., pp. 252–53): "ita aspiciens elementa et rerum multiplicem uarietatem, admiror quidem operum magnitudinem; recogitans autem omnia pertransire, et mundum suo fine senescere, solumque Deum id semper esse, quod fuerit, compellor dicere non semel, sed bis: 'Vanitas uanitatum, omnia uanitas.' In Hebraeo pro uanitate uanitatum, abal abalim scriptum est, quod, exceptis Septuaginta interpretibus, omnes similiter transtulerunt Ατμος ατμιδων sive ατμων, quod nos possumus uaporem sumi [sic] et auram tenuem, quae cito soluitur, appellare." The CCSL text reading sumi must be a typographical error. The PL edition (23, p. 1014), which on the whole varies only slightly, gives fumi. The Septuaginta text, ed. Alfred Rahlfs (Stuttgart, 1935), p. 288, which Jerome cites as the exception, reads Ματαιοτης ματαιοτητων.

85. A practice of exegesis advocated by, among others, Augustine, De doctrina christiana 2.15 (CSEL 80, p. 37): "Nihil enim fere de illis obscuritatibus eruitur, quod non planissime dictum alibi repperiatur."

86. Jerome, Commentarivs 2 (CCSL 72, p. 252): "Tale quid et in psalmo scriptum est: Verumtamen universa uanitas omnis homo uiuens."

87. Ibid.: "Si uiuens homo uanitas est, ergo mortuus uanitas uanitatum."

88. Ibid.: "Possumus igitur et nos in hunc modum, caelum, terram, maria, et omnia quae hoc circulo continentur, bona quidem per se dicere, sed ad Deum comparata, esse pro nihilo."

89. VBA 20 (PL 73, p. 144): "et cum ad consueta Christi munimenta confugerem, tanquam per fenestram fumus laberetur, evanuit"; in the same chapter (ibid., p. 146), "animae Dominum semper cogitantis jugis recordatio . . . quae daemonum ludos quasi fumum expellens."

90. VM 24.7–8 (CSEL 1, p. 134): "ad hanc ille uocem statim ut fumus euanuit"; similarly, 6.3 (ibid., p. 116): "statimque de conspectu eius inimicus euanuit." On these instances as evidence of the influence of Antony's Life, see Jacques Fontaine, Sulpice Sévère: Vie de Saint Martin, vol. 2 (SC 135, pp. 1010–11, 1037).

91. LVP 10.2 (MGH SRM 1.2, p. 707), where Saint Friardus's companion, Secundellus, is filled with vana gloria when tempted to thaumaturgy by a demon; after he is corrected by the saint, the demon returns, but this time, at the sign of the cross, confusus evanuit. For an instance of evanescere used in a nondemonic context, see GM 5 (ibid., p. 490).

92. Ps. 36:20 (I cite both versions, "Hebrew" and "Gallican" Psalters, since they vary considerably here): "impii peribunt et inimici Domini gloriantes ut monocerotes consumentur sicut fumus consumitur"; "peccatores peribunt inimici vero Domini mox honorificati fuerint et exaltati deficientes quemadmodum fumus defecerunt"; likewise, Ps. 67:2: "Exsurgat Deus et dissipentur inimici eius et fugiant qui oderunt eum a facie eius sicut deficit fumus deficiant"; Sap. 5:15 "spes impii . . . tamquam fumus qui a vento diffusus est"; see also Fontaine, Vie, vol. 2 (SC 135, p. 1037), who, in addition to mentioning other relevant biblical and hagiographic texts, also alludes to passages in classical literature depicting "infernal shades" disappearing like smoke.

93. I wish to distinguish the present use of the terms type and typology from the way these words are applied to describe specific categories of sanctity such as the martyr type and monk type, an issue that will be addressed later. Here, I am primarily concerned with typological aspects of the LVP that are based on or closely related to a hermeneutical approach associated with Christian biblical exegesis. Because this form of typology in the LVP seems to me to operate at different levels simultaneously, I have not attempted to categorize it except in the most general of terms. For a more precise typological scheme and terminology specifically suited to hagiographic literature, see Van Uytfanghe, Stylisation biblique, pp. 17–21, who distinguishes and explains what he regards as the three major typological variants in the hagiographic sources (adnominatio, assimilatio, comparatio). On the significance of biblical typology in the Histories and the influence of typological thought on Gregory's writing, see Felix Thürlemann, Der historische Diskurs bei Gregor von Tours: Topoi und Wirklichkeit (Bern, 1974), pp. 86–100.

94. For a summary of the major trends in typological interpretation, see Peter Jentzmik, Zu Möglichkeiten und Grenzen typologischer Exegesis in Mittelalterlicher Predigt und Dichtung (Göppinger, 1973), pp. 6–114.

95. See Tibor Fabiny, The Lion and the Lamb: Figuralism and Fulfillment in the Bible, Art and Literature (New York, 1992), pp. 2, 47–58; Gerhard von Rad, Old Testament Theology, vol. 2: The Theology of Israel's Prophetic Traditions, trans. D. M. G. Stalker (Edinburgh, 1965), pp. 17–39; Michael Fishbane, Biblical Interpretation in Ancient Israel (Oxford, 1985), pp. 350–79.

96. G. W. H. Lampe, "The Reasonableness of Typology," in Essays on Typology, ed. G. W. H. Lampe and K. J. Woollcombe (London, 1957), p. 10: "For the Jew of the first century

. . . to see the past episodes in Israel's history as a foreshadowing of the future, and to express the significance of the present in terms of the past, was entirely natural."

97. Joshua 3:7: "dixitque Dominus ad Iosue hodie incipiam exaltare te coram omni Israhel ut sciant quod sicut cum Mosi fui ita et tecum sim."

98. Compare Philo, *De vita Mosis*, 1.32, 39, in *Philo: With an English Translation*, vol. 6 (Loeb edition), ed. and trans. F. H. Colson (Cambridge, Mass., 1936), pp. 366–67, 388–89.

99. Joshua 4:22–23: "per arentem alveum transivit Israhel Iordanem istum siccante Domino Deo vestro aquas eius in conspectu vestro donec transiretis sicut fecerat prius in mari Rubro quod siccavit donec transiremus," with Fishbane, *Biblical Interpretation*, p. 351; see also Frye, *Code*, p. 83.

100. For ancient exegesis, see Leonhard Goppelt, *Typos: The Typological Interpretation of the Old Testament in the New*, trans. Donald Madvig (Grand Rapids, 1982), pp. 23–58; for modern: Fabiny, *Lion*, pp. 48–49.

101. Frye, *Code*, pp. 80–81.

102. The affinity between Christian biblical interpretation and a Marxian view of history is noted by Henri de Lubac, *Exégèse Médiévale: les quatre sens de l'Écriture* (Paris, 1959), p. 12: "Ainsi de bons marxistes rendent-ils justice à un saint Thomas d'Aquin. Ainsi le socialisme du siècle dernier louait-il volontiers le christianisme primitif de l'avoir en quelque sorte préfiguré"; see Frye, *Code*, pp. 80, 86. For an extensive discussion of this and related issues, see José Porfirio Miranda, *Marx and the Bible: A Critique of the Philosophy of Oppression*, trans. John Eagleson (New York, 1974).

103. Frye, *Code*, p. 79.

104. "Sed regnavit mors ab Adam usque ad Mosen etiam in eos qui non peccaverunt in similitudinem praevaricationis Adae qui est forma futuri". On the other two possible interpretations of this passage, see K. J. Woollcombe, "The Biblical Origins and Patristic Development of Typology," in *Essays on Typology*, p. 67.

105. See 1 Cor. 15:22; 1 Peter 3:21.

106. Certainly, this is what Gregory also assumes, *LVP* 7, pref. (*MGH SRM* 1.2, p. 690), when he attributes one origin to both Testaments: "Et ipse Dominus utriusque conditor Testamenti."

107. Augustine, *Qvaestionvm in Heptatevchvm libri VII*, 73 (*CCSL* 33, p. 106): "et in uetere nouum lateat, et in nouo uetus pateat"; translation is that found in Fry, *Code*, p. 79.

108. On the Adamic typological interpretations of patristic authors, see Jean Daniélou, *From Shadows to Reality: Studies in the Biblical Typology of the Fathers*, trans. Wulstan Hibberd (London, 1960), pp. 11–56.

109. Ibid.

110. Ibid., p. 12: "All the work of the Prophets, which is of cardinal importance in the Old Testament, rests on a twofold movement. It recalls the great works of God in the past, but it recalls them only as a foundation for a faith in great works to come. It is at the same time both commemorative and prophetic. . . . This double character is true in the first place of Paradise. There is no question of nostalgia for some remote ideal, as in the case of the Greek descriptions of a golden age. . . . There is no striving to bring back again these past events . . . the question is not of return (*Wiederkehr*) but of a new creation."

111. Ezekiel 47:12: "et super torrentem orietur in ripis eius ex utraque parte omne lignum pomiferum non defluet folium ex eo et non deficiet fructus eius per singulos menses adferet primitiva quia aquae eius de sanctuario egredientur et erunt fructus eius in cibum et folia eius ad medicinam."

112. See, for instance, *Virtutum sanctae Geretrudis continuatio* 1 (*MGH SRM* 2, p. 471).

113. See Fabiny, *Lion*, p. 8.

114. Frye, *Code*, pp. 80–81: "What typology really is as a mode of thought, what it both assumes and leads to, is a theory of history, or more accurately of historical process: an assumption that there is some meaning and point to history, and that sooner or later some event or events will occur which will indicate what that meaning or point is, and so become an antitype of what has happened previously. Our modern confidence in historical process, our belief that despite apparent confusion, even chaos, in human events, nevertheless those events are going somewhere and indicating something, is probably a legacy of Biblical typology: at least I can think of no other source for its tradition."

115. Similarly, *LVP* 11.2 (MGH SRM 1.2, p. 711); 19.1 (ibid., p. 737).

116. For typology as an interpretive tool, see, in general, Fabiny, *Lion*, who attempts to approach typology as a form of reader-response criticism.

117. In fact, Fortunatus is careful to state that Christ did more and that the greater accomplishment is in proportion to the importance of the person performing the miracle; see *VMarc* 6 (MGH AA 4.2, p 51).

118. Similar to the general conclusion of Jentzmik, *Möglichkeiten*, Hartmut Hoefer, *Typologie im Mittelalter: Zur Übertragbarkeit typologischer Interpretation auf weltliche Dichtung* (Göppingen, 1971), argues that a stricter use of the term is now necessary because previous scholars have exaggerated the role played by a typological system in nonbiblical and secular literature. In large part, the work of Jentzmik and Hartmut is a reaction against Auerbach, who attributed considerable importance to typology for the interpretation of medieval literature in general: *Typologische Motive in der mittelalterlichen Literatur* (Krefeld, 1953); idem, "Figura," in *Scenes from Drama of European Literature*, trans. Ralph Manheim (New York, 1959), pp. 11–74; idem, "Typological Symbolism in Medieval Literature," *Yale French Studies* 9 (1965): 3–10. It should also be noted that neither Jentznik nor Hoefer addresses the issue of typology in hagiographic literature. For remarks on Auerbach's views in light of hagiographic literature, see Earl, "Literary Problems," pp. 18–20; Thürlemann, *Der historische Diskurs*, pp. 87–88.

119. See Daniélou, *Shadows*, p. 1; Fabiny, *Lion*, pp. 10–12.

120. "Et omnia quaecumque petieritis in oratione credentes accipietis"; "omnia quaecumque orantes petitis credite quia accipietis et veniet vobis"; this biblically based belief is central to Gregory's thought; see Nie, *Views*, pp. 95, 136.

121. See Thürlemann, *Der historische Diskurs*, pp. 89–93.

122. *LVP* 3, pref. (MGH SRM 1.2, p. 672): "Qui non inmerito Abrahae illi conparatur seni pro magnitudine fidei, cui quondam dixerat Deus: *Exi de terra tua et de cognatione tua et vade in terram, quam monstravero tibi.* Reliquit autem hic non solum terram propriam, sed etiam illam veteris hominis actionem, et induit novum hominem, qui secundum Deum formatus est in iustitia, sanctitate et veritate." Although the editor and the translator do not note the direct borrowing, the text of Ephesians 4:24 is explicitly inserted into the last sentence of this passage: "et induite novum hominem qui secundum Deum creatus est in justitia et sanctitate veritatis."

123. In the *Histories*, the debate Gregory and Chilperic have with a Jew also focuses on the interpretation of biblical texts: LH 6.5 (MGH SRM 1.1, pp. 268–72). Wallace-Hadrill's comments on the passage, *Frankish Church*, p. 53, are pertinent: "The arresting point is not that Christians should have sought the conversion of a Jew; this was common enough; but that the minds of all three—Jew, king and bishop—should move so naturally over the books of the Old Testament. The Bible is the past of all three as well as their term of reference." But see also Gregory, *DVSM* 3.50 (MGH SRM 1.2, p. 644), where an encounter between Jew and Christian is more along the lines of the religious conflict portrayed in Fortunatus's accounts.

124. On typology as the mouthpiece of theology, see Daniélou, *Shadows*, p. 44.

125. On the *novus heremita*, see LVP 7.2 (MGH SRM 1.2, p. 687); similarly, Sulpicius, *Dial.* 1.24 (CSEL 1, pp. 176–77). For the context, see Claire Fanger, "The Dynamics of Holy Power

as Reflected in Narrative Structure in the Lives of St. Martin and St. Anthony," *Florilegium* 9 (1987): 35–51.

126. See A. C. Charity, *Events and Their Afterlife: The Dialectics of Christian Typology in the Bible and Dante* (Cambridge, 1966), pp. 17–57; von Rad, *Old Testament*, pp. 357–87.

127. See Fontaine, *Vie*, vol. 1 (SC 133, p. 68); Van Uytfanghe, "L'empreinte biblique," p. 572.

128. *Praesentium signorum . . . munera* is the phrase Gregory uses to describe miracles in his day: *DVSM* 1, pref. (*MGH SRM* 1.2, p. 585). Again, the temporality expressed by the phrase indicates that he sees miraculous events in his own time as contemporary indications of God's continuing plan; see Goffart, *Narrators*, p. 134.

129. The passage comes close to becoming, at first, allegory. Perhaps in this case, the two are closely related. Auerbach, "Figura," p. 42, claims that three of the four senses of Scripture have their roots in typology; see also Earl, "Literary Problems," p. 20.

130. *LVP* 18, pref. (*MGH SRM* 1.2, pp. 733–34): "Legiferi vatis oraculum, cum de principio principium fandi sumpsisset . . . fuisset effatus, ait: *Et fecit Deus duo luminaria magna et stellas. Et posuit ea in firmamento caeli, ut praeessent diei ac nocti et lucerent in firmameto caeli.* Sic nunc et . . . luminaria magna dedit, Christum scilicet et eclesiam eius, quae luceant in tenebris ignorantiae et inluminent sensus humilitatis nostrae, sicut Iohannes euangelista de ipso Domino ait, quia: *Hic est lux mundi.* . . . Posuit etiam in eo et stellas, patriarchas videlicet, prophetas apostolosque. . . . Ex horum ergo doctrina et usque in nostris fuerunt temporibus, qui in hoc saeculo quasi astrorum iubar, non solum meritorum radiantes luce, verum etiam dogmatum magnitudine corruscantes, orbem totum radio suae praedicationis inlustraverunt, euntes per loca singula praedicando ac monasteria ad divinum cultum locando . . . sicut de Urso Leobatioque, abbatibus fidelium fratrum relatio signat." I have followed James, *Life*, p. 121, verbatim for the translation of the opening lines, where the text seems corrupt.

131. According to Frye, *Code*, pp. 82–83: "it [typology] is essentially a revolutionary form of thought and rhetoric."

132. The typology of heaven and hell can also extend to sickness and health. Martin, for instance, whose cures are a type of salvation, extinguishes the fevers of the sick, whose illnesses are described as a type of the infernal fires in hell; *DVSM* 4, pref. (ibid., 1.2, p. 649): "Confidimus enim, quod, sicut hic morborum genera resecant, illic saevas tormentorum poenas avertant, et, sicut hic mitigant febres corporeas, illinc restingant aeternas." The typology is remarkably consistent because the secular alternative to Martin's healing power, doctors, can typify death; *DVSM* 2.19 (ibid., p. 616): "medici . . . mortis tormenta figurant"; *figura*, as noted earlier, was the word used in the Vulgate for *typos*.

133. *LVP* 5, pref. (ibid., 1.2, p. 677): "Quanta omnipotens Deus suo dicatis nomine indulgeat, quantaque eisdem pro fideli servitio benignitatis ope conpenset, magna quidem se pollicetur redditurum in caelo, sed quae accepturi sunt plerumque hoc declarat in saeculo. Nam saepius de servis liberos, de liberis efficit gloriosos iuxta illud psalmographi dictum: *Suscitans a terra inopem et de stercore erigens pauperem, ut collocet eum cum principibus populi sui.* De hoc et Anna, uxor Helcanae, ait: *Saturati prius pro pane se locaverunt, et familici saturati sunt.* Ex hoc et ipsa Redemptoris nostri genetrix virgo Maria dicebat: *Deposuit potentes de sede et exaltavit humiles.* Sic et ipse Dominus in euangelico ait: *Erunt primi novissimi et novissimi primi.* Inlicet ergo amore suo divina misericordia corda inopum, ut de parvis magnos statuat ac de infimis Unigeniti sui faciat coheredes. Praefecit enim de hac mundana aegestate in caelo, quo scandere non potuit terrenum imperium; ut accedat illuc rusticus, quo accedere non meruit purpuratus."

134. Ibid.: "Sic nunc de beato Portiano abbate, quem non modo de onere mundani servitii eruit, verum etiam magnis virtutibus sublimavit atque post mundum et praessuras saeculi in requie aeterna constituit; locavitque eum inter angelorum choros, de quibus exclusus est dominus ille terrenus."

135. Slaves had to be freed before entering the clerical or monastic life to prevent masters from later claiming a right to church property; see Graus, "Gewalt," p. 90.

136. LVP 5.1 (MGH SRM 1.2, p. 678): "Tunc abba, vocatum beatum, ait: 'Inpone, quaeso, manus tuas super oculos eius.' Cumque ille refutaret, tandem abbatis devictus precibus, super oculos domini sui signum beatae crucis inposuit, statimque, disrupta caligine, sedato dolore, praestinae redditus est sanitati." For a discussion on this episode in Portianus's Life, see Graus, Volk, p. 138.

137. However, there is evidence suggesting that Fortunatus does depict incarceration as a type of hell (darkness) and liberation as a type of salvation (light), characterizations that lend a typological depth to the accounts of liberation, though such stories lack the extensive typological treatment through which Gregory reveals a story's meaning; see VG 30 (MGH SRM 7.1, p. 390); VA 16 (MGH AA 4.2., p. 31).

138. See Brennan, "Deathless Marriage," p. 85.

139. LVP 12, pref. (MGH SRM 1.2, pp. 711–12): "dilectio enim Dei hominem a terrenis sublevat, ad caelos evocat, paradyso locat, in quo felicium animae, ex illius vitis vitalis sumpto vini novi liquore, aepulantur in regno Dei. Desiderare ergo oportebat homines huius vitis haurire mysterium, ut accedere valerent ad illum tam iocundae habitationis amoenissimum locum. Quod si istae quas nunc cernimus vites, quae per traduces extensae, emissis palmitibus, pampino intextae, dependentibus uvis, amoena nos contemplatione laetificant, dum non solum proferunt copiam fructuum, verum etiam oportuno nos umbraculo protegunt igniti solis ab aestu, quas scimus post adsumpto fructu temporis legitimi deciduis foliis quasi aridas reddi; quanto magis illa desiderare debemus, quae nullo fine deficiunt neque ullo temptationis aestu marcescunt; ubi, spe praeterita, res ipsa quae sperabatur et tenetur et fruitur." Translation relies slightly on James, Life, p. 191.

140. The Histories, in fact, tell how unpredictable nature is: LH 7.45 (ibid., 1.1, p. 365); 4.31 (ibid., pp. 163–66); 5.34 (ibid., pp. 238–41).

141. Significantly, the natural calamities (see previous note for references) are also associated with the end of the world; see Nie, Views, p. 50; against Nie, Goffart, Narrators, p. 187, argues that Gregory tends "to depreciate apocalyptic thinking."

142. See Daniélou, Shadows, pp. 22–25, who notes the stress in patristic thought on the immediacy of paradise, its hodie (as expressed in Luke 23:43: "hodie mecum in paradiso"); the believer's accessibility to the heavenly kingdom is also succinctly stated in Luke 17:21: "ecce enim regnum Dei intra vos est."

143. LVP 12, pref. (MGH SRM 1.2, p. 712): "sicut nunc beatus Aemilianus novis nostris temporibus heremita fecisse probatur." Compare Passio Sanctarum Perpetuae et Felicitatis 1 (ACM, p. 105); see Heffernan, "Philology," p. 315.

144. See Douglas Burton-Christie, The Word in the Desert: Scripture and the Quest for Holiness in Early Christian Monasticism (New York, 1993), pp. 231–33.

145. LVP 12.1 (MGH SRM 1.2, p. 712): "Hic igitur, relictis parentibus ac facultate propria, ad heremi deserta petivit et se intra secreta silvarum Ponticiacensium Arverni territurii abdidit, in qua, decisa silva, modicum deplanans campum, rastro ipsam effodiens humum, vitae elicebat alimentum. Habebat et hortum parvulum, quem aqua superveniente rigabat, de quo holus ad refectionem nullo inpinguato adipe praesumebat. Solatium vero absque Dei adiutorio nullum habens, cohabitatores enim bestias avesque illi erant, qui ad eum cotidie tamquam ad Dei famulum confluebant. Vacabat enim ieiuniis et oratione, nec eum ab hac causa ulla mundanae sollicitudinis occasio inpedire poterat, quia praeter Deum aliud nihil habebat." With only a minor modification, the translation is that of James, Life, pp. 91–92.

146. LVP 12.2 (ibid.): "[Brachio] Consalutatus autem ac osculatus a sene, invitatur ad resedendum. Quibus consedentibus, ait senex: 'Video te, fili dilectissime, in grandi elegantia conpositum, et sequi ea quae magis detrimentum animae praeparent quam salutem. Relinque,

quaeso, terrenum dominum et sequere Deum verum. . . . Subde te eius servitio, qui ait: *Venite ad me omnes qui laboratis et onerati estis, et ego reficiam vos.* Ipse est Dominus, cuius onus leve est, cuius iugum suave est, cuius cultus et tribuit praesentia et vitam largitur aeternam. Sic enim ait: *Si quis renuntiaverit omnibus quae possedet, centuplum accipiet et insuper vitam aeternam possedebit.*' Haec et his similia sene viriliter disserente, sues inlaesus silvas petiit, puerque discessit ab eo non sine grandi admiratione, quod aprum, quem inchoaverat sequi ferum, in conspectu senis mansuetum adstare videbat ut agnum." James's translation, *Life*, pp. 92–93.

147. *LVP* 11, pref. (ibid., p. 709): "Semper enim paupertas saeculi regiam reserat caeli atque utentes se non modo praeparat polo, vere etiam glorificatos miraculis inlustres esse declaret in mundo, quo fiat, ut, dum illa ergastularis contritionis revinctio paradisi ianuam patefecit."

148. *LVP* 11.2 (ibid., p. 710): "Sumebat interdum piscem de flumine, rare quidem, sed cum voluisset, opitulante Domino, confestim aderat."

149. *LVP* 11.2 (ibid., p. 711): "oravit ad Dominum, ut ei in ipso cellulae suae habitaculo fontis venam ostenderet; sed non defuit virtus illa caelestis, quae quondam sitientibus populis aquas produxit a silice. Statimque igitur ad huius orationem gutta laticis a caute prorumpens, coepit solum stillis fequentibus inrigare. . . . limphas divinitus sibi indultas suscipiebat, de quibus tantum ei ministrabatur per dies singulos, quantum ipsi pueroque sufficeret, qui ei minister fuerat datus."

150. *LVP* 14.2 (ibid., p. 719): "Erat enim monachis hortus, diversorum holerum copia ingenti refertus arborumque fructuum et amoenus visibus et fertilitate iocundus; sub quarum arborum umbraculo, susurantibus aurae sibilo foliis, beatus senex plerumque sedebat."

151. Ibid.: "collectis . . . tam pomis quam holeribus, imposuit umeris eius, et aperto ostio, dimisit eum, dicens: 'Vade in pace, et ne ultra repetas, quae . . . gessisti."

152. *LVP* 14.1 (ibid., p. 718): "In hac ergo rupe cavati montis habitationis, ut diximus, necessaria praeparabat, formans in antris ex ipso lapide scamnum et sellulam sive lectulum, in quo post laborem multum fessi corpusculi requiem indulgeret."

153. *LVP*, pref. (ibid., p. 662); 1, pref. (ibid., p. 663); 19, pref. (ibid., p. 736); 11, pref. (ibid., p. 709); 13, pref. (ibid., p. 715); 6, pref. (ibid., p. 679); 7, pref. (ibid., p. 686).

154. *LVP* 16, pref. (ibid., p. 724).

155. However, besides the case of Senoch, there is other evidence in the *LVP* indicating that Gregory had a limit to his toleration of ascetic eccentricities; he praises Leobardus, *LVP* 20.3 (ibid., p. 743), for not letting his hair and beard grow too long as some hermits do: "Verum non ille, ut quidam, dimissis capillorum flagellis aut barbarum dimissione plaudebat, sed certo tempore capillum tondebat et barbam."

156. *LVP* 13.1 (ibid., p. 715). But Scripture is used to justify the behavior: "tormentum sibi, quo corpusculum plus gravaret, adhibuit, non inmemor illud apostoli, quia: *Non sunt condignae passiones huius temporis ad futuram gloriam quae revelabitur in nobis* (Rom. 8:18). Lapidem namque grandem, quem duo homines vix levare potuerunt, cervici impositum tota die, dum Deo caneret, per cellulam deportabat; nocte autem ad additamentum iniuriae in virga quam manu gerebat duos defixerat sudes, desuper acumina parans, quos ad mentum suum, ne somnum caperet, subponebat. Denique ad extremum vitae tempus, corruptum pectus a pondere saxi, sanguinem per os eiecere coepit; quod per parietes praesentes proiciens spuebat."

157. Class is included here because the movement to the desert was probably carried out, for the most part, by the lower classes, whereas the spread of monasticism in Gaul and the acquisition of episcopal sees by Gallican "saints" were evidently phenomena peculiar to the upper class; see Graus, *Volk*, pp. 111–12; however, Brown, *World*, p. 101, emphasizes the role of "well-to-do eccentrics" in the development of Egyptian monasticism. On the various social ranks represented in the *LVP*, see Castagno, "Il vescovo," pp. 242–45.

158. See Elliott, *Roads*, pp. 131–67.

159. Other Lives showing some prominent features associated with hagiographic romance are: *LVP* 1 (*MGH SRM* 1.2, pp. 663–68); 9 (ibid., pp. 702–5); 10 (ibid., pp. 705–9); 11 (ibid., pp. 709–11); 13 (ibid., pp. 715–17); 14 (ibid., pp. 717–20); 20 (ibid., pp. 741–44).

160. Obviously, the state of a holy body in death could also be profitably treated in terms of paradisiacal typology because the washed bodies, uncorrupted flesh, and sweet smell Gregory often describes in the *LVP* and elsewhere are all physical indications of the eternal life. Again, such a body itself is the antitype of the withering vine, or death. Dead saints because of their incorruptibility reveal what heaven is like, perhaps another concrete way they teach about paradise; see Brown, *Cult*, pp. 75–77; Nie, *Views*, pp. 123–27. Here, it is also worth noting that Gregory gives more information about the care of the dead than does Fortunatus, especially with regard to the washing of the corpse: *LVP* 6.7 (*MGH SRM* 1.2, p. 685); 7.4 (ibid., pp. 689–90); 9.3 (ibid., p. 705); 10.4 (ibid., pp. 708–9); 12.3 (ibid., p. 715); 14.4 (ibid., p. 720); 20.4 (ibid., p. 744).

161. *LVP* 14, pref. (*MGH SRM* 1.2, p. 717): "*Dilegite inimicos vestros* (Matt. 5:44)" followed by episodes showing that "erat enim ei magna patientia" (14.2 [ibid., p. 719]).

162. *LVP* 8, pref. (ibid., p. 690): "*Priusquam te formarem in utero, novi te* (Jer. 1:5)" followed by "episcopum gero in utero" (8.1 [ibid., p. 691]).

163. *LVP* 1.3 (ibid., p. 665): "Lupicinus igitur abba cum minus haberet, unde tantam susteneret congregationem, revelavit ei Deus locum in heremo, in quo antiquitus thesauri reconditi fuerant."

164. *LVP* 4.5 (ibid., p. 677): "Senuit autem sacerdos Dei et in tantum in aetate provectus est, ut sputos oris terram proicere non valeret, sed, adhibitum labiis truclionem, in eo salibas oris exponeret."

165. *LVP* 12, pref. (*MGH SRM* 1.2, pp. 711–12): "Quantum disciplina caelestis se custodientibus praebeat, quantumque non custodita neglegentibus inrogare debeat, per os psalmografi Spiritus sanctus pandit: *Adprehendite, inquit, disciplinam, ne quando irascatur Dominus, et pereatis a via iusta* (Ps. 2:12). De bonis autem Salamon ait: *Disciplina pacis erit super eum* (Isa. 53:5). Disciplina ergo haec timorem Domini facit."

166. *LVP* 12.3 (ibid., p. 714): "Cum ad priorem cellulam resederet, in monasterium Manatinse, qui per incuriam abbatis intepuerat, ordinatur, ut scilicet eius studio congregatio ipsa canonicae regeretur. Erat enim castissimus conversationis, sed et alios strenue distringebat castam agere vitam. Qui erat suavis colloquio et blandus affectu, in transgressoribus vero regulae ita severus habebatur, ut aliquotiens putaretur esse crudelis."

167. Daniélou, *Shadows*, p. 64.

168. See Goppelt, *Typos*, p. 42. However, Harry Wolfson, *Philo: Foundations of Religious Philosophy in Judaism, Christianity and Islam*, vol. 1 (Cambridge, Mass., 1947), p. 378, stresses that Philo does not discard the literal meaning; on Philo's use of Greek philosophy, see, in general, Wolfson's *Religious Philosophy: A Group of Essays* (Cambridge, Mass., 1961).

169. Jerome, *Commentarivs*, pref. (*CCSL* 72, p. 249): "Memini me ante hoc ferme quinquennium, cum adhuc Romae essem et Ecclesiastem sanctae Blesillae legerem, ut eam ad contemptum saeculi prouocarem, et omne quod in mundo cerneret, putaret esse pro nihilo, rogatum ab ea, ut in morem commentarioli obscura quaeque disserem, ut absque me posset intellegere quae legebat."

170. *LVP* 9, pref. (*MGH SRM* 1.2, p. 702): "Offerebant ergo donaria auri argentique, aeris ac ferri metalla, gemmarum etiam micantium pulchritudinis ac fila bissi duplicati coccique bis torti; nonnulli pelles arietum rubricatas pilosque caprarum. Sed cum haec omnia doctores eclesiarum esse allegorica tradidissent et in reliquis donariis gratiarum genera demonstrassent, in illis caprarum pilis laudationum verba conparaverunt. Ita nunc et nos steriles sensu, inperiti studio, squalentes in actu, etsi aurum argentumque vel gemmas filaque duplicata ac torta non

offerimus, saltim vel pilos caprarum, id est verba, quae sanctorum . . . prodant miracula."
James's translation, *Life*, p. 78.

171. See Smalley, *Study of the Bible*, pp. 2–12.

172. See Frye, *Code*, pp. 223–24.

173. Fishbane, *Biblical Interpretation*, p. 352: "Typological exegesis thus celebrates new historical events in so far as they can be correlated with older ones. . . . For if legal and other aggadic exegeses emphasize the verbal aspects of ongoing divine revelation, typological exegesis reveals its historical concreteness. Typological exegesis is thus not a disclosure of the *sensus plenior* of the text, in the manner of other forms of inner-biblical exegesis. It is rather a disclosure of the plentitude and mysterious workings of divine activity in history."

174. Castagno, "Il vescovo," pp. 235–64.

175. *LVP* 15.2 (MGH SRM 1.2, p. 722): "Sed cum per eum Dominus super infirmos multas faceret virtutes, et ille ita se dixit includere, ut numquam humanis aspectibus appareret, consilium suasimus, ut non se perpetuo in hac conclusione constringeret, nisi in illis tantum dumtaxat diebus, qui inter depositionem sancti Martini ac dominici natalis solemnitatem habentur [i.e., Nov. 11–Dec. 25], vel in illis similiter quadraginta, quos ante paschalia festa in summa duci abstenentia, patrum sancxit auctoritas, reliquis vero diebus infirmorum gratia populis se praeberet."

176. *LVP* 7.2 (ibid., 1.2, p. 687): "Iam in ieiuniis, elymosinis, orationibus atque vigiliis tam efficax tamque devotus erat, ut in medio mundi positus, novus effulgeret heremita."

177. See Geary, *Before France*, p. 129.

178. *LVP* 7.1 (MGH SRM 1.2, p. 687): "in comitatu autem positus, regionem illam per 40 annos, iustitia comitante, correxit; et tam severus atque districtus fuit in malefactoribus, ut vix ei ullus reorum posssit evadere." Yet, after he dies, as his body is being carried past a prison during the funeral procession, Gregory portrays him as the special patron of the condemned (7.3, [ibid., p. 689]): "et ecce vincti carceris ad beatum corpus clamare coeperunt, dicentes: 'Miserere nostri, piissime domne, ut, quos vivens in saeculo non absolvisti, vel defunctus [et] caeleste regnum possedens digneris absolvere.' . . . His ergo expectantibus, subito reseratis carceris ostiis, trabis illa qua vinctorum pedes coartabantur, repulsis obicibus, scinditur media, confractisque catenis, omnes pariter dissolvuntur."

179. It seems likely that behind the designation of the saint as a "new hermit" lie the traces of the earlier conflict between Eastern and Western asceticism that is heightened in Sulpicius's depiction of Martin. The monk-bishop of Tours is presented not only as the equal of the holy men of Egypt but also as superior to them because he leads a holy life in the bustle of the world (in *medio coetu et conuersatione populorum*), precisely the conditions under which Saint Gregory of Langres attains sanctity and merits the distinction "new hermit"; see *Dial.* 1.24–25 (CSEL 1, pp. 176–78), with Fanger, "Dynamics," pp. 35–51.

180. Gregory also stresses the possibility of martyrdom through asceticism: *LVP* 2, pref. (MGH SRM 1.2, p. 668); 7, pref. (ibid., pp. 686–87); 10, pref. (ibid., p. 705).

181. *LVP* 11.3 (ibid., p. 711): "diaconatus ac praesbiterii sortitus est gradum. . . . Nulli tamen cellulam egressus se praebuit contemplandum, nisi tantum per fenestellam extendens manum, salutare signaculum inponebat."

182. *LVP* 11.1 (ibid., p. 709): "Qui non deliberat laborare, indigne postulat manducare"; an allusion to 2 Thess. 3:10 (though not noted in the edition): "si quis non vult operari nec manducet"; Scripture is used against a saint elsewhere: *LVP* 20.1 (MGH SRM 1.2, p. 741). In Antony's *Life*, the devil quotes Scripture to harass monks: *VBA* 16 (PL 73, p. 139).

183. *LVP* 9.1–2 (MGH SRM 1.2, p. 703): " 'Aut cum reliquis fratribus cibum sume, aut certe descede a nobis. Non enim rectum videtur, ut dissimules cum his habere victum, cum quibus eclesiasticum implere putaris officium. . . . ' Iam heremi sitebat adire secretum. . . ."

184. *LVP* 9.3 (ibid., p. 704): "congregatis monachis, ut solitudinem libero potius fungeretur arbitrio, abbatem instituit, qui gregi monasteriali praeesset. Octavum enim et decimum in hoc heremi loco expleverat annum."

185. *LVP* 2 (ibid., pp. 668–72); 4 (ibid., pp. 673–77); 6 (ibid., pp. 679–86); 7 (ibid., pp. 686–90); 8 (ibid., pp. 690–702); 17 (ibid., pp. 727–33).

186. *LVP* 6.2 (ibid., p. 681): "Referre enim saepe erat solitus vir beatus haec cum lacrimis et dicebat: 'Vae mihi, quia non persteti, ut in hac causa finirer.'" For comments on this passage, see Graus, *Volk*, p. 100.

187. *LVP* 16.1 (*MGH SRM* 1.2, pp. 724–25).

188. As with McCready, *Signs*, pp. 91–92: "It is abundantly clear that, for Gregory [the Great] miracles cannot be gratuitous wonders. He was compulsively interested in the larger religious significance that his miracle stories possessed. In this respect the difference between Gregory the Great and Gregory of Tours could scarcely have been wider." He elaborates (at n. 29): "For the most part, Gregory of Tours is content to celebrate the miracle-working powers of the saints he exalts; unlike Gregory the Great, he [Gregory of Tours] seems largely unaware of any larger spiritual significance of their miracles." For a more balanced comparison, see Joan Petersen, *The Dialogues of Gregory the Great in Their Late Antique Cultural Background* (Toronto, 1984), p. 131.

189. The desire for a better life is especially apparent in the story of Martius, *LVP* 14.1 (*MGH SRM* 1.2, p. 718): "Cumque ad illam aetatis legitimae perfectionem venisset et tamquam sidus egregium in hac urbe fulgeret, adhuc aliquid sibi deesse putans, haud procul ab ea secessit. Acceptoque sarculo, montem lapideum caedere coepit, in quo cellulas sculpens, habitacula sibi parvula fecit, scilicet ut artius subrietatis catena constrictus, facilius Deo omnipotenti precum tura laudationumque holocaustomata cordis mundi altare proferret, recolens, Dominum dixisse per euangelium: *Intra in cubiculum, et clauso ostio, ora Patrem tuum; et Pater tuus, qui videt in absconso, reddet tibi* (Matt. 6:6)." McCready, *Signs*, p. 67, n. 7, following the view of Boesch Gajano, among others, argues that, in Gregory of Tours's depiction of saints, "miracles are of the essence." Certainly, the account from Martius's *Life* and the others like it suggest that this view should be modified.

190. Although Brachio has visions and his body remains uncorrupt in death, Gregory never claims that this saint performed any miracles; Leobatius, of whom we hear very little, performs no miracles; Lupicinus, the companion of Romanus, performs no miracles; compare Graus, *Volk*, p. 119, n. 408: "Es gibt allerdings auch in der Merowingerzeit Heilige, deren Legende noch keine Wunder aufzuzählen wissen (z.B. Aemilianus herem. und Brachio abb . . .)." But Graus's remark overlooks the episode of the wild boar in Aemilianus's *Life*. Even so, that is the only miracle the saint performs. There is also a scarcity of miracles in the stories of Portianus, Abraham, and Illidius. Concerning Illidius, see McCready, *Signs*, p. 67, n. 7, who seems not to take into account the possible role of audience in determining the content of the Merovingian *Vitae*.

191. *LVP* 9.1 (*MGH SRM* 1.2, p. 702): "Discede longius, o rustice. Tuum est enim opus oves pascere, meum [vero] litteris exerceri; qua de re nobiliorem me ipsius officii cura facit, cum te huius custodiae servitus vilem reddit." James's translation, *Life*, p. 78.

192. *LVP* 9.1 (ibid., pp. 702–3): "Quod ille audiens et hanc increpationem quasi a Deo sibi transmissam putans, reliquit oves in campi planitiae et scolas puerorum nisu animi agile atque cursu velocissimo expetivit, traditisque elementis ac deinceps quae studio puerili necessaria erant, ita celeriter, memoria opitulante, inbutus est, ut fratrem vel in scientia praecederet vel alacritate sensus, adnuente divini Numinis auxilio, anteiret. Dehinc Nunnioni, qui quondam cum Childeberto Parisiorum rege magnus habebatur, ad exercendum commendatus est." James's translation, *Life*, p. 79.

193. *LVP* 12.2 (ibid., p. 713): "cum esset adhuc laicus, in nocte bis aut tertio de stratu suo consurgens, terrae prostratus, orationem fundebat ad Dominum. Nesciebat enim, quid caneret, quia litteras ignorabat. Videns autem saepius in oratorium litteras super iconicas apostolorum reliquorumque sanctorum esse conscriptas, exemplavit eas in codice. Cumque ad occursum domini sui clerici vel abbates assiduae convenirent, hic e iunioribus quem primum potuisset arcessire secretius interrogabat nomina litterarum, et ob hoc eas intellegere coepit. Antea autem, inspirante Domino, et legit et scripsit, quam litterarum seriem cognovisset. Exin mortuo Sigivaldo, ad antedictum senem properat, et cum eodem duos vel tres annos faciens, psalterium memoriae conmendavit." R. A. Markus includes this text among the rare and early evidence supporting the use of icons in the West: "The Cult of Icons in Sixth-Century Gaul," in *From Augustine to Gregory the Great: History and Christianity in Late Antiquity* (London, 1983), pp. 152–53.

194. *LVP* 20.2 (MGH SRM 1.2, p. 742): "ibique se, propriis manibus membrana faciens, ad scribendum aptavit; ibi se, ut Scripturas Sanctas intellegeret ac Davitici carminis psalmos, qui dudum excesserant memoriae, reteneret, exercuit. Sicque Divinarum Scripturarum lectionibus eruditus, cognovit, verum esse, quod ei Dominus prius inspiravit in corde." As Krusch notes (ibid., n. 2), the practice of preparing parchment was also one of the duties Martin designated for the younger monks at Marmoutier: *VM* 10.6 (CSEL 1, p. 120).

195. *LVP* 20.2 (MGH SRM 1.2, p. 742): "In qua cellula delectabatur ieiuniis, orationi, psallentio, lectioni, nec umquam a divinis officiis et oratione cessabat; scribebat interdum, ut se a cogitationibus noxiis discuteret." For similar reasons, Antony also encouraged his monks to write: *VBA* 28 (PL 73, p. 151).

196. So Krusch thinks, MGH SRM 1.2, p. 742, n. 3; James, *Life*, p. 157, n. 7, concurs.

197. *LVP* 20.3 (MGH SRM 1.2, p. 742): "librosque et vita patrum ac institutione monachorum, vel quales qui recluduntur esse debeant, vel cum quali cautela monachis vivere oporteat, abscedens ab eo, direxi. Quibus relictis, non solum cogitationem pravam a se discussit, verum etiam tantum sensum acumine erudivit, ut miraretur facundia elocutionis eius." James's translation, *Life*, p. 133.

198. *LVP* 20.3, (ibid., p. 743): "In qua cellula viginti et duos annos in hoc opere degens, tanta Domini gratia confortatus est, ut, pusulis malis salibam oris sui perunctis, vim veneni saevientis obpraemeret."

199. *LVP*, pref. (ibid., p. 662): "Et quaeritur a quibusdam, utrum vita sanctorum an vitas dicere debeamus. A. Gellius quoque et conplures philosophorum vitas dicere voluerunt. Nam Plinius auctor in tertio artis grammaticae libro ait: *Vitas antiqui cuiuscumque nostrum dixerunt; sed grammatici pluralem numerun non putaverunt habere vitam.* Unde manifestum est, melius dici vitam patrum quam vitas, quia, cum sit diversitas meritorum virtutumque, una tamen omnes vita corporis alit in mundo."

200. James, *Life*, p. 6; Wallace-Hadrill, *Frankish Church*, p. 79. The passage is frequently commented on: Elliott, *Roads*, pp. 5–6; Earl, "Literary Problems," p. 96; Olsen, "De Historiis," p. 411; Smith, "Early Medieval Hagiography," p. 69. Bynum, *Holy Feast*, p. 87. Ward, *Miracles*, p. 210, also cites this text, giving it an interpretation that seems to distort what Gregory actually states: "Gregory of Tours had said that all the saints have all their miracles in common and what was said of one could equally well be said of another."

201. Wallace-Hadrill, *Frankish Church*, p. 79.

202. Translation and edition are those of Bertram Colgrave, *The Earliest Life of Gregory the Great* (Laurence, Kans., 1968), pp. 130–32: "Sed neque et illud moveat quemquam si quid horum de alio quolibet sanctorum fuisset effectum, cum sanctus apostolus per mysterium unius corporis membrorum, sanctorum scilicet vitam conparando concordat ut simus ad invicem alter alterius membra. Fitque officium, verbi gratia, oculorum et aurium, manibus ac pedibus, sic profuturum sicut illis in commune, et ita omnia in omnibus licet non eundem actum habent.

Inde etiam scimus sanctorum esse omnia per caritatem corporis Christi, cuius sunt membra communia. Unde si quid horum que scripsimus de hoc viro non fuit, quae etiam non ab illis qui viderunt et audierunt per ore didicimus, vulgata tantum habemus, de illo eius etiam esse in magno dubitamus minime, quod iam hic sanctus vir, in sua prefata sapientia, satis evidenter docet, ut amantium semper in alterutrum fiat quod cernitur in aliis."

203. See Wallace-Hadrill, *Frankish Church*, p. 79.

204. Of all those who comment on the passage, Heffernan, *Sacred Biography*, p. 7, makes the most astute observations: "Gregory's conclusion is most important as it reveals his understanding of the relationship between theological truth and language. Notice that his argument moves beyond purely grammatical concerns into the realm of theology. The precedents of Gellius, Pliny, and the grammarians notwithstanding, the essential reason for his choice of the singular when composing a book of more than one life is based on the developing Christian idea that the saints share collectively in the luminous life of the incarnate Christ. In sum, sanctity is derived from the sacred, which is radically singular" (citing Eph. 5:8–14 and Rom. 12:3–10).

205. *LVP* 10, pref. (*MGH SRM* 1.2, p. 705): "Multi enim sunt gradus, per quos ad caelorum regna conscenditur, de quibus, ut opinor, et David dicit, quia: *Ascensus in corde disposuit* (Ps. 83:6). Accipientur ergo hi gradus diversorm operum ad cultum divinum profectus."

206. *LVP* 16, pref. (ibid., p. 724): "Solitarium atque multiplex donum eclesiis populisque terriginis caelestis potentia praestat, cum largitur iugiter saeculo non modo peccatorum suffragatores, verum etiam vitae doctores aeternae; quod unicum cernitur, dum a magestate divina tribuitur multiplex, quia cunctis qui expetere voluerint affluenter indulgetur." James's translation, *Life*, p. 109.

207. See Frye, *Code*, p. 18.

CHAPTER 4

1. Margo King, "Hagiography, Western European," in the *Dictionary of the Middle Ages*, vol. 6, ed. Joseph Strayer (New York, 1985), p. 66, is mistaken about the number of women: "The title of another work, the *Vitae patrum* is reminiscent of the desert; in it he commemorates eleven abbots, six bishops, four recluses and two holy women." Gregory briefly discusses Monegund and her miracles again in GC 24 (*MGH SRM* 1.2, p. 763). Throughout the GC and GM, Gregory also wrote other pieces on holy women, but they are short sketches, mostly recording *virtutes*, rather than the more substantial and biographical *Vita* of Monegund found in the *LVP*: GC 5 (ibid., p. 751), 16 (ibid., p. 756–57), 18 (ibid., p. 758), 33 (ibid., p. 768), 42 (ibid., p. 774), 63 (ibid., p. 785), 102 (ibid., p. 813) 104 (ibid., pp. 814–16); GM 5 (ibid., pp. 489–92), 37 (ibid., pp. 511–12), 50 (ibid., p. 523), 90 (ibid., pp. 548–49); the female martyrs of Lyon are mentioned by name at 48 (ibid., p. 521). Likewise, in addition to his *Life of Saint Radegund*, Fortunatus also wrote other works related to this saint and dedicated several of his poems to her and Agnes, the woman Radegund appointed as abbess after the monastery of Saint-Croix was founded in Poitiers: *carm.* 8.2 (*MGH AA* 4.1, pp. 180–81), 8.5–10 (ibid., pp. 193–95), 11.2–26 (ibid., pp. 258–70).

2. *LVP* 19, pref. (*MGH SRM* 1.2, p. 736): "Insignia divinorum beneficiorum carismata, quae humano generi caelitus sunt indulta, nec sensu concipi nec verbis effari nec scripturis poterunt conprehendi; cum ipse Salvator mundi ab illo rudis saeculi exordio patriarchis se praestat videri, prophetis adnuntiari, ad extremum semper virginis intactaeque Mariae dignatur utero suscipi."

3. Ibid.: "et praepotens immortalisque Creator mortalis carnis patitur amictu vestiri, mortem pro hominis peccato mortui reparationem adire victorque resurgere. Qui nos gravium

facinorum spiculis sauciatos ac latronum insidiantium vulneribus adfectos, infuso mero oleique liquore, ad stabulum medicinae caelestis, id est eclesiae sanctae dogma, perduxit."

4. *LVP* 7, pref. (ibid., pp. 686–87): "Egregiae sanctitatis viri . . . quos . . . martyrii agonizatio certa coronat; . . . atque ipsi sibi persecutores facti, dum in se sua peremebant vitia, tamquam martyres probati, peracto cursu agonis legitimi, triumpharent. Quod nullus sine Dei ope valebit efficere, nisi dominici adiutorii protegatur vel parma vel galea"; in *LVP* 12, pref. (ibid., p. 715), Gregory speaks similarly of the "athletae Christi" who "in isto agone contendent"; see also *LVP* 1, pref. (ibid., p. 663), 14.1 (ibid., p. 718); *GM* 52 (ibid., p. 525), 53 (ibid.), 72 (ibid., p. 536), 103 (ibid., p. 559).

5. *LVP* 19, pref. (ibid., p. 736): "Qui nos exemplis sanctorum vivere incessabili praeceptionis suae munire cohortatur nobisque non modo viros, sed etiam ipsum inferiorem sexum, non segniter, sed viriliter agonizantem, praebet exemplum. Qui non solum viris legitime decertantibus, verum etiam feminis in his proeliis faborabiliter desudantibus siderea regna participat." It is worth noting that the liturgical *Officium b. Monegundis* (*AASS* 28, July, vol. 1, p. 281), which borrows heavily from Gregory's *Vita*, shows a similar contrast between the "frail" female body and the strong fighter: "Beata namque Monegundis, cujus hodie celebramus solemnia, fragili in corpore mundi illecebras, gratia Dei concedente, fortiter superavit." Also included in the office is Prov. 31:10: "Mulierem fortem quis inveniet? Procul et de ultimis finibus pretium ejus."

6. *LVP* 19, pref. (*MGH SRM* 1.2, p. 736): "sicut nunc beata Monigundis, quae, relicto genitale solo, tamquam regina prudens, quae audire sapientiam Salamonis adivit, ita haec beati Martini basilicam, ut eius miracula cotidianis indulta momentis miraretur, expetiit, hauriretque de fonte sacerdotali, quo possit aditum nemoris paradisiaci recludere." James's translation, *Life*, p. 124.

7. Goffart, *Narrators*, p. 150.

8. *LVP* 5, pref. (*MGH SRM* 1.2, p. 677), is the only other *Vita* that mentions the Virgin Mary.

9. See, in general, Wemple's study, *Women in Frankish Society*, which investigates these issues in the context of the Merovingian church and society; see also Portmann, *Die Darstellung der Frau*, pp. 7–59; for the pre-Merovingian background, especially the classical and patristic sources on which the early church based its philosophical and theological understanding of women, see Aspegren, *Male Woman*, who traces the evolution of misogynistic tendencies throughout the development of Western intellectual history; see also Gillian Clark, *Women in Late Antiquity: Pagan and Christian Life-Styles* (Oxford, 1993); J. Laporte, *The Role of Women in Early Christianity* (New York, 1982).

10. *LVP* 19.1 (*MGH SRM* 1.2, p. 736): "Igitur beatissima Monigundis, Carnotenae urbis indigena, parentum ad votum copulata coniugio, duas filias habuit, super quibus valde gavisa laetabatur, dicens, quia: 'Propagavit Deus generationem meam, ut mihi duae filiae nascerentur.' "

11. Ibid.: "Sed hoc mundiale gaudium praevenit saeculi huius amaritudo, dum puellae modica febre pulsatae, metam naturae debitum concluserunt."

12. See Wittern, *Frauen*, pp. 88–89.

13. In the earlier literature, however, Perpetua maintains close ties with her child and suffers great anguish when separated from her infant son: *Passio sanctarum Perpetuae et Felicitatis* 3 (*ACM*, pp. 108–11).

14. See the illuminating remarks of Dyan Elliott, who also cites other examples from hagiographic literature in addition to Monegund's *Vita*: *Spiritual Marriage: Sexual Abstinence in Medieval Wedlock* (Princeton, 1993), p. 86; Graus, *Volk*, p. 104; Wemple, *Women*, p. 59.

15. Jerome's account of Paula's response to the death of her daughters and husband bears a resemblance to Monegund's behavior; see Nie, "Consciousness," pp. 132–33.

16. *LVP* 19.1 (*MGH SRM* 1.2, p. 737): "Factum est autem quodam die, ut memorata puella, quae ei consueverat famulari,—et credo inimici astu seducta, cui semper bonis iniurias inrogare mos est,—se ab eius famulatu subtraheret, dicens: 'Non potero ego cum haec domina permanere, quae in tali abstenentia commoratur, sed potius utar saeculum ac cibum potumque in abundantia sumam.' " Although Monegund may still be living in the manner of "an aristocratic woman," the *Vita* explicitly states that she had only *puellulam unam*, and the fact that the slave rebelled because of the rigorous life she had to lead with the saint suggests that Wemple, *Women*, p. 61, has painted too rosy a picture: "She retained, at the time of her divorce, her residence at Chartres, where as a recluse, she lived for a while in the manner of an aristocratic woman. Attended only by a few maidservants, she cultivated her garden, raising medicinal herbs, and took care of the poor." While the saint, as we shall see shortly, certainly leaves her husband, there is never any mention of a canonically sanctioned divorce, as Wemple claims.

17. *LVP* 19.1 (*MGH SRM* 1.2, p. 736): "Ex hoc genetrix maesta deplorans orbatamque se lugens, non diebus, non noctibus a fletu cessabat, quam non vir, non amicus, non ullus propinquorum poterat consolari. Tandemque in se conversa, ait: 'Si nullam consolationem de obitu filiarum capio, vereor, ne ob hoc laedam dominum meum Iesum Christum. Sed nunc haec lamenta relinquens, cum beato Iob consolata decantem: *Dominus dedit, Dominus abstulit. Quomodo Domino placuit, ita factum est; sit nomen Domini benedictum.*' Et haec dicens, exuta veste lucubri, iussit, sibi cellulam parvulam praeparari, in qua unam tantummodo fenestellulam, per quam modicum lumen possit cernere, praecepit aptari; ibique, contemptu mundi ambitu, spreto viri consortio, soli Deo in quo erat confisa, vacabat." James's translation, *Life*, pp. 124–25.

18. *LVP* 19.1 (ibid., p. 737): "Quintus enim iam fluxerat abscessionis eius dies, quod haec religiosa neque farinam consuetam neque aquam acceperat; sed perstabat inmobilis et fixa manens in Christo, in quo quisque locatus, nec venti turbine nec fluctuum inpulsione dilabitur; nec sibi illa de mortali cibo vitam, sed de verbo Dei . . . putabat inferri. . . . Sed quoniam corpus humanum absque aesu terreno sustentari non quaeit, prostrata in oratione, petiit, ut, qui manna populo esurienti de caelo lymphasque sitienti produxit e saxo, ipse quoque alimentum, quo parumper corpusculum fessum confortaretur, dignaretur indulgere." James's translation, *Life*, p. 125.

19. See *LVP* 14.2 (ibid., p. 719).

20. *LVP* 19.1 (ibid., p. 737): "Habebat enim contiguum cellulae parvulum viridiarium; in eo enim pro quadam relevatione prodere erat solita. In quo ingressa, dum intuens herbas loci deambulans, mulier eam, quae triticum supra tectum suum siccare posuerat, quasi de eminentiori loco, curis obpleta mundanis, inportunae prospexit, moxque oculis clausis, lumen caruit." James's translation, *Life*, p. 126.

21. *LVP* 19.2 (ibid., pp. 737–38): "His signis glorificata inter parentes, ne vanae gloriae lapsum incurreret, sancti Martini antestitis basilicam, relicto coniuge cum familia vel omni domo sua, fideliter expetivit. . . . ad basilicam sancti Martini Monegundis beata pervenit, ibique prostrata coram sepulchro, gratias agens, quod tumulum sanctum oculis propriis contemplare meruerat, in cellulam parvulam consistens, cotidie orationi ac ieiuniis vigiliisque vacabat. Sed nec ille locus ab eius virtute fuit inglorius." James's translation, *Life*, pp. 126–27.

22. Ibid.

23. Although married, Hilary opposes his daughter's wish to do the same and prays for her to die so that she will remain chaste: *VH* 13 (*MGH AA* 4.2, p. 6). For comments on this, see Elliott, *Spiritual Marriage*, p. 89. As his source, Fortunatus claims, *VH* 6 (*MGH AA* 4.2, p. 3), to be citing in the *Vita* a letter that Hilary wrote urging her to renounce an earthly spouse for a heavenly one; Koebner, *Venantius Fortunatus*, pp. 81–82, argues that the letter is spurious.

24. *LVP* 7.1 (*MGH SRM* 1.2, p. 687): "Coniugem de genere senatorio habens Armentariam nomine, quam ad propagandam generationem tantum dicitur cognovisse, de qua et filios, Domino largiente, suscepit. Aliam vero mulierem, ut iuvenilis adsolet fervor, inardescere non contigit."

25. *LVP* 7.2 (ibid.): "Post mortem autem uxoris ad Dominum convertitur, et electus a populo, Lingonicae urbis episcopus ordinatur."

26. But there are instances in which women demand their conjugal rights from their clerical husbands: GC 75 (ibid., p. 793); 77 (ibid., p. 794); see Wemple, *Women*, p. 134.

27. However, in the desert literature, male saints who flee on the wedding night sometimes encounter later a woman wandering in the desert who comes to the hermit's cell and tells the story of how her husband left her on the night of marriage; moved by the story, they are seduced and discover that the woman was a disguised demon; see Elliott, *Roads*, pp. 110–11.

28. *LVP* 19.2 (*MGH SRM* 1.2, 738): "Dum autem haec agerentur, audita vir ille fama beatae, convocans amicos vicinosque suos, pergit post eam et reducit ad propria et eam in cellula in qua prius habitaverat intromisit. At illa non cessabat ab opere quod consueverat, sed exercebatur in ieiuniis obsecrationibusque, ut tandem locum in quo habitare desiderabat possit adquaerere. Inchoat iterum iter desideratum, inplorans beati Martini auxilium, ut qui dederat desiderium tribueret et effectum. Pervenit ad basilicam, revertitur in cellula illa in qua prius fuerat commorata; ex hoc perstetit inconcussa nec est amplius a viro quaesita." James's translation, *Life*, p. 127. In light of the explicit reference in this text to the husband's resistance, the following statement made by Wemple, *Women*, p. 59, is misleading: "Saint Monegund's husband raised no objection when she decided to become a recluse after the death of her two daughters." Similarly, McNamara, *Sainted Women*, p. 53, also overlooks the husband's opposition: "Gregory portrays her [Monegund] as an exemplary type of the married woman who, with her husband's support, turned the bitter disappointment of her children's death into a source of spiritual nourishment for others."

29. According to Elliott, *Spiritual Marriage*, p. 3, "the term 'spiritual marriage' is not without ambiguity since it has been used to describe any number of quasi-nuptial situations. . . . The bishop's marriage with his see, Christ's union with the church, or the mystical marriage of God with the soul are all described as spiritual marriages." The last definition (*mutatis mutandis*, that is, taking into account that the texts we are examining do not speak much about the soul's union with God) is how the term is being used in the present discussion.

30. *LVP* 2, pref. (*MGH SRM* 1.2, p. 669): "De quo ea tantum capere potui, ut cognoscerem, Iesum Christum, filium Dei, ad salutem mundi venisse atque amicos eius, qui, accepta cruce austerae observantiae, sponsum secuti sunt, dignis obsequiis honorare." James's translation, *Life*, pp. 35–36.

31. See Bugge, *Virginitas*, p. 60.

32. *LVP* 9.1 (*MGH SRM* 1.2, p. 703): "Regressusque ad domum, patre defuncto, repperit matrem suam adhuc superstitem. Cui illa ait: 'Ecce genitor tuus, o dulcissime nate, obiit; ego vero absque solatio degeo. Requiram puellam pulchram ingenuamque, cui copulatus solatium praebeas maternae viduitati.' At ille respondit: 'Non coniungor mundanae coniugi, sed quae concepit animus cum Domini voluntate perficiam.' Cui cum genetrix non intellegens quaereret, quid hoc esset, prodere noluit, sed abiit ad Archadium Biturigae urbis episcopum petiitque, sibi comam capitis tondi adscirique se in ordine clericorum. Quod episcopus, Domino volente, sine mora conplevit." James's translation, *Life*, p. 79. A similar tonsure to avoid marriage, though with the support of the saint's mother, occurs in the *Vita sanctae Geretrudis* 2 (ibid., 2, p. 456).

33. *LVP* 6.1 (ibid., 1.2, p. 680): "Denique abba pro hac causa nuntios mittit ad patrem, interrogantes, quid de puero observari iuberet. At ille parumper contristatus, ait: 'Primogen-

itus,' inquid, 'erat mihi, et ideo eum volui coniugio copulari; sed si eum Dominus ad suum dignatur adscire servitium, illius magis quam nostra voluntas fiat.' " James's translation, *Life*, p. 53.

34. *LVP* 16.1 (ibid., pp. 724–25): "Qui dum esset iuvenili aetate florens, a parentibus sponsali vinculo obligatur. Cumque, ut aetati huic convenit, amori se puellari praestaret affabilem et cum poculis frequentibus etiam calciamenta deferret, contigit, ad urbem Toronicam, Domino inspirante, veniret. Erat enim tunc temporis monasterium basilicae sancti Martini propinquum, in quo Silvinus abba gregem Deo devotum regulari sceptro regebat. Ad hoc vir iste devotus accedens virtutesque cernens beati Martini, ait infra se: 'Ut conitio, melius est servire inpollutum Christo, quam per copulam nuptialem contagio involvi mundano. Relinquam sponsam territurii Biturigi et adnectar catholicae per fidem eclesiae, ut quae credo corde etiam opere merear effectui condonare.' " With only minor modifications, the translation is that of James, *Life*, pp. 109–10.

35. *LVP* 1.1 (ibid., p. 664): "cum ad legitimam transisset aetatem, genitore cogente, cum animi non praeberet consensum, sponsali vinculo nectitur."

36. *LVP* 12.2 (ibid., p. 713): "et cum eodem duos vel tres annos faciens, psalterium memoriae conmendavit. Quem eius germanus plerumque interficere voluit, cur nollet matrimonio copulari."

37. Concerning the class from which the saint comes, Gregory says that Leobardus was not of the senatorial rank but that he was nonetheless freeborn; *LVP* 20.1 (ibid., p. 741): "Igitur beatissimus Leobardus Arverni territurii indigena fuit, genere quidem non senatorio, ingenuo tamen, qui ab initio Deum in pectore tenens, cum non floreret natalibus, gloriosis meritis praefulgebat"; see Castagno, "Il vescovo," pp. 243–44.

38. *LVP* 20.1 (*MGH SRM* 1.2, pp. 741–42): "cum ad legitimam pervenisset aetatem, cogentibus iuxta consuetudinem humanam parentibus, ut arram puellae, quasi uxorem accepturus, daret, inpellitur. Illo quoque respuente, ait pater: 'Cur, dulcissime fili, voluntatem paternam respuis nec iungere vis conubio, ut semen excites nostro de genere saeculis sequentibus profuturum? Casso enim labore exercemur ad operandum, si possessor deerit ad fruendum. Vel cur inplemus domum opibus, si de genere nostro non processerit qui utatur? Quid mancipia dato pretio nostris ditionibus subiugamus, si rursum alienis debent dominationibus subiacere? Oboedire filiis voci parentum, Scripturae testantur divinae; et tu cum inoboediens esse parentibus probaris, vide, ne te caelestibus eruere nequeas ab offensis.' Haec patre loquente, licet haberet alium filium, facile tamen tali aetatulae persuasit voluntati propriae contraire. Denique, dato sponsae anulo, porregit osculum, praebet calciamentum, caelebrat sponsaliae diem festum. Interea genitor, genetrix mortis somno sopiti migraverunt a saeculo, vitae praesentis curriculo iam peracto. Hic vero, cum germano tempore luctus expleto, oneratus donis nuptialibus, fratris pergit ad domum; quem in tantum repperit vino madidum, ut nec cognosceret nec reciperet propria in domo germanum. Ille vero suspirans et lacrimans, secessit in partem et venit ad tugurium, in quo fenum fuerat adgregatum, ibique conligato praebens equiti pabulum, decubuit super fenum ad quiescendum. Expergefactus autem media nocte, surgit de stratu suo, erectisque ad caelum manibus, gratias agere coepit omnipotenti Deo, quod esset, quod viveret, quod aleretur donis eius, et alia huiuscemodi prosecutus. Cum suspiria longa protraheret atque lacrimis crebris genas ubertim rigaret, Deus omnipotens, qui illos quos praescivit et praedestinavit conformes fieri imaginis Filii sui, conpunxit cor eius, ut, relicto saeculo, manciparetur ad cultum divinum." With only a minor modification, the translation is that of James, *Life*, pp. 131–32.

39. *LVP* 20.2 (ibid., p. 742): "Cumque per viam iam alacris pergeret, volvere intra se coepit, quid ageret, quo abiret. Dixitque: 'Expetam Martini beati tumulum, unde procedit virtus alma super infirmos. Credo enim, quod et mihi eius oratio iter reseret ad Deum, qui

deprecatus Dominum mortuos reduxit a tartaro.' Et sic viam carpens oratione comite, sancti Martini basilicam est ingressus.''

40. *LVP* 9.2 (ibid., p. 703): "venit ad vicum Nereensim, ibique aedificato oratorio ac sancti Martini reliquiis consecrato.''

41. Baudonivia also shows Radegund as having trouble with her pursuing husband: *VR* 2.6–7 (ibid., 2, p. 382). Wemple, *Women*, p. 184, suggests that the depiction of the husband in pursuit of his saintly wife is the peculiar feature of Fortunatus's account: "In contrast to Fortunatus's portrayal of Radegund as the withdrawn wife and reluctant queen whose main objective was to transcend her femininity and escape from her husband, Baudonivia described Radegund as an outgoing and emotional woman.'' Another account also thought to be written by a woman describes the saint fleeing from a suitor: *Vita sanctae Balthildis* 3 (*MGH SRM* 2, pp. 484–85). The including of a "chase scene" in *Vitae* is, therefore, as much a strategy of female hagiographers as of male ones.

42. *DVSM* 2.58–59; 3.41 (*MGH SRM* 1.2, pp. 628–29; 642).

43. *LVP* 19.2 (ibid., p. 738); he simply gives the feminine form *monachas*, indicating that a small religious community had formed around Monegund. Monastic sanctity is one of the few types open to women, with the full range of types being severely limited, given that women are barred from the clerical ranks. The important implications are summarized by Graus, *Volk*, pp. 117–18: "Aber dieser Type [i.e., the holy bishop] konnte natürlich (ähnlich wie der viel seltenere des heiligen Priesters) nur für Heilige männlichen Geschlechts angewandt werden; *Frauen* blieben ausgeschlossen. Die Frau konnte Märtyrerin und Klausnerin sein. In der Kirchenorganisation hatten nur die Nonne und die Äbtissin ihren Platz. Darum unterscheiden sich auch in den meisten Legenden die heiligen Frauen etwas von ihren männlichen Pendants. Besonders erhält sich bei den Frauen—wohl auch durch direkten Einfluss des biblischen Berichtes über Maria und Martha (Luke 10, 38 ff.)—viel prägnanter die Bevorzugung der vita contemplativa und zwar auch dann, als bei den männlichen Heiligen sich der aktive Type schon längst durchgesetzt hatte. Ausserdem spielte bei der Frau auch ihr Stand eine viel grössere Rolle. Massgebend für die Einschätzung wurde die Deutung des Gleichnisses vom Sämann durch Hieronymus. . . .

Ausser bei der Märtyrerin und Büsserin kommt also für den Hagiographen nur die jungfräuliche oder verwitwete Heilige in Betracht. Die verheiratete Heilige, die heilige Frau im eigentlichen Sinne des Wortes, kennt die christliche Legende überhaupt nicht, obzwar sie ja in der hl. Anna ein biblisches Vorbild hatte. Wenn die verheiratete Frau in der Merowingerzeit "heilig'' werden wollte, so musste sie sogar die kanonischen Gebote (die eine Einwilligung des Mannes erforderten) übertreten und den Ehemann kurzerhand verlassen [citing the Lives of Monegund and Radegund]. . . .

Im allgemeinen haben jedoch die Frauenvitae durch die besondere Wertskala für die Frauen, durch ihre Ausschliessung von Priesteramt gewisse Spezifika im Vergleich mit den Legenden männlicher Heiliger. Aber auch bei den Frauen lässt sich ein "Einbauen'' in die kirchliche Organisation feststellen. Bezeichnenderweise verschwindet die bekehrte Büsserin (wovon schon die Rede war) und die Asketin wandelt sich in die mustergültige Nonne und besonders in die Äbtissin, die höchste kirchliche Funktion, die für Frauen überhaupt erreichbar war.''

The difference highlighted by Graus does not lead to the creation of a new saint type but restricts the application of previous types in the depiction of women. In the end—and this view, though never addressed, is contrary to all the current scholarship arguing for a new female model that appears in the Merovingian literature—Graus concludes that there are no new saint types introduced during this period of hagiography's development: "Aber eigentliche Neuschöpfungen von Heiligentypen kannte die Merowingerzeit noch nicht.''

44. *LVP* 9.2 (*MGH SRM* 1.2, p. 703): "Ille [Patroclus] autem in cellula qua degebat, con-gregatis virginibus, monasterium instituit puellarum." For other monastic establishments, some of which seem experimental, small and loosely organized around a central figure who is not always present, see *LVP* 1.2–3 (ibid., pp. 664–65); 3.1 (ibid., p. 672); 10.2 (ibid., p. 707); 12.2–3 (ibid., p. 713–14); 14.1 (ibid., p. 718); 15.1 (ibid., p. 721); 18.1 (ibid., p. 734); 20.2 (ibid., p. 742).

45. *LVP* 7.2 (ibid., p. 687).

46. Jerome, *Translatio Latina regulae sancti Pachomii* 88 (*PL* 23, p. 77): "Praeter psiathium, id est, mattam, in loco cellulae ad dormiendum nihil aliud omnino substernet." Given the fre-quency with which *matta* appears in the early monastic sources, McNamara's suggestion, *Sainted Women*, p. 57, n. 12, that *mattas* could be "a vernacular Germanic word" does not seem likely.

47. *LVP* 19.2 (*MGH SRM* 1.2, p. 738): "Ibique paucas collegens monachas, cum fide integra et oratione degebat, non sumens panem nisi hordiacium, non vinum nisi parumper in diebus festis, et hoc ipsum nimio latice temperatum; nullum habens stratum feni paleaeque mollimen, nisi tantum illud quod intextis iunci virgulis fieri solet, quas vulgo mattas vocant; hoc super-ponens formulae, hoc solo supersternens; hoc erat cotidianum scamnum, hoc culcita, hoc plumella, hoc erat stragulum, hoc omnis lectuli necessitudo; sic docens easdem facere quas secum adscivit. Ibique in Dei laudibus degens, multis infirmis, oratione facta, salutaria inper-tiebat medicamenta." James's translation, *Life*, p. 127.

48. *LVP* 19.4 (ibid., p. 739): "Iam enim tempus vocationis eius adpropinquabat, et defessa corpori solvebatur. Quod cum viderent sanctimoniales, quas secum habebat, flebant valde, dicentes: 'Et cui nos, mater sancta, relinques? Vel cui conmendas filias, quas in [hoc] loco pro Dei intuitu congregasti?' " Notice also that the passage of leadership goes quite smoothly from a *mater* to a *pastorem*: "At illa parumper lacrimans, ait: 'Si pacem sanctificationemque sequamini, Deus erit protectio vestra, habebitisque sanctum Martinum antestitem pastorem magnum.' "

49. *LVP* 15.4 (ibid., p. 724); Sulpicius, *Ep.* 2.6–8, 15–19 (*CSEL* 1, pp. 143, 145); see also *GC* 104 (*MGH SRM* 1.2, p. 814).

50. Gal. 3:27–28: "quicumque enim in Christo baptizati estis Christum induistis non est Iudaeus neque Graecus non est servus neque liber non est masculus neque femina omnes enim vos unum estis in Christo Iesu."

51. *LVP* 19.3 (*MGH SRM* 1.2, p. 739): "Mulier erat caeca, quae adducta ad eam, deprecata est, ut ei manus inponeret, At illa respondit: 'Quid vobis et mihi, homines Dei? Nonne sanctus Martinus hic habitat, qui cotidie inlustrium virtutum opere refulget? Illuc accedite, ibi obse-cramini, ut ipse vos visitare dignetur. Nam ego peccatrix quid faciam?' Illa vero in sua petitione perdurans, aiebat: 'Deus per omnes timentes nomen suum cotidie opus exercet egregium; ideoque supplex ad te confugio, cui praestita est Divinitatis gratia curationum.' Tunc commota Dei famula, luminibus sepultis manus inposuit, statimque reseratis cataractis, mundum late patentem quae fuerat caeca prospexit." James's translation, *Life*, p. 128.

52. On her monasticism, see Prinz, *Frühes Mönchtum*, p. 37; Wemple, *Women*, p. 156.

53. *VR* 1, prol. (*MGH SRM* 2, p. 364): "Redemptoris nostri tantum dives est largitas, ut in sexu muliebri celebret fortes victorias et corpore fragiliores ipsas reddat feminas virtute mentis inclitae gloriosas. Quas habentes nascendo mollitiem facit Christus robustas ex fide, ut quae videntur inbecilles, dum coronantur ex meritis, a quo efficuntur, laudem sui cumulent Crea-toris, *habendo in vasis fictilibus thesauros* [italics added] caeli reconditos; in quarum visceribus cum suis divitiis ipse rex habitator est Christus. Quae mortificantes se saeculo . . . quaerentes vivere Deo, ad gloriam Redemptoris sunt copulatae paradiso." Although not noted by Krusch, For-tunatus is following the text from Corinthians: "habemus autem thesaurum istum in vasis fictilibus."

54. See Nie, "Consciousness," pp. 125–26, 137, 139–49, who detects in the description of Radegund's youth and her asceticism the influence of Jerome's account of Paula, as well

as Eugenia's *Vita* and the story of Thais on the works of Fortunatus and Baudonivia; see also Brennan, "Deathless Marriage," pp. 74, 76.

55. VR 1.2 (MGH SRM 2, p. 365): "Quae puella inter alia opera, quae sexui eius congruebant, litteris est erudita, frequenter loquens cum parvulis, si conferret sors temporis, martyra fieri cupiens. Indicabat adolescens iam tunc merita senectutis, obtinens pro parte quae petiit. Denique, dum esset in pace florens ecclesia, ipsa est a domesticis persecutionem perpessa. Iam tunc id agens infantula, quidquid sibi remansisset in mensa, collectis parvulis, lavans capita singulis, conpositis sellulis, porrigens aquam manibus, ipsa inferebat, ipsa miscebat infantulis."

56. VR 1.5 (ibid., pp. 366–67): "Item nocturno tempore cum reclinaret cum principe, rogans se pro humana necessitate consurgere, levans, egressa cubiculo, tam diu ante secretum orationi incumbebat, iactato cilicio, ut solo calens spiritu, iaceret gelu penetrata, tota carne praemortua, non curans corporis tormenta mens intenta paradiso, leve reputans quod ferret, tantum ne Christo vilesceret. Inde regressa cubiculum, vix tepefieri poterat vel foco vel lectulo. De qua regi dicebatur, habere se potius iugalem monacham quam reginam. Unde et ipse irritatus."

57. VR 1.25 (ibid., p. 372–73): "Itaque post tot labores, quas sibi poenas intulerit, et ipse qui voce refert perhorrescit. Quadam vice, dum sibi latos tres circulos ferreos diebus quadragesimae collo vel brachiis nexuit, et tres catenas inserens, circa suum corpus dum alligasset adstricte, inclusit durum ferrum caro tenera supercrescens. Et transacto ieiunio, cum voluisset catenas sub cute clausas extrahere nec valeret, caro per dorsum atque pectus super ferrum catenarum est incisa per circulum, ut sanguis fusus ad extremum exinaniret corpusculum." Translation relies slightly on McNamara, *Sainted Women*, p. 81.

58. VR 1.26 (ibid., p. 373): "Item vice sub altera iussit fieri laminam in signo Christi oricalcam, quam accensam in cellula locis duobus corporis altius sibi inpressit, tota carne decocta. Sic, spiritu flammante, membra faciebat ardere. Adhuc aliquid gravius in se ipsa tortrix excogitans una quadragesimarum super austerum ieiunium et sitis torridae cruciatum, adhuc lima cilicii membra tenera setis asperis dissipante, iubet portare aquamanile ardentibus plenum carbonibus. Hinc discedentibus reliquis, membris trepidantibus, animus armatur ad poenam, tractans, quia non essent persecutionis tempora, a se ut fieret martyra. Inter haec, ut refrigeraret tam ferventem animum, incendere corpus deliberat, adponit aera candentia, stridunt membra crementia, consumitur cutis, et intima, quo attigit ardor, fit fossa. Tacens tegit foramina, sed conputrescens sanguis manifestabat, quod vox non prodebat in poena. Sic femina pro Christi dulcedine tot amara libenter excepit. Hinc actum est, quod ipsa abdiderit, hoc miracula non tacerent."

59. Aigrain, *Sainte Radegonde* (Paris, 1910), p. 160: "Je ne crois pas qu'il y ait dans l'histoire des saints beaucoup d'exemples de pareilles violences faites à la nature." Similarly, McNamara, *Sainted Women*, p. 81, n. 71, states: "These and other extreme tortures appear to be unique to Radegund. No other saint in this collection [of translated Lives] imposed so much exotic self-inflicted pain. . . . Fortunatus may have been overanxious to promote her claims to a place among the martyrs. . . . The spread of formal rules for monks and nuns in the seventh century would in any case put an official limit to similar exercises in endurance."

60. A later version of the *Life*, which will be noted shortly, suggests that the shirt is simply stripped off (*cilicio exuitur*); McNamara, *Sainted Women*, p. 73, translates: "Then she would prostrate herself in prayer under a hair cloak." This rendition does not seem to express adequately the bare bodily exposure implied by the phrase *iactato cilicio*.

61. Perhaps there is a correspondence between the areas in which the chains are placed and where noble women wore jewelry; see Peter Lasko, *The Kingdoms of the Franks* (London, 1971), pp. 55–57, for the grave goods of a Merovingian queen; see also James, *The Franks*, pp. 112–13.

62. McNamara, *Sainted Women*, p. 81, translates the comparative adverb *altius* as "most deeply." Although a similar translation was given previously ("very deeply"), we should not neglect the other meaning of *altus* as "high," in which case the word would convey the sense that the plate is being applied to the upper body, thus lending additional support for interpreting *locus duobus* as a reference to breasts.

63. McNamara gives a literal and accurate translation of the phrase *in signo Christi*, rendered as "in the sign of Christ." I have done the same. But one wonders what exactly is meant here by *signo* and whether it refers to an image of the cross (which seems unlikely because *crucis* would be the obvious word to use) or to an actual representation of Christ that is on the plate, in which case the saint's flesh would be branded by the image of Christ, much as a seal ring or signet, objects also designated by the word *signum*, impress an image on a document. Against the interpretation that the image is of Christ rather than a cross is the Middle English verse, which reads: "A plate of coper the sygne of the crosse hauyng / which layrd in the fyre in her cell solitary." Significantly, however, the poem suppresses the reference to *locis duobus*. On the poem, see chapter 5, n. 6. In *The Life and Opinions of Tristram Shandy*, ed. Ian Watt (Boston, 1965), p. 429, Laurence Stern mentions a similar object as being a relic at the eighteenth-century convent of Saint Radegund.

64. Here, it is important to note that the twelfth-century version of Radegund's *Life* (*AASS* 57, August, vol. 3, pp. 88–89), in which Hildebert of Le Mans "polishes" the Latin of Fortunatus and Baudonivia, leaves no doubt that the saint has conquered femininity by being a "woman brave beyond a woman": "Aenun quippe vas ardenti plenum carbone, sibi praecipiens apponi, familiaris egredi jubet, obserat cellulam, cilicio exuitur et femina supra feminam, fortis, armatur ad poenam." Perhaps Hildebert prefers merely to hint at where the plate is being applied, by saying only that the hair shirt was removed (*cilicio exuitur*). Notice that this version leaves out any explicit reference to a specific place being scorched on the body, such as *locis duobus*. Instead, as he continues the narrative, he refers generally to *membris*. A comparative form of *altus* also appears, followed by *intima fervore*, a phrase that helps to remove the ambiguity of *altius* found in Fortunatus's text, thus lending support to McNamara's translation of the word as "deeply": "Praeparato ergo ad crucem animo, in ignem se projicit; carbo quaeritur ardentior, et versatis desuper artubus, cutem et carnem quaesitum rumpit et penetrat incendium. Mora in igne longior tenerem corpus altiori vulnere persequitur. Candens aes advolvitur membris, intima fervore consumuntur."

65. The possibility that Fortunatus is acting as a reliable reporter in recounting the self-tortures of Radegund has been suggested, with reservations, by Pauline Stafford, *Queens, Concubines and Dowagers: The King's Wife in the Middle Ages* (Athens, Ga., 1983), p. 10: "Fortunatus's portrait is repellent to the modern eye, but exercised a powerful appeal in the Middle Ages as a type of consecrated womanhood. How accurate a description it is of Radegund is a more difficult question. We should be wary of outright dismissal of medieval asceticism from a modern, rationalist standpoint. Yet Fortunatus's ascetic Radegund is sometimes difficult to reconcile with the abbess to whom he dedicated charming classical poems."

66. See McNamara, *Sainted Women*, p. 81, n. 71.

67. LH 9.40 (MGH SRM 1.1, p. 464); VR 2.16 (ibid., 2, pp. 388–89); see Graus, *Volk*, pp. 113, 408.

68. LH 9.40 (MGH SRM 1.1, p. 464): "cum ponteficis sui saepius gratiam quaereret nec possit adipisci, necessitate commota, cum abbatissa sua, quam instituerat, Arelatensim urbem expetunt."

69. GC 104 (ibid., p. 815): "Ecce frater noster Maroveus huius urbis episcopus non est coram"; VR 2.23 (ibid., 2, p. 393): "Triduo expectatus est pontifex, quia vicos circuiebat; sed quia non venit, supradictus vir apostolicus [i.e. Gregory of Tours] . . . eam cum digno sepelivit honore."

70. On the controversy surrounding the cross relic and the animosity between Bishop Maroveus and Radegund, as described in Gregory's *Histories*, see Brennan, "St. Radegund and the Early Development of Her Cult at Poitiers," *Journal of Religious History* 13 (1985): 345–50.

71. See Wemple, *Women*, pp. 136–42; McNamara, *Sainted Women*, p. 75, n. 53.

72. Brennan notes, "Deathless Marriage," p. 77, that certain Merovingian church councils even banned the ordination of deaconesses "because of the perceived weakness of women."

73. *VR* 1.35 (*MGH SRM* 2, p. 375): "Deinde manu beatae visa est oleum aegrotae super caput effundere et nova veste contegere."

74. *VR* 1.29 (ibid., p. 374): "ipsam aegrotam ad se fecit in cellulam deportari et in tepida deponi. . . . Exiit salubris de tepida; quae vinum nec odorabat, accepit, bibit et refecta est."

75. See Collins, "Observations," p. 112.

76. *VR* 1.17 (*MGH SRM* 2, p. 370): "balneo parato, ipsa succincta de savano, capita lavans egenorum, defricans, quidquid erat, crustam, scabiem, tineam, nec purulenta fastidiens, interdum et vermes extrahens, purgans cutis putredines, singillatim capita pectebat ipsa, quae laverat. Ulcera vero cicatricum, quae cutis laxa detexerat, aut ungues exasperaverant, more euangelico oleo superfuso, mulcebat morbi contagium." Concerning Radegund's charity, Samuel Dill, *Roman Society in Gaul in the Merovingian Age* (London, 1926), p. 376, remarks: "The meanest, most disgusting offices, such as no modern pen would venture to describe, were performed by a queen of France. . . . It is enough to say that on certain days Radegund received a crowd of the poor and diseased, washed them from head to foot in the bath, tended their sores and ulcers, and even joyfully clasped a leprous woman in her embrace!"

77. A servant's reaction to this practice, *VR* 1.19 (*MGH SRM* 2, p. 371), is similar to Dill's: " 'Sanctissima domina, quis te osculetur, quae sic leprosos amplecteris?' Illa respondit benivole: 'Vere, si me non osculeris, hinc mihi cura nec ulla est.' "

78. *VR* 1.38 (ibid., p. 376).

79. *VR* 1.11 (ibid., 368): "fractis vinculis, soluti occurrunt sanctae de carcere. Quo cognito, reos se viderunt, qui beatae mentiti sunt, dum, qui rei fuerant, de catenis soluti sunt."

80. *VR* 1.38 (ibid., p. 376): "Adhuc in ipso sopore manum trahit per fauces eius, et gulam diu deliniens, insuper et hoc dicens: 'Veni, ut tibi melior a Deo sanitas conferatur.' Et videbatur sic rogare: 'Per meam vitam ut propter me relaxes illos quos habes in carcere.' " With Radegund's and Genevieve's intervention on behalf of prisoners in mind, McNamara, *Sainted Women*, p. 74 n. 47, states: "The intervention of women on behalf of prisoners may indicate an aspect of the division of labor whereby the harsh military face of kingship could be softened through the merciful quality of queenship without making the king appear weak or indecisive." In light of the frequency with which holy bishops are portrayed securing the release of prisoners and the fact that the sources clearly show there is nothing inherently "merciful" about queenship, the association of this activity specifically with royal women is untenable.

81. Pornographic in Frye's sense, *The Secular Scripture*, p. 24: "it is the function of pornography to stun and numb the reader, and the function of erotic writing to wake him up."

82. Nie's article, "Consciousness," pp. 101–61, is an exception.

83. See W. H. C. Frend, *Martyrdom and Persecution in the Early Church: A Study of a Conflict from Maccabees to Donatus* (Oxford, 1965), pp. 19, 44, 57–58.

84. 2 Macc. 7:27: "ait patria voce fili mi miserere mei quae te in utero decem menses portavi et lac triennio dedi et alui et in aetatem istam perduxi". A poem on the Maccabean mother and her sons, probably written by Hilary of Arles (403–449), also highlights the mother as a female nurturer, "*Versus in Natali Machabaeorum Martyrum*" (PL 50, p. 1277): "Interea fecunda parens, jam crine soluto, / stabat, et hortanti similis jam pectore nudo / ubera protendens, natorum alimenta suorum / non confusa aperit."

85. 2 Macc 7:21: "singulos illorum hortabatur patria voce fortiter repleta sapientia et femineae cogitationi masculinum animum inserens." Following modern English translations

of the passage, I have opted to see a juxtaposition between *femineae cogitationi* and *masculum animum*, partly because this reading anticipates what we shall find in other texts that will be examined shortly. However, one could also translate *inserens* as "introducing into" or "mingling *masculum animum* with *femineae cogitationi*," a rendition that would bring out the complex character of the heroine as a tender mother who also knows how to rouse her children to martyrdom by giving affectionate as well as bold encouragement. This complexity, in fact, seems to be a feature of the mother's profile that the verses cited in the previous note highlight. Also somewhat difficult to translate here is *animum*. Again, modern translations give "courage," which certainly fits the context, but the proximity of the word to *sapientia* and *cogitationi* suggest that the word could also refer to the reasoning faculty or even "spirit," which are the more common connotations of *animus*.

86. On Perpetua's visions and martyrdom, see Peter Dronke, *Women Writers*, pp. 1–17; Heffernan, *Sacred Biography*, pp. 185–230; Elizabeth Petroff, *Medieval Women's Visionary Literature* (New York, 1986), pp. 3–69; Aspegren, *Male Woman*, pp. 133–43; Nie, "Consciousness," pp. 116–23; Brown, *Body*, pp. 74–77, 141, 154.

87. *Passio santarum Perpetuae et Felicitatis* 10 (ACM, pp. 116–19): "Pridie quam pugnaremus, uideo in horomate hoc: venisse Pomponium diaconum ad ostium carceris et pulsare uehementer. Et exiui ad eum et aperui ei. . . . Et dixit mihi: Perpetua, te expectamus; ueni. Et tenuit mihi manum et coepimus ire per aspera loca et flexuosa. Uix tandem peruenimus anhelantes ad amphitheatrum et induxit me in media arena. . . . Et aspicio populum ingentem adtonitum; et quia sciebam me ad bestias damnatam esse, mirabar quod non mitterentur mihi bestiae. Et exiuit quidam contra me Aegyptius foedus specie cum adiutoribus suis pugnaturus mecum. Ueniunt et ad me adolescentes decori, adiutores et fautores mei. et expoliata sum et facta sum masculus; et coeperunt me fauisores mei oleo defricare, quomodo solent in agone. Et illum contra Aegyptium uideo in afa uolutantem. Et exiuit uir quidam mirae magnitudinis ut etiam excederet fastigium amphitheatri, discinctatus, purpuram inter duos clauos per medium pectus habens, et galliculas multiformes ex auro et argento factas, et ferens uirgam quasi lanista, et ramum uiridem in quo erant mala aurea. Et petiit silentium et dixit: Hic Aegyptius, si hanc uicerit, occidet illam gladio; haec, si hunc uicerit, accipiet ramum istum. et recessit." Here and in the next quoted passage, the translations are those of Musurillo, *The Acts of the Christian Martyrs* (Oxford, 1972).

88. Ibid., 118–19: "et accessimus ad inuicem et coepimus mittere pugnos. Ille mihi pedes adprehendere uolebat; ego autem illi calcibus faciem caedebam. Et sublata sum in aere et coepi eum sic caedere quasi terram non calcans. at ubi uidi moram fieri, iunxi manus ut digitos in digitos metterem et apprehendi illi caput; et cecidit in faciem et calcaui illi caput. Et coepit populus clamare et fauisores mei psallere. Et accessi ad lanistam et accepi ramum. Et osculatus est me et dixit mihi: Filia, pax tecum. Et coepi ire cum gloria ad portam Sanauiuariam. Et experrecta sum. Et intellexi me non ad bestias, sed contra diabolum esse pugnaturam; sed sciebam mihi esse uictoriam." Significantly, in interpreting the vision, the martyr considers her contest as a fight against the devil, not wild beasts, so that even at this early stage in the literature's development we can already see how the spiritual struggle against demonic forces, which is the chief occupation of the bloodless martyr and marks a later hagiographic development, can have vestiges in an authentic *passio* recounting actual persecution.

89. Though Nie, "Consciousness," p. 120, perceptively comments: "Perpetua finds herself transformed into the appearance of a man. The trainer/Father, however, continues to speak of and address her as a woman."

90. See Stevan Davies, *The Revolt of the Widows: The Social World of the Apocryphal Acts* (Carbondale, Ill., 1980), pp. 50–69; Elaine Pagels, *Adam, Eve, and the Serpent* (New York, 1988), p. 20; Ross Kraemer, "The Conversion of Women to Ascetic Forms of Christianity, *Signs* 6.21 (1980): 298–307.

91. *Passio beatissimae virginis et martyris Teclae* (ed. Mombrizio, *Sanctuarium seu vitae sanctorum*, vol. 2, p. 561): "Interea haec Tecla ait ad Paulum: Tondeo me: et sequor te: quocumque ieris."

92. On the "erotic pattern" in the relationship between Paul and Thecla, see Aspegren, *Male Woman*, pp. 105–7; see also Brown, *Body*, p. 155–59.

93. Although it is well represented in the manuscript tradition, Mombrizio's edition does not include this passage. But the edition of Gebhardt, *Passio s. Theclae* 40 (TU, NF 7.2, pp. 114–116) gives several important variants: A: "succinxit se super vestem suam et cooperuit se anabulario more uirili et abiit Zmirnam"; Ba: "se ipsam cinxit tunicam suam uirili more componens, et sumpto habitu masculino perrexit in Mirraside"; Bb: "se ipsam cinxit tunicam suam uirili more componens et sumpto virili habitu perrexit in Mirareidem prouinciam"; omitted in Bc; Ca: "Et [replicauit] sibi altiorem tunicam in habitu uiri"; Cb: "Et replicauit tunicam et in tunica in habitu uirili introiuit in domnum"; Cc: "Et replicauit tunicam suam in habitu uirili"; Cd: Et replicauit sibi tunicam et uestita est habitu uirili incisis crinibus."

94. *Passio beatissimae virginis et martyris Teclae* (ed. Mombrizio, p. 563): "Paule lauacrum accepi: Qui enim operatus est tibi in euangelio operatus est et mihi in lauacro." Again, as with Perpetua, the masculinization comes after an experience of nakedness: "Haec cum audisset proconsul: iussit uestimenta eius afferri et indui Teclam. Illa autem ait: Qui me expoliatam ac nudam de igne eripuit: qui inter feras constitutam saluam conseruauit: ipse me induet in die iusti iudicii sui uestimento salutaris." John Anson, "The Female Transvestite in Early Monasticism: The Origin and Development of a Motif," *Viator* 5 (1974): 6, connects Thecla'a masculine appearance to her baptismal experience: "Evidently Thecla's disguise must be intimately linked with her baptism; for in the speech where she first proposes to cut her hair, she also asks for baptism, and when she finally baptizes herself only then does she go to Paul in the garments of a man."

95. *The Coptic Gospel of Thomas*, trans. Beate Blatz (NTA 1, pp. 110–11), with Brown, *Body*, p. 113. Blatz lists no Latin translations of this particular version of Thomas's Gospel in the exhaustive summary of sources and transmission of the text (though, according to Blatz, Jerome, Ambrose, and Bede knew of this version, with all three giving a paraphrase regarding its heterodoxy that is ultimately based on Origen's assessment); see also Jeane Doresse, *The Secret Books of the Egyptian Gnostics: An Introduction to the Gnostic Coptic Manuscripts Discovered at Chenoboskion* (London, 1960), pp. 334–35. However, the so-called Infancy Gospel ascribed to Thomas was widely known through Latin versions: *Evangelica apocrypha*, ed. Constantinus de Tischendorf (Leipzig, 1876), pp. 164–80; see also Montague James, *The Apocryphal New Testament* (Oxford, 1924), p. 49.

96. Aigrain, *L'hagiographie*, pp. 229–30; see also Anson, "Female Transvestite," pp. 12–13.

97. *Vitae patrum* 8.131 (PL 73, p. 1204): Basianilla "in hodiernum usque diem certamina acriter exsequitur"; 8.134 (ibid.): Avita, along with her husband and daughter, "perfecte in honesto certamine decertantes"; 8.135 (ibid.): "virgines, nempe ad decem millia . . . in omni virtutis institutione militant; . . . insignes feminae, et divinum certamen studio exsequentes." Related to theme of women who overcome femininity in spiritual warfare is the description of Asella, 8.133 (ibid.): "mulier longe mitissima"; see also 8.139 (ibid., 1206): "Erat quaedam alia virgo religiosae vitae operibus viriliter insistens." The tradition continues in the Martin literature, with the story of a female hermit: Sulpicius, *Dial.* 1.11 (CSEL 1, pp. 192–93).

98. See McNamara, "Muffled Voices: The Lives of Consecrated Women in the Fourth Century," MRW DE, pp. 23–24.

99. *Vitae patrum* 10.170 (PL 74, pp. 204–5); this story about what "two fathers" discovered is typical: "Die vero quadam aspicimus de longinquo speluncam brevem, ad quam tendentes, cum jam speluncae propinquaremus, cernimus exiguum fontem, et circa fontem herbas modicas, et vestigia hominis; dicebamusque apud nos ipsos: Vere hoc in loco servus Dei est.

Ingressi igitur neminem vidimus; solummodo autem cujusdam vagientis vocem audiebamus. Cum ergo diu quaesissemus, invenimus veluti praesepium, et in eo jacentem quemdam, appropinquantesque servo Dei rogabamus ut loqueretur nobis. Cum vero nihil responderet nobis, tunc accedentes tenuimus eum, et corpus quidem ipsius adhuc erat calidum, anima autem ad Dominum migraverat. Tunc vero agnovimus, quia in ingressu nostro intra speluncam requieverat. Fodimus ergo in ipsa spelunca, unusque ex nobis pallium quo erat indutus, accepit, ut in ipso senis corpus involveret. Sumentes autem illud de loco in quo jacebat, cum ipsum ex more curaremus invenimus esse mulierem, et glorificavimus Deum. Completoque super illud officio, sepelivimus." Ward, *Harlots*, p. 62, gives important historical and theological comments on such stories and the significance they have in understanding gender and sanctity: "The assumption of male dress points to the very practical need for a woman living alone in the desert to protect herself. But there is more to it than that. The way to have a place in the world of early monasticism was to transcend gender differences either by life in a single sex community, or by undertaking a solitary form of life in which it was more prudent, for example in the desert where there were hostile marauders, for a woman to dress as a man. Either way opened the path of return, for men and for women, to the paradisal state of unfallen Adam, or rather, the heaven of the new Adam, where 'there is neither male nor female' (Gal. 3.28). However, an exception to this pattern of withdrawal suggests that a change of dress was neither universal nor fundamental: amma Sarah lived alone by the Nile for sixty years without wearing male attire or joining a convent of nuns. She says that for the first thirteen she had to fight daily against the demon of lust, and it is significant that she dealt with this in exactly the same way as the other hermits; 'she never prayed that the warfare should cease but she said O Lord give me strength for the fight. . . . '

"The idea of 'becoming a man' through undertaking monastic life is connected with the freedom offered women by Christianity itself. Life in the desert, *anachoreisis*, was a practical demonstration of freedom from the limitations and responsibilities of society. It seems that it was very often the wealthy women of the ancient world who were able to take advantage of the desert as an arena of freedom . . . ; and the further stage of freedom was to enter the monastic world of the desert where gender was, by definition, of no significance at all. Prudent and wise, aware of the strength of both sexuality and the pull of the hearth for men and for themselves, these women took care not to present themselves in any way as a female. This has nothing to do with the rejection of femininity; in fact it was an assertion of it; before God, all souls are feminine, and it is this femininity that the women claim, as do the men of the desert."

100. Anson, "Female Transvestite," pp. 1–32, cites the modern studies; see also E. Patlagean, "L'histoire de la femme déguisée en moine et l'évolution de la sainteté féminine à Byzance," *Studi Medievali* 17.3 (1976): 597–623; for the earlier research on this subject, see the references in Graus, *Volk*, p. 130, n. 461.

101. On the textual history and date of composition, see Robert Meyer, trans., *Palladius: The Lausiac History* (London, 1965), pp. 7–15.

102. *Vitae patrum* 8.97 (PL 73, pp. 1198–99): "I thought it necessary to recall in this book the manly and honorable women, to whom God has granted rewards equal to the men who have lived a life according to *virtus*. He has rendered to these women the crown of those who have pleased Him, so that they who are more feeble may not be renounced as frail and effeminate, and seek a pretext as an excuse, like those who are too weak in the struggles for *virtus* and in living an honorable life." Here and in the following passage *virtus* is better left untranslated since both senses of the word seem applicable to the present context. The "power" or "manliness" displayed by leading an ascetic life leads to, or perhaps is, the "moral perfection" known as "virtue."

103. The work appears in PL 74 as part of an appendix to the *Vitae patrum* collection. Rosweyde identified it as part of the *Lausiac History*; see Delehaye, *Work*, p. 19.

104. *Heraclidis paradisus* 28 (PL 74, p. 314): "I think it quite necessary that, for the sake of eternal memory, I devote a page of our book to the women having, as previously mentioned, manly and honorable habits. To these women our God granted struggles and rewards [that are] not inferior to the male sex, so that He may deem unworthy every plea for an excuse from others [who are] negligent. For those who seem [to be] of the inferior sex say that they cannot attain the esteemed glory of *virtus*."

105. *GC* 16 (MGH SRM 1.2, pp. 756–57): "Fuit et Papula valde religiosa, quae cum saepius parentibus flagitaret se in monasterio locari puellarum, eo quod in domo parentum, curis saeculi inpedientibus, Deo servire non possit; et illi prae amore nolent eam a se separari, totondit comam capitis sui, indutaque veste virili, Turonicam diocesim adiens, in congregatione se contulit monachorum; ibique in ieiuniis orationibusque degens, virtutibus deinceps multis emicuit. Erat enim tamquam vir inter viros, nec ulli erat cognitus sexus eius. Parentes autem requerentes eam, numquam repperire potuerunt. Interim abbatem monasterii ad quod venerat defuncto, monachi propter virtutes assiduas hanc elegunt, ignorantes sexum. Quod illa totis viribus rennuit. Triginta autem annos in monasterio fuit, a nullo agnita quid esset. Ante tertium autem diem, quam ab hoc mundo migraret, id monachis patefecit; et sic defuncta, ab aliis mulieribus abluta, sepulta est, multis se deinceps virtutibus manifestans esse ancillam Dei. Nam et frigoritici et aliis morbis obpraessi saepe ad eius tumulum sanitati redduntur." The variant reading for *abbatem*, *abbate*, was followed.

106. Though whether she actually held the position of abbot is, in my view, ambiguous: "monachi . . . hanc elegunt. . . . Quod illa totis viribus rennuit." *Rennuit* may simply refer to her initial unwillingness to hold high office because of her humility but would not necessarily mean that her refusal was final or accepted by the other monks.

107. The story of Papula, in particular, shares several specific features with the account of Eugenia, who also secretly leaves her parents, cuts her hair, wears male attire, and enters a monastery, where she declines to serve as abbot after the community elects her; see *Vita sanctae Eugeniae virginis ac martyris* (PL 73, pp. 606–24); the story is discussed by Nie, "Consciousness," pp. 123–32, who follows Delehaye, *Étude sur le Légendier Romain* (Brussels, 1936), pp. 176, 182, 186, in dating the text before the early sixth century.

108. See Rosemary Rader, "The Martyrdom of Perpetua," in *Women Writers of the Early Church*, ed. Patricia Wilson-Kastner (New York, 1981), p. 3, with Aspegren, *Male Woman*, pp. 133–34. Heffernan, however, argues against this position: "Philology," pp. 321–25.

109. Wemple, "Female Spirituality," pp. 41, 46–48; McNamara, *Sainted Women*, p. 235–36; Schulenburg, "Saints' Lives," p. 290.

110. See McNamara, *Sainted Women*, p. 235.

111. Because there is no agreed-upon edition to use (as noted in the introduction, McNamara and Wemple rely on various editions when discussing the work), I cite McNamara's translation, *Sainted Women*, p. 243, which includes the visions omitted in the MGH text: "the angel of the Lord came to comfort the blessed virgin Aldegund, saying: 'Peace be to you. Be comforted. Act manfully.' " The *Vita*'s conclusion echoes the exhortation found in the vision: "she vanquished the devil's power, overcame the weakness of the female sex, manfully rising above worldly delights."

112. Ibid., pp. 112–13.

113. MGH Ep. Mer. 1, p. 451: " 'Viriliter agite, confortetur cor vestrum' (Ps. 30:25). . . . Quam fortiter et viriliter, si viri fuissetis, pugnature eratis contra inimicos vestros, ne corpus percuteretur, tam constanter et viriliter pugnate contra diabolum, ut non vestras animas occidat per consilia et cogitationes pessimas." Concerning the disputes surrounding the dating of this

text, see the relevant studies cited by McNamara, *Sainted Women*, p. 113. Similar to this passage and to Gregory's preface to Monegund's *Life*, other sources probably dating from around the Merovingian era also characterize female saints as acting *viriliter*: Vita Genovefae virginis Parisiensis 5 (MGH SRM 3, p. 216): "Ait ei [Genovefae] sanctus Germanus: 'Confide, filia, viriliter age . . . ' "; Vita Rusticulae sive Marciae abbatissae Arelatensis 22 (ibid., 4, p. 348): "Septuagesimum septimum agens aetatis suae annum, cum adversum se diabolum iugiter dimicantem Christi iuvamine roborata viriliter triumphare valuisset in terris, ad praemia parata laeta evocatur ad caelos." For similar exhortations in later hagiography, see Bynum, *Holy Feast*, p. 28.

114. Of course, this is not always the case. For an epistolary source that seems consciously to express, largely through extensive citation of biblical texts carefully inserted into her prose, a distinctively female perception, see the letter written by an anonymous nun to an abbess, composed probably between 500–600: MGH Ep. Mer. 1, pp. 716–18 (*Additamentum*). The letter has recently been translated, with an introduction, in the revised edition of Marcelle Thiébaux's *The Writings of Medieval Women: An Anthology* (New York, 1994), pp. 125–33. Riché, *Education*, p. 293, without elaborating, speculates that Baudonivia could have been the author of this anonymous work.

115. Consider, too, the speech attributed to Eugenia, *Vita sanctae Eugeniae* 15 (PL 73, p. 614), in which she seems to justify her preference for living as a man by a scriptural text advocating the equality between men and women (Gal. 3:28): "Tanta enim est virtus nominis ejus, ut etiam feminae in timore ejus positae virilem obtineant dignitatem; et neque ei sexus diversitas fide potest inveniri superior, cum beatus Paulus apostolus, magister omnium Christianorum, dicat quod apud Dominum non sit discretio masculi et feminae, omnes enim in Christo unum sumus (Gal. 3:28). Huius ergo normam animo fervente suscepi, et ex confidentia quam in Christo habui, nolui esse femina, sed virginitatem immaculatem tota animi intentione conservans, virum gessi constanter in Christo. Non enim infrunitam honestatis simulationem assumpsi, ut vir feminam simularem; sed femina viriliter agendo, viro gessi, virginitatem quae in Christo est fortiter amplectendo." Significantly, the speech is given while the saint is dressed as a monk. Immediately following her words, she tears her tunic and appears as a woman. For comments, see Nie, "Consciousness," pp. 126–27.

116. "Sadistic politics": Sheila Delany, *A Legend of Holy Women: A Translation of Osbern Bokenham's Legends of Holy Women* (Notre Dame, 1992), p. xxxiii.

117. See Graus, *Volk*, p. 130, n. 461. Graus also states that the "motif" of the disguised woman eventually disappeared from hagiography but survived in medieval erotic literature.

118. Gregory the Great, *Dial.* 1.4, 1–2 (SC 260, p. 38): "Cumque hac in re ab omnipotente Deo remedium continuis precibus quaereret, nocte quadam adsistente angelo eunuchizari se uidit, eiusque uisioni apparuit quod omnem motum ex genitalibus membris eius abscideret, atque ex eo tempore ita alienus extitit temptatione, ac si sexum non haberet in corpore.

"Qua uirtute fretus ex Dei omnipotentis auxilio, ut uiris ante praeerat, ita coepit postmodum etiam feminis praeesse."

119. The examples offered by Brown, *Body*, pp. 17–25, regarding male, Graeco-Roman attitudes toward sexual intercourse are also relevant here. In particular, Artemidorus's account of an athlete's dream of castration raises the same fundamental issue about gaining power through phallic loss that is found in the description of Equitius: "he dreamed that he cut off his genitals, bound his head and was crowned [as a victor]. . . . As long as he remained a virgin [*aphthoros*], his athletic career was brilliant and distinguished. But once he began to have sexual intercourse, he ended his career ingloriously." Quoted in Brown, *Body*, p. 19; Artemidorous, *Oneirocritica* 5.95, ed. R. A. Pack (Leipzig, 1963) p. 324; R. White, trans., *The Interpretation of Dreams* (Ridge Hill, N.J., 1975), pp. 242–43.

120. Partner addresses the interpretive difficulties of this passage within the context of modern theoretical approaches to the question of gender: "No Sex, No Gender," *Speculum* 68.2 (1993): 419-23.

121. On the revolt, see Scheibelreiter, "Königstöchter im Kloster: Radegund (d. 587) und der Nonnenaufstand von Poitiers (589)," *Mitteilungen des Instituts für österreichische Geschichtsforschung* 87 (1979): 1-37.

122. *LH* 10.15 (*MGH SRM* 1.2, p. 504): "Chrodieldis . . . adserens, eam virum habere in monasterium, qui indutus vestimenta muliebria pro femina haberetur, cum esset vir manifestissime declaratus atque ipsi abbatissae famularetur assiduae, indicans eum digito: 'En ipsum.' Qui cum in veste, ut diximus, muliebri coram omnibus adstetisset, dixit, se nihil opus posse virile agere ideoque sibi hoc indumentum mutasse." Translation relies slightly on Lewis Thorpe, trans., *Gregory of Tours: The History of the Franks* (London, 1974), p. 570.

123. The bishops could have condemned the practice by citing Deut. 22:5: "non induetur mulier veste virili nec vir utetur veste feminea abominabilis enim apud Deum est qui facit haec." There is also some early conciliar evidence prohibiting cross-dressing; see Anson, "Female Transvestite," p. 11.

CHAPTER 5

1. Although exact dates of composition cannot be determined, the first *Life* is thought to have been written shortly after Radegund's death; according to Krusch, *MGH AA* 4.2, pp. xvi–xvii: "Vita Radegundis reginae, quam post mortem sanctae (a. 587) a Fortunato compositam esse certum est." Regarding the second, he proceeds: "Eum scriptorem [i.e., Fortunatus] Vitae illius Baudonivia Pictaviensis monialis, quae iussu 'Dedimiae abbatissae vel omnis congregationis' librum secundum Vitae Radegundis paulo post a. 600 adiecit . . . laudavit." See also idem, *De Vita sanctae Radegundis libri duo* (*MGH SRM* 2, p. 359); idem, *Georgii Florenti Gregorii episcopi Turonensis libri octo miraculorum* (ibid., 1.2, p. 461); Louise Coudanne, "Baudonivie, moniale de Sainte-Croix et biographe de sainte Radegonde," *EM* (Paris, 1953): 45–46; Coudanne believes that the second *Life* was written just after Fortunatus's death to avoid affronting him. On the history of Radegund, with attention given to her *Vitae*, see Aigrain, *Sainte Radegonde* (Paris, 1918). Aigrain's biography is still the standard. Brittain's *Saint Radegund* is also a useful and too often overlooked study of the saint and the hagiographic literature. Jean Aubrun's *Radegonde: Reine, Moniale et Sainte* (Poitiers, 1986) is mainly devotional. Scholarly and devotional is the collection of papers and modern sermons, *La riche personalité de Sainte Radegonde: Conférences et homélies prononcées à Poitiers à l'occasion du XIVe centenaire de sa mort* (587–1987) (Poitiers, 1987). Especially useful on the history of Radegund and her monastery from its origin to the modern era, with recent bibliography, plates, maps, and architectural plans of Sainte-Croix, is the study of Yvonne Labande-Mailfert et al., *Histoire de l'abbaye Sainte-Croix de Poitiers: Quatorze siècles de vie monastique* (Poitiers, 1987). For all the other various studies on Radegund and her Lives, consult the recent and exhaustive bibliography of Affeldt, *Frauen im Frühmittelalter*.

2. See Jean Leclercq, "La Sainte Radegonde de Venace Fortunat et celle de Baudovinie [sic]," in *Fructus Centesimvs: Mélanges offerts à Gerard J. M. Bartelink à l'occasion de son soixante-cinquième anniversaire*, ed. A. A. R. Bastiaensen et al. (Dordrecht, 1989), p. 207.

3. *VR* 2, prol. (*MGH SRM* 2, p. 378): "Non ea quae vir apostolicus Fortunatus episcopus de beatae vita conposuit iteramus, sed ea quae prolixitate praetermisit, sicut ipse in libro suo disseruit, cum diceret: *De beatae virtutibus sufficiat exiguitas, ne fastidiatur ubertas, nec reputetur brevissimum, ubi de paucis agnoscitur amplitudo* [*VR* 1.39]. Ergo, inspirante divina potentia, cui beata Radegundis placere studuit in saeculo et cum quo regnat post saeculum, non polito, sed rustico temptamus de his quae gessit sermone appetere et de multis eius miraculis pauca conplectere." Coudanne,

"Baudonivie," p. 47, contends that here *prolixitate* has the opposite meaning of "prolixity," the word being one of the *véritables contre-sens* (*prolixitate avec le sens de: brièveté*). But no other examples of *contre-sens* occur in Baudonivia's narrative, and the use of the word in this passage does not seem to require an explanation beyond its immediate grammatical context.

4. A similar need gave rise to the second book of Caesarius's *Vita* (MGH SRM 3, pp. 433–501).

5. In the twelfth century, Hildebert, bishop of Le Mans, compiled a life of the saint based entirely on rearranging and polishing the biographies of Fortunatus and Baudonivia; see *AASS* 37, August, vol. 3, p. 84; in his words, "ad Fortunati simul et Baudoniviae sanctimonialis scripta recurri." The thirteenth-century encyclopedist Vincent of Beauvais, although drawing a little from material pertaining to Radegund supplied by Gregory of Tours, gives a sometimes verbatim summary of Fortunatus and Baudonivia: *Speculum quadruplex sive speculum maius*, vol. 4, 21.79, 85–91 (Graz, 1965), pp. 843, 845–47. Relying almost entirely on Vincent's compilation was Antoninus of Florence's fifteenth-century Latin *Chronicle*, a work that, in turn, was heavily used in a Middle English poem perhaps written around 1500 or earlier, probably by Henry Bradshaw (d. 1513): *The Lyfe of Saynt Radegund* (Cambridge, 1926). The poem is edited by Brittain, whose introduction (at pp. xii–xvi) traces the compilations of the *Vitae* beginning with Hildebert. This poem supplements the material of Antoninus with eleven passages drawn from Fortunatus and six from Baudonivia and also adds folkloric material. In general, all the compilers give versions that have rearranged and sometimes drastically summarized but not significantly departed from the original biographies. However, beginning with Hildebert, all the versions insist on Radegund's virginity being intact after her marriage to Clothar and on her abbatial status, a rank that both Lives claim Radegund refused out of humility (Agnes was the appointed abbess). The desire to regard her as an abbess still persists, as the title to McNamara's chapter on Radegund, *Sainted Women*, p. 60, indicates: "Radegund, Queen of the Franks and Abbess of Poitiers." See also Leclercq, "Sainte Radegonde," p. 214.

6. Krusch, "*Prooemivm*" (MGH AA 4.2, p. XVII): "Fortunati liber et Baudoniviae in plerisque codicibus coniuncti sunt, ita ut hic illum ut secundus excipiat." See also Coudanne, "Baudonivie," p. 45.

7. Magdalena Carrasco, "Pictorial Hagiography," p. 52, fig. 2.10, pp. 64–65.

8. Ibid., pp. 64–65; see also Leclercq, "Sainte Radegonde," pp. 207–16; Thiébaux, *The Writings of Medieval Women*, pp. 85–124; Wittern, *Frauen*, pp. 89–107; Schulenburg, "Saints' Lives," pp. 285–320; Marta Cristiani, "La sainteté féminine," pp. 385–434; Sabine Gäbe, "Radegundis: sancta, regina, ancilla. Zum Heiligkeitsideal der Radegundisviten von Fortunat und Baudonivia," *Francia* 16.1 (1989): 1–30; Wemple, *Women*, pp. 181–87; idem, "Female Spirituality," pp. 42–45; McNamara, "Legacy of Miracles," pp. 36–52; idem, *Sainted Women*, pp. 60–65; Etienne Delaruelle, "Sainte Radegonde," pp. 64–74; Graus, *Volk*, pp. 407–11.

9. Schulenburg, "Saints' Lives," pp. 297–301, gives an excellent, clear, and concise overview of the main trends.

10. VR 2.20 (MGH SRM 2, p. 391): "Tu, gemma preciosa, noveris, te in diademate capitis mei primam esse gemmam." Fortunatus relates no visions in his account of Radegund; see appendix.

11. What Carrasco, "Pictorial Hagiography," p. 65, discovered about the two Lives as iconography seems to correspond with what the later compiled versions attempted to achieve, both the visual and the literary interpretations contrasting sharply with what moderns see: "A number of scholars have suggested that the texts of Fortunatus and Baudonivia exemplify differing models of sanctity, conditioned by the point of view of the author: one masculine, the other feminine; one the external perspective of the beneficiary of Radegund's patronage; the other the internal perspective of a member of Radegund's convent. Fortunatus emphasizes Radegund's humility and asceticism; Baudonivia emphasizes her royal status, her political

activity, and her maternal, quasi-clerical role in guiding her convent. The miniatures offer an interpretation of Radegund's personality that essentially fuses these two perspectives into a single image, at once priestly, maternal and ascetic.''

12. Gäbe's article, "Radegundis," pp. 1–30, with its extensive research, is an obvious exception.

13. Limitations noted by Graus, *Volk*, pp. 28–29, 89–90.

14. But Wemple, *Women*, p. 302, n. 405, concedes: "Krusch, of course, treats some male hagiographers similarly.''

15. Krusch, *De vita sanctae Radegundis libri duo* (MGH SRM 2, p. 360): "Stilo mulier admodum rudi utitur: anacolutha atque vocabula barbara abundant, *toti* semper pro *omnes* accepit. Scribere nesciens, quascumque legerat vitas sanctorum spoliavit. Epistulam praemissam fere totam ex verbis Fortunati, quibus in V. Marcelli, Hilarii, Radegundis utitur, composuit. Praeterea Vitam S. Caesarii Arelatensis c. 8. 9. 19. 20. exscripsit. Tamen veniam Baudoniviae probae dabis, imbecillitatem suam confitenti: *parvum*, inquit, *habens intellegentiae eloquium*, et infra: *non polito sed rustico temptamus de his quae gessit sermone appetere.* Later (ibid., pp. 362–63), he complains of the second *Life's* orthography and claims that Baudonivia's writing is worse than that found in Merovingian charters: "in altero vero libro codicem optimum 1a secutus sum, cum, quomodo Baudonivia scripserit, ignoremus, idque solum conici possit, quod monialis linguae Latinae parum gnara ratione scribendi peiore ea, quae in chartis illis Merowingicis deprehenditur, usa sit.'' See also Krusch's remarks in his introduction to Marcellus's *Vita*: MGH AA 4.2, p. xx.

16. Krusch, "Prooemivm" (MGH AA 4.2, p. xvii): "Itaque Pictaviensibus monialibus iam brevi tempore postquam Fortunatus scripsit, eius Vita minime suffecisse videtur, cum Baudoniviae eam iterum tractandam mandarent. Vere multa sunt quae historiam mulieris magis quam poetae miracula commendent.'' In light of this remark, Wemple's criticism of Krusch, "Female Spirituality,'' p. 42, ought to be modified: "Neither Krusch nor later scholars perceived that Baudonivia had a better understanding of the nature of a woman's spiritual experience than had the learned poet.'' Although Krusch does not openly acknowledge the spiritual aspects of Baudonivia's biography (the spiritual quality of the literature itself is generally not of interest to him, regardless of whether the author is male or female), he certainly does regard Baudonivia's account as a better report of Radegund's life. Krusch's first remark obviously indicates that he thought Baudonivia, in spite of whatever linguistic deficiencies he later attributed to her, the better biographer, a fact that Wemple overlooks in her assessment.

17. Aigrain, *L'hagiographie*, p. 302: "la *Vie de sainte Radegonde* présente de si étranges lacunes, que les moniales de Sainte-Croix demandèrent à l'une d'elles, Baudonivie, de les combler''; see Schulenburg, "Saints' Lives,'' p. 298.

18. AASS 37, August, vol. 3, p. 48: "Verum cum utraque haec Vitae pars conscripta sit scabro ac difficili stylo, quem tamen propter venerandam antiquitatem mutare aut mollire non licet, ei subjungemus Acta ejusdem Sanctae, quae venerabilis Hildebertus ex Fortunato et Baudonivia post annum 1197 collegit, alio ordine disposuit, ac plerumque clariore phrasi expressit.''

19. Bonnet, *Latin*, pp. 84–85: "Enfin si l'on est moins frappé de la barbarie du langage chez quelques autres écrivains contemporains—une femme, par exemple, la nonne Baudonivia, quoique postérieure à Grégoire, paraît écrire bien plus correctement que lui—l'une des causes en est peut-être que nous ne lisons pas leurs ouvrages tels qu'ils sont sortis de leurs mains; copistes du IXe siècle et éditeurs du XVIe ont rivalisé pour les dépouiller de ces aspérités qui paraissaient choquantes aux humanistes de la Renaissance et que les critiques de nos jours encore se resolvent si difficilement à rétablir.''

20. Riché, *Education*, p. 293: "Nuns from royal or aristocratic backgrounds were generally more educated. One of them, Baudonivia, author of a *Vita Radegundis*, wrote correct Latin and knew how to draw from hagiographic models.''

21. Wemple, *Women*, p. 181. The only scholar Wemple cites here as having been influenced by Krusch's negative criticism is Graus, *Volk*, p. 409. Yet there is no indication whatsoever that Graus is following Krusch's unfavorable assessment, especially because no mention is ever made of Baudonivia's Latinity, the only aspect of Baudonivia's *Vita* that Krusch viewed unfavorably. All that occurs in this section of *Volk* is a rather balanced and straightforward comparison of the two Lives, neither one being "disparaged." If Krusch did influence Graus's judgment, then it could only have been for his awareness of how Baudonivia stresses aspects of Radegund's character that went unmentioned in Fortunatus's account, such as the second author's emphasis on Radegund as a model nun, concerning which Graus says (at p. 409, n. 636): "Dies fehlt wiederum bei Fortunat," a statement that obviously coincides with Wemple's own view. Furthermore, given the deficiencies Graus finds in Krusch's work throughout the early sections of *Volk*, it is entirely unfounded to claim that he would uncritically follow the latter's position on this or any other matter. It is not Krusch's assessment of Baudonivia but Wemple's inaccurate assessment of the previous research that has actually influenced scholars. Echoing Wemple's remark quoted previously, but again without substantiation, Schulenburg, "Saints' Lives," p. 297, states: "In the past, scholars in general have failed to take seriously the *liber secundus* by Baudonivia. They have frequently dismissed this *vita* as an invalid or unauthoritative source or have viewed it as merely a complementary text, a simple appendix or addition to the primary *vita* by Fortunatus. . . . The lack of interest in Baudonivia as an early hagiographer and the devaluation of her *vita* as an authoritative text seem also to have been predicated, at least in part, on Baudonivia's position as female author." In turn, citing Schulenburg "zur wissenschaftlichen Unterbewertung" of Baudonivia's *Life* is Wittern, *Frauen*, p. 171.

22. Goyau, *Christianisme et culture féminine*, pp. 38–39: "Baudonivie est une figure unique, et nous montre, sous un nouvel aspect, la culture féminine au VIe siècle. . . . Elle donne une voix, voix pure, humble, charmante, au silence du cloître. Elle lui donne une expression." In perhaps one of the highest tributes that she thought could be given to the second *Life*, Goyau compares Baudonivia's portrait of Radegund to the fourteenth-century *Little Flowers of Saint Francis*: "Baudonivie nous a laissé, sur la vie de Radegonde, un chef-d'oeuvre littéraire qui mériterait d'être aussi connu que les *Fioretti*. Ce sont, en réalité, des *Fioretti* du VIe siècle que l'on doit à l'aimable religieuse poitevine."

23. Wemple, *Women*, p. 183; idem, "Female Spirituality," pp. 42–49; McNamara, *Sainted Women*, pp. 8–9.

24. *VR* 2, prol. (MGH SRM 2, pp. 377–78): "*Iniungitis mihi opus agere non minus inpossibile, quam sit digito caelum tangere*, ut de vita sanctae dominae Radegundis, quam obtime nostis, aliquid dicere praesumamus. *Sed istud illis debetur iniungi, qui habentes intra se fontem eloquentiae. Unde quicquid illis iniungitur, carmine irriguo copiosius explicatur. Verum aecontra, quicumque angustae intellegentiae sunt nec habent affluentiam eloquii, per quam vel alios reficere vel suae siccitatis possint inopiam temperare, tales non solum per se aliquid dicere* [non] *appetunt, verum etiam, si quid eis iniunctum fuerit, pertimescunt.* Quod in me hoc recognosco, quae sum pusillanimis, parvum habens intellegentiae eloquium, *quoniam, quantum doctis proloqui, tantum indoctis utile fit tacere. Nam illi de parvis magna disserere, isti de magnis nesciunt vel parva proferre; et ideo quod ab aliis quaeritur, ab aliis formidatur.* Cum sim ego minima omnium minimarum, quam *ab ipsis cunabulis ante sua vestigia peculiarem vernulam familiariter enutrivit, ut inpensi muneris de eius claro opere, etsi non plene, vel ex parte conplexa perstringerem, quatenus, dum sui gregis auribus eius gloriosae vitae praeconia, etsi non digno,* devoto tamen eloquio, benignissimae vestrae voluntati oboediens pareo, vestra me oratione iuvari peto, quae sum minus docta, plus devota." As presented in Krusch's edition, the italicized texts (appearing within quotation marks in this translation) indicate borrowings from Fortunatus's Lives of Hilary and Marcellus.

25. Later in the *Life*, Baudonivia also relies heavily on Caesarius's *Rule* and *Vita*; see William Klingshirn, "Caesarius' Monastery for Women in Arles and the Composition and Function

of the *Vita Caesarii*," *Revue Bénédictine* 100 (1990): 474–80; McNamara, *Sainted Women*, p. 90, n. 94.

26. Although not nearly as bombastic as Fortunatus, Gregory also stresses his inadequacies as a writer throughout the *LVP*: pref. (ibid., 1.2, p. 663); 2, pref. (ibid., pp. 668–69); 8, pref. (ibid., p. 691); 9, pref. (ibid., p. 702); on the humility topos in Gregory's prefaces, see Tore Janson, *Latin Prose Prefaces: Studies in Literary Conventions* (Stockholm, 1964), pp. 162–67; on this convention in early hagiographic literature, see Strunk, *Kunst und Glaube*, pp. 52–53, 74–76; on the humility topos in general, see Ernst Curtius, *European Literature and the Latin Middle Ages*, trans. Willard R. Trask (New York, 1953), pp. 407–13.

27. See Brennan, "St. Radegund," p. 343.

28. E. Jane Burns, *Bodytalk: When Women Speak in Old French Literature* (Philadelphia, 1993), pp. 16–17.

29. See the excellent discussion of McCready, *Signs*, pp. 155–74, who also cites the relevant studies.

30. *VR* 2.7–8 (MGH SRM 2, pp. 382–83): "Although merciful to others, she cast judgement on herself; dutiful to others, she treated herself harshly with abstinence; generous to others, she was tight with herself, so that, made drunk with fasting, she would not be satisfied unless she triumphed over her body.

Completely occupied in these pursuits, as was made known in the first book, she immediately deserved to be free for God alone. However, at this time she was covered with stronger arms, disposed without ceasing to prayers, vigils and reading."

31. A phrase echoing Fortunatus's *Vita sancti Germanii* 76 (MGH AA 4.2, 27): "superato corpore de se triumphatum in pace . . . adquireret."

32. This is the opinion given by Collins, "Observations," p. 111, with respect to the Latin syntax of Fortunatus. I consider it applicable to the context in which Baudonivia uses the word, particularly because of *tamen*'s proximity to the comparative adjective *fortioribus*. However, not all are in agreement with Collins; for other considerations on the use of *tamen* in this period, see Bonnet, *Latin*, p. 316; A. Meneghetti, "La Latinità di Venanzio Fortunato," *Didaskaleion: Studi Filologici di Letteratura Christiana Antica* 6 (1917): 80.

33. Leclercq, "Sainte Radegonde," p. 210: "Cette auto-torture est un martyre délibéré."

34. The role of reading is discussed later in this section.

35. *VR* 2.21 (MGH SRM 2, p. 392): "Ubi iam ad finem vitae venit sanctum eius corpusculum, longum trahens martyrium pro amore Domini"; see Nie, "Consciousness," p. 149.

36. *VR* 2.8 (ibid., p. 383): "peregrinis ipsa cibos ministravit ad mensam, ipsa suis manibus lavit et tersit infirmantum vestigia. Non famulae permisit sibi dare solatium, quod devota concursitabat inplere sevitium; se autem in tam ardua abstinentiae districtione conclusit, usquequo infirmitas permisit, ut mens intenta Deo terrenum iam nec requireret cibum"; compare Sulpicius, *VM* 2.5–6 (CSEL 1, p. 112): "uno tantum seruo comite [Martinus] contentus, cui tamen uersa uice dominus seruiebat, adeo ut plerumque ei et calciamenta ipse detraheret et ipse detergeret, cibum una caperent, hic tamen saepius ministraret."

37. *VR* 1.17 (MGH SRM 2, p. 370): "Hinc tribus ferculis inlatis, farcitis deliciis, stans ante prandentes ieiuna, praesens conviviis, ipsa incidebat panem, carnem, quidquid adponeret. Languidis autem et caecis non cessabat ipsa cibos cum cocleare porrigere, hoc praesentibus duabus, sed se sola serviente, ut nova Martha satageret, donec potulenti fratres laeti fierent conviviis."

38. *VR* 1.23, 24 (ibid., p. 372): "ferens foetores stercoris"; "sola ferebat in sarcina. Aquam de puteo trahebat et dispensabat per vascula. Holus purgans, legumen lavans, flatu focum vivificans, et ut decoqueret escas, satagebat exaestuans, vasa de foco ipsa lavans, discos lavans et inferens. Hinc, consummatis conviviis, ipsa vascula diluens, purgans nitide coquina, quidquid erat lutulentum, ferebat ima purgamina."

39. As is indicated from the fact that she exchanges hair shirts with a holy man: VR 2.4 (ibid., p. 381).

40. VR 2.4, 7 (ibid., pp. 380–81, 382).

41. There is no need to cite the studies stressing this point because, to a varying degree, everyone from Goyau to Graus calls attention to her royal status. I believe this aspect has been tremendously overemphasized.

42. Bernoulli, *Die Heiligen*, p. vii. Delehaye, of course, embraced a similar view about hagiography in general, but, unlike Bernoulli, he seems to regard the "popular imagination" with contempt. According to Graus, *Volk*, pp. 26–37, the romantic view of hagiography was useful for Catholic scholars. With the literature as a product of the masses, the role of clerics (i.e., those who officially represented the church as opposed to, in Delehaye's words, "the aggregate" lacking "keen intelligence or an enlightened morality") in hagiographic production could be reduced to mere editors who preserved the entertaining tales told by ignorant people; see *Legends*, pp. 16–39, 49–59. In the face of Protestant criticism that pointed to saints' Lives as evidence of priestly deception, the romantic view of hagiography was thus apologetically expedient for Catholic researchers.

43. E.g.: *Vita sanctae Balthildis* 2, 11 (MGH SRM 2, pp. 484, 496); *Vita sancti Arnulfi* 8, 21 (ibid., pp. 435, 441); *Vita Elegii episcopi* 1 (ibid. 4, pp. 664, 669); *Vita sanctae Mahthildis* 5 (MGH SS 4, p. 286); *Vita sanctae Segolenae* 15, ed. J. Mabillon, *Acta santorum ordinis sancti Benedicti*, vol. 3.2 (Paris, 1688–1701), p. 545. On the similarities between Mahthildis's Life and Fortunatus's *Life of Saint Radegund*, see Auerbach, *Literary Language*, pp. 157–59; Graus, *Volk*, pp. 410–11; ibid., p. 479, for a textual comparison of the Lives of Segolena and Radegund. Significantly, of the four Lives that would exercise the greatest influence on the hagiography of the "Belgian cycles," Van der Essen, *Étude critique*, p. 436, lists Fortunatus's *Life of Saint Radegund* and two of the other Lives mentioned here that also relied on his narrative: "En comparant les cycles des divers diocèses entre eux, on peut constater que quatre *Vitae* anciennes ont exercé une assez grande influence sur l'esprit des hagiographes, qui se sont empressés de plagier ces modèles au point de vue du style et de la composition. Ce sont les *Vitae Radegundis, Arnulfi, Eligii*, et la *Vita Richarii* d'Alcuin"; also claiming that Fortunatus's account became a model for other *Vitae* is Eileen Conheady, "The Saints of the Merovingian Dynasty: A Study of Merovingian Kingship" (Ph.D. diss., University of Chicago, 1967), p. 39.

44. *Vita sancti Arnulfi* 8 (MGH SRM 2, p. 435): "Porro abstinenciae illius normam narrare quis valeat, vel maxime cum interdum post triduana seu amplius protracta ieiunia panem ordeacio seu limphae poculo victitaret. Indutus namque iugiter intrinsecus tonice occulte cilicio sicqui exesis iam membris vigilis adque ieiuniis geminum ingerebat cruciatum" (compare VR 1.15, 20); again at 21 (ibid., p. 441): "spretis dumtacxat mollibus et preciosis vestibus, cilicio exornabat" (compare VR 1.22); *Vitae sanctae Balthildis* 11 (ibid., p. 496): "Ita humilitatis magnae fortiter exhibebat exemplum, ut ipsa quoque in quoquina ministraret sororibus et munditias vilissimas, etiam deambulationes stercorum, ipsa mundaret" (compare VR 1.24); on this aspect of Balthild's Life, Krusch, *Vita sanctae Balthildis* (ibid., p. 478), states: "Sanctae pia servitia describenti Radegundis, cuius 'actus' c. 18. citantur, Vita a Fortunato composita ei ante oculos fuisse videtur."

45. *Vita sanctae Balthildis* 2 (ibid., p. 484): "honore congruo ministrans senioribus, ita ut de earum pedibus calciamenta detraheret et ipsa tergeret ac dilueret, aquam quoque ad lavandum afferret et vestimenta earum festinanter pararet" (compare VR 1.23); *Vita sancti Arnulfi* 21 (ibid., p. 441): "Adscitis quippe aliquantulis secum monaculis necnon et leprosis, sub quibus manibus propriis fidelissimam servitutem iugiter inpendebat, calciamenta a pedibus detraens adque detergens, capita et pedes illorum crebrius abluens" (compare VR 1.23, 17, 24.); *Vita Elegii episcopi*, pref., (ibid., 4, p. 664): "enarrare temptabo eiusque vitae cursum, licet sermone inculto, ingenti tamen amoris obtentu ferre conabor in publicum" (compare VR 1, prol.).

46. As suggested by Aigrain, *Sainte Radegonde*, p. 160.

47. Significantly, Baudonivia sometimes feminizes words, *VR* 2.16 (*MGH SRM* 2, p. 389): "povitrix obtima, gubernatrix bona"; perhaps a counter to Fortunatus's *tortrix*.

48. *VR* 2.8 (ibid., p. 383): "De abstinentiae rigore vel servitii anterior liber multa docuit. In tantum enim se propter Deum pauperem fecit, ut ceteris exemplum praeberet. Manicam, quam brachio indueret, non habebat, nisi de caliga sua sibi duas fecit manicas; sed ita se pauperem tractabat, ut hoc nec abbatissa sentiret. *Quis enim eius pacientiam, quis caritatem, quis fervorem spiritus, quis discretionem, quis benignitatem, quis zelum sanctum, quis iugem meditationem die noctuque in lege Domine poterit explicare? Qui cum a meditatione salmorum aut praedicatione cessare videretur, lectrix ante eam una monacharum legere non desistebat* (*Vita Caesarii*, 1.24). In tantum de corde vel ore illius Dei laus non discedebat, ut, cum quadam vice vidisset postitiariam monasterii transeuntem nomine Eodegundem, ubi eam voluit appellare, pro eius nomine 'alleluia' clamavit. Hoc milies fecit, numquam de ore illius detractio, numquam mendatium, numquam maledictum contra qualemcumque personam processit; et non solum non detraxit cuiquam, sed nec detrahentem patienter audivit."

49. *VR* 2.8 (ibid., p. 383): "Pro persequentibus se semper oravit et orare docuit. Congregationem, quam in nomine Domini plena Dei desiderio congregavit, in tantumque dilexit, ut etiam parentes vel regem coniugem se habuisse nec reminisceretur. Quod frequenter nobis dum praedicaret, dicebat: 'Vos elegi filias, vos, mea lumina, vos, mea vita, vos, mea requies totaque felicitas, vos, novella plantatio. Agite mecum in hoc saeculo, unde gaudeamus in futuro. Plena fide plenoque cordis affectu serviamus Domino; in timore, in simplicitate cordis quaeramus eum, ut cum fidutia ei dicere possimus: "Da, Domine, quod promisisti, quia fecimus quod iussisti." ' "

50. See Leclerq, "Sainte Radegonde," p. 216. Given the difference between the two Lives in the amount of direct speech inserted into the narratives, Nelson's position, "Women and the Word," p. 66, at least in light of Radegund's *Vitae*, may overlook the significance of dialogue: "In the Lives of women saints, direct speech crops up very frequently. . . . It is significant that such articulate women could be depicted for a milieu and where the stereotype of feminine silence already had a secure place. But here genre has triumphed over gender: direct speech and lively dialogue are characteristic of *Vitae*." Yet extensive "direct speech" is not characteristic of Fortunatus's *Life of Saint Radegund*.

51. Brennan, "Career," pp. 67–68: "The nuns emerge as the patrons of the poet, who see to it that he is well supplied with mountains of food (11.9) and a milk delicacy that Agnes has prepared for him with her own hands (11.14–15). Meat and vegetables arrive on silver plate and marble dishes, and chicken in a glass salver (11.10.3–8). The poet is supplied with dinners at which he and his companions nearly swim in wine (11.23.5–10)." On the enclosed monastic life of women at this time, see Schulenburg, "Strict Active Enclosure and Its Effects on the Female Monastic Experience, 500–1100," *MRW DE*, pp. 51–86.

52. See Nie, "Consciousness," pp. 148–49.

53. See McNamara, "Ordeal," pp. 293–326. In addition to the monastic rule, there is also the model of Martin's sanctity, with that saint doing similar humble chores for his religious companion: *VM* 2.5–6 (*CSEL* 1, p. 112); Fontaine, "Hagiographie et politique," pp. 114–15, 136–37, stresses the influence of the Martinian ideal of sanctity on both Lives of Radegund.

54. The rule of Caesarius, which Radegund's convent followed, required all nuns to read for two hours every day; *Règle des vierges* 18, 19, in *Césaire d'Arles. Oeuvres monastiques*, vol. 1: *Oeuvres pour les moniales*, ed. Adalbert de Vogüé and Joel Courreau (SC 345, p. 192): "Omnes litteras discant. Omni tempore duabus horis, hoc est a mane usque ad horam secundam lectioni uacent." On reading and Caesarius's rule, see Mary McCarthy, *The Rule for Nuns of St. Caesarius of Arles: A Translation with a Critical Introduction* (Washington, D.C., 1960), pp. 25, 85, 136–37; see also Riché, "Sainte Radegonde et le monachisme féminin de son temps," in *La riche personalité*

de Sainte Radegonde (Poitiers, 1988), p. 27; Aigrain, *Sainte Radegonde*, p. 115; Brittain, *Saint Radegund*, p. 23. It should also be noted that, although in his *Vita Radegundis* Fortunatus does not emphasize the role reading played in the saint's life, he does mention in his poetry that she read the Greek and Latin Fathers: car. 8.1 (MGH AA 4.1, pp. 53–56).

55. VR 2.9 (MGH SRM 2, pp. 383–84): "Undecumque servus Dei venisset, sollicite percontabatur, qualiter Domino serviret. Si quid novi ab eo agnovisset, quod ipsa non faceret, continuo cum omni alacritate sibi prius inposuit; post congregationem tam verbo docuit, quam exemplo ostendit. Cum ante eam vicibus psalmus cessasset lectio numquam discessit, non die, non nocte, non dum vel paululum corpus suum refecit. Cum lectio legebatur, illa sollicitudine pia animarum nostrarum curam gerens, dicebat: 'Si non intellegitis quod legitur, quid est, quod non sollicite requiritis speculum animarum vestrarum?' Quod etsi minus pro reverentia interrogare praesumebatur, illa pia sollicitudine maternoque affectu, quod lectio continebat, ad animae salutem praedicare non cessabat. . . . Et dum nocte quasi vel unius horae spatium videretur somnum carpere, semper lectio legebatur. Quae legebat, in se somni marcorem sentiens, putabat, eam iam paululum requiescere. Ubi a lectione cessasset mens intenta ad Christum, tamquam si diceret: *Ego dormio, et cor meum vigilat*, aiebat; 'Quare taces? Lege, ne cesses.' "

56. Although scholars generally acknowledge the liturgical function of hagiographic material, researchers who study the Lives rarely indicate how complex and even confusing this issue is; see Catherine Dunn, *The Gallican Saint's Life and the Late Roman Dramatic Tradition* (Washington, D.C., 1989), pp. 17–34, 73–101; Hen, *Culture*, pp. 80–120.

57. On the distinction between *legentes* and *audientes* in Merovingian hagiography, see Collins, "Observations," p. 107.

58. VR 2, pref., (MGH SRM 2, p. 377): "Dominabus sanctis meritorum gratia decoratis Dedimiae abbatissae vel omni congregationi gloriosi dominae Radegundis Baudonivia humilis omnium."

59. Burns, *Bodytalk*, p. 1.

60. VR 1, pref., (MGH SRM 2, pp. 364–65): "In quo est pariter numero illa, cuius vitae praesentis cursum, licet tam privato sermone, ferre temptamus in publico, ut, cuius est vita cum Christo, memoria gloriae relicta celebretur in mundo."

61. See Fontaine, "Hagiographie et politique," p. 132; Schulenburg, "Saints' Lives," pp. 299–300.

62. Perhaps some of Fortunatus's poems could also have served a similar function; see Brennan's comments, "Deathless Marriage," p. 95, regarding Fortunatus's *De virginitate* as "a mirror of nuns."

63. McCarthy, *Rule for Nuns*, pp. 76–79, 195–96, n. 48, rightly stresses that the readings "were drawn from the various books of Scripture and from the Acts of the Martyrs." However, Baudonivia's own text indicates that contemporary hagiographic material was also being read and studied. Furthermore, Krusch notes, MGH AA 4.2, pp. xx, that Fortunatus's *Life of Marcellus*, on which Baudonivia relied, was likely in the monastic convent at Sainte-Croix. His opinion is based on the poem Fortunatus appended to Marcellus's *Vita*, which the poet addressed to Radegund: "hinc tibi nunc absens Marcelli munera misi, / cui dedit excelsum vita beata locum, / et si displiceant indigno verba relatu, / conplaceant animo signa superna tuo." Krusch then gives the following comment: "Libellum a Radegunde in bibliotheca monasterii S. Crucis Pictaviensis collocatum paulo post Baudonivia legit."

64. For comments on the passage in the context of maternal sanctity, see Nie, "Consciousness," p. 147.

65. On Radegund's role as provider, see McNamara, "A Legacy of Miracles," pp. 36–52.

66. Sulpicius relates a series of attacks against pagans, Martin even being spurred on by angels who appear to him in military attire: VM 13–14 (CSEL 1, pp. 122–24).

67. *VR* 2.2 (*MGH SRM* 2, p. 380): "dum iter ageret, saeculari pompa se comitante, interiecta longinquitate terrae ac spatio, fanus, qui a Francis colebatur, in itinere beatae reginae quantum miliario uno proximus erat. Hoc illa audiens, ibi a Francis fanum coli, iussit famulis fanum igni conburi, iniquum iudicans, Deum caeli contempni et diabolica machinamenta venerari. Hoc audientes Franci universaque multitudo cum gladiis et fustibus vel omni fremitu diabolico conabantur defendere; sancta vero regina inmobilis perseverans, Christum in pectore gestans, equum quem sedebat in antea non movit, antequam et fanus perureretur." Wemple never discusses this episode; McNamara mentions it briefly in a sentence: "Living Sermons: Consecrated Women and the Conversion of Gaul," *MRW PW*, p. 21.

68. The punitive miracles are also especially prominent in the later *virtutes* attributed to Radegund: Bodenstaff, "Miracles de Sainte Radegonde," pp. 433–77.

69. *VR* 2.12 (*MGH SRM* 2, pp. 385–86): "Vinoberga una ex eius fuit famulabus, qui ausu temerario in cathedra beatae reginae post eius discessum sedere praesumpsit. Quo facto, iudicio Dei percussa, sic ardebat, ut viderent omnes fumum de ea in altum procedere, et illa coram omni populo proclamaret, confitens se peccasse; propterea arderet, quia in beatae sede consederat. Tribus diebus et tribus noctibus unum incendium passa, vociferans clamabat: 'Domina Radegundis, peccavi, male egi, indulge, refrigera membra duro cruciatu exusta. . . .' In tanta poena ipsam omnis populus videns, pro ea precabatur, tamquam si praesens esset, dicens, quia, ubicumque ex fide invocatur, adest: 'Domina bona, parce ei, ne tanto cruciatu infelix deficiat. Sic beatissima ad preces omnium benigne indulgit, ignem ferventem conpescuit." Wemple, "Female Spirituality," p. 44, comments briefly on this passage: "An extension of Radegund's role as mother was her function as *domina*, which she discharged with strictness and kindness even after her death." In fact, it is not maternal at all but is the standard punitive miracle previously observed in Fortunatus's *Vitae* and represented throughout hagiography. McNamara, *Sainted Women*, p. 94, offers a less positive assessment: "This story and the events surrounding the revolt of 589 in the nunnery provide depressing evidence that the monastic ideal of social equality was not observed at Poitiers."

70. The discussion of Hope Mayo highlights some of the problems raised by the similarities in the *regulae* of men and women: "The Sources of Female Monasticism in Merovingian Gaul," *SP* 16, ed. Elizabeth Livingstone (Berlin, 1985), pp. 32–37.

71. *VR* 2.10 (*MGH SRM* 2, p. 384).

72. *VR* 2.16 (ibid., p. 389): "Non minorem iniuriam est passa sancta crux per invidiam, quam Dominus, qui . . . vocatus et revocatus ante praesides et iudices, omnem maliciam pacienter sustinuit, ut quod creaverat ne periret."

73. *VR* 1.17 (*MGH SRM* 2, p. 370): "sed se sola serviente, ut nova Martha satageret"; see Brennan, "St. Radegund," p. 347; Nie, "Consciousness," p. 145, who also notes (at p. 105) that in his poetry Fortunatus compared Radegund to Mary of Bethany (or, possibly, Mary Magdalene) and several other prominent holy women of early Christianity.

74. Gregory the Great, *Homiliae in Hiezechihelem prophetam* 1.3.9 (*CCSL* 142, p. 37): "Quod bene in Euangelio duae illae mulieres designant, Martha scilicet et Maria. *Martha etenim satagebat circa frequens ministerium; Maria autem sedebat ad pedes Domini, et uerba eius audiebat* (Luke 10:40). Erat ergo una intenta operi, altera contemplationi. Vna actiuae seruiebat per exterius ministerium, altera contemplatiuae per suspensionem cordis in uerbum."

75. *VR* 2.10 (*MGH SRM* 2, p. 385): "Pedes omnium manibus propriis lavans, savano tergens et osculans, et, si permissum fuisset, ad similitudinem Mariae fusis crinibus extergere non renitebat."

76. Luke 10:40: "Martha autem satagebat circa frequens ministerium". On the conflation of biblical women named Mary, see Nie, "Consciousness," p. 137.

77. Luke 10:41–42: "et respondens dixit illi Dominus Martha Martha sollicita es et turbaris erga plurima porro unum est necessarium Maria optimam partem elegit quae non auferetur

ab ea"; Gregory the Great, *Homiliae* 1.3.9 (CCSL 142, pp. 37–38), comments: "Et quamuis actiua bona sit, melior tamen est contemplatiua, quia ista cum mortali uita deficit, illa uero in immortali uita plenius excrescit."

CHAPTER 6

1. Hen, *Culture*, pp. 192–93, also notes the influence of Martin's *Vita* on this episode; his argument that the evidence of literary borrowing renders the account historically unreliable, along with his suggestion that the *fanum* could have been a "local pub," is unconvincing.

2. *Vita Rusticula*, pref. (MGH SRM 4, p. 339); the author identifies himself in the dedication as "Florentius Presbyter."

3. *Vita sanctae Balthildis* 3 (MGH SRM 2, p. 484).

4. *Legends*, pp. 25–26.

5. In addition, we can wonder what criteria could be established to determine which of the surviving "anonymous hymns," also mentioned in Wemple's comment, are the products of female composers.

6. See Fontaine, *Vie* 2 (SC 133, p. 188), who describes hagiography as "la cristallisation littéraire des perceptions d'une conscience collective."

7. Virginia Woolf, *A Room of One's Own* (1929; reprint London, 1959), p. 69.

8. See Partner's "Introduction" to "Studying Medieval Women: Sex, Gender, Feminism," *Speculum* 68.2 (1993): 305–6.

9. Van Uytfanghe, *Stylisation biblique*, p. 191, referring to Radegund, Balthild, Gertrude, and Rusticula, observes, "l'hagiographie mérovingienne a mis en scène des femmes qui, en dépit de leur place subordonnée dans la hiérarchie ecclésiale, s'étaient acquis une stature spirituelle et sociale considérable dans l'Eglise et la société de leur temps. Du moins en tant que *saintes* à vénérer et à imiter, elles se trouvaient sur un pied d'égalité avec les saints masculins."

10. Unfortunately, Waldron's thorough study, "Expressions of Religious Conversion among Laymen Remaining within Secular Society in Gaul: 400–800 A.D.," in which the main sources that document lay religious life are painstakingly collected and analyzed, has been neglected by all but a few scholars studying the religious milieu of late antique Gaul.

BIBLIOGRAPHY

PRIMARY SOURCES

Ambrose. *De Cain et Abel*. Ed. Charles Schenkl. CSEL 32.1, pp. 22–409. Vienna, 1896.
Ambrosiasti qvi dicitvr commentarivs in epistvlas Paulinas (Ambrosiaster). Ed. Henry Vogels. 3 vols. CSEL 81.1–3. Vienna, 1966–69.
Artemidorous. *Oneirocritica*. Ed. R. A. Pack. Leipzig, 1963.
Athanasius. *Vita b. Antonii abbatis* (Latin version by Evagrius). PL 73, pp. 126–94.
Augustine. *De civitate Dei*. Ed. Bernard Dombart and Alphonse Kalb. 2 vols. CCSL 47–48. Turnhout, 1955.
———. *De doctrina christiana*. Ed. William Green. CSEL 80. Vienna, 1963.
———. *Qvestionvm in Heptatevchvm libri VII*. Ed. I. Fraipont. CCSL 33. Turnhout, 1958.
Baudonivia. *Vita sanctae Radegundis*. Ed. Bruno Krusch. MGH SRM 2, pp. 377–95. Hannover, 1888.
Bea, Augustino, ed. *Liber Ecclesiastae qui ab Hebraeis appelatur Qohelet. Nova e textu primigenio interpretatio Latina cum notis criticis et exegeticis edita curis*. Rome, 1950.
Bede. *Vita sancti Cuthberti*. Ed. and trans. Bertram Colgrave. In *Two Lives of Saint Cuthbert: A Life by an Anonymous Monk of Lindisfarne and Bede's Prose Life*. Cambridge, 1940.
Bradshaw, Henry. *The Lyfe of Saynt Radegund*. Ed. F. Brittain. Cambridge, 1926.
Caesaria II, Abbess of Saint Jean of Arles. "*Dominabus sanctis Richilde et Radegundi Caesaria exigua*." Ed. W. Gundlach. MGH Ep. Mer. 1, pp. 450–53. Berlin, 1892.
Caesarius of Arles. *Césaire d'Arles. Oeuvres monastiques*, vol. 1: *Oeuvres pour les moniales*. Ed. Adalbert de Vogüé and Joel Courreau. SC 345. Paris, 1988.
———. *Sermones*. 2 vols. Ed. G. Morin. CCSL 103–4. Turnhout, 1953.
———. *Césaire d'Arles: sermons au peuple*. 3 vols. Ed. M.-J. Delage. SC 175, 243, 330. Paris, 1971.
Colgrave, Bertram, ed. and trans. *The Earliest Life of Gregory the Great*. Laurence, Kans., 1968.
Concilia Galliae a. 314–a. 506. Ed. C. Munier. CCSL 148. Turnhout, 1963.
Concilia Galliae a. 511–a. 695. Ed. Carlo de Clerq. CCSL 148A. Turnhout, 1963.

Cyprian. *Epistulae*. PL 4, pp. 193–438.

De virtutibus s. Geretrudis. Ed. Bruno Krusch. MGH SRM 2, pp. 464–71. Hannover, 1888.

Florentius. *Vita Rusticula sive Marciae abbatissae Arelatensis*. Ed. Bruno Krusch. MGH SRM 4, pp. 339–51. Hannover, 1902.

Fortunatus, Venantius. *Liber de virtutibus sancti Hilarii*. Ed. Bruno Krusch. MGH AA 4.2, pp. 7–11. Berlin, 1877.

———. *Opera poetica*. Ed. F. Leo. MGH AA 4.1, pp. 1–270. Berlin, 1881.

———. *Vita sanctae Radegundis*. Ed. Bruno Krusch. MGH AA 4.2, pp. 38–49. Berlin, 1877.

———. *Vita sancti Albini*. Ed. Bruno Krusch. MGH AA 4.2, pp. 27–33. Berlin, 1877.

———. *Vita sancti Germanii*. Ed. Bruno Krusch. MGH AA 4.2, pp. 11–27. Rev. ed., MGH SRM 7.1, pp. 372–418. Hannover, 1919.

———. *Vita sancti Hilarii*. Ed. Bruno Krusch. MGH AA 4.2, pp. 1–7. Berlin, 1877.

———. *Vita sancti Marcelli*. Ed. Bruno Krusch. MGH AA 4.2, pp. 49–54. Berlin, 1877.

———. *Vita sancti Martini*. In *Opera poetica*. Ed. F. Leo. MGH AA 4.1, pp. 293–370. Berlin, 1881.

———. *Vita sancti Paterni*. Ed. Bruno Krusch. MGH AA 4.2, pp. 33–37. Berlin, 1877.

———. *Vita Severini*. Ed. Wilhelm Levison. MGH SRM 7.1, pp. 206–24. Hannover, 1840

Gebhardt, Oskar Leopld von, ed. *Die Lateinisch Übersetzungen der Acta Pauli et Theclae*. TU, NF 7.2. Leipzig, 1902.

Ghesquière, Joseph. *Acta sanctorum Belgii selecta*. 6 vols. Brussels, 1783–1794.

Gregory the Great. *Dialogorum libri quatuor de miraculis patrum Italicorum*. Ed. Adalbert de Vogüé. SC 251, 260, 265. Paris, 1978–1980.

———. *Homiliae in Heizechihelem prophetam*. Ed. M. Adriaen. CCSL 142. Turnhout, 1971.

Gregory of Tours. *De miraculis beati Andreae apostoli*. Ed. Max Bonnet. MGH SRM 1.2, pp. 821–46. Hannover, 1885.

———. *De passione et virtutibus sancti Iuliani martyris*. Ed. Bruno Krusch. MGH SRM 1.2, pp. 562–84. Hannover, 1885.

———. *De virtutibus sancti Martini episcopi*. Ed. Bruno Krusch. MGH SRM 1.2, pp. 584–661. Hannover, 1885.

———. *Liber in gloria confessorum*. Ed. Bruno Krusch. MGH SRM 1.2, pp. 744–820. Hannover, 1885.

———. *Liber in gloria martyrum*. Ed. Bruno Krusch. MGH SRM 1.2, pp. 484–561. Hannover, 1885.

———. *Liber vitae patrum*. Ed. Bruno Krusch. MGH SRM 1.2, pp. 661–744. Hannover, 1885.

———. *Libri historiarum X*. Ed. Bruno Krusch and Wilhelm Levison. MGH SRM 1.1, rev. ed. Hannover, 1951.

———. *Passio sanctorum martyrum septem dormientium apud Ephesum*. Ed. Bruno Krusch. MGH SRM 1.2, pp. 847–53. Hannover, 1885.

Gundlach, W., ed. *Quaedam sanctimonialis laudata respondens ipsa quoque laudibus effert quandam abbatissam, ut videtur, illustri genere natam atque rogat, ut crebo sibi erudiendae scribat* (500–600). MGH Ep. Mer. 1 (anonymous letter in *Additamentum*), pp. 716–18. Berlin, 1892.

Hennecke, E. *New Testament Apocrypha*. Ed. W. Schneemelcher. Trans. R. Wilson. 2 vols. London, 1963–1965.

Heraclidis paradisus (Appendix ad vitas patrum). PL 74, pp. 243–342.

Hilary of Arles. *Versus in natali Machabaeorum martyrum*. PL 50, pp. 1276–86.

Hildebert of Le Mans. *Vita sanctae Radegundis*. AASS 37, August, vol. 3, pp. 83–92.

James, Montague. *The Apocryphal New Testament*. Oxford, 1924.

Jerome. *Commentarivs in Ecclesiasten*. ed. Marc Adriaen. CCSL 72, pp. 247–361. Turnhout, 1959.

———. *Translatio Latina regulae sancti Pachomii*. PL 23, pp. 62–82.

———. *Vita malchi monachi captivi*. PL 23, pp. 55–62.

Jonas of Bobbio. *Vitae Columbani abbatis discipulorumque eius libri duo.* Ed. Bruno Krusch. MGH SRM 4, pp. 1–152. Hannover, 1902.

Lippe, Robert, ed. *Missale Romanum.* 2 vols. Henry Bradshaw Society 17. London, 1899.

Mombrizio, Bonino, ed. *Sanctuarium seu vitae sanctorum.* 2 vols. Paris, 1910.

Passio sanctarum Perpetuae et Felicitatis. Ed Herbert Musurillo. ACM, pp. 105–31. Oxford, 1972.

Passio sancti Irenaei episcopi Sirmiensis. Ed. Herbert Musurillo. ACM, pp. 294–301. Oxford, 1972.

Passio sanctorum Mariani et Iacobi. Ed. Herbert Musurillo. ACM, pp. 194–213. Oxford, 1972.

Passio sanctorum Montani et Lucii. Ed. Herbert Musurillo. ACM, pp. 215–39. Oxford, 1972.

Passio Thrudperti martyris. Ed. Bruno Krusch. MGH SRM 4, pp. 352–63. Hannover, 1902.

Philo. *De vita Mosis.* In *Philo: With an English Translation,* vol. 6 (Loeb edition). Ed. and trans. F. H. Colson. Cambridge, Mass., 1936.

Plummer, Charles, ed. *Vitae sanctorum Hiberniae.* 2 vols. Oxford, 1910.

Rahlfs, Alfred, ed. *Septuaginta id est Vetus Testamentum graece iuxta LXX interpretes.* 2 vols. Stuttgart, 1935.

Ratcliff, E. C., ed. *Expositio liturgiae Gallicanae.* Henry Bradshaw Society 98. London, 1971.

Remigius of Reims. *Epistulae.* In *Epistulae Avstrasicae.* Ed. W. Gundlach. CCSL 117, pp. 403–508. Turnhout, 1957.

Robinson, F. N., ed. *The Works of Geoffrey Chaucer.* Cambridge, 1957.

Rufinus of Aquileia. *Historia monachorum sive de vita sanctorum patrum.* PL 21, pp. 387–462. New edition: Eva Schultz-Flügel. In *Patristische Texte und Studien* 34. Berlin, 1990.

Sulpicius Severus. *Dialogi.* Ed. Charles Halm. CSEL 1, pp. 152–216. Vienna, 1866.

————. *Epistulae.* Ed. Charles Halm. CSEL 1, pp. 138–51. Vienna, 1866.

————. *Sulpice Sévère: Vie de Saint Martin.* Ed. and trans. Jacques Fontaine. 3 vols. SC 133–35. Paris, 1967–1969.

————. *Vita sancti Martini episcopi et confessoris.* Ed. Charles Halm. CSEL 1, pp. 109–37. Vienna, 1866.

Tertullian. *De paenitentia.* Ed. and trans. Charles Munier. SC 316. Paris, 1984.

Tischendorf, Constantinus de, ed. *Evangelica apocrypha.* Leipzig, 1876.

Vincent of Beauvais. *Speculum quadruplex sive speculum maius.* 4 vols. Graz, 1965.

Virtutum sanctae Geretrudis continuatio. Ed. Bruno Krusch. MGH SRM 2, pp. 471–74. Hannover, 1888.

Vita sanctae Aldegundis, abbatissae Malbodiensis. Ed. Wilhelm Levison. MGH SRM 6, pp. 79–90. Hannover, 1913.

Vita sancti Amantii episcopi. Ed. Bruno Krusch. MGH AA 4.2, pp. 55–64. Berlin, 1877.

Vita Aridii abbatis Lemovicini. Ed. Bruno Krusch. MGH SRM 3, pp. 581–612. Hannover, 1896.

Vita sancti Arnulfi. Ed. Bruno Krusch. MGH SRM 2, pp. 426–46. Hannover, 1888.

Vita Audoini episcopi Rotomagensis. Ed. Wilhelm Levison. MGH SRM 5, pp. 553–67. Hannover, 1910.

Vita sanctae Balthildis reginae. Ed. Bruno Krusch. MGH SRM 2, pp. 477–508. Hannover, 1888.

Vita Bertuini episcopi. Ed. Bruno Krusch. MGH SRM 7.1, pp. 175–82. Hannover, 1902.

Vitae Caesarii episcopi Arelatensis libri duo auctoribus Cypriano, Firmino, Viventio episcopis, Messiano presbytero, Stephano diacono. Ed. Bruno Krusch. MGH SRM 3, pp. 433–501. Hannover, 1896.

Vita Eligii episcopi Noviomagensis. Ed. Bruno Krusch. MGH SRM 4, pp. 663–741. Hannover, 1902.

Vita Fursei abbatis Latiniacensis. Ed. Bruno Krusch. MGH SRM 4, pp. 440–49. Hannover, 1902.

Vita Genovefae virginis Parisiensis. Ed. Bruno Krusch. MGH SRM 3, pp. 215–38. Hannover, 1896.

Vita sanctae Geretrudis Nivialensis. Ed. Bruno Krusch. MGH SRM 2, pp. 453–64. Hannover, 1888.

Vita sancti Goaris confessoris Rhenani. Ed. Bruno Krusch. MGH SRM 4, pp. 402–23. Hannover, 1902.

Vita Landelini abbatis Lobbiensis et Crispiniensis. Ed. Bruno Krusch. MGH SRM 6, pp. 438–44. Hannover, 1913.

Vita Landiberti episcopi Traiectensis vetustissima. Ed. Bruno Krusch. MGH SRM 6, pp. 353–84. Hannover, 1913.

Vita sancti Leobini. Ed. Bruno Krusch. MGH AA 4.2, pp. 73–82. Berlin, 1885.

Vita sanctae Mahthildis (vita posterior). Ed. G. H. Pertz. MGH SS 4, pp. 282–302. Hannover, 1826.

Vita Nivardi episcopi Remensis auctore Almanno monacho Altivillarensis. Ed. Wilhelm Levison. MGH SRM 5, 157–71. Hannover, 1910.

Vita Odiliae abbatissae. Ed. Wilhelm Levison. MGH SRM 6, pp. 24–50. Hannover, 1913.

Vita Richarii sacerdotis Centulensis primagenia. Ed. Bruno Krusch. MGH SRM 7.2, pp. 438–53. Hannover, 1920.

Vita sancti Romani abbatis. Ed. Bruno Krusch. MGH SRM 3, pp. 131–43. Hannover, 1896.

Vita Sadalbergae abbatissae. Ed. Bruno Krusch. MGH SRM 5, pp. 40–66. Hannover, 1910.

Vita sanctae Segolenae abbatissae Traclarensis. In Acta sanctorum ordinis sancti Benedicti, vol. 3.2, pp. 540–50. Ed. J. Mabillon. Paris, 1688–1701.

Vita Vedastis episcopi Atrebatensis duplex. Ed. Bruno Krusch. MGH SRM 3, pp. 399–432. Hannover, 1896.

Vita Vincentiani confessoris Avolcensis. Ed. Wilhelm Levison. MGH SRM 5, pp. 116–28.

Vitae patrum. PL 73.

Weber, Robert, et al., ed. *Biblia Sacra iuxta vulgatam versionem.* Editio minor. Stuttgart, 1984.

MODERN STUDIES AND TRANSLATIONS

Affeldt, Werner. *Frauen im Frühmittelalter: Eine ausgewählte kommentierte Bibliographie.* Frankfurt am Main, 1990.

————, et al., eds. *Frauen in Spätantike und Frühmittelalter.* Sigmaringen, 1990.

Aigrain, René. *L'hagiographie: ses sources, ses méthodes, son histoire.* Paris, 1953.

————. *Sainte Radegonde.* Paris, 1918.

Allard, Paul. *Les esclavaes chrétien depuis les premiers temps de l'Église jusqú à la fin de la domination romaine en occident.* Paris, 1914.

————. "Slavery." *The Catholic Encyclopedia*, vol. 14, pp. 36–39. New York, 1912.

Altman, Charles F. "Two Types of Opposition and the Structure of Latin Saints' Lives." *Medievalia et Humanistica*, vol. 6. Ed. Paul Clogan, pp. 1–11. Cambridge, 1975.

Anson, John. "The Female Transvestite in Early Monasticism: The Origin and Development of a Motif." *Viator* 5 (1974): 1–32.

Apostle, Hippocrates, trans. *Aristotle's Metaphysics.* Grinnel, Iowa, 1979.

Aspegren, Kerstin. *The Male Woman: A Feminine Ideal in the Early Church.* Stockholm, 1990.

Aubrun, Jean. *Radegonde: Reine, Moniale et Sainte.* Poitiers, 1986.

Auerbach, Erich. "Figura." In *Scenes from Drama of European Literature.* Trans. Ralph Manheim. New York, 1959.

————. *Literary Language and Its Public in Late Latin Antiquity and in the Middle Ages.* Trans. Ralph Manheim. London, 1965.

————. *Mimesis: The Representation of Reality in Western Literature.* Trans. Willard Trask. Princeton, 1953.

————. "Typological Symbolism in Medieval Literature." *Yale French Studies* 9 (1965): 3–10.

————. *Typologische Motive in der mittelalterlichen Literatur.* Schriften und Vortrage des Petrarca-Instits Köln. Krefeld, 1953.

Balfour, I. "The Fate of the Soul in Induced Abortion in the Writings of Tertullian." In *Studia Patristica* 16 (= TU 129), ed. Elizabeth Livingstone, pp. 127–31. Berlin, 1985.

Beck, Henry G. *The Pastoral Care of Souls in South-East France during the Sixth Century.* Analecta Gregoriana 51. Rome, 1950.

Bell, Rudolph. *Holy Anorexia.* Chicago, 1985.

Bergengruen, Alexander. *Adel und Grundherrschaft im Merowingerreich.* Wiesbaden, 1958.

Bernoulli, Carl. Die Heiligen der Merowinger. Tübingen, 1900.

Bieber, Margarete. The History of the Greek and Roman Theater. Princeton, 1961.

Bischoff, Bernhard. "Die kölner Nonnenhandschriften und das Skriptorium von Chelles." In Mittelalterliche Studien, vol. 1: Ausgewählte Aufsätze zur Schriftkunde und Literaturgeschichte, pp. 16–34. Stuttgart, 1966.

Blatz, Beate, trans. "The Coptic Gospel of Thomas," in NTA 1, pp. 110–133.

Bloch, Marc. Slavery and Serfdom in the Middle Ages. Trans. William Beer. Berkeley, 1975.

Bodenstaff, H. "Miracles de Sainte Radegunde: XIII et XIV siècle." AB 23 (1904): 433–77.

Boesch Gajano, Sofia. "Il santo nella visione storiografica di Gregorio di Tours." In Gregorio di Tours, pp. 27–91. Todi, 1977.

Bonnet, Max. Le Latin de Grégoire de Tours. Paris, 1890.

Borchardt, C. F. A. Hilary of Poitiers' Role in the Arian Struggle. The Hague, 1966.

Bosl, Karl. "Der 'Adelsheilige': Idealtypus und Wirklichkeit: Gesellschaft und Kultur im merowingerzeitlichen Bayern des 7. und 8. Jahrhunderts." In Mönchtum und Gesellschaft im Frühmittelalter, ed. Friedrich Prinz, pp. 354–86. Darmstadt, 1976.

Boyer, Régis. "An Attempt to Define the Typology of Medieval Hagiography." In Hagiography and Medieval Literature: A Symposium, ed. Hans Bekker-Nielsen, Peter Foote et al., pp. 27–36. Odense, 1981.

Bradley, George. Lectures on Ecclesiastes. Oxford, 1885.

Brehaut, Ernst, trans. The History of the Franks by Gregory Bishop of Tours. New York, 1969.

Brennan, Brian. "The Career of Venantius Fortunatus." Traditio 41 (1985): 49–78.

———. "Deathless Marriage and Spiritual Fecundity in Venantius Fortunatus's De Virginitate." Traditio 51 (1996): 73–97.

———. "St. Radegund and the Early Development of Her Cult at Poitiers." Journal of Religious History 13 (1985): 340–54.

Brittain, F. Saint Radegund: Patroness of Jesus College Cambridge. Cambridge, 1925.

Brown, Peter. The Body and Society: Men, Women and Sexual Renunciation in Early Christianity. New York, 1988.

———. The Cult of the Saints: Its Rise and Function in Latin Christianity. The Haskell Lectures on History of Religions, n.s. 2. Chicago, 1981.

———. "The Saint as Exemplar in Late Antiquity." Representations 1.2 (1983): 1–25.

———. Society and the Holy in Late Antiquity. Berkeley, 1982.

———. The World of Late Antiquity: From Marcus Aurelius to Muhammad. London, 1971.

Brunhölzl, Franz. Geschichte der lateinischen Literatur des Mittelalters, vol. 1: Von Cassiodor bis zum Ausklang der karolingischen Erneuerung. Munich, 1975.

Bugge, John. Virginitas: An Essay in the History of a Medieval Ideal. The Hague, 1975.

Burns, E. Jane. Bodytalk: When Women Speak in Old French Literature. Philadelphia, 1993.

Burton-Christie, Douglas. The Word in the Desert: Scripture and the Quest for Holiness in Early Christian Monasticism. New York, 1993.

Bynum, Caroline Walker. "Did the Twelfth Century Discover the Individual?" JEH 31 (1980): 1–17.

———. Holy Feast and Holy Fast: The Religious Significance of Food to Medieval Women. Berkeley, 1987.

———. The Resurrection of the Body in Western Christianity, 200–1336. New York, 1995.

Cabrol, J., and H. Leclercq. Dictionnaire d'archéologie chrétienne et de liturgie. 15 vols. Paris, 1907–1953.

Cardot, Fabienne. L'espace et la pouvoir: Étude sur l'Austraise merovingienne. Paris, 1989.

Carlyle, R. W. and A. J. A History of Medieval Political Theory in the West. 2 vols. London, 1903.

Carrasco, Magdalena. "Sanctity and Experience in Pictorial Hagiography: Two Illustrated Lives of Saints from Romanesque France." In Images of Sanctity in Medieval Europe, ed. Renate Blumenfeld-Kosinski and Timea Szell, pp. 33–66. Ithaca, 1991.

Castagno, Adele. "Il vescovo, l'abate e l'eremita: tipologia della santità nel Liber Vitae Patrum di Gregorgio di Tours." In *L'agiographia latina nei secoli IV–VII*. Augustinianum 24, pp. 235–64. XII Incontro di studiosi dell'antichità cristiana. Rome, 1984.

Chadwick, Owen, trans. *Western Asceticism*. Philadelphia, 1958.

Chance, Jane, ed. *Gender and Text in the Later Middle Ages*. Gainesville, Fla., 1996.

Charity, C. A. *Events and Their Afterlife: The Dialectics of Christian Typology in the Bible and Dante*. Cambridge, 1966.

Chase, Alston. "The Metrical Lives of St. Martin of Tours by Paulinus and Fortunatus and the Prose Life by Sulpicius Severus." HS 43 (1932): 51–76.

Cherewatuk, Karen, and Ulrike Wiethaus, eds. *Dear Sister: Medieval Women and the Epistolatory Genre*. Philadelphia, 1993.

Chitty, Derwas J. *The Desert a City: An Introduction to the Study of Egyptian and Palestinian Monasticism under the Christian Empire*. Oxford, 1966.

Chomsky, Noam. *Chronicles of Dissent: Interview with David Barsamian*. Monroe, 1992.

Clark, Gillian. *Women in Late Antiquity: Pagan and Christian Life-Styles*. Oxford, 1993.

Cloche, P. "Les élections épiscopales sous les merovingiens." *Moyen Âge* 26 (1924–1925): 203–54.

Collins, Richard. "Observations on the Form, Language and Public of the Prose Biographies of Venantius Fortunatus and the Hagiography of Merovingian Gaul." In *Columbanus and Merovingian Monasticism*, ed. H. B. Clarke and M. Brennan, pp. 105–31. British Archaeological Reports, International Series 113. Oxford, 1981.

Conheady, Eileen. "The Saints of the Merovingian Dynasty: A Study of Merovingian Kingship." Ph.D. diss., University of Chicago, 1967.

Corbett, John H. "Changing Perceptions in Late Antiquity: Martin of Tours." *Toronto Journal of Theology* 3.2 (1987): 236–51.

———. "*Praesentium signorum munera*: The Cult of the Saints in the World of Gregory of Tours." *Florilegium* 5 (1983): 44–61.

———. "The Saint as Patron in the Work of Gregory of Tours." *Journal of Medieval History* 7 (1981): 1–13.

Coudanne, Louise. "Baudonivie, moniale de Sainte-Croix et biographe de sainte Radegonde." In *Études mérovingiennes: Actes des Journées de Poitiers*, 1952, pp. 41–51. Paris, 1953.

Cristiani, Marta. "La sainteté féminine du haut Moyen Âge: Biographie et valeurs." In *Les fonctions des saints dans le monde occidental (IIIe–XIIIe siècle)*, pp. 385–434. Collection de l'Ecole francaise de Rome 149. Actes du colloque organisé par l'Ecole francaise de Rome avec le concours de l'Universite de Rome, 27–29 Octobre 1988. Rome, 1991.

Cunningham, Lawrence. "Religious Booknotes." Review of *Sainted Women of the Dark Ages*, ed. and trans. Jo Ann McNamara and John Halborg, with E. Gordon Whatley. *Commonweal* 120.3 (February 12, 1993): 26.

Curtius, Ernst Robert. *European Literature and the Latin Middle Ages*. Trans. Willard R. Trask. New York, 1953.

Dalton, O. M. *The History of the Franks*. 2 vols. Oxford, 1927.

Daniélou, Jean. *From Shadows to Reality: Studies in the Biblical Typology of the Fathers*. Trans. Wulstan Hibberd. London, 1960.

———. *The Ministry of Women in the Early Church*. Trans. Glyn Simon. London, 1961.

Davies, Stevan. *The Revolt of the Widows: The Social World of the Apocryphal Acts*. Carbondale, Ill., 1980.

Delany, Sheila, trans. *A Legend of Holy Women: A Translation of Osbern Bokenham's Legends of Holy Women*. Notre Dame, 1992.

Delaruelle, Etienne. "Sainte Radegonde, son type de sainteté et la chrétienté de son temps." In *Études mérovingiennes: Actes des Journées de Poitiers*, 1952, pp. 65–74. Paris, 1953.

Delehaye, Hippolyte. *Cinq leçons sur la méthode hagiographique*. SH 21. Brussels, 1934.

————. *Étude sur le Légendier Romain*. SH 23. Brussels, 1936.

————. *The Legends of the Saints*. Trans. V.M. Crawford. London, 1961.

————. *Les passions de martyrs et les littéraires*. SH 14. Brussels, 1921.

————. *Sanctus: Essai sur le culte des saints dans l'antiquité*. SH 17. Brussels, 1927.

————. *The Work of the Bollandists through Three Centuries: 1615–1915*. Princeton, 1922.

Delooz, Pierre. *Sociologie et canonisations*. Liège, 1969.

Demyttenaere, Albert. "The Cleric, Women and the Stain: Some Beliefs and Ritual Practices concerning Women in the Early Middle Ages." In *Frauen in Spätantike und Frühmittelalter*, ed. Werner Affeldt, pp. 141–65. Sigmaringen, 1990.

Derouet, J. L. "Les possibilités d'interpretation sémiologique des textes hagiographiques." *RHEF* 62 (1976): 152–62.

De Smedt, Charles. "Les fondateurs du Bollandisme." In *Mélanges Godefroid Kurth*, vol. 1: *Mémoires historiques*, pp. 295–303. Liège, 1908.

Dill, Samuel. *Roman Society in Gaul in the Merovingian Age*. London, 1926.

Doignon, Jean. *Hilaire de Poitiers avant l'exil: Recherches sur la naissance, l'enseignement et l'épreuve d'une foi épiscopale en Gaul au milieu du IV siècle*. Paris, 1971.

Dolbeau, François, Martin Heinzelmann, and Joseph-Claude Poulin. "Les sources hagiographiques narratives composées en Gaule avant l'an mil (SHG). Inventaire, examen critique, datation (avec Annexe)." *Francia* 15 (1987): 701–31.

Doresse, Jeane. *The Secret Books of the Egyptian Gnostics: An Introduction to the Gnostic Coptic Manuscripts Discovered at Chenoboskion*. London, 1960.

Dronke, Peter. *Woman Writers of the Middle Ages: A Critical Study of Texts from Perpetua (d. 203) to Marguerite Porete (d. 1310)*. Cambridge, 1984.

Dunn, E. Catherine. *The Gallican Saint's Life and the Late Roman Dramatic Tradition*. Washington, D.C., 1989.

Earl, James Whitney. "Literary Problems in Early Medieval Hagiography." Ph.D. diss., Cornell University, 1971.

Eckenstein, Lina. *Woman under Monasticism: Chapters on Saint-Lore and Convent Life between A.D. 500 and A.D. 1500*. Cambridge, 1896.

Elliott, Alison. *Roads to Paradise: Reading the Lives of the Early Saints*. Hanover, Pa., 1987.

Elliott, Dyan. *Spiritual Marriage: Sexual Abstinence in Medieval Wedlock*. Princeton, 1993.

Erickson, C., and K. Casey. "Women in the Middle Ages: A Working Bibliography." *Medieval Studies* 37 (1975): 340–59.

Eriksen, Robert. *Theologians under Hitler: Gerhard Kittel, Paul Althaus and Emmanuel Hirsch*. New Haven, 1985.

Fabiny, Tibor. *The Lion and the Lamb: Figuralism and Fulfillment in the Bible, Art and Literature*. New York, 1992.

Fanger, Claire. "The Dynamics of Holy Power as Reflected in Narrative Structure in the Lives of St. Martin and St. Anthony." *Florilegium* 9 (1987): 35–51.

Finnis, John. *"Historical Consciousness" and Theological Fractions*. The Etienne Gilson Series 14. Toronto, 1992.

Fishbane, Michael. *Biblical Interpretation in Ancient Israel*. Oxford, 1985.

Flaubert, Gustave. *The Temptation of St. Antony*. Trans. Lafcadio Hern. New York, 1910.

Fontaine, Jacques. "Le culte des saintes et ses implications sociologiques. Réflexions sur un récent essai de Peter Brown." *AB* 100 (1982): 17–41.

————. "Hagiographie et politique, de Sulpice Sévère à Venance Fortunat." *RHEF* 62 (1976): 113–40.

————, ed. and trans. *Sulpice Sévère: Vie de Saint Martin*. 3 vols. SC 133–135. Paris, 1967–1969.

Fouracre, Paul. "Merovingian History and Merovingian Hagiography." *Past and Present* 127 (1990): 3–38.

Fouracre, Paul, and Richard Gerberding. Late Merovingian France: History and Hagiography (640–720). Manchester, 1996.

Frend, W. H. C. Martyrdom and Persecution in the Early Church: A Study of a Conflict from Maccabees to Donatus. Oxford, 1965.

Frye, Northrop. Anatomy of Criticism: Four Essays. Princeton, 1957.

————. The Great Code: The Bible and Literature. San Diego, 1982.

————. The Secular Scripture: A Study of the Structure of Romance. Cambridge, 1976.

Gäbe, Sabine. "Radegundis: sancta, regina, ancilla. Zum Heiligkeitsideal der Radegundisviten von Fortunat und Baudonivia." Francia 16.1 (1989): 1–30.

Gaiffier, Baudouin de. Études critiques d'hagiographie et d'iconologie. Brussels, 1967.

Galatariotou, Catia. The Making of a Saint: The Life, Times and Sanctification of Neophytos the Recluse. Cambridge, 1991.

Garbe, Ulrike. Frauen des Merowingerhauses: Königinnen und Mägde, Heilige und Dirnen. Ein Beitrag zur Sittengeschichte der Zeit des Kulturbruchs (Reden und Aufsätze zum nordischen Gedanken, Heft 38). Leipzig, 1936.

Geary, Patrick J. Before France and Germany: The Creation and Transformation of the Merovingian World. Oxford, 1988.

————. Living with the Dead in the Middle Ages. Ithaca, 1994.

George, Judith. Venantius Fortunatus: A Latin Poet in Merovingian Gaul. Oxford, 1992.

Gibbon, Edward. The History of the Decline and Fall of the Roman Empire. 7 vols. Ed. J. B. Bury. London, 1925.

Gill, Penny. Review of Sainted Women of the Dark Ages, ed. and trans. Jo Ann McNamara and John E. Halborg with Gordon Whatley. Church History 63.3 (1994): 437.

Gingsburg, Christian. Coheleth, Commonly Called the Book of Ecclesiastes. London, 1861.

Goffart, Walter. Barbarians and Romans, A.D. 418–584: The Techniques of Accommodation. Princeton, 1980.

————. "The Conversions of Avitus of Clermont, and Similar Passages in Gregory of Tours." In "To See Ourselves as Others See Us": Christians, Jews, "Others" in Late Antiquity, ed. J. Neusner and E. S. Frerichs, pp. 473–97. Chico, Calif., 1985.

————. "From Historiae to Historia Francorum and Back Again: Aspects of the Textual History of Gregory of Tours." In Religion, Culture, and Society in the Early Middle Ages: Studies in Honor of Richard E. Sullivan, ed. T. F. X. Noble and J. J. Contreni, pp. 55–76. Kalamazoo, 1987.

————. The Narrators of Barbarian History (A.D. 550–800): Jordanes, Gregory of Tours, Bede, and Paul the Deacon. Princeton, 1988.

————. "Two Notes on Germanic Antiquity Today." Traditio 50 (1995): 9–30.

Goodich, Michael. Vita Perfecta: The Ideal of Sainthood in the Thirteenth Century. Stuttgart, 1982.

Goppelt, Leonhard. Typos: The Typological Interpretation of the Old Testament in the New. Trans. Donald Madvig. Grand Rapids, 1982.

Goyau, Lucie Félix-Faure. Christianisme et culture féminine. Paris, 1914.

Graus, Frantisek. "Die Gewalt bei den Anfänge des Feudalismus und die 'Gefangenenbefreiung' der merowingischen Hagiographie." Jahrbuch für Wirtschaftsgeschichte 1 (1961): 61–156.

————. "Sozialgeschichtliche Aspekte der Hagiographie der Merowinger- und Karolingerzeit: Die Viten der Heiligen des südalemannischen Raumes und die sogenannten Adelsheiligen." In Mönchtum, Episkopat und Adel zur Gründungszeit des Klosters Reichenau, ed. Arno Borst, pp. 131–76. Sigmaringen, 1974.

————. Volk, Herrscher und Heiliger im Reich der Merowinger. Studien zur Hagiographie des Merowingerzeit. Prague, 1965.

Gregorio di Tours. 10–13 Ottobre 1971. Convegni del Centro di studi sulla spiritualità medievale 12. Todi, 1977.

Harnack, Adolf von. Militia Christi: The Christian Religion and the Military in the First Three Centuries. Trans. David Gracie. Philadelphia, 1981.

Head, Thomas. Hagiography and the Cult of the Saints: The Diocese of Orléans, 800–1200. Cambridge, 1990.

Heffernan, Thomas J. "Philology and Authorship in the Passio Sanctarum Perpetuae et Felicitatis." Traditio 50 (1995): 315–25.

———. Sacred Biography: Saints and Their Biographers in the Middle Ages. New York, 1988.

Heinzelmann, Martin. Bishofsherrschaft in Gallien. Zur Kontinuität römischer Führungsschichten vom 4. bis zum 7. Jahrhundert: soziale, prosopographische und bildungsgeschichtliche Aspekte. Munich, 1976.

———. Gregor von Tours (538–594): "Zehn Bucher Geschichte": Historiographie und Gesellschaftskonzept im 6. Jahrhundert. Darmstadt, 1994.

———. "Neue Aspekte der biographischen und hagiographischen Literatur in der lateinischen Welt (1.–6. Jahrhundert)." Francia 1 (1973): 27–44.

———. "Sanctitas und 'Tugendadel.' Zu Konzeptionen von 'Heiligkeit' im 5. und 10. Jahrhundert." Francia 5 (1977): 741–52.

Hélin, Maurice. A History of Medieval Latin Literature. Trans. Jean Snow. New York, 1949.

Hen, Yitzhak. Culture and Religion in Merovingian Gaul A.D. 481–751. Leiden, 1995.

Hilaire et son temps: Actes du Colloque de Poitiers 29 Septembre–3 Octobre 1968 à l'occasion du XVI centenaire de la mort de saint Hilaire.

Hoare, F. R., trans. The Western Fathers, Being the Lives of SS. Martin of Tours, Ambrose, Augustine of Hippo, Honoratus of Arles and Germanus of Auxerre. New York, 1954.

Hoefer, Hartmut. Typologie im Mittelalter: Zur Übertragbarkeit typologischer Interpretation auf weltliche Dichtung. GAG 54. Göppingen, 1971.

Inwood, Brad, and L. P. Gerson, trans. Hellenistic Philosophy: Introductory Readings. Indianapolis, 1988.

Irsigler, Franz. "On the Aristocratic Character of Early Frankish Society." In The Medieval Nobility: Studies on the Ruling Classes of France and Germany from the Sixth to the Twelfth Century. Ed. and Trans. Timothy Reuter, pp. 105–36. Amsterdam, 1978.

James, Edward. "Beati Pacifici: Bishops and the Law in Sixth-Century Gaul." In Disputes and Settlements: Law and Human Relations in the West, ed. J. Bossy, pp. 25–46. Cambridge, 1983.

———. The Franks. Oxford, 1988.

———, trans. Gregory of Tours: Life of the Fathers. Liverpool, 1985.

———. The Origins of France: From Clovis to the Capetians, 500–1000. New York, 1982.

Janson, Tore. Latin Prose Prefaces: Studies in Literary Conventions. Stockholm, 1964.

Jentzmik, Peter. Zu Möglichkeiten und Grenzen typologischer Exegesis in Mittelalterlicher Predigt und Dichtung. GAG 112. Göppingen, 1973.

Kech, Herbert. Hagiographie als christliche Unterhaltungsliteratur: Studien zum Phänomen des Erbaulichen anhand der Mönchenviten des hl. Hieronymus. GAG 225. Göppingen, 1977.

Kelly, J. N. D. Jerome: His Life, Writings and Controversies. London, 1975.

Kemp, Erik. Canonization and Authority in the Western Church. Oxford, 1948.

Kern, Edmund. "Counter-Reformation Sanctity: The Bollandists' Vita of Blessed Hemma of Gurk." JEH 45.3 (1994): 412–34.

Kieckhefer, Richard. Unquiet Souls: Fourteenth-Century Saints in Their Religious Milieu. Chicago, 1984.

King, Margo. "Hagiography, Western European." In Dictionary of the Middle Ages, vol. 6. Ed. Joseph Strayer, pp. 64–71. New York, 1985.

Kitchen, John. "Saints, Doctors and Soothsayers: The Dynamics of Healing in Gregory of Tours's De Virtutibus Sancti Martini." Florilegium 12 (1993): 15–32.

Kleinberg, Aviad. Prophets in Their Own Country: Living Saints and the Making of Sainthood in the Later Middle Ages. Chicago, 1992.

Klingshirn, William. "Caesarius' Monastery for Women in Arles and the composition and Function of the Vita Caesarii." Revue Bénédictine 100 (1990): 474–80.

Klingshirn, William. *Caesarius of Arles: The Making of a Christian Community in Late Antique Gaul.* Cambridge, 1994.

———. "Charity and Power: Caesarius of Arles and the Ransoming of Captives in Sub-Roman Gaul." *JRS* 75 (1985): 183–203.

Kneepkens, C. H. " 'Nil in ecclesia confusius quam ymni isti cantantur': A Note on the Hymn *Pange, lingua gloriosi.*" In *Frvctvs Centesimvs: Mélanges offerts à Gerard J. M. Bartelink à l'occasion de son soixante-cinquième anniversaire,* ed. A. A. R. Bastiaensen et al., pp. 193–205. Instrvmenta Patristica 19. Dordrecht, 1989.

Knowles, David. *The Evolution of Medieval Thought.* New York, 1962.

———. *Great Historical Enterprises: Problems in Monastic History.* London, 1963.

Koebner, Richard. *Venantius Fortunatus. Seine Persönlichkeit und seine Stellung in der geistigen Kultur des Merowingerreiches.* Beiträge der Kulturgeschichte des Mittelalters und der Renaissance 22. Leipzig and Berlin, 1915.

Kraemer, Ross. "The Conversion of Women to Ascetic Forms of Christianity." *Signs* 6.21 (1980): 298–307.

Krusch, Bruno. "Georgii Florentii Gregorii episcopi Turonensis libri octo miraculorum." In MGH SRM 1.2, pp. 451–484 (introduction to Gregory's hagiographic writings).

———. "Prooemium." In MGH AA 4.2, pp. v–xxxiii (introduction to Fortunatus's *Vitae*).

Kurth, Godefroid. *Études franques.* 2 vols. Paris and Brussels, 1919.

Labande-Mailfert, Yvonne, et al. *Histoire de l'abbaye Sainte-Croix de Poitiers: Quatorze siècles de vie monastique.* Mémoires de la Société des antiquaires de l'Ouest. 4ème série, Tome XIX, Années 1986–1987. Poitiers, 1987.

Laistner, M. L. *Thought and Letters in Western Europe.* Ithaca, 1957.

Lampe, G. W. H. and K.J. Woollcombe. "The Reasonableness of Typology." In *Essays on Typology,* ed. G. W. H. Lampe. London, 1957.

Laporte, J. *The Role of Women in Early Christianity.* New York, 1982.

Lasko, Peter. *The Kingdom of the Franks.* New York, 1971.

Le Blant, E., ed. *Inscriptions chrétiennes de la Gaule antérieures au VIIIe siècle.* 2 vols. Paris, 1856–1865.

Leclercq, Jean. *The Love of Learning and the Desire for God: A Study of Monastic Culture.* Trans. Catherine C. Misrahi. New York, 1977.

———. "La Sainte Radegonde de Venace Fortunat et celle de Baudovinie [sic]." In *Fructus Centesimvs: Mélanges offerts à Gerard J. M. Bartelink à l'occasion de son soixante-cinquième anniversaire.* Ed. A. A. R. Bastiaensen et al., pp. 207–16. Instrvmenta Patristica 19. Dordrecht, 1989.

Lefkowitz, Mary. "The Motivations for St. Perpetua's Martyrdom." *Journal of the American Academy of Religion* 44.3 (1976): 417–21.

Lehmann, Andrée. *Le rôle de la femme dans l'histoire de France au Moyen Age.* Paris, 1952.

Lesne, Emile. *Histoire de la propriété ecclésiastique en France,* vol. 1: *Epoques romaine et merovingienne.* Paris, 1910. Lille, 1926.

Lifshitz, Felice. "Beyond Positivism and Genre: 'Hagiographical' Texts as Historical Narrative." *Viator* 25 (1994): 95–113.

Longnon, A. *Geographie de la Gaule au VIe siècle.* Paris, 1878.

Loomis, C. G. *White Magic: An Introduction to the Folklore of Christian Legends.* Cambridge, Mass., 1948.

Lot, Ferdinand. *The End of the Ancient World and the Beginnings of the Middle Ages.* Trans. Philip and Mariette Leon. New York, 1931.

Lubac, Henri de. *Exégèse médiévale: les quatre sens de l'Écriture.* 2 parts in 4 vols. Paris, 1959–1964.

Lucius, Ernst. *Die Anfänge des Heiligenkults in der christlichen Kirche.* Ed. Gustav Anrich. Tübingen, 1904.

MacCarthy, Fiona. "The Power of Chastity." *New York Review of Books* 43.20 (December 19, 1996): 31–33.

Malone, Edward E. *The Monk and the Martyr: The Monk as Successor of the Martyr.* Catholic University of America Studies in Christian Antiquity 12. Washington, D.C., 1950.

Malsbary, Gerald. "The Epic Hagiography of Paulinus of Périgueux." Ph.D. diss., University of Toronto, 1987.

Manitius, Max. "Zur Frankengeschichte Gregors von Tours." *Neues Archiv* 21 (1986): 549–57.

Marié, Georges. "Sainte Radegonde et le milieu monastique contemporain." In *Études mérovingiennes: Actes des Journées de Poitiers, 1952,* pp. 219–25. Paris, 1953.

Marignan, A. *Études sur la civilisation française,* vol. 2: *Le culte des Saints sous les Mérovingiens.* Paris, 1899.

Markus, R. A. "The Cult of Icons in Sixth-Century Gaul." In *From Augustine to Gregory the Great: History and Christianity in Late Antiquity,* pp. 151–57. London, 1983.

Martindale, John, ed. *Prosopography of the Later Roman Empire,* 3 vols. Cambridge, 1992.

Mayo, Hope. "The Sources of Female Monasticism in Merovingian Gaul." In *Studia Patristica* 16 (= TU 129), ed. Elizabeth Livingston, pp. 32–37. Berlin, 1985.

McCarthy, Mary Caritas, trans. *The Rule for Nuns of Saint Caesarius of Arles: A Translation with a Critical Introduction.* Washington, D.C., 1960.

McCready, William. *Signs of Sanctity: Miracles in the Thought of Gregory the Great.* Studies and Texts 91. Toronto, 1989.

McGonagle, Sara. "The Poor in Gregory of Tours: A Study of the Attitude toward the Poor as Reflected in the Literature of the Time." Ph.D. diss., Columbia University, 1937.

McKeon, Richard, trans. *The Basic Works of Aristotle.* New York, 1941.

McKitterick, Rosamond. "Frauen und Schriftlichkeit im Frühen Mittelalter." In *Weibliche Lebensgestaltung im frühen Mittelalter.* Ed. H. W. Goetz, pp. 65–118. Köln, 1991.

McNamara, Jo Ann. "Cornelia's Daughters: Paula and Eustochium." *Women's Studies* 11 (1984): 9–27.

———. "A Legacy of Miracles: Hagiography and Nunneries in Merovingian Gaul." In *Women of the Medieval World: Essays in Honor of John Mundy,* ed. Julius Kirschner and Suzanne Wemple, pp. 36–52. New York, l985.

———. "Living Sermons." In *Medieval Religious Women,* vol. 2: *Peace Weavers,* ed. John A. Nichols and Lilian T. Shank, pp. 19–38. Kalamazoo, 1987.

———. "Muffled Voices: The Lives of Consecrated Women in the Fourth Century." In *Medieval Religious Women,* vol. 1: *Distant Echoes,* ed. John A. Nichols and Lillian T. Shank, pp. 11–29, Kalamazoo, 1984.

———. "The Need to Give: Suffering and Female Sanctity in Medieval Europe." In *Images of Sainthood in Medieval Europe,* ed. Renate Blumenfeld-Kozinski and Timea Szell, pp. 199–221. Ithaca, 1991.

———. "The Ordeal of Community: Hagiography and Discipline in Merovingian Convents." *Vox Benedictina* 3.4 (1986): 293–326.

———. *Sisters in Arms: Catholic Nuns through Two Millennia.* Cambridge, Mass., 1996.

——— and John E. Halborg with E. Gordon Whatley, eds. and trans. *Sainted Women of the Dark Ages.* Durham, 1992.

Meneghetti, A. "La Latinità di Venanzio Fortunato." *Didaskaleion: Studi Filologici di Letteratura Christiana Antica* 6 (1917): 1–166.

Merton, Thomas. *The Last of the Fathers: Saint Bernard of Clairvaux and the Encyclical Letter Doctor Mellifluus.* New York, 1954.

———, trans. *The Wisdom of the Desert: Sayings from the Desert Fathers of the Fourth Century.* New York, 1960.

Meyer, Robert, trans. *Palladius: The Lausiac History.* London, 1965.

Meyer, W. *Der Gelegenheitsdichter Venantius Fortunatus. Abhandlungen der Königlichen Gesellschaft der Wissenschaften zu Göttingen, philologisch-historische Klasse,* NF, Band 4, No. 5. Berlin, 1901.

Miranda, José Porfirio. *Marx and the Bible: A Critique of the Philosophy of Oppression.* Trans. John Eagleson. New York, 1974.

Mollat, Michel. *The Poor in the Middle Ages.* Trans. Arthur Goldhammer. New Haven, 1986.

Monod, Gabriel. *Études critiques sur les sources de l'histoire mérovingienne, 1ère partie, Introduction, Grégoire de Tours, Marius d'Avenches*. Paris, 1872.

Morris, Colin. "Individualism in Twelfth-Century Religion: Some Further Reflections." JEH 31 (1980): 195–206.

Morrisson, Karl. *I Am You: The Hermeneutics of Empathy in Western Literature*. Princeton, 1988.

Murphy, Roland. "Ecclesiastes (Qoheleth)." In *Jerome Biblical Commentary*, vol. 1. Ed. Raymond Brown et al. Englewood Cliffs, N.J., 1968.

Murray, Alexander. "Peter Brown and the Shadow of Constantine." JRS 73 (1983): 191–203.

Musurillo, Herbert. *The Acts of the Christian Martyrs*. Oxford, 1972.

Nelson, Janet L. "Commentary on the Papers of J. Verdon, S. F. Wemple and M. Parisse." In *Frauen in Spätantike und Frühmittelalter*, ed. Werner Affeldt, pp. 325–32. Sigmaringen, 1990.

———. "Queens as Jezebels: The Careers of Brunhild and Balthild in Merovingian History." In *Politics and Ritual in Early Medieval Europe*, pp. 1–48. London, 1986.

———. "Women and the Word in the Earlier Middle Ages." In *Women in the Church: Papers Read at the 1989 Summer Meeting and the 1990 Winter Meeting of the Ecclesiastical History Society*, ed. W. J. Sheils and Diana Wood, pp. 43–78. Oxford, 1990.

Newman, Barbara. *From Virile Women to WomanChrist: Studies in Medieval Religion and Literature*. Philadelphia, 1995.

Newman, John Henry. *Historical Sketches*. 3 vols. New York, 1917.

Nie, Giselle de. " 'Consciousness Fecund through God': From Male Fighter to Spiritual Bride-Mother in Late Antique Female Sanctity." In *Sanctity and Motherhood: Essays on Holy Mothers in the Middle Ages*, ed. Anneke B. Mulder-Bakker, pp. 101–61. New York, 1995.

———. Review of *Venantius Fortunatus: A Latin Poet in Merovingian Gaul*, by Judith George. *Speculum* 70.1 (1995): 143–46.

———. *Views from a Many-Windowed Tower: Studies of Imagination in the Works of Gregory of Tours*. Amsterdam, 1987.

Nisard, Charles. "Des poésies de Sainte Radégonde attribuées jusqu'ici à Fortunat," RH 37.2 (1888): 49–57.

Nunn, H. P. V. *An Introduction to Ecclesiastical Latin*. Oxford, 1958.

O'Faolain, Julia. *Women in the Wall*. London, 1975.

Olsen, Alexandra Hennessey. " 'De Historiis Sanctorum': A Generic Study of Hagiography." *Genre* 13 (1980): 407–29.

Pagels, Elaine. *Adam, Eve, and the Serpent*. New York, 1988.

Partner, Nancy. "Introduction" to "Studying Medieval Women: Sex, Gender, Feminism." *Speculum* 68.2 (1993): 305–8.

———. "No Sex, No Gender." *Speculum* 68.2 (1993): 419–43.

Patlagean, Evelyne. "L'Histoire de la femme déguisée en moine et l'évolution de la sainteté féminine à Byzance." *Studi Medievali* 17 (1976): 597–623.

Patterson, Orlando. *Slavery and Social Death: A Comparative Study*. London, 1982.

Peeters, Paul. "Father Hippolyte Delehaye: A Memoir." In *The Legends of the Saints*, Hippolyte Delehaye. Trans. Donald Attwater. New York, 1962.

———. *Figures Bollandiennes contemporaines*. Brussels, 1948.

Perry, T. A. *Dialogues with Kohelet: The Book of Ecclesiastes. Translation and Commentary*. University Park, Pa., 1993.

Peters, Edward, ed. *Monks, Bishops and Pagans: Christian Culture in Gaul and Italy, 500–700*. Philadelphia, 1975.

Petersen, Joan M. *The Dialogues of Gregory the Great in Their Late Antique Cultural Background*. Studies and Texts 69. Toronto, 1984.

———. "The Spirituality and Miracles of St. Radegund." In *Monastic Studies: The Continuity of Tradition*, ed. Judith Loades, pp. 34–47. Bangor, 1990.

Petroff, Elizabeth. *Medieval Women's Visionary Literature*. New York, 1986.

Pontal, Odette. *Histoire des conciles mérovingiens*. Paris, 1989.

Portmann, Marie-Louise. *Die Darstellung der Frau in der Geschichtsschreibung des früheren Mittelalters*. Basler Beiträge zur Geschichtswissenschaft 69. Basel, 1958.

Power, A.D. *Ecclesiastes or the Preacher*. London, 1952.

Prinz, Friedrich. "Aristocracy and Christianity in Merovingian Gaul." In *Monographien zur Geschichte des Mittelalter* 11: *Gesellschaft-Kultur-Literatur. Rezeption und Originalitat im Wachsen einer europäishen Literatur und Geistigkeit*, ed. Karl Bosl, pp. 153–65. Stuttgart, 1975.

———. "Aspekte Frühmittelalterlicher Hagiographie." In *Mönchtum, Kultur und Gesellschaft: Beitrage zum Mittelalter*, ed. Alfred Haverkamp and Alfred Heil, pp. 176–98. Munich, 1989.

———. *Frühes Mönchtum im Frankenreich. Kultur und Gesellschaft in Gallien, den Rheinlanden und Bayern am Beispiel der monastischen Entwicklung (4. bis 8. Jahrhundert)*. Munich and Vienna, 1965.

———. "Gesellschaftsgeschichtliche Aspekte frühmittelalterlicher Hagiographie." *Zeitschrift für Literaturwissenschaft und Linguistik* 3 (1973): 17–37.

———. "Heiligenkult und Adelsherrschaft im Spiegel merowingischer Hagiographie." *Historische Zeitschrift* 204 (1967): 529–44.

Raby, Frederick. *A History of Christian-Latin Poetry from the Beginnings to the Close of the Middle Ages*. Oxford, 1927.

Rad, Gerhard von. *Old Testament Theology*. 2 vols. Trans. D. M. G. Stalker. Edinburgh, 1965.

Rader, Rosemary. *Breaking Boundaries: Male/Female Friendship in Early Christian Communities*. New York, 1983.

———. "The Martyrdom of Perpetua." In *Women Writers of the Early Church*. Ed. Patricia Wilson-Kastner, pp. 1–32. New York, 1981.

Rice, Carl. "The Phonology of Gallic Clerical Latin after the Sixth Century." Ph.D. diss., Harvard University, 1902.

La riche personalité de Sainte Radegonde: Conférences et homélies prononcées à Poitiers à l'occasion du XIVe centenaire de sa mort (587–1987). Comit du XIVe Centenaire. Poitiers, 1987.

Riché, Pierre. *Education and Culture in the Barbarian West: Sixth through Eighth Centuries*. Trans. John Contreni. Columbia, S.C., 1976.

———. "Sainte Radegund et le monachisme féminin de son temps." In *La riche personalité de Sainte Radegonde*, pp. 17–33. Poitiers, 1988.

Roberts, Jennifer. "Gregory of Tours and the Monk of St. Gall: The Paratactic Style of Medieval Latin. *Latomus* 39 (1980): 173–90.

Rousseau, Philip. *Ascetics, Authority, and the Church in the Age of Jerome and Cassian*. Oxford, 1978.

Russell, Bertrand. *A History of Western Philosophy*. New York, 1945.

Russell, James. *The Germanization of Early Medieval Christianity: A Sociohistorical Approach to Religious Transformation*. New York, 1994.

Salin, Edouard. *La civilisation mérovingienne: d'après les sépultures, les textes et le laboratoire*. 4 vols. Paris, 1949–1959.

———. "Les conditions de vie au temps de Radegonde et de Fortunat." In *Études mérovingiennes: Actes des Journées de Poitiers, 1952*, pp. 269–72. Paris, 1953.

Sas, L. F. "Changing Linguistic Attitudes in the Merovingian Period." *Word* 5 (1949): 131–35.

Scheibelreiter, Georg. *Der Bischof in merowingischer Zeit*. Vienna, 1983.

———. "Der Frühfrankische Episkopat: Bild und Wirklichkeit." *Frühmittelalterliche Studien* 17 (1983): 131–47.

———. "Königstöchter im Kloster: Radegund (d.20587) und der Nonnenaufstand von Poitiers (589)." *Mitteilungen des Instituts für österreichische Geschichtsforschung* 87 (1979): 1–37.

Schulenburg, Jane Tibbets. "Saints' Lives as a Source for the History of Women, 500–1100." In *Medieval Women and the Sources of Medieval History*, ed. Joel Rosenthal, pp. 285–320. Athens, Ga., 1990.

———. "Sexism and the Celestial Gynaeceum from 500 to 1200." *Journal of Medieval History* 3 (1978): 117–33.

———. "Strict Active Enclosure and Its Effects on the Female Monastic Experience, 500–1100." In *Medieval Religious Women*, vol. 1: *Distant Echoes*, ed. John A. Nichols and Lilian T. Shank, pp. 51–86. Kalamazoo, 1984.

Sheppard, Lancelot. *The Saints Who Never Were.* Dayton, 1969.

Sigal, Pierre-André. *L'Homme et le miracle dans la France médiévale, XI–XIIe Siècles.* Paris, 1985.

Smalley, Beryl. *The Study of the Bible in the Middle Ages.* New York, 1952.

Smith, Julia M. H. "Review Article: Early Medieval Hagiography in the Late Twentieth Century." *Early Medieval Europe* 1.1 (1992): 69–76.

Smith, Kendall. "The Use of the High-Soled Shoe or Buskin in Greek Tragedy of the Fifth and Fourth Centuries B.C." *HS* 16 (1905): 123–64.

Stafford, Pauline. *Queens, Concubines, and Dowagers: The King's Wife in the Early Middle Ages.* Athens, Ga., 1983.

Stancliffe, Clare E. *St. Martin and His Hagiographer: History and Miracle in Sulpicius Severus.* Oxford, 1983.

Stern, Laurence. *The Life and Opinions of Tristram Shandy*, ed. Ian Watt. Boston, 1965.

St-Michel, Denise. *Concordance de l'Histoire Francorum de Grégoire de Tours.* 2 vols. Montreal, 1979.

Stoeckle, Maria. *Studien über Ideale in Frauenviten des VII–X. Jahrhunderts.* Munich, 1957.

Stroheker, K. F. *Der senatorische Adel im spätantiken Gallien.* Tübingen, 1948.

Strunk, Gerhard. *Kunst und Glaube in der lateinischen Heiligenlegende: Zu Ihrem Selbstverständnis in den Prologen.* Medium Aevum: Philologische Studien 12. Munich, 1970.

Sullivan, Donald. "Jean Bolland (1596–1665) and the Early Bollandists." In *Medieval Scholarship: Biographical Studies on the Formation of a Discipline*, vol. 1: *History*, ed. Helen Damico and Joseph B. Zavadil, pp. 3–14. New York, 1995.

Sutcliffe, F. E., trans. *René Descartes: Discourse on Method and the Meditations.* Penguin Classics. London, 1968.

Talbot, C. H., trans. "The Hodoeporicon of Saint Willibald." In *Soldiers of Christ: Saints and Saints' Lives from Late Antiquity and the Early Middle Ages*, ed. Thomas F. X. Noble and Thomas Head, pp. 141–64. University Park, Pa., 1995.

Tardi, Abbé. *Fortunat: Étude sur un dernier représentant de la poésie Latine dans la Gaule mérovingienne.* Paris, 1927.

Theis, Laurent. "Saints sans familles? Quelques remarques sur la famille dans le monde franc à travers les sources hagiographiques." *RH* 255 (1976): 3–20.

Thesavrvs lingvae Latinae editvs avctoritate et consilio academiarvm qvinqve Germanicarvm Berolinensis Gottingensis Lipsiensis monacencis Vidobonensis. 10 vols (in progress). Leipzig, 1900– .

Thiébaux, Marcelle. *The Writings of Medieval Women: An Anthology.* New York, 1994.

Thorpe, Lewis, trans. *Gregory of Tours: The History of the Franks.* London, 1974.

Thürlemann, Felix. *Der historische Diskurs bei Gregor von Tours: Topoi und Wirklichkeit.* Geist und Werk der Zeiten 39. Bern, 1974.

Van Dam, Raymond. trans. *Gregory of Tours, Glory of the Confessors.* Liverpool, 1988.

———, trans. *Gregory of Tours, Glory of the Martyrs.* Liverpool, 1988.

———. "Images of Saint Martin in Late Roman and Early Merovingian Gaul." *Viator* 19 (1988): 1–27.

———. *Leadership and Community in Late Antique Gaul.* The Transformation of the Classical Heritage 8. Berkeley, 1985.

———. *Saints and Their Miracles in Late Antique Gaul.* Princeton, 1994.

Van der Essen, Léon. Étude critique et littéraire sur les Vitae des saints mérovingiens de l'ancienne Belgique. Louvain, 1907.

Van Uytfanghe, Marc. "Les avatars contemporains de l''hagiologie': A propos d'un ouvrage récent sur saint Séverin du Norique." Francia 5 (1977): 639–71.

———. "L'empreinte biblique sur la plus ancienne hagiographie occidentale." In Le Monde latin antique et la Bible, ed. Jacques Fontaine and Charles Pietri, pp. 565–611. Bible de tous les temps 2. Paris, l985.

———. "L'hagiographie et son public à l'époque mérovingienne." In Studia Patristica 16 (= TU 129), ed. Elizabeth Livingstone, pp. 54–62. Berlin, 1985.

———. "Histoire du latin, protohistoire des langues romances et histoire de la communication." Francia 11 (1983): 579–619.

———. "Latin mérovingien, latin carolingien et rustica romana lingua: Continuité ou discontinuité?" Revue de l'Université de Bruxelles 1 (1977): 65–89.

———. "Modèles bibliques dans l'hagiographie." In Le Moyen Âge et la Bible, ed. Pierre Riché and Guy Lobrichon, pp. 449–88. Bible de tous les temps 4. Paris, l984.

———. Stylisation biblique et condition humaine dans l'hagiographie mérovingienne 600–750. Brussels, 1987.

Vauchez, André. La Sainteté en occident aux derniers siècles du moyen âge: d'après les procès de canonisation et les documents hagiographiques. Rome, 1988.

Verlinden, Charles. L'esclavage dans l'Europe médiévale, vol. 1: Péninsule ibérique-France. Bruges, 1955.

———. "Slavery (History of)." New Catholic Encyclopedia, vol. 13, pp. 282–87. Washington, D.C., 1967.

Vieillard-Troiekouroff, May. Les monuments religieux de la Gaule d'après les oeuvres de Grégoire de Tours. Paris, l976.

Waddell, Helen. trans. The Desert Fathers. London, 1936.

———. The Wandering Scholars. Boston, 1929.

Waldron, Harry. "Expressions of Religious Conversion among Laymen Remaining within Secular Society in Gaul, 400–800 A.D." Ph.D. diss., Ohio State University, 1976.

Wallace-Hadrill, J. M. The Frankish Church. Oxford, 1983.

———. The Long-Haired Kings and Other Studies in Frankish History. London, 1962.

Ward, Benedicta, trans. Harlots of the Desert: A Study of Repentance in Early Monastic Sources. Oxford, 1987.

———. The Lives of the Desert Fathers: The Historia monachorum in Aegypto. Including a translation of the Historia monachorum by Norman Russell. Oxford, 1981.

———. Miracles and the Medieval Mind: Theory, Record and Event, 1000–1215. London, 1982.

———, trans. The Sayings of the Desert Fathers. London, 1975.

———, trans. The Wisdom of the Desert Fathers: Apophthegmata Patrum (The Anonymous Series). Oxford, 1975.

Wasyliw, Patricia. Review of Sainted Women of the Dark Ages, ed. and trans. Jo Ann McNamara and John Halborg, with E. Gordon Whatley. Speculum 71.2 (1996): 467–468.

Wattenbach, Wilhelm and Wilhelm Levison. Deutschlands Geschichtsquellen im Mittelalter. Vorzeit und Karolinger, vol. 1: Die Vorzeit von den Anfängen bis zur Herrschaft der Karolinger. Weimar, 1952.

Weber, Katharina. "Kulturgeschichtliche Probleme der Merowingerzeit im Spiegel frühmittelalterlicher Heiligenleben." In Studien und Mitteilungen des Benediktinerordens und seiner Zweige, NF 17, pp. 347–403. Munich, 1930.

Weber, Max. On Charisma and Institution Building: Selected Papers. Ed. S. N. Eisenstadt. Chicago, 1968.

———. The Sociology of Religion. Trans. Ephraim Fischoff. Boston, 1964.

Weidemann, Margarete. Kulturgeschichte der Merowingerzeit nach den Werken Gregors von Tours. 2 vols. Römisch-Germanisches Zentralmuseum, Forschungsinstitut für Vor- und Frühgeschichte. Monographien Bd. 3.1 and 3.2. Mainz, 1982.

Weinstein, Donald, and Rudolph Bell. *Saints and Society: The Two Worlds of Western Christendom,* 1000–1700. Chicago, 1982.

Wemple, Suzanne F. "Female Spirituality and Mysticism in Frankish Monasteries: Radegund, Balthild, and Aldegund." In *Medieval Religious Women,* vol. 2: *Peace Weavers,* ed. John A. Nichols and Lilian T. Shank, pp. 39–54. Kalamazoo, 1987.

———. *Women in Frankish Society: Marriage and the Cloister 500 to 900.* Philadelphia, 1981.

White, R., trans. *The Interpretation of Dreams.* Ridge Hill, N.J., 1975.

Wilson, Stephen, ed. *Saints and Their Cults: Studies in Religious Sociology, Folklore and History.* New York, 1983.

Wittern, Susanne. *Frauen, Heiligkeit und Macht: Lateinische Frauenviten aus dem 4. bis 7. Jahrhundert.* Stuttgart, 1994.

Wolfson, Harry. *Philo: Foundations of Religious Philosophy in Judaism, Christianity and Islam,* 2 vols. Cambridge, Mass., 1947.

———. *Religious Philosophy: A Group of Essays.* Cambridge, Mass., 1961.

Wood, I. N. "Administration, Law and Culture in Merovingian Gaul." In *The Uses of Literacy in Early Medieval Europe,* ed. Rosamond McKitterick, pp. 63–81. Cambridge, 1991.

———. "Early Merovingian Devotion in Town and Country." In *The Church in Town and Countryside,* ed. Derek Baker, pp. 61–76. Studies in Church History 16. Oxford, 1979.

———. "Forgery in Merovingian Hagiography." In *MGH Schriften,* vol. 33 (= *Fälschungen im Mittelalter 5*), pp. 369–85. Hannover, 1988.

———. *The Merovingian Kingdoms 450–751.* London, 1994.

———. "The *Vita Columbani* and Merovingian Hagiography." *Peritia* 1 (1982): 63–80.

Woodward, Kenneth. *Making Saints: How the Catholic Church Determines Who Becomes a Saint, Who Doesn't, and Why.* New York, 1990.

Woolf, Virginia. *A Room of One's Own.* 1929; reprint, London, 1959.

Woollcombe, K. J. "The Biblical Origins and Patristic Development of Typology." In *Essays on Typology,* ed. G. W. H. Lampe and K. J. Woollcombe. London, 1957.

Wyschogrod, Edith. *Saints and Postmodernism: Revisioning Moral Philosophy.* Chicago, 1990.

Zwierlein, Stephan. *Venantius Fortunatus in seiner Abhängigkeit von Vergil.* Würzburg, 1926.

INDEX